D0295217

FORE!

FORE!

THE BEST OF
JOHN HOPKINS
ON GOLF

First published 2013 by
Elliott and Thompson Limited
27 John Street, London WC1N 2BX
www.eandtbooks.com

ISBN: 978-1-90965-318-4

Text © John Hopkins 2013

The Author has asserted his right under the Copyright, Designs and Patents Act, 1988, to be identified as Author of this Work.

All rights reserved. No part of this publication may be reproduced, stored in or introduced into a retrieval system, or transmitted, in any form, or by any means (electronic, mechanical, photocopying, recording or otherwise) without the prior written permission of the publisher. Any person who does any unauthorized act in relation to this publication may be liable to criminal prosecution and civil claims for damages.

Picture credits
© Charles Briscoe-Knight: pages 19, 77, 177, 205, 289, 325; © Getty Images: pages 7, 35, 42, 60, 131, 156, 183, 222, 233, 250, 270, 303, 315; © AFP/Getty Images: pages 148, 193, 123; © Augusta National/Getty Images: page 86; © Bob Thomas/Getty Images: page 103

9 8 7 6 5 4 3 2 1

A CIP catalogue record for this book is available from the British Library.

Printed and bound in the UK by TJ International Ltd

Jacket design: kid-ethic.com
Typeset by Marie Doherty

*For John Lovesey, who hired me and
then taught me how to write.*

CONTENTS

CONTENTS

FOREWORD

One day in London, in late 2012, Lorne Forsyth of Elliott & Thompson and I sat down for lunch to discuss my writing a book about rugby; about the Lions, in fact. We did so, batting around a few ways of doing this as we ate. Something told me that it wasn't going to fly and so I slipped across the table a brown folder containing some cuttings of my golf writing. "I was looking through these and I wondered whether there were the makings of a book in there," I asked. A few weeks later and the deal was done.

Then came the difficult task of working out how to present the material. Although I have covered and written about more than 130 major championships, doing it event by event did not seem to be the answer. There were plenty of candidates, such as Tom Watson's near miss at the 2009 Open, or Tiger Woods at Augusta in 1997, his first victory in a major championship, or Europe's success at Muirfield Village in 1987, the first Ryder Cup victory in the US.

Perhaps I balked because I had another idea. I had been writing full-time about golf for more than 30 years. The first article on any sport that I wrote for *The Sunday Times*, which was the first newspaper I worked on, was on golf. It appeared in January 1970. That might have been a sign that golf was going to be a very important part of my life. The last piece I wrote in full-time employment at *The Times* came on March 26, 2010, the day of my 65th birthday. It was an interview with Alex Salmond, the leader of the Scottish Nationalist Party and the most important politician in Scotland, who was keen on golf and once had been a half-decent player. So I decided that collecting my articles month by month should allow me to show off the breadth of the material I had covered.

One year on after that lunch with Lorne Forsyth, I have finished. It represents a life's work and I am happy with both the book and my work. I should be. Goodness knows how many times people have said to me that I had the best job in the world. When I renewed my US visa in 2008, an official at the embassy in London peered at my documents, noted that I was *The Times*'s golf correspondent and said with a smile: "Call this a job?" Then he added: "Who's going to win the Masters?" Virtually all my working life has been spent writing, almost all about sport and by far the greatest part of that life writing on golf.

Three sports interest me above all others – squash, rugby and golf. I have tried playing all three, but I was no good at rugby and not very good at squash. I lived, however, on the edge of Stinchcombe Hill golf course in Dursley in Gloucestershire and thus able to spend hours playing or practising, I acquired the basic skills of golf. The first obstacle was finding left-handed clubs for a boy of seven or eight. My father came up with the solution. He simply turned me round so that I looked at the hole over my left shoulder instead of my right. I have no recollection of anger or frustration. Though I bat left-handed and I wrote naturally left-handed until a teacher simply forced me to put a pen in my right hand and use it, I feel completely comfortable playing golf this way.

And play it I did. My first round as an eight-year-old was in the region of 144. I got to 7 handicap when I was 14 and then stalled. Henry Longhurst's articles on golf in *The Sunday Times*, 52 each year for 25 years, were compulsory reading in our house when I was growing up. By the time I was 15 or 16 I had become besotted by the game. I appealed to Longhurst for advice. "I am good at English and quite good at golf," I wrote. "How do I become a golf correspondent?" His reply was quick and encouraging. "Write, write and write," he commanded and so I did. In 1980, after returning from covering the Lions tour of South Africa in my capacity as rugby correspondent of *The Sunday Times*, I switched to becoming the golf correspondent of that paper. In 1993 I joined *The Times* in the same role.

To compile this book I spent many hours poring over the golf articles I had written over the years, pulling them down from shelves in my garage and taking them out of their plastic folders dated for each month. If I had once or twice thought I ought to get rid of them in a massive clear-out, I am so glad now I didn't.

A colleague was once nicknamed the optician because his conversation was full of "I"s. A project such as this is very bad for your ego because it is likely to make you start too many sentences with the first-person pronoun. From time to time one needs to be brought down to earth and not long ago I was. One of my grandsons had been watching me on a Sky golf programme on television and for a few seconds had moved close to the screen, as if to make sure he could hear and see what his grandfather was saying. Then he turned away and ran off. His mother asked him what Grandpa had been saying. "Dunno," the little shaver replied. "Lots of blah-blah-blah."

There is a lot in the following pages. I hope it is not all blah-blah-blah.

John Hopkins, Cowbridge, July 2013

JANUARY

Nearly every January for the best part of 30 years, I have cheerfully thrown a bundle of winter clothes into a suitcase, jumped into my car and driven to Rye in East Sussex. I do so with a sense of excitement, my pulse quickening the moment I cross the level crossing just outside the old town and see it, honeycomb-shaped, on a hill in the distance.

I go there to cover the President's Putter, the wonderfully eccentric competition that could only be played in the first week of January, by the members of the Oxford and Cambridge Golfing Society. In the first month of the year the East Sussex town is often blasted by an east wind and the ground can be too firm to take a divot. It always seems to be cold. At roughly the same time, the first tournament on the PGA Tour in the United States is taking place in Hawaii and a European Tour event will be held somewhere, almost certainly not in Europe. Hawaii or Rye? There is no contest. It has to be Rye.

The President's Putter is a competition of short putters and long memories, of fast play and slow meals, of low shots and high winds. The essential point about the Putter is that golf is played at a time when few people in the northern hemisphere want a competitive game, and played by people who care about golf and don't take themselves too seriously. Some of them are also very good. I have had more stimulating discussions and arguments about the game over dinner during the Putter than in the rest of the year combined.

One year, for a stunt, I caddied for the exuberant Jeremy Caplan. He wore a red sweater that against the dark green grass of the Rye course "made him look like a tomato on a bed of lettuce", I wrote. On another occasion I caddied for Ted Dexter, the famous cricketer. He and the Putter had quite a history. At the time I caddied for him, he was the second-oldest winner, the oldest finalist and, pushing 60, a force to be reckoned with. He played off four at Sunningdale and were it not for his ailments would surely have been lower. He had had operations on his left foot, right knee, left leg and twice they had dug into his broad back to relieve the pressure. "The truth is," he said, "the old undercarriage isn't what it should be any more."

The opportunity to caddie for him was nearly missed. This is how Dexter tells it: "Hopkins asked if he could do it and I thought it would be a bit of fun and so I said 'yes'. He said 'Good. I'll see you mid-morning Thursday and we'll have a cup of coffee and discuss tactics.' I'm afraid I had to tell him that we were off at 8.16. He went a bit quiet after that."

Often in January I went abroad. If there were significant events on the European Tour in Cape Town or California, Sydney or San Francisco, *The Times* generally afforded me the opportunity to be there. The space accorded to golf in those days was greater than now and the budgets accommodated such trips more easily too.

In 1999 I covered some early tournaments on the Sunshine Tour, a couple of weeks split between Cape Town and Stellenbosch with an occasional excursion to Franschhoek. In Johannesburg a week earlier, I had interviewed Bafana Hlophe, a Zulu whose name means, oddly and ironically, white boy. He was competing in his first event on the European Tour. Coming across stories like Hlophe's was one reason why I liked South Africa. Another was meeting Hettie Els, Ernie's mother, a small figure with a soft voice and, though I did not experience it, a firm fist inside the softest of gloves.

Nearly 20 years earlier I had been stuck in a snowdrift in central Germany with Mark Ellidge, a photographer with *The Sunday Times,* for whom I then worked. He and I were visiting Bernhard Langer at his parents' home in Anhausen, near Augsburg, where he lived when he was not travelling. We had been served *Krapfen* (doughnut-like cakes) and *Apfelkuchen* with *Schlagsahne* (apple slices and whipped cream) by his mother, a small warm lady who spoke no English but followed every word of our conversation, eyes sparkling. It did not take much persuading by us to get Langer to take a bag of golf clubs out into a wintry scene so that we could photograph him with an onion-topped church in the background, rather like St Adelgundis, where he had been an altar boy.

It was when we came to drive away that we ran into difficulties. I had a spell behind the wheel of our rented car and so did Ellidge. There was a lot of high revving and wheel spinning and plumes of snow flew away from the wheels. There wasn't much forward progress, however. "Out of the way, John," Langer said. "This is how you do it." And with that he engaged the clutch, kept the engine revving as quietly as possible and slowly the vehicle responded to Langer's delicate touch just as on so many greens his ball would obey the instructions of his hands, scoot across a putting surface and plunge into the hole.

Once I return from Rye, I regard the golfing year as having begun. The Christmas torpor is long behind me. After covering the President's Putter, I feel as though I have just teed off on the 1st hole. How am I going to play? What am I going to be able to report on? Who will win the major championships? In January, enveloped in a post-Rye glow, the magic that has entranced me about golf from my early years returns. The game is afoot.

The President's Putter

Golf Illustrated, January 2012

In the grand scheme of things golfing, the President's Putter is so far down the pecking order as to be almost invisible. Yet the Putter has a very unusual position and thoroughly deserved reputation in golf. It is an event of huge importance but little significance.

It is a yearly reaffirmation that there is more to golf than 72-hole strokeplay events competed for by professionals earning more in one season than most people do in a lifetime. Each January, the amateur competitors of the Oxford and Cambridge Golfing Society who compete in the President's Putter remind us that before there were professionals there were amateurs and that almost every leading professional was first an amateur.

It is competed for by male (and occasionally female) golfers, who have represented one or other university. The winner will have played eight rounds of matchplay in four days. Olympic mottoes are clear in our minds in the lead-up to this summer's London Games, including the one about the taking part being important. Those 139 entrants in the 2012 Putter demonstrated as clearly as their predecessors had that it is not the winning that matters, but the taking part – the true amateur ideal.

Few embody the spirit of the Putter more than Malcolm Peel, a 78-year-old farmer from Northamptonshire. One year recently he was first off at Rye and two hours and 38 minutes later he was back in the clubhouse, windswept and ruddy-faced. "First off and first back," he said cheerfully after losing 7 and 6, a margin he called a dog's licence because that is what one such cost in old money. Thus ended his 45th attempt to win the Putter, an event he would no more forget or ignore than he would his own birthday.

"I missed one Putter in 1958 when I got married," Peel said before pausing and frowning. "Now when did I get married?" he asked himself out loud. Reassured that he had got the year right and would not be in danger of having a four-iron wrapped around his head by his wife, he added: "I missed a few more years, too, but I've played almost every year, starting in 1955."

The Ryder Cup is thrilling. The Open is exciting. The Masters a visual treat. The Putter is an annual demonstration of extreme eccentricity by polymaths of varying golfing standards played over a doughty links course in the worst weather of any event in the world. With any luck it takes place in conditions when many would think twice about putting the dog out. In fact, the worse the weather, the better it is.

That has always been the spirit of the event and one hopes it will always remain so. It would be as daft to play the Putter in July as it would the Open in January. In 1963, a proposition to move the Putter to a more sensible time of year was defeated 57-2.

Winds of 40mph? Difficult, but playable. Rock-hard fairways and greens? Tricky, but you just have to land the ball well short of where you want it to end up. Biting wind? Wrap up well and get on with it. In one really cold year a competitor wore three pairs of socks, underwear, pyjamas, trousers, rain trousers, a heavy shirt, six sweaters, two scarves, two pairs of gloves and a balaclava topped by a woollen bobble hat. Rain squalls? Keep playing and get into the clubhouse for a few restoring glasses of Kummel, known as the putting mixture, as quickly as possible.

It was started in 1920, the year after a request from the O&CGS to Rye Golf Club "to hold a two [sic] day meeting at some date in January next." Why Rye, you might ask. Unlike Bletchley, which was settled on as the site where the Enigma code was cracked during the Second World War because it was halfway between Oxford and Cambridge and therefore not identified with one more than the other, Rye, down in the bottom right-hand corner of England, is not near either.

The answer is that many of the great and good in the Society, men such as Bernard Darwin, the eminent golf correspondent of *The Times*, were also members of the East Sussex club which had, in 1899, invited Oxford and Cambridge to play their home matches at Rye. When Society members wanted to start an annual competition, where better to hold it?

From the start the Putter became a competition that spanned all ages. In 1924, two of the semi-finalists had combined ages of 101. This year Michael Grint, a retired lawyer aged 77 who had played in the winning Oxford team in 1957, was the oldest competitor. Asked his age, he replied: "I say I'm five over fours." Martin Yates, 69, the oldest man to reach the fifth round, and Peter Gardiner-Hill, 85, the presiding eminence grise, a past captain of Rye, a past president of the O&CGS, and a past captain of the Royal & Ancient Golf Club, was the oldest spectator. He was probably the most enthusiastic, too. On Thursday afternoon, in winds of up to 40mph, Gardiner-Hill wrapped himself well and spent an hour or so watching the golf.

Darwin did as much as anyone to promote the virtues of Rye as a golf course. He wrote about the Putter long before *The Times* gave its writers a byline. When he won in 1924, his account in *The Times* of his victory referred to himself in the third person and included the following extract: "I do not think Mr Darwin will be hurt in his feelings by any remark I make about him and so I will say that he is one of the most enigmatical golfers of my acquaintance. You never can tell to what depths of futility he may fall…"

Years later, as a successor of Darwin's on *The Times*, I delighted in the annual ritual of a drive through the marshes to Rye, a town shaped like a beehive, to spend my days watching men who had been to Oxford and Cambridge play golf as if they hadn't and my nights listening to a wind roaring in from the Urals and rattling the windows as it raced up and down chimneys.

I caddied for Ted Dexter, the imperious cricketer/golfer, and later for Peter Gracey. The low point with Dexter came when I forgot to rake a bunker and had to chase back down the 3rd fairway to repair the damage to a bunker on the 2nd; the high point when I talked him into playing a five-iron second shot on the 15th (he had wanted to play a six-iron) and the ball ended six feet from the flag.

Gracey was rather different. He was 73 and making his 46th appearance and I began my report by wondering: "What drives a man of 73 to leave his home and hearth on a bitter winter morning to play golf against men half his age and half his handicap? What drives the same man to do it the year after, wearing only one sweater, with a hole under the armpit, and one sleeve rolled up regardless of the cold?"

Before every shot a ritual was enacted, one as serious as the taking of communion. Gracey would arrive at the ball, take off his brown leather gloves and hand them over, taking care not to drop the hand warmers he kept inside them. In return he would be given the club of his choice. There is no discussion, no practice swing, no wasted time.

"Thank you," he said as he handed over his gloves. "Thank you," he said as he received his club. "Thank you," he said as he returned his club to his caddy. "Oh bugger," he said when he hit a bad shot.

Two facts have become obvious in the past 20 years. The standard of golf has been rising, at least if measured by falling handicaps. This year's four semi-finalists had combined handicaps of +5: two were +2, one +1 and one scratch. It is also interesting to note that the age of the winners has been rising. In 2001, Bruce Streather defied form and convention by winning aged 54 and this year Andrew Stracey was successful aged 58. It is something to do with improved fitness, the developments in the clubs and balls and the rather quirky nature of Rye golf course, over which skill and cunning can and often do triumph over youth and power.

With only 34 bunkers (nearby Royal St George's has that many in the first ten holes and Muirfield in the first eight) and a yardage a little over 6,300, Rye might seem to be a pushover. Far from it. Positioning is important, good chipping and putting paramount: "…the problem at many holes is not necessarily getting down in two or more but in avoiding taking more than three more," Gerald Micklem noted in 1984.

Distance is not essential – as long as you drive into the correct place. It has one par-five, nine par-fours over 400 yards and a par of 68. Its four short holes are wonderful. Darwin said the most difficult shots in golf were the second shots at the short holes at Rye.

It is an observation by one who has attended the Putter for a number of years that its participants and a good many of the spectators dress similarly. At the Putter you will see more blazers than in an Aquascutum sale. If the Putter had not been invented then the production of quilted jackets, mustard and raspberry cord trousers and blue blazers would be reduced and the popularity of Labrador dogs would be diminished.

Everyone, it seems, has a nickname: "Dog", "Camel", "Black Man", "Italian", "Swampy", "Binman". David Normoyle, an American who came to Cambridge to do a one year's masters in history and ended up doing a three-year PhD with a thesis called "Bernard Darwin and the Development of Golf Literature", is nicknamed Mr Dottie Pepper, because that is to whom he is married.

Golf writer Bernard Darwin holds the President's Putter at the Oxford and Cambridge Golfing Society tournament in Rye, January 1932.

On the Thursday night of this year's Putter, ten members of the Society gathered for dinner in the Hope Anchor Hotel, one of the Society's spiritual homes. Almost everyone wore a blue blazer and grey trousers and the dark, striped Society tie and when they sat at a long table facing one another, five down one side and five down the other, it was almost certainly as they had sat to eat meals at their prep schools some 50, 60, 70 years before. One man had the same room in the hotel since 1990 and stayed in the hotel for 20 years before that.

In quick succession the conversation touched on political correctness, the devotion shown by the Welsh to the stand-off half in rugby, who had done what to whom in such and such a Varsity match, the length of time those at the table had been staying at the hotel, the quality of the food, the decline in popularity of another hotel in Rye, the fun of bridge, the speed of play on the golf course, the diaries of his golf kept by Gerald Micklem, one of the great figures in postwar golf, the fortunes of North Hants Golf Club and Justin Rose, its most famous member, the increasing use of the distance-measuring choices and Tiger Woods. Notable by their absence were discussions about money, church, sex, drugs, rock and roll.

On Friday it was as if the Gods were keen to make amends for the dirty, gusting winds and rain squalls that hit south-east England the previous day, when a four-club wind roared over the course. Weather is a part of most golf tournaments, sometimes a very influential part. In this event, it assumes great importance because it is almost always ignored. The inaugural Putter was held in comparatively mild weather. "There was a strong south-west wind with a touch of wet mist in the air; the course provided a searching test and it would have been a malicious delight to see two of the best professionals fish for their fours and threes," Darwin wrote. The coldest Putter was probably 1963, when Rye was snowbound and the event was moved to Littlestone and a competitor came off the course and apologised for being unable to speak on the grounds that his cheeks were frozen.

In 2005 the wind was so biting that some players wore more sweaters than an artichoke has leaves. In 1997, after three inches of snow had fallen early in January, it was played one month later. In 1979 it was called off altogether for the first and only time. Weather conditions are most appropriate when, as somebody once put it: "I enjoyed the having played rather more than the playing."

Not least of the attraction of Rye is the golf clubhouse itself, a four-square, sturdy building two miles outside the town set among the dunes, discreet and unobtrusive. It is a collegiate sort of place where eating, drinking and talking are given as much attention as a tricky downhill three-footer to win a hole. Henry

James was elected a member in 1898 and used the club mainly for tea. Its standard lunch once was buttered eggs and ham, followed by cheese.

The course is almost never closed, except when snow is on the ground. It does not flood easily and its springy turf resists the tramp of thousands of golfers. Peter Gardiner-Hill was sitting in the clubhouse on Friday morning discussing this and that when he was asked whether Rye had winter tees and greens. His eyebrows shot skywards. "Winter tees!" he asked in that inimitable voice of his. "Winter greens! What are they? The only time we can't play golf is when snow is on the ground or the course is flooded."

On Friday afternoon, as dusk gathered outside, Andrew Stracey draped his long limbs over the arm of the Darwin chair in the Society corner of the clubhouse. The Darwin chair came from Down House where Charles, Bernard's grandfather, lived and worked on *The Origin of Species*. At that stage of the competition Stracey was one of the few who could say he was playing as well now as when he was an undergraduate, and perhaps better. "He's a good scratch," someone said, adding: "and you can't say that about many players."

Stracey used to own an advertising company with 115 employees, but he sold that ten years ago and took to playing golf more seriously. At 55, he leaped into senior golf with enthusiasm, winning the Irish Seniors, and coming second in the Welsh Seniors (twice) and the English Seniors. A graceful swinger who uses his long legs to good effect to generate the power to give the ball a good whack, Stracey looks comfortable from tee to green and uncomfortable on the putting surface.

In one of the Sunday morning semi-finals Stracey had to go to the 20th to beat Ben Keogh and win the right to face Mark Benka, the defending champion, who had beaten Amir Habibi more easily. The final turned out to be a contest of good ball striking by two men who would never be described as good putters. Benka has had the yips, but says now that a claw grip rather like the one that Sergio Garcia uses has been a lifesaver for his golf. Stracey's putter grip is twice the normal size.

Stracey was three up on the 16th tee, lost that hole, but won the 17th and the match. He had played golf almost without blemish, which was more than could be said for his sickly green and shrieking yellow waterproof jacket. "He could become the first car parking attendant to win the Putter," a spectator whispered out of the corner of his mouth. Stracey blamed his wife. "I wanted to buy a black one, but she said black was boring and made me buy this."

At this point little mattered to Stracey other than at the age of 58 and at his 35th attempt and his fourth final he had finally won the Putter. Standing over his bag he had a moment's private exultation, clenching his hand and doing a quiet and unobtrusive fist pump as the applause from perhaps 100 spectators banked around the green died down. Then in the blinking of an eye, as gloom gathered and the lights of Rye twinkled in the distance, he was presented with a small medal inscribed with the words "primus inter pares" on it. Soon his golf ball would be hung on the hickory-shafted putter – used by Hugh Kirkcaldy when he won the 1891 Open – and put in a glass case and kept in the Society's corner in the clubhouse, near the Darwin chair. Stracey grinned like the Cheshire Cat. Now he was really and truly the first among equals.

Bold Davies seeking to blossom afresh

The Times, January 10, 1995

It was late on a winter's afternoon and Laura Davies was not answering the telephone at her home in Ottershaw, Surrey. Perhaps she was out playing golf? Hardly. The best woman golfer in the world, the woman who won tournaments on five tours last year, often wants nothing to do with golf and this was one of those occasions. She had been gardening and now she was relaxing in the bath.

Ah yes, gardening. A straw hat on her head, basket under her arm and a pair of secateurs in her hand. Some gentle clipping behind the potting shed. That sort of gardening?

Wrong again.

The idea that Davies would do that was as laughable as the notion that she would play short at a par-five. Davies goes for everything she does and gardening is no exception. "I've been striding into the brambles, sorting out the rhododendrons, helping on the tractor," Davies said, summoning up a vivid picture in the mind's eye. "We've got 5½ acres here and 60 per cent of it is undergrowth," she said. "There is a lot to do. I love it."

Love is a word Davies uses a lot. Gambling, shopping, sport and fast cars are all loves in a life she pursues with the frenzy of someone being chased in the fast lane. She can afford to indulge herself. She won nearly $1 million in 1994, the record-breaking year when she became the first European, of either sex, to top the United States money list.

Davies sets off today for two tournaments in Florida at the start of her 1995 campaign. It would be sensational if she matched her performances in 1994, when she won at least once in Europe, the United States, Asia, Australia and

Japan. For Davies, it all came down to consistency. "I had 33 starts, 22 top tens [finishes]," Davies said. "Not bad, was it? That was what pleased me. My attitude was so much better.

"In the British Open at Woburn, I was five over par after the first ten or 12 holes yet I finished fourth. I wanted to do better last year and I did. I controlled myself better. Before, I used to rush. The quicker I got, the more shots I dropped; and the more shots I dropped, the quicker I got. Now, I tell myself off when I hit a bad shot."

Achieving more than any other woman golfer before her was not enough for Davies to be voted the BBC television sports personality of the year. Davies was at the ceremony, but as a rubbernecker, not as a recipient. In golf, particularly women's golf, her being overlooked was seen as a slight, though Davies is characteristically low-key and laid-back about it.

"Believe me, I like winning at everything," Davies said. "But the public don't know who I am. Nigel Mansell's on TV every Sunday, so is Damon Hill. I didn't think I had a chance of winning. The fact that I was in the running was an honour. I'm not worried about it; it was out of my hands. My attitude these days is that there is no point in worrying about something I can't do anything about."

From Davies's point of view, the evening was a success anyway. She is an uncomplicated lover of sport, and open and generous about her heroes, among whom she moved that night. "I love people who are a bit different," she said. "I think Mansell is terrific. I stayed up last night until four o'clock in the morning watching the cricket. That Darren Gough is brilliant."

One wonders where it will all end for Davies? She is 31. Can she continue to improve at the rate she has? The time when she played in the 1984 Curtis Cup at Muirfield seems light years away. For that matter, so does her startling virtuoso performance in the second Solheim Cup, at Dalmahoy, Edinburgh, in 1992, when she was unbeaten and led Europe to a stunning triumph.

Davies, however, has one characteristic that makes it inadvisable to predict normal patterns for her to follow. She is remarkably gifted. She is able to fly in the face of accepted golf wisdom as easily as she launches a 300-yard drive.

Furthermore, she is level-headed, unable to be spoilt by the siren voices of success and certainly not downcast by the dreariness of failure. Her feet are almost off the ground when she hits a drive, but they are planted firmly on terra firma at all other times.

One vignette involving Davies in 1994 remains clear in the memory. It came during the four-balls in the Solheim Cup and Davies and Alison Nicholas, her perennial partner, a par-five and a par-three, were facing Brandie Burton and Dottie Mochrie.

At the 16th, Mochrie pulled her second shot left of the green near a spectator stand. There followed ten minutes of discussion as to the best position for her to drop her ball. Davies, not noted for her patience at the best of times, could hardly stand it. Finally, she turned to her colleague and remarked: "If that was me, I'd have put my ball in my skyrocket [pocket] ages ago and said, 'it's all yours, partner'. I don't know what all the fuss is about. Why don't they just get on with it?"

That was Davies in 1994, quick, uncomplicated, entertaining and hugely successful; a woman who could never be accused of letting her work intrude on her pleasure. "You've got to have fun," she once said, "otherwise golf would be too much like a real job." It was her year in 1994. May 1995 be her year, too.

Following Darwin and the evolution of Welsh golf

The Times, January 11, 1995

One hundred years ago today men from golf clubs all over Wales climbed aboard railway trains and headed for Shrewsbury. Coming from Borth, Aberdovey and Merionethshire, from Rhyl and Caernarvonshire, from Porthcawl and The Glamorganshire, they made their way to the Raven Hotel, where that evening they agreed to found the Welsh Golfing Union (WGU). Not for the first time, the Welsh were ahead of the English. The English Golf Union was formed in 1924.

It might seem odd for a Welsh organisation to be founded in a county town in England but in those days it was easier to reach Shrewsbury from north and south Wales than from any town in the Principality. One who made regular train journeys was Bernard Darwin, grandson of Charles, who later became golf correspondent of *The Times*.

It was R.M. Ruck (later Major General Sir Richard), a relative of Darwin, who had called the founding meeting of the WGU. The Ruck family founded Aberdovey Golf Club. With antecedents like these, it was not long before Darwin was roped in, too. He joined the executive committee of the WGU in 1898. Darwin, who wrote like an angel, was one of the greatest of sporting essayists. Almost as much as golf, he loved train journeys and referred to them constantly, though not always favourably. "To get from north to south Wales is not so easy a matter as might be supposed," he once wrote. "It entails much waiting at junctions, which have been placed in some of the most melancholy and deserted spots on the face of the earth."

In an essay entitled "Aberdovey" he describes a journey from London to that mid-Wales town where he spent many of his childhood holidays. Its course, he wrote, "my soul loves best of all the courses in the world". Rereading this essay and feeling the excitement that coursed through Darwin prompted me to recreate this journey.

It could not have begun more felicitously. Darwin wrote of arriving at Euston by cab, of tipping a porter sixpence, of taking a corner seat in a carriage, and of having arrived "absurdly early". Taxis and porters combined to deliver me, complete with golf clubs and suitcase, and an item that Darwin would not have heard of, let alone possess, a portable computer, equally early to the station.

A train that should have already departed was waiting on the platform and duly began to move unenthusiastically towards the Midlands. "The stations will whirl past," Darwin wrote, and they did until Birmingham New Street. A screen on platform 7B showed that the Aberystwyth train left at 14.07. At the bottom of the screen were the words Regional Railways, a less mellifluous name than The Cambrian Railway, three words that so excited Darwin.

Then came dirty Wolverhampton, Telford Central, Wellington and Shrewsbury. "At Shrewsbury," Darwin wrote, "will be encountered my two kind hosts and other golfers bound for the same paradise… then we shall pack ourselves into another carriage, for the second half of our journey… I should not be surprised if we even attempted to waggle each other's clubs in the extremely confined space at our disposal."

Last Monday almost every seat was taken as the small, two-carriage "Sprinter" train pointed its nose at the English/Welsh border. In fading light it sped deep into Wales, the luscious green and hedged fields around Welshpool replacing the industrial wastelands of Wolverhampton. Welshpool (*Y Trallwng* in Welsh) was followed by Newtown (*Drenewydd*) and Caersŵs (*Caersws*).

"The train comes into a country of mountains and jolly, foaming mountain streams. It pants up the steep hill to a solitary little station called Talerddig," Darwin wrote. I shall take Darwin's word for all that. Of jolly, foaming mountain streams I saw little because it was dark and rain pounded the windows. Of Talerddig, I saw nothing. Dr Beeching and his railway cuts had seen to that.

Then came Machynlleth ("Let a Saxon try to pronounce that!" Darwin wrote). The pretty and newly painted station had an Edwardian glass roof reaching out to protect passengers on both platforms. It was the penultimate stop. The journey that had begun six hours earlier was nearly over. "Then on again through the darkness, til we stop once more," was as true now as when Darwin wrote it. "There is a wild rush of small boys outside our carriage window, fighting and clamouring for the privilege of carrying our clubs." That wasn't quite the same. Aberdovey was reached in pitch darkness. One passenger alighted onto a station that was totally deserted. The train whirred away into the night, heading north for Pwllheli (let a Saxon try pronouncing that!).

I trudged away from the station wondering whether Darwin would recognise Aberdovey in January 1995. Over my shoulder was the wonderful golf course, ahead of me the neat little town. Despite a film of rain, I knew exactly how Darwin had felt because I felt the same way. His words would do for me. Not for the first time he had written it better. "Nunc dimittis – we have arrived at Aberdovey."

Rise of Spaceman and The Don

The Times, January 31, 2000

Readers of this column who have long memories will remember how in part one of the story entitled "The Golfing Adventures of Spaceman and The Don", Luke Donald, also known as The Don, left his home in Beaconsfield to take up a place at university in Chicago, and was named the best collegiate golfer of the year in the United States in June 1999.

Part two of the story begins with the toppling of The Don from his position of superiority in American college golf by Paul Casey, also known as Spaceman, a member at Burhill Golf Club in Surrey, who is on a golf scholarship at Arizona State University.

Now Casey is ranked No 1 and Donald No 2. Never before have golfers from these shores achieved such success in such a competitive arena – not even Sandy Lyle or Nick Faldo, who both attended American universities for a time in the 1970s. If this time last year it could be said that the best college golfer in the States was English, now it can be said that the two best are English.

"I am not sure about the rankings," Donald said. "I won two tournaments and finished sixth and thirteenth in two others, while Paul came second and eleventh in the two he played, yet he overtook me. It's a funny system."

Donald and Casey are both 22. They grew up within 50 miles of each other in the south of England and were rivals at junior level, before Donald went to Northwestern University to study for a liberal arts degree, while Casey won a scholarship to the university where Phil Mickelson studied in the early 1990s.

Donald is the better-known of the two, having played junior and youth golf for England, but Casey, who has not yet represented his country, returned to England last summer to compete in the English Amateur, knowing that victory in that would cement his place in the Walker Cup team. He achieved that aim impressively; the two men were then paired together at Nairn and won all their matches.

Donald is quiet, thoughtful, calm and composed. His nickname, The Don, comes obviously enough from his surname. "Sometimes he is known as Don Corleone," Casey said. "The Americans sometimes call him Cool Hand Luke, which he doesn't like." Casey, who is more outgoing, just as disciplined and no less composed, is known as Spaceman.

"Why am I known as Spaceman?" Casey mused. "Because I am a little out there. I used to hit it all over the place and get up and down from outrageous positions. I used not to be so focused."

The quiet strength that the two men share is striking. They are confident and articulate and have a British modesty allied to an American self-assurance. "Paul is very powerful, has a good short game and believes in himself," Donald said. "Luke is emotionally very stable. Everything about him is solid," Casey responded.

But whereas Donald was calmer and more matter of fact about the time he was leading the US rankings, ahead of so many well-known names, Casey is clearly quite excited to be in that position now.

"It is good fun to be first and second in the US," Casey said. "It keeps the Americans quiet. They love to talk about themselves and it is nice to shut them up. I think it gets their goat that Luke or myself is No 1. They are frustrated that foreigners have come over and are taking their glory. They don't like it and that spurs us on even more, of course.

"Luke and I play well together because we both think we are good golfers who value and respect each other's games," Casey continued. "One week I see him win, the next he sees me win. Luke has a quiet confidence. There is not a shot he can't play and I like to think the same is true of me. The strength of his game is that his all-round game is strong rather than any one aspect of it."

Last week, Donald and Casey were representing the English Golf Union at the Lake Macquarie Greater Invitational Amateur in Australia, a 72-hole stroke-play event at a course 1½ hours from Sydney. Donald finished second, nine under par, Casey took third place on a countback, eight under par. Casey earned a rare accolade from the club captain. "He is the best striker of the ball I have seen in the 30 years of this competition," Richard Flanagan said.

It is encouraging for British amateur golf that both intend to remain as amateurs until they finish their studies. That means Peter McEvoy, the captain, will have both of them available for Great Britain and Ireland's defence of the Eisenhower Trophy, the world amateur team event, in Berlin later this year, as well as for the defence of the Walker Cup at Sea Island, Georgia, next year.

"I think I could play on tour," Casey said. "But give me 1½ years to develop my game more, to get my degree and I will have more success later. I am still learning."

McEvoy is unstinting in his praise for both men. "Luke is close to being the finished article," McEvoy said. "He is a Peter Thomson type of golfer, a Neil Coles or a Hale Irwin, very consistent and very accurate, a complete player. Paul has more of the Tony Jacklin in his heyday about him. He is very powerful and a formidable player, but he has some improving to do. Both will turn pro in time and I expect both to do very well."

"I harbour hopes that the pessimism will be confounded"
The Times, January 2, 2013

He stood tall and erect, a slim figure with an authoritative air, surveying the scene at Royal St George's. There was mud to the left of him, mud to the right. He had something like a cagoule spread over his shoulders, a hat with muffs that dropped down over each ear and a pair of binoculars dangling around his neck. He was ready for any contingency at his club when it staged the Open in 2011.

I never saw Christopher Martin-Jenkins at Lord's or the Oval or Trent Bridge, but I can imagine him at those places from the way he was at golf clubs such as Sandwich, Wentworth and Sunningdale. He looked at home in these clubs, in an appropriately coloured sports jacket and club tie. Clearly he understood the rhythms and peculiarities of golf and a golf club as well as he did those of cricket.

At The Grove he had been due to play with a group of colleagues, but he forgot to turn up. Alerted as to his faux pas and apologetic to a fault, he raced up by car in time to join us for lunch, making some typically self-deprecating remark: "I am sorry. I am a complete prat. Please forgive me."

The Martin-Jenkins swing caught my eye on the 6th tee of the East course at Wentworth some years ago. As he addressed his ball, there came a wry comment about one of our group: "Seventeen handicap? My foot." Then followed the swing, an elegant, languid swish in which it was possible to detect the influences of cricket, and particularly batting. He was strong through the ball. If on that occasion it looked better than it performed, on many other occasions it would perform as well as it looked.

He loved Pulborough, the West Sussex golf club where his name was on a few honours boards. We never did have the game there that we had been promising one another.

"You have not taken in that I can never play golf again, whatever happens to the other affected areas, hip and liver, because I was given a fasciotomy which went wrong," he wrote, understandably somewhat acerbically, in an e-mail last month. "Secretly I harbour hopes that all the pessimism will be confounded."

It wasn't and when our small golf group gathers at Sunningdale next month for our annual competition, a minute's silence will be called for in memory of a cricket writer who looked so at home in golfing surroundings. We will remember him with affection as one who could slice, hook, top, sclaff, foozle and dunch with the best of us and then be a genial companion in the clubhouse afterwards.

Jack Nicklaus still out in front as he shoots 70

The Times, January 21, 2010

He is 70 today and somewhere in a fast-running stream in the Rocky Mountains, a man in a check shirt with thinning fair hair will arch his back and cast for a fish.

Jack Nicklaus being Jack Nicklaus, he will probably catch one, too. It would be wrong if it were any other way. Perhaps the greatest golfer of all time can expect a bumper catch on the day he enters his eighth decade.

He had a birthday present on Sunday when he and Tom Watson, ten years his junior, won a senior skins game in Hawaii. "Good gracious," Nicklaus said, using a very Jack Nicklaus phrase. "I play one tournament a year and I win one. That's 100 per cent. That's pretty good, isn't it?"

Good indeed, and no more than he deserves. "The thing that made Jack a great champion was talent, great strength and also a wonderful putter – and really the best mind I have ever seen on a golf course," Gary Player said. "You never saw him getting upset. You could never tell if he had hit a bad shot. He always had great patience."

Nicklaus was unquestionably the golfer of the twentieth century, while at the same time being a good husband and father, qualities not attributed to the present world No 1. Nicklaus did it with skill and grace, often flying home from tournaments to attend his children's football, basketball and baseball games, while knocking off 18 professional major titles and a couple of amateur ones as well.

These days the hallelujahs come long and loud. "I think he has been a wonderful player," Arnold Palmer, his friend and rival, said. "He has been very, very good for the game. He's probably the best of all time, and that's very good."

For Ben Crenshaw, what was so striking about Nicklaus was his will to win. "He won in a lot of different conditions, different countries, and to me he played with more common sense than almost anybody," Crenshaw said. "Jack just had a competitive nature and his will was remarkable. He has been so great to everybody and he has meant so much to our game."

Nearly 20 years ago, during a weekend spent with Nicklaus while he visited courses he was designing in Britain, Ireland and France, he told me he considered his crowning achievement was marrying the former Barbara Bash.

She was so devoted that she watched him play golf on their two-day honeymoon. One night she suffered a miscarriage and did not wake her husband because he was competing in a tournament and needed his rest.

"Marrying Barbara was the best thing that ever happened to me," Nicklaus said. "I could never have done it without her. When Michael [their fourth son] left college I told Barbara I had a new rule about tournaments. If she doesn't go, I don't go."

Talk of Nicklaus being a successful family man inevitably brings us to Tiger Woods. Nicklaus was the golfer of the past century; Woods wants to be the golfer of this century. The two, one twice as old as the other, seem inseparable in conversation, like dollars and cents. Comparisons follow the mention of their names and almost always they favour Nicklaus.

"Please don't ask me to feel sorry for [Woods]," reads a letter in an American golf magazine. "He wanted all the trappings of fame and fortune but none of the responsibilities. He may come back and surpass Jack's 18 majors. Jack Nicklaus is a man to be admired as a brilliant player, husband and father. Tiger Woods will never be Jack Nicklaus."

Nicklaus's total of 18 major championships is the benchmark and one that Woods, who has 14, wants to pass. Who is to say what will happen now? Woods's extraordinary fall from grace has emphasised one of the game's great talking points: will he beat Nicklaus's record?

Jack Nicklaus playing in the 2005 Open, which was
to be the last of his professional career.

"Let's see him do it first," Nicklaus said a couple of years ago, not conceding an inch. More recently he said: "The guy's awfully good. I think he'll probably pass my record, but he still has to do it."

Two years ago, when Woods was recovering from surgery to his left knee, Nicklaus telephoned his pursuer. "I told him, 'Tiger, you know nobody ever wants their records to be broken,'" Nicklaus said. " 'Certainly I don't want you breaking my records. However, I don't want you not breaking my records because you're not healthy. I don't want outside forces preventing you from performing as an athlete.'"

Yet that is what is happening. "Tiger has his own personal problems right now and they're none of my business," Nicklaus said.

"This is a tough year for him. If he comes back and plays the Masters, Pebble Beach [the US Open] and St Andrews [the Open], which are his meat, I think Tiger will do well. I expect him to come back and be Tiger. If he doesn't come back and doesn't play those almost three gimmes, then he'll have a harder time breaking my record."

Just as Nicklaus knew how to line up a putt and how not to putt until he was ready, so he has no difficulty in putting in perspective the Woods episode.

"The game had Bobby Jones, the game had Walter Hagen, Arnold Palmer, Gary Player, Tom Watson, Lee Trevino, Nicklaus," the "Golden Bear" said in a telephone interview before Christmas. "The game always survived that. The game will continue to go forward.

"Tiger is a big influence, probably the largest one we ever had. And, certainly, we hope he comes back and plays. It's not all about one person. The game is a big game."

Happy birthday, Jack.

That's what they call "experience"

Golf International, January/February 2010

We have all seen the wildlife programmes in which a lioness is curled up under a tree with her cubs around her. They are noisy, arguing with one another, annoying her until suddenly she reaches out a paw and clips the smallest and noisiest cub around the head. It gives a yelp and then it quietens down.

That is what Lee Westwood, 36, did to Rory McIlroy, 20, in the Dubai World

Championship that decided the Race to Dubai. He cuffed McIlroy around the ear, gave him a good kicking.

At the start of the week Westwood was second, £114,000 behind McIlroy, the Race to Dubai leader, yet the Englishman taught his young stablemate a lesson in all aspects of the game – the playing of it, the mental approach to it, what to say and what not to say, what to do and what not to do, when to talk and when to keep quiet. In short, Westwood beat him all ends up.

It helped that Westwood's golf was exceptional. He hardly made a mistake in 72 holes. One can sense that when it was all over and McIlroy had gone away to think about it he must have felt quite bruised at what had been done to him. One hopes that he learnt from it. He will win plenty in his time and when he does he might regard the third week in November 2009 as having been hard but beneficial.

Westwood and McIlroy had begun sparring on a BBC online forum. "They [Westwood and Darren Clarke] think the nickname they have given me ['Titch'] is hilarious so I guess I'm stuck with it until they get too old and fat to play on tour any more," McIlroy said.

This was McIlroy's first mistake. Confidence is one thing; irreverence is another. When McIlroy is older and heavier, he will be more mindful of gibes made about age and weight.

"We're just having a laugh," Westwood said, "and I'm a little better at it than he is because I've got 16 years' more experience. I can normally wind him up." This is exactly what Westwood did. In the opening exchanges, Westwood landed more blows than McIlroy.

When the two of them were paired together for the first round, Westwood's psychological dominance was soon to surface again. He loved the confrontational nature of it. He was confident and he dictated the terms, how much they talked, what they talked about and so on. Having gone round in 66, two strokes fewer than McIlroy, he was in his element, the more so because he realised McIlroy was not.

"I didn't think I would find it as difficult as I did," McIlroy said later before making another error. He owned up to the world that he did not want to play with Westwood again. What was the message here? That Westwood was proving too much for him?

Westwood later said that had the roles been reversed he would not have said such a thing, even if he had thought it. "But then I've been on tour 16 years and he has been on tour three years and it's something he'll learn over time." Round two to Westwood as well.

After 27 holes McIlroy had overtaken Westwood and led by two strokes. Westwood said he was not aware of this. "I have no interest in anybody else's game this week," Westwood explained. Take this with a pinch of salt. It is hard to imagine that Westwood had not caught a glimpse of a scoreboard that showed how well McIlroy was doing but the last thing he was going to do was to acknowledge a rival's success publicly. Round three to Westwood.

By Sunday Westwood was two strokes ahead of Ross McGowan and five of McIlroy. He continued to demonstrate the rare calm and unusual degree of confidence that he had all week. Did this get through to his challengers, particularly McIlroy? If it did, it was meant to. "I think the way you are, the way you portray yourself can be intimidating to other people," Westwood admitted on Sunday. "I am not saying it was but it certainly helped." Round four to Westwood.

One further factor might have influenced Westwood. It was that McIlroy had disregarded Westwood's, Darren Clarke's and Ernie Els's advice, as well as that of Chubby Chandler, his manager, to remain mainly in Europe. On the eve of the tournament McIlroy publicly admitted he was going to join the PGA Tour in the US. I dare say this gave Westwood more motivation to teach his young rival a lesson.

One last thing. What colour shirt did Westwood wear on Sunday? Red, the same as Tiger Woods. Westwood was doing what Woods demonstrates so often, namely that the hitting of a shot is only part of golf. Having a strong mind and dominating rivals is the other half.

All in all, Westwood outplayed and out-thought McIlroy quite strikingly. "Sometimes what you say off the course and the mind games you play are as important as the pressure you can put on people on the golf course," Westwood said.

He certainly demonstrated this to be true down in Dubai.

Blackball, not fourball

The Sunday Times, January 29, 1989

It was Ludovic Kennedy who the other day raised the subject of prejudice in golf. In his recently published autobiography, he recounts how he was blackballed when his name was put forward for membership at Muirfield; as a result, he believes, of his championing the cause of Patrick Meehan, a man wrongly jailed for murder.

"I was so sad about this because I am a clubbable person by nature, and have never regarded a game of golf as anything but an occasion of social exchange," he wrote.

What caused Kennedy more concern was that shortly after this episode he was also blackballed by the Senior Golfers' Society. (A point hotly disputed by the SGS, who maintain that he was merely unsuccessful in six successive ballots.) "I was annoyed about that," Kennedy said last week. "I thought that was a very dirty trick."

Kennedy is not the first to discover that what matters in golf is not only your handicap but, sadly, also your politics, religion, colour and sex. For all that golf gives the impression of being honest and sociable, it is only up to a point, Lord Copper.

Talk to a Jewish person about joining a golf club in London and there'll be a hollow laugh. As the Jewish character Lionel Richards, in a short story by Brian Glanville, discovers when he tries to become a member of a golf club, there has been both overt and covert discrimination. "Yes, I am a [Jew]," says Richards in *Join the Club,* "…but what's that got to do with playing golf?"

"I'm afraid we have a Jewish quota," replied the club secretary.

"What does that mean?"

"It means we can't admit you."

Years ago this led to Jews deciding to form their own golf clubs, which were and are non-sectarian: among them Dyrham Park, Hartsbourne, Coombe Hill, Potters Bar and Abridge in Essex, are in or near London. The Association of Jewish Golf Clubs and Societies has 12 member clubs, including Moor Allerton near Leeds, the oldest Jewish club in Europe, and Bonnyton in Glasgow.

Nearly 30 years ago, allegations of discrimination against Jews were made against Hertfordshire golf club Moor Park. "There are no quotas here any more," said John Davies, the club secretary, last week. "We have quite a few Jews on our committee. In fact, a couple of years ago we had a Jewish captain. I would say that between five and seven per cent of our members are Jewish."

The new outcasts in golf are the Japanese. Their ambassador has playing facilities in Sunningdale, but his fellow countrymen have had to buy a golf club, make weekend raids on accommodating London clubs or take their turns at Ealing driving range.

Perhaps a lack of opportunity and exposure to the game are among the reasons why golf has remained the plaything of the middle classes. The Professional Golfers' Association says there are 3,400 pros, assistant pros and retired members in Britain and Ireland. Just two of them are black – Jim Howard at Pontypool and Roland West at Altrincham municipal course.

I know many golf clubs where the attitude of the male members towards the female members resembles that of Victorian fathers to their children. Never mind that we have a Queen on the throne, and are led by a female prime minister. Women, sometimes patronisingly referred to as "girls", are tolerated, and that is about all.

The Equal Opportunities Commission is recommending that legal measures be taken against clubs that offer membership to both men and women and then discriminate against women.

"Discriminatory rules within mixed-sex private clubs, including golf clubs, are the source of constant complaint to the commission," said Joanna Foster, chair of the EOC. "Clearly this is now an unacceptable situation which the EOC has recommended the government should resolve by amending the Sex Discrimination Act to bring such clubs within its scope."

"There's nothing to beat a round of golf," says Ludovic Kennedy, recalling a lifetime's involvement in the game.

I might suggest that there is nothing to match it for those who are white, Christian, middle-class, Anglo-Saxon and male.

Baker-Finch ponders parting shot

The Times, January 29, 1998

Ian Baker-Finch, the 1991 Open champion, was at home in Australia at 10 o'clock on Monday night. He was sitting in front of a television set surrounded by his family. For the moment, the 37-year-old Australian was not thinking about his retirement from competitive golf, which had made news around the world. This is because he says he has not decided to retire and because he was engrossed in watching the Australian Open tennis tournament. So when his mobile telephone rang, the last person he expected to find on the end of it was a journalist from Britain.

At this point it would have been no surprise if Baker-Finch had decided to put the telephone down. After all, he had refused to take any of the other calls made to him by journalists since the retirement story had appeared. This time, though, the innate courtesy of the Australian surfaced, the courtesy that has made him so popular at tournaments around the world these past 19 years.

He started to talk. "The words 'I have decided to retire' never passed my lips," Baker-Finch said slowly. "I am taking an extended rest. This is not retirement. I am just having a look at what has happened. I am not practising as much as before. I said I felt I was playing better than I had for a long time by not playing much. Really, what I would like to be able to do is to change my name, come back in a different body and go and play without the pressure of being Ian Baker-Finch. My problem is I can't do that and I have to live with that. I realised when I tried to play the British Open last year that I should not have. Although I had practised well, my insides would not allow me to play."

Golfers have nothing but sympathy for Baker-Finch. They remember how well he swung the club and scored when he triumphed at Royal Birkdale in July 1991 and they have watched his recent fall from grace with the uneasy feelings one has when one sees a friend go off the rails. They might have mixed reactions to the antics of John Daly, but Baker-Finch's troubles have generated enormous compassion.

Just about everyone in golf remembers the way he drove twice out of bounds on the 1st hole of the 1995 Open at St Andrews and the anguish he suffered before, during and after that 92 in the Open last summer. They know that since 1993 he has played all four rounds in only three of the 22 tournaments he has entered and they also remember how he disqualified himself after eight holes of the first round of a tournament before Christmas. They can understand the mental torture Baker-Finch must have gone through and their instincts have always been to ask why he continued to put himself through all this anguish.

Golf has a power to inflict pain in a way that few other games have. Often the torture chamber is on the greens, where players from the mid nineteenth century to the last knockings of the twentieth have been victims of the yips. It can be from the tee, too, as it seems to be with Baker-Finch. Or it can be both.

Imagine you are already the champion golfer of your county and one morning you wake up and find yourself improved by a factor of ten, which might put you in the same league as Baker-Finch. Now imagine that, on another day, you wake up and find that your talent has gone. It must be the most difficult thing in the world to accept this.

"It would be easy to say 'that's it, I've had enough'," Baker-Finch said. "My fellow pros ask me 'why do you put yourself through it?' The thing is I still have the desire. I had nine birdies when I played the other day and it is hard realising that I can still play and yet knowing that, when it matters, I am not the same person.

"It is very difficult to realise I cannot compete, that I cannot put aside the bad thoughts. When I was playing well, these bad thoughts passed. But now they are like a self-sabotage mechanism that destroys everything."

No one wants to see as nice a man as Baker-Finch continue to suffer. He said on Monday night that he wanted to announce his retirement at a time and place of his own choosing. I can only urge him to do it soon, not only for his sake and that of his family, but for all those friends and fans to whom he has brought so much pleasure down the years. Sometimes the obvious course is both the correct and the courageous one. Stop now. That would be the sensible decision.

FEBRUARY

I was stuck in traffic on the M25 when the telephone went. It was 6.45 on a weekday evening and I was due at Moor Park Golf Club at 7pm that night. "I'm in one of those jams where you move at a snail's pace one minute and 50mph the next," I said to the caller, a club official with an understandable hint of anxiety in his voice. "I think I'm about 20 miles away."

I have done a little after-dinner speaking at golf clubs, but though this was after a light dinner it was not the traditional sort of speech. Instead I was to talk about the newly released golf film, *The Legend of Bagger Vance*, and, indeed, about golf in films generally. It was slim subject matter. Golf has been poorly served by Hollywood – or has Hollywood been poorly served by golf?

There have been baseball and boxing films, a memorable one about rugby league, but hardly any about golf, which surely has the capability of putting on to the screen mouth-wateringly beautiful scenery at the very least. Think of golf and films and you come up with the match between James Bond and Goldfinger in the eponymous film, with *Caddyshack*, and with *Follow the Sun*, about Ben Hogan, which may be the best golf film ever made.

The evening at Moor Park was reminiscent of evenings I used to spend with my father at Stinchcombe Hill Golf Club in Gloucestershire when a film in *Shell's Wonderful World of Golf* series was being shown. Another series was made at the turn of the millennium and not long ago I watched Jack Nicklaus and Gary Player compete against one another over Sunningdale's New Course while some of my friends who are members there tried to look conspicuous in the background.

I might be biased but I found it as compelling at the start of a new millennium as I had found the previous series nearly half a century earlier. Even now, even after the release of two more golf films, *Tin Cup* and *The Match*, I am puzzled: golf seems a natural subject for a film, a slow-moving, elegant, gentlemanly game in which the scenery is stunning and varied. There are hundreds of storylines. Why aren't there more films about it or at least involving it? I suppose the answer lies in the form of another question: why aren't there more films about sport?

In Februarys past I have eaten breakfast with Player at Blair Atholl, his 1,000-acre estate outside Johannesburg, talked to Ernie Els as he moved towards victory in the South African PGA Championship at The Wanderers in Johannesburg, listened to the sane voice of Peter Thomson in Perth, Western Australia, speaking out against appearance money and wishing that Greg Norman would compete in tournaments in Australia for smaller remuneration.

When he was the world No 1 and living in the US, Norman, born in Queensland in 1955, must have felt that he couldn't please everyone. Controversy swirled around his pearly-coloured hair. There were those in Australia who applauded him for his success around the world and those who criticised him for not returning more often to the country of his birth to give golf there a boost and, when he did so, for accepting huge appearance fees. In February 1996 he was competing in Perth and there was so much criticism that in *The Times* I described him as wary, more guarded and less relaxed than usual.

"It's the tall poppy syndrome," Frank Williams, his manager, said. "If a man has a Rolls Royce in the United States, Americans will look at it and say 'I want one of those'. If you parked a Rolls Royce in Collins Street in Melbourne, it is likely to be scratched."

Seeing a national figure so ill at ease and coming under so much criticism in his home country was surprising and in an article written while I was in Perth I concluded: "This week, a great white shark is at bay on land – his own land. It is a shame."

With his striking hair and an Australian easiness, Norman was good for journalists. He would always talk, even if sometimes he didn't say anything. Quite often he did. Seeing a group of us at a tournament on Hilton Head Island in the US in the days after his collapse in the last round at the 1996 Masters, he said, cheerily: "Fingers sore from all the typing, boys?"

That collapse gave rise to one of the best stories about Norman. On the Saturday night of the third round of that Masters, after which he had a lead of six strokes over Nick Faldo, Norman found himself in the lavatory of the locker room at Augusta National standing alongside the late Peter Dobereiner, the revered golf writer. "Well, Greg," Dobereiner said. "Even you can't fuck it up from here." Sadly, Norman could and did.

One February I wrote perhaps my hundredth story about Faldo, this time as he was making his first steps in his career as a golf analyst and commentator on television in the US. That this sometimes sullen and taciturn man could become a star of golf coverage there remains one of the game's surprises. Yet he has, which goes to show that the journalists who presented a picture of Faldo as a prickly non-communicator who cared only about his golf certainly may have got the first part of that description wrong. I know. I was one of them.

February does not have a major championship, and it has only one World Golf Championship tournament. It might seem to be a nothing month. Yet by February both the European and American professional golf seasons are well under way and, as you are about to read, I always found it to be anything but a nothing month.

Tiger Woods's wooden act of theatre does little to restore aura of greatness

The Times, February 20, 2010

In the 15 years since Tiger Woods made his first appearance in Europe, competing as a member of the victorious four-man United States team in the Eisenhower Trophy in Paris, I have seen him countless times. I have seen him angry and tired, victorious and defeated, smiling and morose, but I have never seen him as he appeared during his 14-minute confession on television yesterday, perspiring, tieless and uncomfortable, close to tears.

Suddenly those moments on a golf course when he wheels away after holing a putt and raises his right arm, fist clenched, bicep rippling, were miles away. His 14 major championships were of no use to him now. For all that he is probably the best-known sportsman in the world and the No 1 golfer, he was a tall, lonely-looking figure for 840 seconds yesterday morning, slightly stooping as he stood at a lectern reading his mea culpa.

He was a man out of context, out of character, out of sorts. He had an audience of female members of his staff positioned on either side of Kultida, his mother, as well as friends and business associates. Notah Begay, a fellow professional, was in the front row, as was Tim Finchem, commissioner of the PGA Tour in the US. But of Elin, his wife, there was no sign.

It was said that Woods had to apologise and he did not shrink from doing so – to his wife, his family, his friends, his fans, his business associates, to young students who are involved in his Foundation. He did it again and again. At various times he described himself as having been wrong, foolish, selfish, irresponsible. He said that he was sorry in one way or another eight times. Nor did he make any attempt to shift the blame. He was the one to blame, he said. He used the first-person pronoun 108 times.

"I have bitterly disappointed all of you," he said. "I have made you question who I am and how I could have done the things I did. I am embarrassed that I have put you in this position. For all that I have done, I am so sorry. I have let you down and I have let down my fans. I was unfaithful. I had affairs. I cheated. What I did is not acceptable and I am the only person to blame.

"I stopped living by the core values that I was taught to believe in. I knew my actions were wrong but I convinced myself that normal rules did not apply. I never thought about who I was hurting. Instead I thought only about myself. I ran through the boundaries that a married couple should live by. I thought I could get away with whatever I wanted to.

"I felt I had worked hard my entire life and deserved to enjoy all of the temptations around me. I felt I was entitled. Thanks to money and fame, I didn't have far to go to find them."

Yet on one key issue Woods prevaricated, wrapping his intentions about returning to golf in such convoluted language it is hard to know precisely what he meant. He said he would continue today the course of therapy he is undergoing. He was clear about that, but any hint as to when the man who last competed in a tournament in Australia in November 2009 may return to professional golf was obscured.

"I do plan to return to golf one day," Woods said. "I just don't know when that day will be. I don't rule out that it will be this year."

What is one to make of that? He seemed to be saying that he was more likely to return this year, yet he did not rule out the possibility that it might be next year. He did not give the impression that it will be for next month's Tavistock Cup, at the start of the week of the Arnold Palmer Invitational, or for the Masters in April. Because he was so unclear, there is even a doubt that he will be ready by the Ryder Cup in Newport, Wales, in October, never mind the US Open in

June at Pebble Beach, California – where he won in 2000 – or the Open in July at St Andrews.

Woods being Woods, he could not resist a flash of anger. There was even a hint of finger-wagging. He denied suggestions that he had used performance-enhancing drugs and he took a pop at the media for following his 2½-year-old daughter to school and pursuing his mother. These comments jarred, coming in the midst of an apology.

Overall, this was far from a convincing performance and one wonders what the players whom he once dominated will have made of it. They might have been impressed by his honesty, but they can hardly have had the respect they once had for him reinforced. For them, Woods's aura has gone, like a cloud, perhaps never to return.

His delivery was wooden but he can hardly be blamed for that. He is a golfer, not an actor. The obviously scripted theatrical gestures that he interposed from time to time were inept, unnecessary and exaggerated. His contrived sniff so that he sounded as though he was close to tears; the way he walked slowly from the lectern and buried his head on his mother's shoulder for several seconds; the congratulations he was given at the end by friends and employees; all these jarred horribly.

At one point one even thought of those famous words: "Pass the sick bag, Alice."

Sadly the message that Woods was trying to get across was obscured. This was one of the greatest challenges that Woods has faced in his life and he failed it. He failed to convince us of his sincerity because it all looked too con-trived. Talk, someone once said, is easy. Actions are hard. Let him go away and prove he can do what he repeatedly said he wanted to do and then we will judge him. Then he will have something to say and then we will be more prepared to listen.

For now, looking back on this exercise staged for the TV, a typically public-relations performance, one has to conclude that it achieved little.

Mr Hotchkin's eighteen-hole back garden
The Sunday Times, February 5, 1984

The golfer, a visitor to Woodhall Spa, had just struggled out of the bunker, and clouds of sand were falling from his shoes when a figure in an old, worn raincoat and cap appeared. "Please don't climb out of the front of the bunker again," he asked, a touch of asperity in his voice. "And don't forget to rake your footprints."

In the clubhouse later, the golfer inquired about the odd fellow who had laid down the law. "Oh that," said the secretary, only a slight smile on his face indicating that he was used to such inquiries. "That's the gaffer, the owner of the club, Mr Neil Hotchkin."

Owning a golf course is less unusual than it sounds. But being the gaffer at Woodhall Spa, the beautiful club in Lincolnshire which has been rated among the best 50 in the world, is the sort of responsibility for which many desk-bound golfers would willingly endure years and years of the yips.

Neil Hotchkin, however, was born to it. Woodhall Spa golf course was laid out in 1905 by Harry Vardon and J.H. Taylor on land owned by Stafford Hotchkin, a gentleman farmer and sometime MP, who later remodelled it. Stafford Hotchkin, a much-loved figure at Woodhall Spa, died in 1953.

Though the course was always there, just over the garden wall of The Old Manor House while Neil Hotchkin was growing up, he was more interested in cricket, and preferred to ask Alf Fixter, the club's assistant pro, to bowl at him for hours on end in a net in the garden. Helped by all this practice, Hotchkin scored a record (still unbeaten) 459 runs in the Eton v Harrow cricket matches between 1931 and 1933. At Cambridge, he chose to go racing at Newmarket, and to play soccer.

But now the course dominates his life, overshadowing his passion for Arsenal, where he took over cricket commentator Brian Johnston's season ticket in 1946, and his considerable efforts for English and European amateur golf. Scarcely a day passes that he isn't seen at Woodhall Spa, striding out in his plus twos, or bouncing around in his Land Rover. "I sometimes wonder in which order Neil would put his interests," says his wife, Sally. "I think I would come first, and then it's the golf course – at least, I think that's right, isn't it, Neil?" she added, darting an anxious look across the table at her husband.

The clubhouse at Woodhall Spa is a warm, welcoming place, pleasantly unpretentious, where a fire glows in the grate, and Kummel and decent port are dispensed from the bar. Hotchkin is very much in charge, often to be found sipping beer.

"I've got complete financial control," he says. "I don't have any truck with house or greens committees. The members are very good, and we get along well, but sometimes I do have to say to them, 'If you want that, then the subs will have to go up.'" Under this benevolent autocracy there are only two club committees for the 300 members – one for handicaps, the other, much more important, to look after the wine.

To say he is proud of Woodhall Spa would be an understatement of Jeeves-like proportions. He has the eye of a perfectionist, a man who is offended even by an out-of-place twig. Each week he writes instructions for his greenkeeping staff, what to do in wet weather and in the dry. "I can never catch up with everything I want to do on the course," he moans, only half-joking. "Steve [the secretary] is always allowing people to come and play. I'm trying to stop them so I can get out and do some work."

Hotchkin pointed out an elderly man with clumps of silvery hair peeping out from beneath a tweed cap. His jacket was patched with leather, his tie had seen better days. "That's Ted Atkin," said Hotchkin. "He's 73, and hasn't been to a doctor in his life. Pulls his own teeth, that sort of thing. Never been further than Horncastle or Lincoln in his life. Can't think what I'd do without him."

For their part, a number of Hotchkin's employees can't think what they would have done without the squirearchy established by the Hotchkin family. Alf Fixter, for example, was born nearby, and first came to the club as a two-year-old when his mother was the stewardess.

Hotchkin climbed back into the Land Rover, and headed back to the club-house. He gesticulated at half a dozen spruce trees which had fallen in a recent storm: "That's precisely where we cut all our wood. We don't have to move them at all. We can just start sawing in the morning." The vehicle bumped over the old railway line. "It's home, this place," Hotchkin said quietly. "It's just like my own garden."

The golfing talent that helped unite a nation

The Times, **February 20, 1995**

Ernie Els was at home last week, his home in his home country. Els and Liezl Wehmeyer, his girlfriend who travels the world with him, stayed at his parents' house in Kempton Park, eastern Johannesburg. It was there that Els grew up in an Afrikaner household, and it was there that he returned after his first, faltering attempts to play golf, having taken 83 strokes for nine holes and thinking that the game was so difficult that he would never be good enough to play a full round.

How times have changed. Last year, Els, 25, became the first non-American to win the US Open since 1981. He was recently named South African sportsman of the year, a reward not only for capturing the US Open but also for winning a slew of titles across the world, and nearly £2 million in prize money in 1994.

He is one of the best golfers in the world, among the most popular of South African sportsmen. One had only to follow Els in the PGA championship at the Wanderers Club to see just how popular. More people watched him practise his putting before the third round on Saturday than watched Transvaal play cricket a few hundred yards away.

Later, nearly 2,000 spectators were gathered around the 18th green as he and Simon Masilo, his African caddie, approached it. Most were white, though some were black. There was affection bordering on adulation at the sight of this tall, gangling man with the shock of fair to gingery hair and a face that, far from being locked in a rictus of concentration, would often break into a smile.

"Ernie is a new South African," Johann Rupert, one of South Africa's leading industrialists, said of his young friend. "He is like Morné du Plessis [a past South Africa rugby captain who is now the team's manager], my roommate at university. His appeal crosses the colour barriers. He is idolised in golf because he represents a lot of amateurs. He hits it a mile and gets into trouble. He likes a couple of beers. He is relaxed. He is a clean John Daly if you like."

A hint of a blush passed over Els's strong features when he heard this ringing tribute. "Those are big words from a big man," he said. "I'd like to be something close to what Gary Player has been for this country. Gary has been unbelievable. I'd like to do my best. I'd like to keep us on the map internationally. I'd like to do well overseas and I'd always like to be remembered as a South African."

As a South African or an Afrikaner? "I am an Afrikaner South African," Els said, smiling at the subtlety of the point he was making. "Afrikaans is my first language. I only started to learn English at school when I was ten or so. It is my second language. When I started playing junior golf in this country, golf was 75 per cent English and 25 per cent Afrikaans. I would say it would be 60-40 Afrikaans now."

Els began playing golf with members of his family. The family is known to be tight-knit, loyal, caring. "Afrikaner families instil strict discipline," Dale Hayes, the South African former touring professional, said. "If the father says: 'This is the way you do it', then that is the way you do it."

Nils Els, Ernie's father, provides much of the family's drive; Hattie, his mother, much of the soft, easy-going nature. Both characteristics are evident in Ernie, who is the youngest of their three children.

"They are lovely," John Bland, a South African professional on the European Tour, said. "They care about his golf, but they don't go on at him about it. If

Ernie Els holds the trophy after victory in the final round of the South African
PGA Championship at the Wanderers Club, Johannesburg, in 1995.

Ernie comes in and says he's shot 80, I don't think his dad is going to say: 'You'd better go and hit a bucket of balls.' His dad is more likely to say: 'That's no good. I can do better than that.'"

Els was asked what he thought were the characteristics of the Afrikaner. "When you think of the Afrikaner, you think of Boers, of farmers," he said. "English people look down on Afrikaners. In this country, they call us *Boertjies,* a derogatory term. It's not true. This country was run by Afrikaners. They have held high office. At first, I felt embarrassed that I couldn't speak English, but then, I thought: 'Why should I speak English if they can't speak Afrikaans?'"

It is easy to understand why this husky young man, the personification of a Boer, would vote for the National Party in the historic election that changed the face of his country, though Els himself has not revealed which way he marked his ballot paper. The National Party was the party of the Afrikaner. Furthermore, Els remembers how, when he was doing his national service, he had sat in a large room and been told that the African National Congress was banned and a dangerous organisation that bombed and killed indiscriminately.

Yet listen to him now. "The election was unbelievable," Els said. "I was at our holiday place down in George and I saw on television that people were going out to supermarkets and stocking up. Nobody knew what to expect. Anything could have happened. We thought: 'This could be a civil war.'

"It was really quite tense in this country. Then, I promise you, a miracle happened. On television on election day, I saw people, black and white, standing in queues kilometres long, and everybody was having a chat. It was quite bonding.

"I think we are the favourite people in the world right now. I feel really proud of my country. What has happened should have happened 15 or 20 years ago and then we would have been right through all this.

"I am going to meet [Nelson] Mandela [the president] next week. I can't wait. I am going to be sitting at a table with him. He is a great man. He has done this after being locked away for 27 years on Robben Island. He has been unbelievable."

Through all this, Els talked well, stumbling only when asked whether he was a liberal. "I am for people to have a chance in life," he said after a pause. "If they haven't got a chance, then give them a chance, white or black, and see how good they can become." He gesticulated at the golf enthusiasts who were walking past the tent where we were talking. "I am so happy there is no sign here saying 'whites only'," he said. "I am sure that 95 per cent of the country feel like that.

How can you have apartheid and try and run a country? You are only going to become a third-world country if you do that."

A smile passed over the face of this admirable young man, who seems wise beyond his years and gifted beyond measure. Now that he had come off the golf course, away from the fierce heat and the blindingly clear light of the high veld, one could see that his face was lightly smeared with sun protection cream.

As he talked, he ran a hand through his hair and swigged from a can of beer. He looked happy, at ease, at peace with himself.

There was, though, one thing that worried him. "I don't play that often down here in South Africa," Els said, trying to explain one of the reasons behind his decision to have a house built in Orlando, Florida. "And people just don't give you your privacy any more. It really gets quite bad here. I like to go out with my mates, sit down at the dinner table and eat and have a few beers. But people just come to me all the time. It's one thing being a good golfer, but I am not a better person than anybody else."

"A better person." Three words that revealed so much about Els. God has given him huge talent, his parents have instilled in him inestimable qualities. Golf is lucky to have him. And so, most assuredly, is South Africa.

Strokeplay no match for head-to-head
The Times, February 22, 1999

What do Ian Fleming, P.G. Wodehouse, John Updike, Ring Lardner, Richard Ford, Stephen Potter and Agatha Christie have in common? I shall award you one point for knowing that golf features in the works of these authors, quite often in the case of Wodehouse. I shall award a bonus point to anyone who knows that they wrote quite often about matchplay golf.

In Wodehouse's matches the hero, who usually is hapless, helpless or hopeless, and sometimes all three, is often playing for the hand of a comely girl. On occasions, though, the stakes are eccentric. The American millionaires, Bradbury Fisher and Gladstone Bott, played a rousing match for three railroads and an English butler.

Such matches are a joy to read about because Wodehouse lived and loved golf and understood the rhythms of the game. Consider this passage: "Gladstone Bott ... fussed about for a few minutes like a hen scratching gravel, then with a stiff quarter-swing sent his ball straight down the fairway for a matter of seventy yards, and it was Bradbury Fisher's turn to drive ... It was his [Fisher's] habit, as a rule, to raise his left foot some six inches from the ground, and having swayed forcefully back on to his right leg, to sway sharply forward again and lash out with sickening violence in the general direction of the ball."

Fleming has contributed the widest-known golf match of all time to literature. Anyone who has not read how James Bond defeated Goldfinger in Fleming's book of that name has probably seen a recreation of the match in the film. Although in the book the course is named Royal St Mark's and described as the greatest seaside course in the world, where the club professional was Cyril Whiting, Fleming set it at Royal St George's, where he was a member and past captain, and the then professional was Cyril Blacking.

It is revealing that for more weeks than not, strokeplay golf demands my attention, yet my memories are divided equally between the two. It follows that matchplay has that extra something.

Matchplay encourages the daring stroke because the only penalty is the loss of the hole and not the loss of several strokes and ultimately prize money. Matchplay to strokeplay is rugby union to rugby league, a sports car to a saloon, a devilish little par-four of 340 yards to a 450-yard par-four into a wind.

Strokeplay is unremitting, like being gripped in a vice on the 1st tee and not released until the last putt is holed. It takes forever. It can be boring and often is.

Matchplay was therefore the natural form of golf when a relative and I played the other day. We had not seen each other for a while and had never played together. We met just after nine o'clock, teed off at 9.25 and as we played we talked of this and that. At least Roddy did; I listened. We played off our respective handicaps and I had to hole a three-footer on the 18th to halve a match in which almost every hole was won or lost. The hands on the clock stood at 11.55 as we completed our round, match all square, honour shared, much enjoyment had by both of us.

Matchplay has a way of insinuating itself deep into the consciousness. I have no recollection of my first competitive round, at the age of eight, other than knowing it was 144 strokes. On the other hand, I can remember quite clearly my first serious match. It was against John Jermine in the quarter-finals of the Welsh Boys' Championship at Llandrindod Wells in 1960. I lost, but thank you for asking. Perhaps you would like me to take you through it hole by hole?

This talk of matchplay is relevant because starting on Wednesday is the first significant matchplay competition for professional golfers from all over the world since the US PGA Championship abandoned its traditional matchplay format and went to strokeplay in the late 1950s.

There is a real sense of anticipation at the thought of 64 of the world's best 65 players teeing off against one another in 32 matches. My one wish is that the matches were over 36 holes, not 18, because the longer the match, the less chance is involved. "It's like playing one set of tennis," Colin Montgomerie said. "Anything can happen."

Given the quality and the size of the field in Carlsbad, California, it is certain that at least one match will become clearly written into the annals of golf. There is so much at stake that caution will have to be thrown to the wind. "You will have to go for everything," Ernie Els said recently. "It's 18 holes and, if you lose your match, you are out. There is no second chance."

Many golfers these days, particularly those in the United States, where strokeplay is a way of life, struggle with the concept of matchplay. Believe me, learning how to play against an opponent rather than against a card is a form of golf worth learning.

Freddie Tait, the Amateur champion who once drove the 18th green at St Andrews using a gutta percha ball, was as deft with words as he was prodigious from the tee. "Matchplay is the thing," Tait said. "Strokeplay is so much rifle shooting."

Thomson rails against keeping up appearances

The Times, February 7, 1996

As the Heineken Classic concluded in Perth on Sunday, one of the most interested observers at The Vines was a stocky man with stout brown shoes, a skew-whiff smile and crinkly black hair that rose and fell back from his forehead in waves.

Peter Thomson, five times the Open champion between 1954 and 1965, watched with pleasure as five of his fellow Australians finished in the top ten of the first joint event between the tours of Australia and Europe. But he was disconcerted that appearance money, which he has fought against for years, remains such an important issue in the modern game.

"I am pleased with golf these days, except for the ugliness of appearance money in these parts and in Europe," Thomson, 66, who was president of the Australian Professional Golfers' Association for three decades, said. "Sport is sport. It is not a business or entertainment. The moment entertainment overtakes sport you have wrestling. If you pay people to strut the stage that is disastrous.

"Australian golf has never been stronger but it is under the spell of Greg Norman. It is hard to mount a series of events without him. It would be good if he gave Australian golf more help – by not taking so much money out of the pot. This is a very expensive sponsorship by Heineken and it may or may not be profitable. If Heineken could get the same exposure for half the price there would be no question as to its profitability. Who knows, Heineken may decide it is a poor investment. In my time there has been a procession of sponsors who do it for a year or two and then decide they can no longer afford it.

"Greg and I are not friends. I live in Australia, he in the United States. We are polite when we meet. As a player he is amazing, unique even. His swing is technically correct now. We thought it was perfect when he was 25. But he can make such hard work of some simple shots, it's almost as if he is ungifted. Almost any drive involves tortuous preparation. He can take such a long time to do something that others do in the flick of an eyelid."

Thomson's trenchant views have appeared in the columns of the Melbourne *Age* newspaper for 40 years. He was the first professional to augment his prize-money with income from writing, and one of the first to leave golf and attempt to enter politics.

Memories of his unsuccessful attempt to get into the Victorian state legislature in 1982 have been revived because his son, Andrew, is a candidate in the general election in Australia on March 2. "He is a Liberal and standing in a safe Liberal seat – I expect him to win," Thomson said. "I loved the manipulation of the media, which is what politics is all about. The media like to be tickled. I had a constituency of 44,000 and I knocked on 8,000 doors over 15 months. There were 19,000 Greeks and four out of five of them voted Labour. We Liberals were demolished by a landslide. Had I got in, I would still be there."

Instead, Thomson voyaged to the United States, made a small fortune on the seniors' tour and began the profitable golf course-building firm he now runs. Though his travelling keeps him away from his home in Melbourne for six months of the year, he has discovered the delights of being able to play golf without marking a card. "Pencil-less golf, I call it," Thomson said. "For the first time for 40 years I can play without returning a score. It's wonderful. I always say to people I am two Scotches short of perfect health and two rounds away from competitive pitch."

Norman's early cut leaves sour taste

The Times, February 20, 1998

If Greg Norman has read Shakespeare's *Julius Caesar* I wonder whether he remembers Act I, Scene II, in which the soothsayer in ancient Rome warns Caesar to beware the Ides of March, the fifteenth day of the month. Perhaps some twentieth-century soothsayer should warn Norman not to be in Johannesburg in February, because there seems to be nothing but trouble for him there at that time of the year.

At Houghton Golf Club on Sunday, February 26, 1995, Norman and Nick Price conceded generous putts of 15 feet and nine feet to one another on the 16th green in the third day's singles of the Alfred Dunhill Challenge match between Southern Africa and Australasia. It was meant as a gesture of goodwill in an event won by Southern Africa, but it was received with surprise by players, spectators and officials from around the world, who felt that the spirit of competition had been abused.

At Houghton Golf Club on Sunday, February 15, this year, Norman was competing in an individual event, the Alfred Dunhill PGA Championship. Rain had interrupted this event from the start and when play ended on Sunday, Norman still had nine holes of his final round to complete and was eight under par. Amid controversy, Norman withdrew from the event and flew home to Florida, saying that he had a prior commitment the next day.

Norman's action was greeted with astonishment throughout the world of golf because it seemed disrespectful and Norman is generally known to be an upholder of the game's traditions. "If Norman was getting paid what people said he was, you'd have thought that would have been worth an extra day," Tony Johnstone, who won the event with a score 17 under par, said. The PGA of Southern Africa disqualified Norman and fined him R1,000. "I consider his conduct to be injurious to our tour," Arnold Mentz, the South African PGA Tour commissioner, said.

Around the world, the managers of other players read these remarks and wondered what had come over Norman and his advisers. "Other than matters like health, I can't think of any meeting that can't be moved," one manager said. "If you're in the business, you would not fix a life-and-death meeting for the day after a tournament for precisely this reason." Another manager said: "It is disgraceful. You cannot accept appearance money and not finish a tournament."

Norman is managed by Bart Collins, of Great White Shark Enterprises Inc, in Florida. "There are two points to be made in Greg's defence," Collins said. "The sponsors knew when Greg committed to the tournament that he had this prior

Greg Norman in action during the Dubai Desert Classic at
the Emirates Golf Club in Dubai, United Arab Emirates, 1998.

commitment back in Florida. It was a fundraising function at the Medalist club, Greg's club in Hobe Sound, for Jeb Bush, George Bush's son, who is running for Governor of Florida. Greg had to be at a cocktail party on the Monday evening and to play golf with George Bush on Tuesday.

"Secondly, Greg sought out the sponsors on Sunday night, told them he had to leave and was given the thumbs-up. In other words, he went through the appropriate protocol. To blame Greg is unfair. The ground rules were set. The contract was specifically written to include the days of the tournament. There was not a provision for a holdover."

Ian Bannen, on behalf of Alfred Dunhill, confirmed that the sponsor knew of Greg's prior commitment. "We were aware of it and we did not stand in Greg's way," Bannen said. "However, we were cognisant of the fact that he was contravening the rules of golf and it was a decision only he could make. He put himself into a difficult position. He has to live with it."

Collins said no consideration had been given to returning some of the £250,000 reportedly paid to Norman for appearing in the event. "Why would we volunteer that?" he asked. "It was known from day one that Greg could not stay beyond Sunday. Look at what Greg did for the tournament."

There is no doubt that this affair has left a bad taste in the mouth. The game, which prides itself on its adherence to traditions, appears to have been tarnished and the spectators short-changed. "I am only the tournament co-ordinator and, yes, Alfred Dunhill did know about this before," Louis Martin said. "But I do feel disappointed. Everybody is disappointed; the public is disappointed. It is not for me to say if Greg had been leading by two strokes whether the result would have been the same. It was not right and that is why the Tour fined him."

Norman was said to be embarrassed by the whole business. "This is not a common occurrence by Greg Norman," Collins said. "Greg is not the sort of person who withdraws when playing well. It is against his character."

February has not been a good month for Norman. During the Greg Norman International in Sydney, he said how irritated he was at being asked persistently whether Monica Lewinsky was with President Clinton at his house last March, when the president injured his knee. "Will it ever stop?" Norman said recently. "I keep telling the truth, but I am feeling more and more like some Watergate figure engaged in a terrible cover-up – all because people love to gossip about the president's private life. I say it has gone too far."

Perhaps he had better remain in Florida next February. Better still, he could compete in the Alfred Dunhill PGA championship next year for no appearance fee at all. That would mend a few fences.

Poulter finally pitching with the best

The Times, February 8, 2000

Ian Poulter is a tall man with vaulting ambitions. He dreams of winning not just one major championship but more. Twenty-five years ago, Nick Faldo was cutting a swath through these parts of England – Bedfordshire, Buckinghamshire, Hertfordshire. Poulter, who grew up within a hefty drive of Faldo's birthplace, wants to do the same.

Malcolm Muggeridge, who did not play golf but would have been plus four at writing, entitled one volume of his autobiography *Tread Softly For You Tread On My Jokes*. A raised eyebrow might be in order upon hearing Poulter's ambitions, for this is a man who did not play top-class amateur golf, the traditional preparation for a professional career, as Faldo did and is only now, at 24, competing regularly on the European Tour.

The tournament in Kuala Lumpur this week is only his third on the Tour. But what you cannot do is mock Poulter for aiming for the unrealistic, for believing that he can succeed where a million others have tried and failed. "They are big goals, I know," Poulter said. "But I believe my dreams are realistic. If you believe in yourself and you want it badly enough, provided you work hard enough I think it is all achievable. If I play well, things will start taking care of themselves."

Most golf clubs have a figure like Poulter, the young assistant professional who is behind the counter in the pro shop when you buy some tees, who gives lessons when he can, who is always racing out to the practice ground to hit a few balls, who dreams of walking the fairways alongside Faldo, Bernhard Langer and Lee Westwood.

Poulter is the sort of young man who knows the football scores so that he can answer members' queries, is handy with a snooker cue and listens to members' banter. He also watched the golf transmission on Sky last night. He has read *Golf Weekly*, watched the sporting quiz shows and saw Severiano Ballesteros on *A Question of Sport*.

Such figures are usually popular and Poulter certainly is. At Leighton Buzzard Golf Club, he is the butt of a pleasing mixture of teasing and respect. As he leans on the bonnet of the new Nissan Primera that he has just collected from the showroom or crouches over his golf bag to have his photograph taken, a passing member shouts out: "Don't get his face in the picture."

Later Poulter is eating a massive breakfast of egg, baked beans and sausage in the clubhouse when another member comes over, hand extended. "I just want to say well done, boy. That was a good start," referring to Poulter's 22nd-place finish and a cheque for nearly £4,600 in his first event on the European Tour, in Johannesburg. "The wife sends her best wishes. She likes to say she had a few lessons off you." A spreading blush coloured Poulter's face. "Thanks," he said. "Give her my best."

Ah yes, the thorny subject of lessons. Lessons to complete beginners, to the captain's wife, to 24-handicappers. Faldo never gave them because he became a tournament pro as soon as he turned professional. Poulter, having started as an assistant, has switched only now to playing competitively full-time. Lessons are often the bane of the life of an aspiring young professional who wants to improve his own game, not someone else's.

But not to Poulter. To him they were a challenge, something he had to do while he worked in the shop. He wanted to play golf all day long but he was appreciative of the time off that he was given to compete in local events by Lee Scarbrow, the head professional.

"I liked giving lessons," Poulter said. "It was nice to see someone improving in front of your eyes. I must admit, though, what I really wanted to do was to hit balls myself."

On this particular morning Poulter is dressed fashionably for a young man in golf. His hair is gelled and a necklace jangles at his neck. He wears grey trousers, black shoes and a fawn sweater bearing the name of two of his sponsors, one a local car dealership, the other a local builder. His mobile phone is never far from his hand. It has a telephone on the front and a small computer on the back and he uses it to e-mail news back to his sponsors and talk to friends such as Justin Rose.

"When I sit back and think where I am, I think 'fantastic'. I have worked hard to be here. I would love to be Justin's age and just going out on tour, but if I pass my PGA exams later this month I shall be qualified. I feel I've done my time, done my work. It is now time to go and do the things I've always dreamt of doing. I love going out and playing with the names, knowing I can make the cut and knowing that if I play well I can move up to the top ten; and if I have a nice and good week I should be able to win the tournament."

There is a charm about Poulter and his determination and sound values that make you warm to him. You want him to do well, despite your doubts. And as you follow his progress in the coming months, it would be as well to remember Muggeridge's words. *Tread Softly Lest You Tread On My Dreams.*

Player still driven by need to succeed

The Times, February 1, 1999

The invitation was for breakfast at Blair Atholl, Gary Player's 1,000-acre estate that lies north-west of Johannesburg. Soon after 8am, Player came down a broad staircase and took his place at the wide wooden table. It was the last of the 30 days that he spends annually at this house, one of the three homes he owns in his native country.

Gary Player and I have breakfasted before. Some years ago, he arrived after an overnight journey from South Africa. As he does on most flights, he had worn a tracksuit while in the air, laying down on the floor of the aircraft for some of the time, and had drunk litres of water. Just before landing, he had shaved, changed into a blazer and grey flannels and combed his hair.

As he disembarked, he looked as neat as a pin. He resembled an ageing film star, the effect of his entrance magnified by the fluttering presence nearby of the solicitous British Airways official.

On that day, between doing demonstrations of press-ups, his talk was full of praise for Winston Churchill (the man of the century, he said), Nelson Mandela (a saint), of how he had lost 1lb each year since he turned 50 and of his exercise routine.

He turned a scornful eye on the breakfast tray that had been delivered. "Didn't I ask for tea, wholewheat toast and Flora?" he said.

At Blair Atholl, Player was tucking into a bowl of corn porridge. "If I could take this with me everywhere I went in the world, I would be all right," he said. "It is good roughage. I recommend you put some sugar on it and milk and then mix it all up like this."

Player followed this with one piece of brown wholewheat toast, on which he spread butter and marmalade very thinly. He drank one cup of tea.

As he fuelled himself up for the day ahead, Player talked of the challenges he faces, aged 63. He and Sam Snead are the only men to win golf tournaments in five separate decades. Player has his sights set on winning in 2000, which would be his sixth decade, a record that he is confident will never be beaten.

"This is the only challenge left to me now," Player said. "I want it to be a PGA-sanctioned event, not something in the bush, and preferably in the US or Britain, because that is where the competition is.

"I need the physique, I need to live that long, to retain my golf swing and to remain strong. I have started to increase my exercises to meet the challenge. I am training for the year 2000 already.

"Einstein said that while we might exercise nearly 100 per cent of our bodies, we only exercise 10 per cent of our minds. Think what I could do if I increase that to 15 per cent. I shall be competing with Tom Watson, Tom Kite. They will be 50. I shall be 65. I must have a mind of steel."

If the truth be told, Player has been training all his life. Rarely has anyone been so driven as he is. Driven to make up for his lack of height, he pushes himself hard and when asked why, he quotes an aphorism of his father's: "Luck is the residue of design."

Player loves such sayings. "Trust instinct to the end, even you cannot render any reason" is one he uses often. Another, quoted by Marc, his older son, is: "Turnover is vanity, profit is sanity." A third: "Memories are the cushions of life."

Driven to compete with bigger and stronger rivals, Player set himself a daunting exercise programme to survive alongside Arnold Palmer and Jack Nicklaus, who, with him, formed the Big Three in golf.

"Jack and Arnold are the golfers of the century," Player said. "They behave so well. They are truly global, known everywhere in the world. They are great for the game."

But then the old competitiveness surfaced, the understandable urge to emphasise how he, so much smaller, had outplayed Nicklaus. "You know, Jack outdrove me by 60 yards but I beat him 6 and 5 in the World Match Play."

Player could have referred to a letter that he received after winning a tournament last August just before his 63rd birthday. "You absolutely amaze me," it read. It was signed simply, "Jack".

Driven is the only word to describe Player and his energy, which seems to be increasing with age. Player knows why he is like this, why he has travelled more than any other athlete in history – 11 million miles, or two dozen trips to and from the moon, at the latest count – and won nine major championships and 163 tournaments in all.

He knows why he is the only one of the Big Three still winning tournaments. And, after the breakfast had been cleared away, he revealed why. "I was eight years old," he said. "My father was working hundreds of feet below ground in the goldmines, earning £100 each month. My sister was at school. My older brother Ian wanted to fight in the war, but he was 16 and not old enough. My mother was dying, so I would come home from school and be by myself in the house in the evening.

"I used to think: 'I don't want to be poor, I don't want to live like this.' So I began exercising. I took up challenges and they have become a habit.

"I say a thank-you to the man upstairs for the talent he has loaned me. I believe that when you get old, you eat more, you lounge around, you get cancer, you die. So as I get older, I will always be busy." Then Player was off, to catch a plane to London en route to Hawaii, to Perth, to Japan and the United States.

Breakfast with this man who could give Norman Vincent Peale lessons in positive thinking had been inspiring. As he shook my hand, I concluded that he might achieve that victory in his sixth decade. I, for one, would not bet against it and would be delighted if he did.

Bonallack will be a hard act to follow

The Times, February 8, 1999

Henry Longhurst always said that he had the best job in the world. "I am paid to do what I want to do, which is to write about golf," the distinguished correspondent used to marvel, peering at his shoes through the bottom of a glass of gin.

But among those jobs that could push Longhurst's close is that of the secretary of the Royal and Ancient Golf Club of St Andrews. The incumbent of this office works a wedge shot away from one of the broadest beaches in Britain, used in the opening scenes of *Chariots of Fire*. The room in which he works is big enough to hold a bunker, a putting green and a pitching area as well. From this eyrie overlooking the 1st and 18th holes of the Old Course, half the Kingdom of Fife is visible on a clear day and, from the binoculars mounted on the balcony outside his office, the secretary can identify the make of a ball in the Road Hole bunker and count the dimples, too.

Sir Michael Bonallack has held this job since 1983. "It is nice to know a knight," David Fay, the executive director of the United States Golf Association (USGA), said when Bonallack was honoured last summer. "Michael has been the outstanding administrator in the game. Given what he has done as a British champion golfer and what he has contributed to the game, this is a most deserved honour. It is very rare to find a champion turning into an administrator in such a seamless manner."

Now though, Bonallack is putting out on the 18th green of his career. He will be 65 on December 31 and a successor is being sought to work alongside him for the past few months. A Glasgow-based firm, Genesis Consulting, has drawn up a shortlist to be considered by a five-man selection committee drawn from among the R & A hierarchy.

The chairman of this committee is Ian Webb, a leading Ulster businessman, who is chairman of the general committee. The other four members are Gordon Jeffrey, a retired Liverpool lawyer who made his name by his skilful handling of the R & A's case during the dispute with Ping; Richard Cole-Hamilton, a former chief executive of the Clydesdale Bank and former chairman of Stakis Hotels; Dr David Marsh, a former Walker Cup player who is now a part-time occupational health physician on Merseyside; and Neil Crichton, a solicitor, and auditor of the Court of Session in Edinburgh.

These are the men who are planning for the day when, for the first time for nearly 50 years, the name Bonallack will not ring out in golf. You cannot go anywhere in the world without meeting someone who knows, has played with or against Bonallack or sat on a committee with him.

He has said that his swing resembles that of "a drunk shovelling coal" but he won five English Amateur and five British Amateur titles and competed in nine Walker Cup teams, being the playing captain of the one that won at St Andrews in 1971.

Two weeks ago, he was playing in a pro-am tournament with Ernie Els at Stellenbosch, near Cape Town. Last week, he was in Kenya. He will be off to the US for The Players Championship in March and will act as a referee at the Masters in April. Woe betide any player who thinks they can intimidate him into giving them a free drop.

Seve Ballesteros did precisely this a few years ago when his ball ended in an iffy lie and he called for a ruling. The moment that Bonallack's buggy hove into sight, with Bonallack wearing a blazer, his head covered by a baseball cap, Ballesteros probably knew he had no chance. He stated his case, Bonallack, who has known the odd bad lie in his time, listened unimpressed and then said, correctly and curtly: "Play it."

The man who brought Michael Bonallack to St Andrews is Colin Maclaine, a retired dentist from Lytham St Annes, and one of few Britons who are members of Augusta National. Maclaine, a past captain of the R & A. has recounted the story of how he persuaded Bonallack to take the job when they were sharing a taxi.

"There were 285 applicants and I whittled it down to 16. When we got down to the last four, they all went to be tested by an industrial psychologist. I still have the report on Michael somewhere. I remember the chap said that we should not be put off by his laid-back manner. He said that Michael would open his eyes wide enough to solve the problem in front of him and then go back to sleep again."

Applicants to succeed him include former international players, administrators and businessmen who play golf. It had been thought that the R & A might take this opportunity to make a root and branch change, but after a review three years ago this is not likely.

"The R & A is a highly efficient, tightly run organisation and that is good," Frank Hannigan, Fay's predecessor at the USGA, said. "The R & A has a staff of what, 30? I think it is wonderful. If Michael has been responsible for curbing the growth of bureaucracy, then God bless him."

Bagger suffers from the odd bogey

The Times, February 26, 2001

Golf is a game of such beauty and anguish played out over such stunning scenery that you would have thought it would make an ideal subject for films.

The clink of a putter sending a ball bobbing across a green. "Lights! Camera! Crack!" and a ball is hit out over the sea before it curves back to land on the edge of a fairway only feet from the top of a cliff.

Yet, down the years there has been no affinity between Hollywood and golf. Twentieth Century Fox's film of the novel *The Legend of Bagger Vance* opened in London last week and will soon go on general release in Ireland.

It is directed by Robert Redford, who as a boy watched Ben Hogan win his first tournament after the car crash that nearly killed him, and who has also made baseball and skiing films. He has also been one mean player in his time, once lowering his handicap to six.

Despite Redford's credentials, his film of *Bagger Vance* did poorly in the United States where its makers stand accused of turning a good book into a bad film.

Steven Pressfield's novel is set in Savannah in the early twentieth century. It is an absorbing tale of how Ranulph Junah, whose name is mysteriously changed in the film to Junuh, an outstanding local amateur, returns shell-shocked from the First World War, unable and unwilling to play golf.

In time, he is persuaded to uphold the honour of Savannah and participate in a challenge match between Walter Hagen and Bobby Jones staged at a resort that is on the verge of bankruptcy as a result of the Great Depression.

A caddie named Bagger Vance, a nod by Pressfield in the direction of mysticism and the Bhagavad-Gita, appears and helps Junah and, with a mixture of the sort of homily and mysticism that has been fashionable in golf for some time now, enables Junah to take the match to a conclusion on the 18th green.

The book has some human redemption, a lot of mysticism and a degree of David matching Goliath. It is told by a young boy, Hardy Greaves, whose portrayal in the film is captivating.

All the ingredients are there. That it has done well as a book and is likely to do badly as a film highlights the conundrum as to the way golf has been so poorly served by film. There have been baseball and boxing films, a memorable one about rugby league, but the canon of golf film is hardly worth shaking a nine iron at. Why?

"I love the game," says Pressfield, who played good amateur golf in his early twenties. "It is such an internal game. The enemy is yourself but the rush of hitting a great shot is unforgettable. Perhaps it is because golf is a particularly elusive game and that the nature of it cannot be captured on screen."

One of the few good films about golf was *Caddyshack*. It was a good golf film because it turned a sharp eye onto the peculiarities and pomposities of golf and pricked them one by one. It was both fun and funny.

The golf scenes in the James Bond film *Goldfinger* were memorable and not offensive to those who know about the game, a real danger when actors portray sportsmen. They worked.

And so did *Follow the Sun*, the rather sentimental account of Ben Hogan in which Glenn Ford played the hero in a story that recounted Hogan's struggle, his near-death in a car crash and his comeback when he won three major championships in one year.

Looked at now, *Follow The Sun* is unbelievable, but put in the context of cinematic techniques of the time when it was made, it remains the best golf film there has been.

A few years ago there was a golf film called *Tin Cup*. It bowled along unmemorably enough until it came to the last scenes. Then it offended in two ways: it was historically inaccurate in its portrayal of the US Open being staged on a Florida-style golf course with artificial water hazards.

What is more, it beggared belief in expecting us to accept that the hero would keep whaling away, hitting shot after shot until finally one ball reaches the green and disappears in the hole.

Among golfers there was an outcry of "as if" at this overwrought conclusion. The result was that instead of tumbling out of the cinema and falling into animated conversations about the merits of the whole film, time was spent being scornful of its last scenes.

Films, clearly, are about suspending belief, but in *Bagger Vance* one or two requests are made to our beliefs that are simply too big to be asked. Expecting us to accept Will Smith as a believable Bagger Vance is one.

In the book, Junah was winning tournaments in the early days of the First World War. Assuming he was at least 20 by then, by 1937 he would have been at least 37. This is older than Smith and it takes some believing that a man who has been through all that Junah has been through could be convinced about the mystique of golf (and life) by a man who is younger than himself.

Caddies are supposed to be gnarled, round-shouldered, down at heel, having emerged with honours from the university of life. You ask for the yardage of a shot and they give you the explanation for the meaning of life.

This is what Vance did in the book but not what Smith does in the film. How much better and believable the casting of Bagger Vance would have been with Morgan Freeman, who could have brought age and gravitas to a part that calls out for those characteristics. A wise, old man is a caddie; a callow young thing is a bag-carrier.

Bagger Vance, Redford has said, "is about a man who has lost his authentic swing. I read the book and thought it had all the elements of great storytelling … the classic journey of a hero who falls into darkness and then comes back into the light with the help of a spiritual guide."

It is a good, if florid, film in which the actors who play Jones and Hagen excel. Their golfing prowess is good enough to stem criticism.

On the one day that he was invited onto the set, Pressfield said he was impressed by how seriously everyone took their jobs. Though he will say nothing about what he thinks of the film, which is revealing in itself, he does praise Redford for effort and attention to detail. "He was not cynically exploiting it. He has put his stamp on it and he gave it his all," Pressfield said.

But Redford's all in a film-making sense is not as good as Pressfield's as a writer.

Back-to-front St Andrews is still a tough old course

The Sunday Times, **February 12, 1989**

Michael Bonallack stood on the 1st tee of the Old Course at St Andrews wearing a battered sweater with a hole near the collar and carrying his 30-year-old clubs in a slim bag. "This is going to be interesting," he said, pulling down the peak of his cap and leaning into the strong wind. The man who knows the course backwards was about to play it backwards, with me as his partner.

Few people know the Old Course better. The secretary of the Royal and Ancient Golf Club has competed on the most famous course in the world in amateur and professional events as well as countless friendly matches. Five times Amateur champion, he scored 68 around the Old Course in the 1970 Open and led Great Britain and Ireland to a stunning defeat of the US in the 1971 Walker Cup at St Andrews. All this acquired knowledge was to be of no use to him whatsoever.

He teed up and aimed left of the bridge over the Swilcan Burn towards the green of the Road Hole and its guardian bunker. A strong wind gusted in his face. The hole measured 395 yards but Bonallack, still no mean hitter, doubted he could reach the green even with two woods.

Playing the left-hand (back-to-front) version of the Old Course, which at 6,489 yards is 200 yards shorter, is not a contemporary eccentricity, Bonallack pointed out. It harks back to the days of the feathery ball, the short spoon and the Georgian kings. It is the way the game always used to be played at the home of golf. The Opens of 1873, 1876, 1879 and 1881 were all held on the left-hand course, as was the 1886 Amateur. But then the authorities faced a crisis: the course was getting worn out. They ordained that play should be over the right-hand course and this quickly became accepted as the medal course.

However, it wasn't long before this course began to suffer from the pounding of feet as well. In 1906 *Golf Illustrated* noted "the practice of alternating the left-hand course with the ordinary right-hand course has been re-adopted and the turf already shows signs that the policy of change" produces less wear and tear. Thus began the tradition of alternating, although the left-hand course has been used only a couple of times since the war.

Since he became secretary of the R & A, Bonallack has looked out over the course from his office every working day. "If I had to play one course for the rest of my life, this would be it," he explained. "It presents so many different challenges. It's different every time I play it."

And never more so than when he stood on the 16th tee and aimed towards the 14th green and was actually playing the fourth hole. "I'm not sure what the best line is from here," said Bonallack, who now plays off a handicap of three. If you thought he was confused, you should have seen me. I was about to chip to what I thought was the seventh green when a shout stopped me in my tracks. "Oy," Bonallack shouted, pointing. "Over here. That's the 11th green." Not everything has changed. The 8th, 9th, 10th and 11th holes are still played in the traditional order.

As an attraction, the Old Course is to golfers what the Vatican is to Catholics.

A record 47,000 rounds were played over it last year and if it could be open 24 hours a day then it wouldn't satisfy demand. "I've just had a call from someone in Japan who wanted to book a starting time," Ian Forbes, deputy secretary of the St Andrews Links Trust, had said earlier. "I explained that he would have to play the course backwards. He didn't speak very good English and I think he thought I was taking the mickey."

Almost all the famous bunkers on the Old Course remain a danger when you play the left-hand course. The Spectacle bunkers on either side of the fifth green are a feature of the 14th and the Beardies will have to be negotiated even though you're playing them on the fifth. If there is an exception then it is Hell bunker, which is only 100 yards out from the fifth tee and safe enough, you'd have thought. Not a bit of it. Coming upon it unexpectedly, I nearly fell into it.

It is still possible to putt from the 17th green into the Swilcan Burn, just as the American Tom Shaw did when he was playing in the 1970 Open. I know because I nearly did it. And the menace of the Valley of Sin in front of the 18th green, where so many championships have been won and lost, is hardly diminished by coming at the green from a different angle. It nearly claimed Bonallack's approach shot.

"I enjoyed it," he said, pleased that even in blustery conditions the round had only taken 2 hours and 20 minutes and he'd come in at 38. "It *was* interesting but there were too many blind shots. I prefer the course the right way round."

MARCH

"Is the jazz still good in Bourbon Street? Do the narrow streets of the French Quarter, lined by brick buildings with ornate wrought-iron balconies, exert as great a pull as ever? Does the Café du Monde still serve its delicious slightly bitter coffee and beignets?"

I grant you that is an unusual opening paragraph from a golf tournament. But I was in New Orleans in March 1995 on a three-week assignment, looking forward to the next week's Masters in Augusta and looking back at The Players Championship which had just finished at the Tournament Players Club in Ponte Vedra Beach, near Jacksonville, northern Florida.

For some time when The Players Championship was held in March, this annual 21-day jaunt was a highlight of the third month of the year that often leeched into April. The route was Jacksonville, New Orleans and later Atlanta and then Augusta. Paul Theroux wrote that "extensive travelling induces a feeling of encapsulation, and travel, so broadening at first, contracts the mind" but I have never felt anything other than pleasure at the thought of a trip such as this.

The time in 1982 when The Players moved from Sawgrass Country Club in Ponte Vedra Beach to the specially designed Pete Dye Stadium course at the Tournament Players Club just across the road coincided with it becoming the fifth most important strokeplay tournament in the world. The Masters, the Opens of the US and Britain and the PGA of America's championship, known, probably incorrectly, as the US PGA, retain their pre-eminence but the annual staging of The Players Championship starts a chorus for it to be added to the game's major championships. This is a plea that the heart might answer with a yes but to which the head says no because there are enough major championships held in the US as it is.

For 15 years, my birthday fell when I was on this trip and I celebrated it once with a nine-course tasting menu at a restaurant in New Orleans, and several times with a lip-smacking piece of fish at The Dolphin Depot in Jacksonville. Either that day or some other and sometimes both I would run on Jacksonville's beach, which extended farther than the eye could see in both directions. For a number of years several of us journalists stayed in the Sea Turtle, a large hotel on the edge of the Atlantic, until it was discovered that the reason we couldn't make telephone calls from our rooms back to our offices in London was that the owner had not been paying his rates for years.

I have very happy memories of The Players because covering it in March often represented a dramatic climatic change. One year I remember having a Sunday morning game at Highgate, my club in London, with sodden turf underfoot and a distinct nip in the air. The next time I touched a club was on the practice ground near to The Players Club where the turf was firm, the sky blue and the temperature in the mid seventies.

Augusta National remains the best example of a club that annually hosts a very important tournament and a course that regularly receives a huge amount of work to its greens, tees and fairways but the Stadium course at the TPC is not far behind. "This event has improved year by year and last week we were privy once again to one of the most blatant seduction attempts since Salome's," I wrote from Jacksonville in March 1999. "The Players Championship, in all its glory, was making its case to become a major championship."

When The Players moved from March to May, in part to get better weather and in part to join a monthly run of important events – following the Masters in April and preceding the US Open in June – a little of the early season excitement went out of March. The event still generated stories, though, sometimes coming from the induction ceremonies of famous people in golf at the World Golf Hall of Fame in nearby St Augustine, which take place on the Monday of the week of The Players, and sometimes from interviews with Tim Finchem, the Commissioner of the PGA Tour.

In May 2013 he and I were having a chat in the huge, ornate clubhouse when he leaned back in his chair and ruminated on golf. "I guess I am realising I have fallen in love with practice," he said finally. "This year and last year have been difficult to get anything going after the winter. Now is the time I've got to play between April and late June."

"Are you working on anything?" he was asked. "A couple of years ago you said you were. You were working with one particular professional."

The answer was quick. "If I go off and can't play for two weeks, when I come back it takes me about 40 minutes to conjure up the way I was supposed to be thinking about what I'm doing … it's awkward." He grinned. "The typical woes of the average player."

Then he brightened. "But I have my moments. I played quite well for three or four weeks last summer. I had a career round, 67, out in Colorado. I played 36 holes that day, shot 83 in the morning and 67 in the afternoon. How do you figure that out? It's all between your ears.

"That round was totally out of character. I think I've only broken 70 three or four times ever. So I have this strange score and I kept thinking about it and I kept not thinking about my score in the morning. This is the new me. Then I go off to play in this thing and I play dreadfully. I shot 84, 85."

He started laughing at the incongruity of it all, shaking his head. "I don't know about this game. I just don't know." There was just about the most important man in golf, puzzled and smitten by the game, just like the rest of us.

With the move of The Players to May, March became a time to write features, to talk to Peter Alliss, to interview Arnold Palmer at his golf club in Orlando, Florida, to visit Aberdovey, Bernard Darwin's favourite course in the world, as well as writing a piece that suggested the R & A had missed a trick in not inviting Judy Bell to become the first female member when she was president of the United States Golf Association.

March wasn't a great month for Julius Caesar but covering golf, travelling the world, I never had any trouble in passing the time. The Ides were good to me.

Fallen Faldo still refusing to accept decline

The Times, March 15, 1999

In January this year, Nick Faldo uttered the most depressing words I have heard on a golf course for a long time. He had just completed a bad round at the

Houghton course in Johannesburg, another bad round, and was heading towards the practice ground again. "There are no surprises left in golf, only disappointments," Faldo said. This from the man who was once ranked the best golfer in the world for 80 weeks, whose mental strength obliterated Greg Norman in the Masters three years ago, who has won more major championships – six in all – since 1980 than any other golfer.

When success is around, failure is never far behind because the greater the degree of success, the greater the risk of failure. Faldo has had plenty of success. By many yardsticks, though, he is, at present, a failure. His consistency, once a byword, has gone. Only two of his 12 strokeplay rounds this year have been under par, so it is not surprising that he has missed the halfway cut in four of the five events in which he has competed. He is struggling to remain not in the top 50 but in the top 100 players in the world. His putting, which he used to practise on the linoleum in the kitchen of his parents' home, comes and goes and his ball striking is erratic.

Yet Faldo refuses to countenance the word failure. At its mention, he frowns and grimaces, as a priest might at an obscenity. "There is no point in thinking about it," he said. "You set yourself a goal, in this case to be in the Ryder Cup team, and there is no point in interjecting failure into it, otherwise there is no point in having it as a goal. You might as well give up.

"Sure, I might not make it, but I'm not going to let everyone think it is going to happen. If you think your ball is going to go into the lake, where does it go? That's the whole beauty of having something as a goal. It keeps you going, keeps you positive, keeps you out there. You've got to keep pursuing your goals and, if you can't be bothered to set goals or if a goal is failure, then you've got no chance.

"It is frustrating because I know what I can do. I have done it in the past – stood up there with an iron in my hand and fired it, '*whooooosh*', straight at the flag, but the bottom line is that there is something wrong. It is not something that is in the lap of the gods. It is there and you still have to find it. It is a process of elimination."

Does it ever occur to Faldo that work might not be the answer? His reply came quickly. "No. Work is always the answer.

"I don't believe the answer is sitting in an armchair saying 'well, I'll forget it for a week. It's all going to be all right'. I can't see that theory working at all.

"I come out every day really feeling good. I get up, go out to the golf course thinking 'yesterday we did some really good work. I've got some good things to work on. Let's go out and play and let it all happen. I am really looking forward to it.' Those sort of thoughts. And what happens? Usually, I get a walloping. I think today it is going to change and it doesn't. That's the hardest bit.

"I get angry out there. I get as mad as hell. That is either the wonderful thing or the hardest thing about golf. There are no guarantees in it. Put your clubs down for three months and you're rusty again. You've got to work your way back into it. Not many players don't work at it. All the greats have worked on it.

"I have had a lot of letters from people who have got the answer to my problem. I've had a few belters. I love the one that started off 'It's simple. I can solve your problems' and there were six pages of the tiniest writing you've ever seen in your life. It must have been well over 2,000 words. I didn't even read it. I thought if this is meant to be simple, I need it in two lines – do this, do that."

When you are down as low as Faldo, any recovery can only come in small stages. "You have to take it step by step. The next step is to start playing really solid, start getting some decent scores, get to the right end of the leaderboard. Then, we start looking at winning again. Win a regular event before we start thinking of winning majors, I guess."

And if, in the process, Faldo were not to make the Ryder Cup team? What would that mean? "I am planning to. I am not going to think negatively like that. A couple of months here [in the United States] to sort it out and then I will go back to Europe and start chipping away at the points.

"Nothing is easy at the moment. Yes, there are moments when you begin to wonder about it all. The game is giving you a beating all the time. You have to be very determined, that's the bottom line. You have got to keep chipping away all the time. I'll get there in the end. That's my attitude. I know I will. It ain't gonna beat me. I'm not going to roll over."

Golf's First Lady still remains an outsider

The Times, March 17, 2003

As the story unfolds of the struggle between Augusta National and Martha Burk, the leader of a women's rights group in the United States who wants the all-men golf club to induct female members, another woman goes quietly about her business in the US with a slight smile on her face. Judy Bell, 67, a talkative, friendly woman whose iron-grey hair frames a round face, smiles because she is the central figure in a game of "what if".

What if events in 1996 had been slightly different for Bell? What if she had

USGA president Judy Bell with Ernie Els after the US Open at
the Congressional Country Club in Bethesda, Maryland, 1997.

made history by becoming a member first of the men-only Royal and Ancient Golf Club of St Andrews and then of Augusta National? Such a chain of circumstances might have been sufficient to have prevented the row between Burk's National Council of Women's Organisations and Hootie Johnson, the chairman of Augusta National, that is preoccupying people in golf before Augusta hosts the Masters, which begins on April 10.

These "what ifs" do not require a massive leap of the imagination. Bell was elected president of the United States Golf Association (USGA) in 1996. She was the first woman, and remains the only one, to hold that role in the organisation's 102 years. She was an experienced administrator in both the men's and women's game, a former Curtis Cup player and captain, a past chairman of the USGA's championship committee and a fixture on many of its other committees. Some of her work was done in conjunction with the R & A, which sets the rules throughout the world, except in the US and Mexico, where the USGA has primacy.

Imagine the reflected glory that would have accrued to the R & A if the holder of such impressive credentials had become a member. Instead of being labelled in some colourful quarters as an organisation that is out of touch with modern society, it would be hailed as having been far-sighted and aware of the surge towards gender equality. By the same token, if Bell had become eligible to wear the famous green jacket that marks out members at Augusta, that would have meant no Burk in Augusta next month, no Jesse Jackson, the civil rights leader, protesting in support of Burk, and no Ku Klux Klan protesting at the presence of Jackson in Georgia.

"It's quite a logical hypothesis," Sir Michael Bonallack, who was secretary of the R & A at the time, said. "But the point is that the rules of the club do not allow you to invite people to become members. People who want to become members have to be proposed and seconded by existing members. It would have been great if she had been, but she wasn't and, being a members' club, the R & A has to abide by its rules. It is not true to say that every USGA president has become a member of the R & A. They have not. But a lot of presidents of the USGA were members of the R & A."

There is a sense of a glorious opportunity having been missed here for want of a little daring and a lot of time. In fact, in 1996 there was comment about Bell joining the R & A, but it was never formally discussed. "No one who could make that happen asked me," Bell said. "But certain various members said they wished that it could happen."

This view is confirmed by an R & A member who was in a position of authority at the time. "There were passing comments [about Bell and women]," the former official said. "In every organisation there are people who think outside the box and when Judy became president some of these people wondered whether the R & A would consider such a move. The world has changed these past three or four years and if Judy had become president of the USGA three or four years later it might have happened. As it was it came upon us. Suddenly it happened. The R & A did not have the mechanism to deal with it. And then Judy's term ended and the problem did not exist any longer."

Peter Dawson, Bonallack's successor, believes that if Bell had become the R & A's sole woman member, it would have been brazen tokenism. "How shallow that would be," he said. It was pointed out to him that when Ron Townsend, a black man, was elected Augusta's first non-white member, and the only one for a number of years, it silenced the clamouring for such a move.

"But there is no similarity between racial discrimination and single-sex golf clubs," Dawson said. "Racial discrimination is seated in bigotry and violence. It is to be abhorred. There are 3,000 golf clubs in Britain and 99 per cent of them are mixed. We [the R & A] support the strides towards equality. I think that golf is doing very well.

"If the R & A had elected one woman member, then it would be a quarter of a nanosecond before the media would say that is not enough. I have been here for nearly four years and in that time I have had only two letters on the subject [of equality]. This is a media-driven campaign."

Bell herself felt no strong desire to join the R & A. "In 1996–97 I was on the executive committee of the USGA and I had a lot of contacts in the R & A. I can't see how being a member of the R & A could affect the way I functioned. I was welcomed there. I was comfortable. I didn't have any trouble asking hard questions. I was able to function as president of the USGA. I would not have taken that for two minutes if I hadn't. You would have seen me throw a fit.

"How can you say women would be better off if I had been a member of the R & A? What's it going to benefit? Matter of fact, if I joined tomorrow I can't imagine I would be as effective as when I worked with the R & A as president of the USGA."

Bell has wondered what would have happened if she had been asked to become a member of Augusta. "I am certainly for seeing women go as far as they can on merit," she said. "There are a lot of ways of getting there. Is this the best way? I don't know. I would think about all the same issues I would think about if I joined any club. Does this make any sense on my journey? How much will

I play? I am not in a position to become a member of a club I could not use. I don't care if Augusta is all men. I am comfortable with separation.

"I am sorry but that is where it is. No one can send a letter and expect to change the traditions of a club. Men or women have a right to decide who is in their club. Clubs can decide who they want as members. There is no discrimination between men and women at that event. I don't know as a female where someone is more welcome."

Tiger Woods's efforts to wipe slate clean don't wash with me
The Times, March 23, 2010

Ari Fleischer, the former spokesman for President George W. Bush who persuaded Tiger Woods to give two television interviews on Sunday, has moved on.

Did Fleischer do a good job for Woods, his client? Have the five-minute interviews that Woods gave to Tom Rinaldi of ESPN and The Golf Channel's Kelly Tilghman on Sunday night finally got Woods off the media hook? Will he now be able to turn up for the Masters next month and not be bothered by the public interest that has been generated by his marital infidelities?

Woods did say that his behaviour was "disgusting", but there has hardly been a diminution of interest in what he did and why he did it.

As with so many things that have happened to Woods since he crashed his car on November 27, 2009, all is not what it seems. Short interviews conducted entirely on his terms are hardly soul-baring confessionals.

With luck there will be further attempts to get Woods to explain himself at the Masters. If he deigns to appear in front of the press, he will almost certainly try to answer only golf-related questions but I hope one journalist will have the professional courage to risk being ejected from the press conference by asking Woods non-golf questions.

There are doubts as to whether Woods was telling the truth when he said to Tilghman: "No one [in his inner circle of friends] knew what was going on when it was going on …"

How does that square with the e-mails that a celebrity website posted suggesting that the travel arrangements to Melbourne for one of Woods's alleged girlfriends had been paid for by an employee of his?

Woods has a technique to sound convincing. He widens his eyes and raises his voice slightly. He used it in his laughable mea culpa in Florida last month and he used it on Sunday. It didn't wash in February and it didn't wash this month.

A number of golfers came out in support of Woods yesterday, which was precisely what the interviews were meant to do. Will Ernie Els and Geoff Ogilvy, who criticised Woods for disrupting the Accenture Match Play Championship last month, tell him to his face that he probably should not have hijacked the Masters by making his comeback there either? Is he being fair on his peers?

Will Woods be a changed man, as he said he would be last month? "I need to make my behaviour more respectful of the game," he had said.

Woods may think he can now be welcomed back. If he thinks that ten minutes on television will achieve that, he almost certainly cannot have listened to Fleischer. Perhaps that is why the spin doctor left, not because he was, as he said, creating a diversion. Woods's performance on Sunday left a lot to be desired.

Cheap shots at top Scot are out of bounds
The Times, March 13, 1998

Rummaging around on my desk the other night, I came upon a card. Colin S. Montgomerie BA it said on the top line, with the words "European Tour Golf Professional" in capital letters underlined beneath. In the bottom left-hand corner was his address in Troon, Ayrshire, and in the bottom right his telephone number.

It was a hangover from the mid eighties, the days when Montgomerie was just starting on his career as a pro and felt he needed publicity. Now a multimillionaire, Europe's No 1 these past five years appears to be everyone's punchbag. The latest attack has come from a weekly sports magazine in the United States.

The bilious article was entitled "Here Come Da Scot" and subtitled "Never-popular Colin Montgomerie brings his bluster to the States". The second and third sentences went as follows: "Colin Montgomerie, the Goon from Troon, golf's Gael-force windbag, returns from the European Tour to give us fits at Doral this week. When we last despised him, Monty was leading Europe past our Ryder Cup team after ripping our boys in the press."

To make matters worse, the article was anonymous. No one had the courage to stand up and be counted, just as one of the three people who were quoted was that well-known source, "an insider".

Why does Montgomerie attract such contumely? It is, partly, because he deserves it. He can be churlish, badly behaved and rude. There are moments when the overriding feeling of observers is to grab him and shriek: "Colin, stop behaving like an idiot. You are letting yourself down."

Montgomerie, then, is no saint, but nor is Tiger Woods, who has been known to utter an obscenity after a poor stroke and bang his club on the ground now and then. He swore at a lady official at a tournament earlier this year. But, whereas Woods's behaviour is excused as being passionate, Montgomerie's is considered intemperate and rude.

Montgomerie cannot help the complexion of his face, though he hardly deserves to be described in this article as "the pasty Scot ... a firth-class jerk". The most gratuitous insult hitherto had been David Feherty's nickname for Montgomerie of "Mrs Doubtfire".

Feherty described the Scot when angry as resembling "a bulldog", among other things. It was to Montgomerie's credit that, though hurt by such stinging – and funny – insults, he did not lower himself to respond to them.

Woods gets away with it; Montgomerie does not. Sam Torrance gets away with it; Montgomerie does not. In these columns three years ago I likened Torrance and Montgomerie to characters in a Bateman cartoon. Torrance is "The Scot Who Can Do No Wrong" while Montgomerie is "The Scot They Cannot Warm To".

I suggested that "Sam could covet his neighbour's wife, not to mention his ox and his ass, steal his malt whisky and do cartwheels down the main street of Auchtermuchty while 15 sheets to the wind, and the people who are so reproving of Montgomerie would merely cluck, shake their heads and say 'Och Sam, he's just a gallus [rascal]'."

Montgomerie does not suffer fools gladly. He is highly intelligent and ambitious and one of those rare people who is gifted enough at golf to achieve all that he has having expended half as much perspiration and spent half as much time on the practice ground as his rivals.

In what is beginning to resemble a vendetta against him, critics overlook that he is the finest golfer in Europe week in and week out. Davis Love III says Montgomerie hits the best iron-shots that he has ever seen, admiring particularly the ball flight and accuracy.

No one in golf talks so articulately and concisely as Montgomerie – when he wants to. He says things sometimes that would be better left unsaid. Remarks about Brad Faxon's divorce before the Ryder Cup last year come into that category.

Montgomerie is at his peak, a man who has had two seconds, a third and a tenth in the US Open and a second in the US PGA Championship, losing play-offs in both events. His drive on the 18th in his singles match in the Ryder Cup last year was described recently by Severiano Ballesteros as one of the strokes of the year. It is to be hoped that Montgomerie's reaction to this wave of hostility in the US would be to silence his critics by winning tournaments.

If the events of the past week were a boxing match, and at times Montgomerie must feel that his life resembles a contest against the rest of the world, the referee would have stopped the bout and warned his opponent about low blows. "Gloves up" would have been the command. "A clean fight, please. Box on!"

Evergreen Palmer retains all his zest

The Times, March 22, 1999

More than 40 years ago a young golfer forced himself into the American consciousness with the shattering power of one of his own drives. With a thrilling style of play, a wink, and a hitch of his trousers, Arnold Palmer took the first steps that led to his present status as one of the most revered men in the United States, one of the great sporting icons of the second half of the century.

Palmer was at it again in Florida last week. The man who has won seven major championships was broader in the beam, slower of gait, but still winking, laughing, sighing and wearing his heart on his sleeve. Palmer charmed golf once more while acting as host of a tournament at his club and launching an enchanting book about himself.

Few sportsmen in the United States have earned the level of popularity of this man, who was once asked to run for a career in politics. "I wasn't going to be a politician," he said, laughing. "Too many skeletons in the closet."

He was once summoned by President Richard Nixon and Dr Henry Kissinger and asked how to solve the Vietnam problem. On Palmer's 37th birthday in 1966 came a knock on the door. "You wouldn't have room to put up an old man for the night, would you?" Dwight D. Eisenhower, President of the United States between 1953 and 1961, asked as he stood on the doorstep of Palmer's home.

Look at Palmer now, a Tintin-like curl of snowy hair atop a face weathered as brown as a walnut. A hearing aid is just visible in his right ear. Those massive hands fidget restlessly, scratching at his huge forearms. He has just faced down prostate cancer as he once used to outstare curling three-foot putts.

You don't so much have an interview with Palmer as an audience while he sips at a beer and stuffs crisps into his mouth and receives the greetings of players as a king at court, which, I suppose, is just what he is. There is a magnetism about him that is electric. You just want him to like you, to acknowledge you, to give you a wink. Down the years, Palmer has had a great rivalry with Jack Nicklaus. The two men were strong and gifted, each recognisably shaped by the influences of their dominant fathers.

Nicklaus was the cool one, the product of a Germanic background, Palmer the "let 'er rip" young boy whose father had played golf the same way. Nicklaus was the roundhead, Palmer the cavalier.

It is an odd coincidence that the nature of their rivalry and their differences in personality are continued in their recent books. Nicklaus's is enormous and fact-filled, a stone-cold piece of testimony, Nicklausian to a tee in its thoroughness. Palmer's is folksy, a crafted piece of work that worms its way into your heart as quickly and convincingly as the author himself.

Now Palmer has made his way into the locker room at Bay Hill, after a round in the company of Severiano Ballesteros and Bob Friend. "Give me a beer," he has just roared, needing some solace to ease his unhappiness after a 78, still unwilling to accept that such a score was far from a disgrace for a man who will be 70 in November. It was in this calm locker room that Palmer aired his views on some of today's issues in golf.

On Tiger Woods: "I think that frown all the time and slamming the club down doesn't do anything for his game. He's got the world in his hands. All he has to do is to enjoy it and laugh."

On manners: "Pap [Deacon, Palmer's father] had a thing about living and having good manners. It was just the proper thing in my family and I suppose it was the tradition my father thought very strongly about, whether it means taking your hat off inside or particularly at a dinner table with ladies. It was a fetish with him. It was more than a fetish. It was a positive to take your hat off and it was a positive that you learnt how to use a knife and fork and how to talk to people. Manners and etiquette and proper conduct are a part of what makes a nation such as ours strong and solid. If you lose that, or if it goes away, then you weaken the very nucleus of the country and the people."

On money in team events: "To make winning money a feature of the Ryder or Presidents Cup would be very bad. I think you see the spirit in which the guys play the game without money and I think that's important. If you have to instil that spirit by putting up money, then I think it's bad."

On his father: "Pap was a muscular, mentally tough guy and I loved that. He never backed off anything from the time I was a little fellow. Boy was he strong. He could do ten pull-ups with his left arm and then ten with his right. He was never more than 180lb and I saw him wrestle two 200lb men and pin them to the ground, one in each arm. He reminded me of Spencer Tracy. He was a very quiet person. He was as cavalier as I was. He suffered from infantile paralysis and had a club left foot. As a result he played golf from an open position, his left side was always pointed to the left of the target, and when he was young the shots that he played were always low driving shots at the target. Naturally, I picked that up."

On Severiano Ballesteros: "My father taught me that when you are not sure what to say, don't say anything. He still has a magic touch but his long game is … he hit it out of bounds on the 4th hole. He hit it across two fairways into a lake. Who knows whether you get it back, but at 42 years old you've got lots of time to keep trying. I am not sure what he has to do. I am not sure what he has done up to this point to get it back. He should have one person teaching him and stick with him, somebody who knows, or not anyone and do it himself."

Alliss finds no reason to regret wounding words at Carnoustie

The Times, March 13, 2000

Peter Alliss, television's pre-eminent golf commentator, celebrated his 69th birthday recently with a glass in his hand in the first-class compartment of a plane returning from the United States where he had seen Darren Clarke defeat Tiger Woods in the final of the Andersen Consulting Match Play championship. Alone with his thoughts at 35,000ft, Alliss might have pondered the tradition of golf that his father had begun and he continued first as a player and now as a commentator, or the pleasures of the family of two boys and a daughter he and Jackie, his second wife, have reared.

What he did not think about any more was the final day of the Open

Championship last year, when his commentary created a furore. "Alliss in blunderland" was one headline; "The Open – a nice walk ruined by a garrulous commentator" was another; "Alliss stuck in a bunker" was a third.

The *Daily Mail* started a debate about Alliss and more than 2,000 letters poured into its offices in answer to its calls for a view as to whether Alliss "played out the destruction of Jean Van de Velde's hopes on Carnoustie's 18th hole like Victor Meldrew".

"I was amazed at the response," Alliss said. "More than 2,000 people responded. They said it was six or seven to one in my favour but I heard from inside sources it was actually about eight to one. That was quite humbling."

Were they writing to say you were a good golf commentator, or that what you had said at the Open was OK? "It was a mix. Some said 'leave him alone. We are more than happy.'"

Were you surprised by the fierceness of the criticism? "Some of it, yes. But they did it to my father." But criticism is much more personal now. They call you an old fool, a silly bugger, an old fart, a dinosaur. Do you mind that? "No." Does it bounce off you? "Sticks and stones. It hurts.

"It would be wrong to say it wasn't uncomfortable because I did not know what was going to happen," Alliss said. "I was thinking 'perhaps they're right?' That didn't last very long because letters started coming to the BBC in support. They sent them to me in batches of 100 and there weren't more than three out of 100 that said 'about time, you big poof, bugger off.'"

Alliss was speaking in the house in Hindhead that he and Jackie, a local magistrate, bought 20 years ago when they moved to Surrey from Leeds. A big, warm house that reflects Alliss's personality, it had in the sitting room a television showing pictures of BSkyB's transmission of the golf tournament in Qatar. Alliss was ebullient, offering coffee, telling stories, posing for photographs. He said that when he returned home from San Diego he had said to Jackie, for one of the few times in the past five years: "I thought I was on good form last week."

I wondered whether he had had similar thoughts about Carnoustie. "I never had any thoughts about it because I was so overwhelmed by the golfing disaster of Van de Velde. It was a long day and there were cries down to the TV centre to keep going and the Americans were shouting that it was running into overtime. It wasn't a clean finish on a lovely summer's evening with Jack Nicklaus up the last hole at St Andrews with a two-shot lead. It wasn't tidy.

"I didn't know what to say. It was a chapter of sad things where, in my opinion, someone who played the game professionally, his golfing brain just switched off, it blew a major fuse. You could have put an 18-handicap golfer there and he wouldn't have made a worse mess-up of it."

Did you regret your remark about Van de Velde delaying everyone from going home and having a nice dinner? "Yes, well, slightly. It went on a long time. The whole thing was becoming a bit of nonsense. I would like to do it again but that is instant television. It was one of the saddest sporting occasions that I had ever witnessed."

Around the house, Alliss is known jokingly as the dinosaur. He plays up to it in the same way he likes to present himself as an old soak on television, often saying to a fellow commentator "time for a G and T" when, in fact, he drinks sparingly and never gin and tonic.

He likes to pretend to be firm with his children. When his son's school friends come to visit, Alliss is likely to tell them off for wearing baseball caps around the house or putting a can of beer on the table or for being impolite or rude. And when his daughter brought home a boyfriend he would say to the suitor: "I hope your intentions are honourable towards my daughter. Don't think you can get up to any hanky panky with her, my boy."

"People regard me as a hard-nosed right winger and the old jokes about Genghis Khan, but I do believe I would bring back capital punishment. I would open up a few prisons as they were in 1750 and I would have them on a short chain on a wall for about a week. They would do all their own business, sit in their own muck and then I'd say 'what do you think about that? You've just smashed up Mrs Jones's face. Now if you like that you can come back again next week. And if you snuff it, then bad luck. We'll put you in a box and throw some lime on you and that'll be it because you're no bloody good to anybody.' Anyone who wants to rape women of 85 or murder children, they're … I don't hold with it."

I asked what Alliss would say if Van de Velde walked into the room? "I'd say 'Jean, nice to see you'. I might say something like 'I don't know about you but I am not sure I have totally recovered from Carnoustie'. I might even say 'I hope you don't think I was too jocular, I hope you don't think I was taking the mickey or I hope you don't think I was too flippant because for me, Jean, having been in the game all my life and the Alliss family having been involved in golf for the best part of this century, if I said anything you might have interpreted as being rude then I am sorry.'

"If he said 'I did at the time', I would reply 'well, I hope time has healed it'. I had no intention of making him look stupid. He was doing that well enough on his own."

Unmoved by the Players draw

The Times, March 29, 1999

On Thursday morning, while walking out to watch some competitors in The Players Championship. I passed the 9th green of the Stadium Course at the Tournament Players Club here near Jacksonville, in Florida, and noticed that there were 12 greenkeeping staff at work on it. Some were mowing the green, some the edges of bunkers, others were raking the sand and still more were trimming the whiskery fringes of the green. This was impressive. Even the richest woman in the world rarely has this much attention and expense lavished on her.

Yet this is commonplace at The Players Championship, the most important event in the calendar for the PGA Tour, the body that looks after the touring professionals of the United States. This event has improved year by year and last week we were privy once again to one of the most blatant seduction attempts since Salome's. The Players Championship, in all its glory, was making its case to become a major championship.

There are four championships in the men's game that are regarded as being above all others and thus known as majors. It should be pointed out that they have reached their pre-eminence without direct help from the Royal and Ancient Golf Club and the United States Golf Association. Officials from these two bodies, or any other bodies come to that, do not sit down every so often and decide to create major championships. But why those four?

Robert Tyre Jones, the legendary amateur known as Bobby Jones, is held responsible for this because in 1930 he won what were then the two most important events in the leading golfing countries of the world – the Amateur and Open championships of the US and Britain.

If Jones had won three or five it might be different now, Robert Sommers, the noted historian and writer, said. Jones's biographer, O.B. Keeler, called Jones's cache of titles The Impregnable Quadrilateral, an unforgettable name even to those who do not know what a quadrilateral is, never mind how to spell it.

So the idea of four major championships as the supreme tests was born. And these four it remained for years, even though the Amateur championship in Britain no longer had a stellar field, even though the Masters had begun and been given international fame by Gene Sarazen's holed three-wood from the 69th fairway in 1935, and even though the professionals in the US had been contesting their own championship since 1916. Not until Arnold Palmer burst upon the stage of golf did the final act of deification of a new quartet of events occur.

In his new book Palmer outlines how he and Bob Drum, a journalist from Pittsburgh, more or less together established the modern grand slam on an aeroplane flight to Ireland and Scotland in 1960. Their account has a ring of truth to it.

"Somewhere on my first flight over ... Drum and I got to talking about Jones's great grand slam," Palmer wrote. "Drum remarked to me that it was a shame that the growth of the professional game ... effectively ended the grand-slam concept as it had been known in Jones's day. 'Well,' I said casually over my drink, 'why don't we create a new grand slam?'"

"'What the hell are you talking about?' Drum muttered. Though probably a little more colourfully than that.

"I explained what I was thinking. What would be wrong with a professional grand slam involving the Masters, both Open championships and the US PGA Championship?"

And so the modern grand slam was born. It remains four events, an appropriate number in a game dominated by the word four. For example, level fours, or a round of 72, was widely regarded as a standard for years, play is often in four-balls and when two players hit one ball alternately, it is known as foursomes.

There are par-fives and par-threes on almost every course, but there are nearly always more par-fours. But what makes a major championship? Quality of field is one criterion. It has to be an event that the best players want to win on an outstanding golf course.

A major championship cannot be created one year, downgraded the next. The steady throb of history is the lifeblood of a major championship. In 1987, just after Sandy Lyle had won The Players Championship, he was asked the difference between that championship and the Open. "About 115 years," he replied drily.

Major championship status is bestowed by the public and the game's historians, and by the media. Do not underestimate the media. After all, the man who named the 11th, 12th and 13th at Augusta "Amen Corner" was Herbert Warren Wind, the brilliant essayist, in an article in *Sports Illustrated,* just as it was Drum (and others later), who campaigned for what we now know as the modern grand slam, that shaped public opinion.

Which leaves only the players. Their views and influence are powerful. Last month Tiger Woods was asked whether he thought the new World Match Play Championship would become a major. He said that he did not think so. "Golf is about traditionalists and traditionalists don't ever want to see another major added," Woods said. "It is very difficult to incorporate a new event into what has been there for quite some time. You can't relate and compare. You can't compare yourself versus a Gene Sarazen versus a guy in 2050. I don't see it happening. Definitely not in my lifetime."

Last week Woods was asked if The Players Championship was close to being a major. "No," Woods replied. "Which is the one you want to win – ten Players Championships or six Masters? I think any player would say the Masters because you can draw comparisons on the great ones who have played the game from the Hogans, the Nicklauses, Watsons, Nelsons."

It would seem, then, that The Players Championship has little chance of becoming a major. It can continue its annual attempts at seduction by, among other things, upgrading still further the free car that the players are lent for the tournament and continuing to increase its prize fund – this year's was double that of four years ago and the first prize is greater than the total prize money at many events on the European Tour.

But that does not completely cut the mustard. "The British Open is close to 130 years old and has the title of being a major, the Players does not," Justin Leonard, the 1997 Open and 1998 Players champion, said last week. "Therefore, there is no reason to compare apples to oranges. This is a helluva orange, probably the best orange you could have, but it is not a major."

Aberdovey Golf Club
Links, March 2005

Golfers in Britain have good reason to be grateful for development of the railway network in the nineteenth and twentieth centuries. Had it not been for trains whisking travellers on holiday from London to Turnberry, for example, the rugged Scottish links and Open venue by that name might have remained anonymous. Likewise for Gleneagles in the foothills of the Scottish Highlands, and such English seaside courses as Royal Birkdale and Royal Lytham & St Annes.

Perhaps the country that has benefited most from rail travel is Wales. One of its finest courses, Aberdovey, was for the first half-century of its existence accessible only via the Cambrian Railway, which stretched up and down the mid-Wales coastline. Aberdovey's name resonates among golf aficionados for two reasons, the first being the quality of the course, a sporty links laid out on a narrow strip of land parallel to Cardigan Bay.

On the inward side of the property is the aforementioned railway; on the seaward side, rows of massive dunes that hint at the crashing waves beyond (the sea is visible only from the 12th green and from a few back tees set high in the dunes). These days it matters not whether you arrive at Aberdovey by car or train, for the last few yards of the journey are the same: you cross the railway line, lift the steel latch on a gate, walk 20 paces and there is Aberdovey, spread out before you in all its splendour.

The second reason for Aberdovey's fame is its status as the course Bernard Darwin called home. No one has exerted a greater influence here than the famed golf writer and grandson of naturalist Charles Darwin. Bernard's maternal antecedents founded the club (an uncle placed jam jars in the ground to act as the first holes), and he won a strokeplay competition (with a score of 100) as a 15-year-old in 1892.

For the better part of 40 years, Darwin spent the New Year's holiday and summer vacations as the house guest of an Aberdovey member who lived in town. He was responsible for recruiting first Harry Colt and then James Braid to make architectural revisions to the course (Herbert Fowler later had a hand in it, as well). He was an honorary life member of the club, served as its president for two terms of office and wrote about the club so often in *The Times* that he referred to it as "my King Charles's Head", meaning a place about which he had no journalistic objectivity.

After leaving university, Darwin lived and worked in London. This meant that to reach Aberdovey, he had to take the train. Incomparable essayist that he was, he penned an enchanting passage about the journey, concluding: "The train comes into a country of mountains and jolly, foaming mountain streams. It pants up the steep hill to a solitary little station called Talerddig. Then on again through the darkness 'til we stop once more. There is a wild rush of small boys outside our carriage window, fighting and clamouring for the privilege of carrying one's clubs. Nunc dimittis – we have arrived at Aberdovey."

In the early 1900s one of those youths jostling for Darwin's bag may well have been the son of the club pro. That youngster, Harry Cooper, would later accompany his father to the US, acquire the nickname of "Light Horse" for the speed with which he played, and gain repute as one of the best players never to win a major championship (Cooper lost a play-off with Tommy Armour for the 1927 US Open and settled for second place again at the 1936 US Open).

When you arrive at Aberdovey today, there is no rush of young boys to carry one's clubs, but in many ways what Darwin saw when he got off the train a century ago is the same scene that greets a present-day visitor. The 18th green is only a chip shot away from the clubhouse. Many tees adjoin greens of previous holes, as they do on the Old Course at St Andrews. Golf at Aberdovey is a reminder of what the game was like in a bygone era, a time before noisy earthmovers scraped and shaped the landscape, before water was considered an essential element of a course's defences. As in those days, grazers here are allowed to bring their livestock onto the course (cattle in summer, sheep in winter).

Aberdovey (which in Welsh means "mouth of the river Dovey") measures 6,445 yards from the back tees and includes three par-fives and four par-threes, three of them on the outward nine. One of those par-threes, the 173-yard 3rd, was Darwin's favourite short hole. It requires a blind tee shot to a green that in the writer's day was surrounded by much sand. Darwin said: "the club is rather proud of this ... hole, which consists of a rather terrifying iron shot perfectly blind, over a vast and formidable hill shored up with black railway sleepers onto a little green oasis amid a desert of sand."

It was on this hole that an electric gadget was installed to tell golfers the putting surface was clear. Because golfers could not view the green, according to a report in the *London Globe* of September 24, 1909, "an apparatus has accordingly been fitted on the teeing ground which shows at a glance if the putting green is clear. If it is not, the apparatus is set at 'danger'. As soon as the players have holed out they press a button and the apparatus signals 'all clear'."

Aberdovey's primary defences are undulating terrain, fast greens and wind that blows almost constantly in from the sea. The routing develops like a piece of music: the opening holes are quiet, the middle ones grow bolder and from the 12th onward they become downright frenzied. Just stand on the tee of the 288-yard 16th with a crosswind off the surf and see if you can find the narrow fairway. "No man is a medal winner until he has played that shot and sees the ball lying safely on the turf," Darwin wrote in his tome *Golf Courses of the British Isles*, in 1910.

Even if you make par on this tricky little devil, can you do the same at the 17th and 18th, both stout par-fours that require pinpoint driving and approach play? The 18th, say the locals, is perhaps the best finishing hole in Welsh golf, with the railway line running down the left, and ditches and bunkers on the right.

At the end of the round there is ample opportunity for a toddy or a cup of tea in the handsome new clubhouse, which opened in 1997 after the previous facility had burned down two years before. Thus refreshed, you retrace your steps over the railway line either to catch the train or drive away on your own. As you go, you take with you an overwhelming sense of history, and perhaps a knowing smile as you think back on what Darwin described as "the course that my soul loves best of all the courses in the world".

Old guard clinging to leaderboard

The Times, **March 6, 1998**

Forty. The Big Four-0. When Ian Woosnam reached the milestone on Monday, the last of Europe's famous five golfers to be born in the 11 months between April 1957 and March 1958 officially became middle-aged. Severiano Ballesteros hit the landmark during the Masters last year, Nick Faldo during the Open at Royal Troon. In August, Bernhard Langer was 40 and last month it was the turn of Sandy Lyle. Woosnam grinned: "Wobbly [his caddie, Philip Morbey] gave me a walking stick and we had a bit of a party. I know I had a headache the next day."

Success has brought undreamt-of riches to Woosnam, who now lives in tax exile in Jersey, as well as owning a home in Barbados, and has his own plane for travelling around on his home continent. It flew him to and from Twickenham for the England v Wales rugby international last month. Twenty years ago he drove to almost every venue in a battered caravanette. "It would take a long time to drive here," Woosnam said here in Qatar. "The caravanette would need wings."

For all the material improvements and mental satisfaction that golfers have acquired by their 40s, it does become harder for them to summon up the imp of inspiration, the discipline to go out and hit more practice balls, the urge to compete. At 40, the waistline and the bank balance have expanded, the nerve and the will to win contracted. "I do not have the length I used to have when I was 25 and I do not have as much energy," Ballesteros admitted. "I find it more difficult to travel and playing tournament golf becomes tougher. Yes, I find it harder to concentrate," he said.

At the 1983 Ryder Cup, on the 18th hole of his singles match, Ballesteros played one of the most brilliant strokes the game has seen. To avoid hitting his ball into the face of the bunker, he aimed well left, perhaps as much as 20 yards, before he struck so crisp a shot that he scarcely moved a grain of sand. The ball inscribed a banana-shaped flight and ended on the edge of the green, 240 yards away.

Ballesteros was 26 when he played that stroke of genius. Could he play it now, in his 41st year? "Of course not. When you are 40 you lose flexibility, speed and strength. But I still have the imagination.

"On the other hand, age brings you experience, which you cannot buy. I tell Carmen, my wife, every day how lucky we are to have three great children and the lifestyle we lead from golf. When you are 40 you think differently from the way

Left to right: Nick Faldo, Severiano Ballesteros, Sandy Lyle, Bernhard Langer and Ian Woosnam.

you do at 25: How can I explain it? At 20 I would drive a car at 190 kilometres per hour. At 40, with a family, I drive at 120 kilometres per hour."

Family and children; these are the words they all use. The draw of a growing family exerts an increasing pull on the father, a sort of magnetic field. It gets harder and harder to pack the suitcase for a two or three-week trip and kiss the children goodbye. Ballesteros now travels as much as he can with Carmen and a nanny to supervise their two boys and a girl. In Qatar, Baldomero, Miguel and Carmen Ballesteros wore T-shirts bearing the legend: "Future US Open champion".

"I am Catholic, I believe in God, but I don't practise," Ballesteros said. "I do not mind whether or not my children grow up to be golfers. For me, what I want most for them is a good schooling and education and for them to be good persons. Sport is important."

Greg Norman, who is three years older than Ballesteros, speaks similarly of the difficulty of marrying the demands of work and family. "Everything changes," Norman, who was 40 in 1995, said. "My little boy is 12 and all he wanted to do was get on the junior varsity golf team. He practised and played and got on last week. Frankly, I'd rather be there seeing him play than play in a tournament."

The famous five are competing at a sport in which middle-aged players are not necessarily at a disadvantage. Tournaments can be won by men in their 40s. Nicklaus won the US Open, PGA and Masters after he was 40. Sam Snead was 41 when he won his third Masters and Ben Hogan was 42 when he tied for the US Open and 47 when he nearly won the 1960 US Open. Hale Irwin was 45 when he became US Open champion in 1990. Can Ballesteros, Faldo, Langer, Lyle and Woosnam be as successful?

Jaime Ortiz-Patiño

Golf International, March/April 2013

They paid their respects to Jimmy Patiño, the man who had brought the Ryder Cup to Spain, in a simple Catholic church in southern Spain. Bouquets of flowers were placed on the altar of the Church of Nuestra Señora de la Merced in Sotogrande on a sunny day in January. There was one from Sergio Garcia and family, another from the European Tour, one from Crans Golf Club, another from Patiño's staff. Two urns containing his ashes were placed just beneath the altar.

Several hundred people, including Miguel Angel Jiménez on crutches, Manuel Piñero and Eddie Polland, assembled to participate in the 65-minute ceremony and hear an address from Felipe Patiño, one of Patiño's twin sons. Emma Villacieros, the formidable former president of the Spanish Golf Federation, was there, and so was Maria Acacia, a familiar figure in press rooms on the continent. There were friends and business associates from Sotogrande, from Andalucia, from Switzerland, from Britain, representatives of the World Bridge Federation of which he had been president for ten years. It was a meeting of many of the great and the good. Except it wasn't. There were no officials from Valderrama, though many of the greenkeeping staff lined the church wearing their Valderrama fleece tops.

There were few representatives of the European Tour from Britain. Those who were not there were almost as conspicuous as those who were. It demonstrated that there were some for whom Patiño was a hero, a fighter for good, a man who made his mark in life in mining, art collecting, bridge and, most notably, golf. And there were those for whom he had been difficult, argumentative, excitable and domineering, a man for whom his way was the only way.

Jimmy Patiño's most quoted words may well have been: "I have one golden rule. I have the gold. I make the rules." Those words were said of Valderrama, where he brooked no intervention, but in the eyes of many they were typical of his attitude to any cause he took up. He also famously said he liked committees of odd numbers and three were too many.

Patiño was born in June 1930 in France and grew up in a mansion in Paris waited on by a staff of 12. He attended schools in Switzerland, France, England and the US and went on to study engineering at Lausanne University.

An occasional golfer, a tennis player good enough to have competed in the French and Italian Opens, a competent rally driver and playboy, he first became aware of international golf when the Italian Open was held at Monza and he caddied for Dai Rees in the last round. Instead of payment Patiño received tickets to the 1957 Ryder Cup at Lindrick. He became an enthusiast though he never got lower than 12 handicap.

Patiño lived just outside Geneva in a house that contained Impressionist paintings, an eighteenth-century silver chandelier made for the Queen of Prussia, two silver thrones of the same period made for a royal palace in Berlin and a gaming table made for Marie Antoinette.

In 1967, acting on the advice of an American banker friend, he set off in his electric-blue Ferrari to drive to southern Spain and some days later he came upon the Sotogrande estate, then little more than a golf course and one dozen houses.

There he built himself a home overlooking the 4th tee of Sotogrande Old golf course, which was to be his base for the next 40 years.

Having won control of the family mining business in 1977, Patiño divested himself of it in the early 1980s and went into battle with the Swiss authorities for permission to build a nine-hole golf course in the 20-acre garden of his house in Geneva. His intention was to ask Robert Trent Jones Snr to design it for him. Though permission was denied, he built it anyway, played one round on it and then sold the house and moved to Spain.

Meanwhile, his ten-year reign as president of the World Bridge Federation was coming to an end. Golf now was to consume him.

Sotogrande Old was becoming too crowded for a man used to being able to play whenever he liked. He wanted to buy it so that he and Felipe could continue to play each morning, starting on the 4th at 8am and stopping for breakfast at the turn. In that he failed, so on the advice of a friend he and seven others bought a nearby course called Las Aves (which later became "Valderrama").

In time, Valderrama would stage 16 season-ending Volvo Masters tournaments, two World Golf Championship events and two Andalucian Masters as well as the 1997 Ryder Cup. Winners there included Nick Faldo, Severiano Ballesteros, Sandy Lyle, Bernhard Langer and Tiger Woods. During tournaments he would rise at 3.30, be the first man into the greenkeeping sheds, keep track of each of his workmen throughout the day and then retire to his office overlooking the putting green and have a drink. His daily consumption was measured precisely: four whiskies, two vodkas and a bottle and a half of red wine.

Patiño had impeccable manners, endless charm, lots of money and a determination to achieve whatever he set his mind to. He was an enjoyable dinner companion, gossipy, irreverent and generous. For a number of years he hosted a small group of journalists for lunch during the Masters. At an otherwise ordinary meal, the high point was the red wine, which was often five, six or seven times as expensive as the rest of the meal.

He was an autocrat and autocrats want things done their way. There are stories of his shooting a bull that had strayed on to Valderrama, of having a row over orange peel with a leading European golfer of the time, of overnight building a concrete wall along the side of the 9th hole. He was impatient and could often be rude when he wanted something. For years he campaigned for the Malaga to Cadiz motorway to be widened. He told the story of a stormy meeting with a Minister of Transport who said to him: "I'm not going to spend $300 million to build a road for golf, which is a rich man's sport."

Patiño replied: "You're not spending $300 million to build a road for me, you idiot! You are building a road for the No 1 container port of the Mediterranean! You are building the road to finish the gateway to Africa! To develop your own country! The Ryder Cup is a way to show your country to 500 million people that it is the best place in Europe to play golf!"

Patiño's last years were sad. In 2006 he was removed as president of Valderrama and two years later he was asked to leave his office overlooking the course. He moved into a home nearby and plotted revenge by planning a new course on land he owned nearby. There were rumours that Valderrama had been sold and then that it had not and that his relationship with Felipe had become testing.

In 2012, the night before his fabulous collection of golf memorabilia came up for sale in London, he looked shrunken, ill and forlorn. The next day the sale, which had been expected to realise well over £2 million, went for £1.8 million. In November he had dinner with Angel Gallardo in Crans, saying to Gallardo as he cradled a drink: "This will be my last." At Christmas he fell ill and one night asked his staff not to wake him in the morning. The next day they found him on the floor, semi-conscious, and he was taken to hospital, dying on January 3, aged 82.

A man who had done so much in his life deserved a better and happier ending.

APRIL

Augusta, Georgia, April 1997. No one who was there will forget it. Although I had seen Tiger Woods in 1995 competing for the US as an amateur in the Eisenhower Trophy and in the Walker Cup team that was beaten at Royal Porthcawl by Great Britain and Ireland, it was not until that seminal Masters tournament that the true measure of his exceptional ability struck home. What Woods did then, winning his first major championship by 12 strokes, was the start of a series of occurrences at that wonderful pocket of Georgian tranquillity that made sure his name and Augusta's would be yoked together, much as azaleas and green jackets are words that rarely appear far from the words "the Masters".

On April 15, 1997, *The Times* headlined a story of mine "Golf wakes to the dawn of the Tiger era" and carried the sub-heading: "America hails player whose mastery transcended a tournament and captivated a nation". Woods had run away with the Masters, making golf cool and widening its appeal and footprint hugely by doing so. We weren't to know then how April in Augusta would occur so repeatedly in Woods's timeline.

For example, it was at Augusta two years later that *The Times* revealed that Earl Woods was suffering from prostate cancer and would be unable to watch his son at either the forthcoming US Open or the Open Championship. We did not know either back then that Woods would triumph over that famous course in Georgia three more times in the next 15 years, though we might have suspected something like it, or that Woods's victory in the Masters in 2001 would be his fourth major title in succession, a grand slam if not a calendar grand slam; or that in 2010 Augusta National would be the place where he held his first press conference and played his first tournament having returned to the game after his car crash and other related incidents the previous November.

On April 2, 2009, writing in The Spike Bar, my online golf column for *The Times*, I said I did not think Woods would reach Jack Nicklaus's record of victory in 18 professional major championships, never mind pass it, and I explained why. It gives me little pleasure now to note that the key sentences in this item went as follows: "My money is still on Nicklaus. Woods's injured leg does appear to have recovered but say he attracts another injury, this time to the other leg or to an arm. Say he is injured in a car accident, as Ben Hogan was, or, dare one say it, physically attacked? What happens then?"

Little did I know that seven months later Woods would indeed be hurt in a car crash and that his life would unravel very publicly thereafter and that it would be at Augusta in April 2010 that he would begin his comeback and hold his first press conference.

How does one place Woods in the game's pantheon? Nicklaus is considered to be the best golfer of the twentieth century, though I have more than a sneaking regard for Bobby Jones, the great amateur, who won the four major championships of his era, the Opens and Amateurs of the US and Britain, in one glorious summer in 1930, something that no one has matched. Woods has won four in a row but not in one calendar year. If I had to pigeonhole these three talents, I would do so as follows: Nicklaus is the greatest player, Woods the greatest competitor, Jones the greatest all-rounder, being a successful lawyer as well.

Justin Rose came to the fore very young and has gone on to achieve great things. I remember first seeing him as a tall, fresh-faced teenager at the McEvoy Trophy, traditionally held at Copt Heath in mid April, wobbling on his long legs much as a foal taking his first steps might. He was gawky, that was the only word for it, but the moment he settled into the address position he looked comfortable and composed, as though he had a right to be playing golf.

Ken Rose, his father, and a wise man and good mentor, was never very far away from Justin. "Dad was my best friend," Justin said a couple of months after his father's death. "He was always there for me, whether I had come off the 18th green or wanted some time to myself in the locker room. He said what needed to be said." Often half-hidden by a wide-brimmed straw hat, Ken Rose watched his son climb the world rankings before he died from leukaemia, aged 57, in September 2002.

The Masters is by no means the only golf event that takes place in April but it is the one that gets the most column inches and soundbites, the most television footage. I have been to Augusta on 32 occasions, which means that I have spent nearly nine months of my life there. I have grown to like it, perhaps love it. My first visit was in 1981 and after finding a barber's shop in the clubhouse, I had a good Southern haircut. It lasted for months. Some years later I saw Sam Snead in the same place, having his hair cut. The barber's shop has gone now. So has Snead's hair. And so has Snead.

Golf wakes to dawn of the Tiger era

The Times, April 15, 1997

History has often been made here in Georgia. The old city of Augusta, which once housed the largest cotton exchange in the South and still publishes its oldest newspaper, is where a new era dawned. Just after 5am yesterday, fingers of light broke through to brighten the first day of the Tiger era, golf's sixth since 1896.

It was fewer than 12 hours after Tiger Woods had slipped on his first green jacket as the 61st Masters champion and the first of African-American heritage. He had broken half as many records as he had clubs in his bag and his smile was as wide as his 12-stroke winning margin. Soon, in a television interview, he would speak like a mature man possessed of a dignity that few golfers in the history of the game could rival.

Not for the first time, he would make everyone realise that he was a person whose appeal and skill transcended golf and could make him one of the best-known sporting figures in the world.

"I hope my victory will make kids think that golf is cool," Woods said, occasionally wiping his brow with a pianist's finger and from time to time flashing a disarming smile. "When someone not too far from their age, or even the same age, wins a tournament like this, then they think, 'hey, let's try this game.' I hope they will try it and so will their friends and so will their friends' friends. Golf used not to be cool, it is now."

Gary Player speaks with the authority of a South African when he talks of what Woods could do for the people of that continent. "Tiger has the opportunity

Tiger Woods puts on the green jacket with the help of Nick Faldo at
the presentation ceremony of the 1997 Masters tournament.

to do something for the human race that no other golfer before him has," Player, three times a Masters champion, said. "Imagine the black people in Africa – 400 million watching Tiger Woods win the Masters. There has never been a world champion golfer who is a black golfer."

Woods, 21, toyed with his peers as he demonstrated that he has taken the game to a new level. Some of them, perhaps, were even frightened by what they saw at close range. Was it because Nick Faldo and Colin Montgomerie were so stunned by playing alongside Woods one day that they each took 81 the next? With his unrivalled blend of power and subtlety, his self-control and sense of purpose, Woods can change the face of the game in the way few have done in the past hundred years.

Starting in 1898, Harry Vardon "blazed out in full glory", according to Bernard Darwin. Vardon continued in similar vein for 16 years. Not until he had won his sixth Open, in 1914, and was beaten by Francis Ouimet, the amateur, in a play-off for the 1913 US Open, did Vardon's grip on golf falter.

His successor was quickly identified. Robert Tyre Jones, the gifted amateur from Atlanta, rarely played during the winter and competed in few tournaments in the summer. At 15 he travelled across the United States participating in a series of exhibition matches for the Red Cross. In 1923, aged 21, he won the US Open, and seven years later he capped his extraordinary career by winning the Amateur and Open Championships of the United States and Britain, a feat known as the Impregnable Quadrilateral. Having conquered the world of golf, he retired.

From 1946 until 1955, Ben Hogan was dominant, his year to end all years coming in 1953 when he won the three major championships he entered – the Masters, US Open and Open. Almost immediately, a stocky, thrilling young man from Pennsylvania set the world of golf alight. Arnold Palmer reigned pretty much from 1958 until 1965, electrifying everyone with his slashing swing, a winsome smile and a magnetic personality.

In 1965, Jack Nicklaus raced away with the Masters, winning by nine strokes and causing Bobby Jones to utter: "He plays a game with which I am not familiar." Nicklaus's era ended in 1980 when he won two majors in his fortieth year, although in 1986 he captured the Masters for a sixth time – the eighteenth major of his career.

Not one of these men achieved the modern grand slam, all four professional major championships in one year, though Nicklaus won the Masters and US Open in 1972 and nearly caught Lee Trevino in the Open at Muirfield that summer. Now Woods has a chance. It is not, as the Americans say, "a given". Congressional Country Club, in Washington DC, as do all US Open courses, will have narrow fairways and ankle-high rough, defences that the Augusta National did not have.

If Woods triumphs there, then at Royal Troon in July he will have to cope with fairways that are like rumpled eiderdowns and slower greens with fewer subtleties than those at Augusta. Thus his exceptional length and skill will be less of an advantage. Strong winds could also hand his rivals an advantage. Despite all this, Woods, who has not scored higher than 73 this year, is a legitimate contender for golf's Holy Grail.

"If Tiger is playing well," Nicklaus said both at and about Augusta, "the golf course becomes nothing. I have never seen anyone come on the scene with such publicity, face up to the pressure and outperform it."

"He is the best for his age there has ever been," Byron Nelson said, "so if he continues there is every reason for him to become the best there has ever been." Trevino said: "He copes with the pressure far better than I did, and goodness knows he is a better player than I ever was."

"The grand slam can be done," Woods said. "Phil Mickelson last year won four times. Well, if you can win the right tournaments four times, you have the slam. But it is difficult to win these because they are the majors. In order to win a big tournament you have to have a lot of luck. Then who knows?"

We know that Woods is truly exceptional. Last week proved as much. His win here now ranks him No 3 in the world. What happens over the years may be exceptional, too. For now, it is sufficient to say that what occurred at Augusta National was one of the greatest moments of the game, for sociological reasons as much as for sporting ones. It was the start of Tiger's era, and if what follows is half as good, then it will be some era.

Tiger Woods will not beat Jack Nicklaus's major record

The Times, April 2, 2009

A friend posed an interesting question the other day. Did Jack Nicklaus have more or fewer challengers to his supremacy all those years ago than Tiger Woods does today? After consideration I said I thought that in Nicklaus's day there were more really good golfers who were unafraid to challenge him, though fewer really good golfers in all.

I said that Arnold Palmer and Gary Player with 16 major championships combined, Tom Watson (8) and Lee Trevino (6) as well as Johnny Miller, Seve Ballesteros and Ray Floyd were more genuine contenders to Nicklaus's title as the world's best golfer than Ernie Els, Phil Mickelson, Vijay Singh, Sergio Garcia, Padraig Harrington, Geoff Ogilvy, Retief Goosen are to Woods now. Nicklaus did not spook his opponents the way Woods seems to.

This led to a discussion as to whether or not Woods will reach Nicklaus's total of 18 victories in professional major championships or, indeed, pass it. My view is constant on this and always has been. I will not put any money on Woods even equalling Nicklaus's record.

What? I hear you exclaim. You mean that the man who at 33 has won 14 major championships will not win four more? The player who can will his ball into the hole better than any previous golfer ever has – as he proved in a tournament in Florida on the last Sunday in March when he made up a five-stroke deficit in the last round and holed for a birdie on the 72nd hole to win by one stroke – might only win three more major championships in his career and maybe not even that many? That Woods, who will be 34 at the end of this year, cannot match or comfortably exceed the record of a man who won his sixteenth and seventeenth major championships when he was 40 and his eighteenth and last at 46?

That is exactly what I mean. My money is still on Nicklaus. Woods's injured leg does appear to have recovered but say he attracts another injury, this time to the other leg or to an arm. Say he is injured in a car accident as Ben Hogan was or, dare one say it, physically attacked? What happens then?

Let me call another witness, one Jack Nicklaus. "Tiger's got an unbelievable work ethic and he's so fit," Nicklaus recently told Rick Reilly, the American sports writer. "But that knee makes it a little less certain."

Nicklaus continued: "You guys are all so willing to hand it to Tiger: '[he's the] greatest player ever', like it's already over … I'm just saying the kid is amazing and I'll be the first to congratulate him, but doesn't he actually have to do it first?"

There you have it. For now and until it happens, it's Nicklaus over Woods for me.

Duval's line on life makes easy reading

The Times, April 5, 1999

Consider the world of David Duval as he wakes up this morning amid the dogwood and azaleas of Augusta, Georgia. It is the second week of April and, in golfing terms, that means only one thing. Unfurl the parasols on the lawn behind the Augusta National clubhouse and bring on the peach cobblers and mint juleps. It is time for the Masters.

Augusta is a small town 100 miles east of Atlanta, known for once having had the largest cotton exchange in the Southern states. The Partridge Inn on Walton Way is the oldest hotel in the south of the United States and the *Augusta Chronicle* the oldest newspaper. William Makepeace Thackeray passed through it on a lecture tour and was paid 60 guineas – a plump sum from a plump city, he noted.

For 51 weeks of the year, Augusta goes about its business without impinging much upon the consciousness of the rest of the world. In the remaining week, the eyes of the world are on Augusta National Golf Club and this year, particularly, on Duval, 27, the young man who once could not win a tournament and who now cannot lose one. He went for 92 events before he won his first (including seven times coming second), but, after winning the BellSouth Classic in Atlanta last night, he had beaten his opponents in 11 of the past 34 that he entered. In one event that he won, his final round was a 59, arguably the greatest competitive round ever.

Many of today's golfing heroes have echoes of their forefathers. With Duval, it is Ben Hogan, who had a stare that was just as impassive and who was the last man before Duval to win his first three victories in consecutive appearances. This is not the only connection. When Hogan was 9, his father, Chester, sick with financial worries, put a gun to his head and shot himself. Tragedy visited the Duval household when David was 9 and bone marrow was extracted from his hips in an unsuccessful attempt to save the life of Brent, his 12-year-old brother, who had aplastic anaemia.

Hogan was a voracious practiser, Duval is a voracious reader, whose favourite novel is Ayn Rand's *The Fountainhead,* the story of a young architect who rails against conventional standards. Duval once set himself the task of reading 30 books in one year and managed 31. The week after his 59, while skiing in Idaho, he took a house guest into a room and pointed out the 20 volumes of the *Oxford English Dictionary* given to him as a present by his girlfriend. Duval, whose 59 had taken five hours, marvelled that these dictionaries had taken three quarters of a century to compile. "People are making a big deal out of what I've done, but it's nothing compared to this," he said, holding out one of four volumes containing words beginning with the letter S. "This took ten years."

A young man full of spikiness was how Duval had appeared to me when I first came across him at the 1992 US Open at Pebble Beach. He walked with a cocky swagger, as though he was rather pleased with himself, which, I gathered later, he was. He was pear-shaped, weighing nearly 50lb more then than he does now, and had short, fair hair.

He took a distinctive and somewhat unconventional grip of his club, with both his hands rotated well to the right. That was the first stylistic solecism I noted. The second came during the downswing, when his head swivelled towards the target.

Recently, trying to explain how he was in those days, Duval said: "What is, is. My brother died, my parents divorced … blah, blah, blah. There is nothing I can do about it. Maybe my mechanism has not been to analyse it because it would only hinder me from going on. The bottom line is, I don't believe you are given more than you can handle and you have to find a way to cope. You can level your own playing field by understanding that life only becomes fair when you realise it is unfair. I do not wonder about, or want to share, the way I am. I am not saying my way is right. It might turn off a lot of people, but it's the way I found that suits me."

In past weeks, Duval has demonstrated what Tom Watson once noted, namely that winning breeds charisma. Duval oozed charisma long before he had that 59. He created charisma by his stony face, his obduracy, by the black cap and sunglasses, by his remarkable run of success. Now he is making a conscious effort to relate more to people who are generating such feelings of warmth towards him and he actually made rather a good joke in the aftermath of his victory in The Players Championship on Sunday last week. "It might sound stupid, but I have always found the rough isn't so bad in the middle of the fairways," he said.

At Atlanta, three days later, he had loosened up even more. "Sure I am more comfortable than two years ago. I have been playing for five years now and I am getting used to seeing the people who travel the tour and once you get familiar with the people at each spot, it gets easier to interact. I think I have done a very good job since I have been a pro, watching my time, making sure I did not over-extend myself, investing my earnings, saving money, looking down the road. It hasn't changed much in the past two years I have been doing well. I don't see why it will in the future."

The plaudits are ringing out for Duval in a way that once he would not have thought was possible, but he is no more likely to be swayed by it all than Hogan was. Designing his own line of golf clothing? Hardly. Designing golf courses? Possibly, but daily fee courses, not, as he put it, "places you have to come up with $75,000 to join".

"My main agenda is to leave the world a better place than it was when I came in. I want to be a good role model, conducting myself as a professional, to act as a gentleman when I play."

Penick's legacy a lesson in more than golf

The Times, April 11, 1995

Nine days ago, Harvey Penick, the famous golf teacher, died in hospital in Austin, Texas, at 5.30 in the afternoon. One of his last acts had come a few hours earlier, when he heard that Davis Love III, a pupil of his, had won a tournament and gained entry into the Masters. Penick, a wisp of a man weighing no more than 7st, was fading fast. Raising arms as thin as golf shafts, he clapped twice.

Seven days later, at 5.30 in the afternoon, Ben Crenshaw, another of Penick's pupils, took the lead in the Masters from Love, his friend, and went on to win his second green jacket. When he had done so, Crenshaw broke down with emotion on the 72nd green. He appeared to snap at the waist, like a flower being broken halfway up the stem. He placed his hands on his knees and cried.

Golf is an individual game that has produced some enduring partnerships. Typically, these relationships start as ones of pupil and teacher, of men separated by 30 years, and mature into deep bonds of friendship, love and respect. The partnership between Stewart Maiden, the Scot who emigrated from Carnoustie, and Bobby Jones, who would become the greatest amateur, at East Lake Country Club in Atlanta in the early years of the century was one such.

A second was between Jack Grout and a fat boy with a crew cut and a high-pitched voice at Scioto Golf Club, Columbus, Ohio, in the fifties and sixties. The boy's name was Jack Nicklaus and, from the time the two of them met to the time of Grout's death, Nicklaus hardly saw another teacher.

Then there was Penick, formerly the professional at the Austin Country Club for 48 years, and Crenshaw. "When I was about six and a half, he [Penick] cut down a mashie, put my hands on the club and my grip hasn't changed," Crenshaw said.

For Jones, Nicklaus and Crenshaw, their golf teachers taught them much more than how to play golf. In fact, golf sometimes became a metaphor for life. "It is apt to describe Harvey as a philosopher," Crenshaw said on Sunday evening, fingering his green jacket. "He was the kindest, gentlest individual and he always had time for you. He was always helping you. We tried to learn from this man. He gave us lessons in life, no question."

Maiden, Grout and Penick did not go in for gimmicks or long practice sessions. Maiden gave Jones a famous lesson when the amateur was having trouble with his long irons. It involved Maiden saying fewer than ten words and Jones hitting five balls. After hitting the last, Jones turned to make a remark to Maiden and noticed he was halfway back to his shop.

When Nicklaus was unable to keep his head still during the swing, Grout grabbed a handful of his hair so that any movement would hurt. For years, Nicklaus met Grout before beginning each season. A short session was all that was needed and then Nicklaus would go forth and conquer the world.

When Grout died, in 1989, Nicklaus delivered a moving eulogy. "Farewell my teacher and my guide," he said. "Jack was a friend to everybody. I don't think he had an enemy in the world. He was part of the family. We all loved him."

When Penick died, Crenshaw acted as a pallbearer at the funeral. Four days later, he won the Masters. He did it for Penick. It was his way of thanking the man who had become a father figure to him. "Harvey was with me every step of the way," Crenshaw said.

Brave Edwards dies hours after Watson's tribute
The Times, April 9, 2004

Bruce Edwards, who had been Tom Watson's caddie, and friend, since 1973, died early yesterday at his home in Jacksonville, Florida. Thus ended one of golf's most poignant recent stories, in which Watson strove ceaselessly to find a cure for the amyotrophic lateral sclerosis (ALS) with which Edwards had been suffering since January 2003. It was a race against time and time won. But Edwards always did have a sense of occasion. The last day of his life was the first day of the Masters.

Watson and Edwards were like Don Quixote and Sancho Panza, travelling the world, tilting at windmills, often setting the sails spinning with their deeds. For almost 30 years Watson was the star, Edwards the lesser figure a few paces away from him. At a moving ceremony in Augusta on Wednesday night, the bag was on the other shoulder.

Edwards, too ill to be in attendance, received the Ben Hogan Award from the Golf Writers' Association of America and in a clear, firm voice Watson spoke proudly about his caddie, companion and friend. "Let there be no long faces tonight," Watson began. "I want to thank Bruce for being in such good spirits … and for keeping that wonderful, wonderful attitude up. That's why we love him. That is why this is such a special award tonight for Bruce. I had a good year on the course with Bruce on my bag. We had some good times and some good breaks."

The Ben Hogan Award is given to an individual who has continued to be active in golf despite a physical handicap or serious illness. It is named after the American golfer whose car was hit by a bus while he and Valerie, his wife, were driving out of a small Texas town early one foggy morning in 1949 and who nearly died thereafter. Showing an indomitable spirit, Hogan recovered and although his legs had been badly injured he went on to win three US Opens, two Masters and one Open, including a Masters, a US Open and an Open in one glorious sweep in 1953.

Edwards carried Watson's bag for the whole of last year. It was some year, even by the standards of a man who has won the Open five times and three other major championships and who will be regarded as one of the greatest golfers in the history of the game. Wherever the two went in pursuit of their duty became a place where sentiment and success were mixed in equal, considerable measures.

Watson, 53 at the time, led the US Open after the first round in June and the spectators in Chicago were shouting "Bruce, Bruce" when caddie and player strode up the 18th fairway, their arms around each other's shoulders.

Without Edwards, who was too ill to be exposed to the weather, Watson won the Senior British Open at Turnberry. With Edwards on his bag, he won the Tradition, a major championship on the seniors' tour in the United States, as well as $1.8 million in prize money. When Watson won a $1 million tax-free annuity, he donated it to ALS-related charities. "They keep telling me a cure is just around the corner," Watson said again and again. "Unfortunately, I don't think we're going to get to the corner in time."

Soon after midnight on Wednesday night, Edwards's parents and four closest friends returned to their hotel from the awards dinner. They telephoned Marsha Edwards, who proudly listened to their account of how her husband had been so well spoken of at the dinner. Edwards was too weak to speak, but Marsha held the telephone to his ear so he could hear their words of support.

Dosed with morphine and visibly in pain, Edwards was able to give only a limp smile and a thumbs-up. He died at 6.26 yesterday morning.

True masterclass in evasion leaves us feeling more than a little disappointed

The Times, April 6, 2010

How should we view Tiger Woods after his press conference in Augusta yesterday? With disappointment and with dissatisfaction. Although some questions were answered, too many were left unanswered. This was a frothy, light-as-air soufflé when one had been hoping for something more substantial.

Is it too much to expect that if Woods was prepared to be questioned, then we had a right to expect him to answer those questions? And although some of his answers were germane to the question he had been asked, many were not. Overall, it was a masterclass in evasion and avoidance, of speaking without saying much, of being elliptical, of answering questions but often not the questions he was asked.

We know little more this morning than we did yesterday morning about certain important issues. Why, for instance, did Woods become involved with a Canadian doctor who is known to administer human growth hormone and is under investigation by the police?

Another example. Many of those who listened to his stumbling mea culpa in Jacksonville in February got a clear impression then that he would be away from golf for a long time. Yet only eight days later he had returned from his therapy clinic and was hitting balls, raising the question of why Woods had spoken in the week of the Accenture Match Play Championship when he could have waited another ten days.

Woods was asked about this apparent contradiction and again he gave an answer that barely dealt with the question. "When I gave my speech in February, I had no intentions of playing golf in the near future at all," he said. "I just had barely started practising two days prior to that. That was the first time I hit balls. And then I started hitting more balls and more balls and more balls and I started getting the itch again to start playing again ..."

So his long-term commitment to staying away from golf, to sorting out his marriage, his family, his friends, that all went out of the window because he "started getting the itch again". That is what we are left to conclude from this rambling answer.

It is known there had been disagreement in Woods's camp about how he should handle this scandal. Woods is believed to have wanted to do as little as possible, while various advisers were said to be urging him to come clean in a televised press conference.

Yesterday, Woods was asked why he did not feel the need to do what he was doing now at some earlier date? He prevaricated, asking when he was meant to have said something. "January or December" was the response.

"Not December because I wasn't at a right place for it," he said. "And in January I was in rehab." Did that answer the question? Not really.

To give credit where it is due, while the conference was ended after only 35 minutes, which was rather short, there was no attempt to censor the questions. Woods looked relaxed and composed, much more like the Tiger Woods of old and not at all like the heavily directed, nervous individual who had appeared in front of a hand-picked, sympathetic audience in Florida two months ago.

Yet this is what creates a sense of dissatisfaction. Woods answered nearly fifty questions and he made sure he looked his questioners in the eye when he did so. He declined to say what he was in therapy for and he explained that Elin, his wife, and their children will not be joining him at Augusta.

But did he really convince us that he was genuine in his contrition? Not really. Did he address the key issues? Not really. Does he think that he has played the most difficult shot of this Masters week and that from now on there will be a lot of players saying, "Welcome back, Tiger". Probably.

It is not too much to suspect that after Woods had left the room, he clenched his right fist and pumped the air. He had talked without saying very much. He had sat down in front of journalists and done, in his view, what so many people had been urging him to do within a few days of this scandal starting.

And he had done it with hardly a glove being laid on him. He ducked, he weaved, he blocked. Tiger Woods had pulled off another miracle shot.

Letters show that long march to equality started 90 years ago

The Times, April 16, 2001

Last month, I predicted that Anita Olrog, of Foxhills Golf Club, would make history by becoming the first lady captain of a mixed golf club when she took office later this year. May I take a mulligan? My swing was a bit stiff that day. Perhaps this is what I should have said. When I wrote that Anita Olrog "would become the first lady captain of a mixed golf club" what I really meant was that she was by no means the first, nor the second nor even the third but more likely the fourth or fifth, and that in the early years of the last century two women had captained a mixed golf club in Cheshire.

I know this because various correspondents rushed to correct me and put forward their own nominations. First on the tee was Tony Lewis, chairman of Wales's bid to stage the 2009 Ryder Cup, who wrote that "… Elaine Thomas, the present club captain of Ashburnham GC, became the captain of the mixed club on January 19, 2001". Her achievement, Lewis wrote, "is all the more poignant for Welsh golf in a year when the nation is bidding to host the Ryder Cup. The pillar of the Welsh bid is the merging of the men's and ladies' unions. Indeed, the Welsh Golf Union will be the first to effect the historic merger between the two governing bodies and help to sweep away sexism in golf."

Then came an e-mail from Janet McTear, who teed off with flattery. "Your esteemed golf writer, Mr Hopkins, gives pleasure to many in the manner in which he weaves a tale – but today, no Sir!" McTear pointed out that Joan Lawrence, a much respected player and dministrator in Scottish golf, had been captain of Aberdour Golf Club in Fife.

This was confirmed by Sandy Laing, the secretary of Aberdour GC, who said that Joan Lawrence was elected captain in 1997. I rang Joan Lawrence and discovered that not only had she held that office (as well as having represented Great Britain and Ireland in the 1964 Curtis Cup and captained the Great Britain and Ireland team in the Esperito Santo Trophy in 1971) but she was also in her second year as captain of the Canmore Golf Club in Dunfermline.

But Joan Lawrence was not the first lady captain of a mixed golf club. Ian Macdonald wrote to me about Betty Barbour, who was the first lady to be elected to the committee of Colvend Golf Club in Dumfries and Galloway in the 1970s and later became president from 1977 to 1981. Barbour was something of a local legend because she had won the club championship on 29 occasions.

"Colvend, founded in 1905, has always been without segregation and gender," Macdonald wrote. "Long before the days of political correctness Colvend decided that the position of club captain would, in view of the fact that it could be filled by a woman, be best known as president. The president fulfils all the duties and responsibilities as required of captains of other clubs."

Barbour, now 87, is still a regular at Colvend. "I like to go up there and help with the medals and things," she said. "It came about after an AGM at a local hotel. Somebody said it was about time we had a lady captain and my name was put forward. I thought 'why not?' I remember going to a South of Scotland captains meeting. It was traditionally all men. Someone said to me, 'you're a lady.' I said, 'so what? I'm still captain of Colvend Golf Club.' I thought at the time it was quite good."

"Let's face it, golf clubs had been male prerogatives, hadn't they?" Thomas, a retired head teacher and lecturer at Trinity College, Carmarthen, said. "Some of us felt something had to happen and so did some of the men." In the summer of 1999 Thomas was asked if she would become vice-captain, knowing that this would lead to her becoming captain in due course. "I thought about it for two or three weeks and then decided I had to accept. It was an honour for me and a privilege. I was fighting for the ladies."

Lawrence said that the men at Aberdour treated her with the utmost respect. There were no embarrassing incidents for her during her term of office, or at least if there were she was not telling.

Then came the letter to end all letters. Len Norbury, the secretary of Helsby Golf Club in Cheshire, said that while researching the club's history for its centenary this year it was discovered that a Mrs N.F. Martin and a Mrs D. Edmondson had been elected club captains in 1911 and 1923 respectively.

Thus Mrs Martin deserves the accolade of being described as the first lady captain of a mixed golf club. She had received a "hearty vote of thanks" from the annual meeting in 1909 for "superintending teas" and during her year of office, the captain, "ably assisted by Mrs Brotherton, continued with the never-ending task of providing Saturday afternoon tea".

Perhaps electing a lady captain because she served good teas was an enlightened way of doing things 90 years ago. It would not wash these days.

Daly reaches bottom of barrel at last-chance saloon

The Times, April 1, 1997

John Daly is in trouble again. His escapades since he burst to prominence by winning the 1991 US PGA Championship have been enough to test the patience of a saint. The latest involving the 1995 Open champion occurred last week. When is it all going to end?

Drink is a recurring theme in many of these incidents. In December 1991, he damaged an hotel room in South Africa while he was drunk. In June 1992, he was removed from a New York-bound plane in Denver after a confrontation with a stewardess. He won his first major championship while an alcoholic, his second while on the wagon.

Since 1991, he has twice been suspended from the US PGA Tour and twice attended an alcohol rehabilitation centre. At different times since then, he has failed to sign his card, scuffled in a car park with a man three times his age, picked his ball up during a competitive round as well as being involved in well-publicised marital difficulties. He has been off the wagon, on it and off it again.

Last week, after a drinking session at Sloppy Joe's, a nightclub in Jacksonville, Florida, Daly allegedly did $1,000-worth of damage to his hotel room after a dispute with his wife, before being driven to hospital by Fuzzy Zoeller. On Sunday, Daly announced he was entering the Betty Ford Clinic alcohol rehabilitation programme.

"I have come to realise that this terrible disease is much tougher than I thought," he said in a statement on Sunday. "I apologise to others who struggle with me in fighting this disease. I am going to do my best and, hopefully, we will prevail together."

There was a time when one felt sympathy for Daly, an immature young man of 30, who is unable to cope with the attendant difficulties of being able to hit the ball a long way and being excessively well paid for doing so. Even when his fellow professionals pointed out how he gave up if he did not start with a good first round, he seemed to cut a sympathetic figure.

He gained a new generation of followers when he won the Open Championship at St Andrews in 1995, joining Jack Nicklaus, Johnny Miller and Tom Watson as the only men to have won two major titles before their 30th birthday. He hit the ball massive distances, driving for six of the par-fours during the event, for example.

Yet, he also demonstrated that he was more than a prodigiously long hitter. Four times in one round, he two-putted from more than a hundred feet, including one monster he paced off at 180 feet. The people of St Andrews took him to their hearts.

Such sympathy now seems misplaced because he has played so badly since. He gives the impression of taking people for a ride. In the Johnnie Walker Classic, in Australia, this year, for which he was handsomely rewarded for appearing, he began with a 77 and then added a 79 for a 36-hole total that was 12 over par. He finished 146th out of 154 competitors. One week later, in another tournament for which he was paid to appear, he finished 65th and the promoter said: "You cannot play cards all night, drink, smoke and eat hamburgers and expect to play top-class golf. You can't blame the world, only yourself."

The truth is golf no longer needs Daly as it once did. The hundreds of spectators who used to turn up to marvel at his prodigious hitting have been replaced by thousands who are drawn to watch Tiger Woods. At present, Woods appears to have the credentials to become the greatest name in the game. He is nearly ten years younger than Daly and hits the ball farther. He tries his best, behaves with decorum and appeals to a much wider audience.

An article about Woods in a local paper in Jacksonville last week explained this rather well. "Tiger is … Mr Multi Racial – part black, part white, part Indian, part Asian, part you, part me," it went. "There is a little bit of Tiger in every single one of us. And that is why we adore him. He is we."

Daly no longer does many of these things. He desperately needs help. His is a rare talent on the course when he cares to demonstrate it – and a sublime talent to destroy himself off it. This time, he should stay away from the game for a long time. Enough is enough.

Darwin prize for youth evolution
The Times, April 3, 1996

As darkness falls this afternoon, a promising young amateur golfer, perhaps not yet out of his teens, will take possession of a magnificent silver salver, two feet in diameter. He will have recorded the lowest score of the day at Rye, that jewel of a course in East Sussex, and thus will have won the first Bernard Darwin Youths' Salver, a new national 36-hole amateur competition for golfers aged under 21.

Our young hero will know a Vardon grip from an interlocking, a titanium shaft from a graphite, a two-piece ball from a three-piece. But will he have any idea of the historical significance of what he holds in his hands? Will the name Darwin mean anything to him? If it does not, then an inscription on the salver itself should help him. It reads: "To Bernard Darwin in affectionate gratitude for the happiness which he has given to thousands by his writings on Golf in *The Times* 1907–1953."

Darwin, *The Times* golf correspondent in those days before bylines, never needed to be identified. There was no other sportswriter – and few other writers – whose prose was as clean and correct as Darwin's, who once wrote an introduction to the *Oxford Book of Quotations*. He wrote mainly about golf, but also about Victorian England, Charles Dickens – on whom he was an authority

– and often those whimsical fourth leaders in *The Times* on a Saturday morning, pieces that were always identifiable by his habit of including obscure Dickensian references.

Golf, though, which Darwin played well enough to have represented his country, was his love, and aficionados link his name inextricably with the Welsh club, Aberdovey. It was to the mid-Wales town, where he spent so many childhood summers, that Darwin journeyed by train and wrote about it so vividly that it remains one of the best of all sporting essays. Aberdovey, he wrote, "is the course my heart loves most in all the world."

Rye, however, a course he first came to know in the late nineteenth century and later came to know well because of the staging there of the Oxford and Cambridge Golfing Society's President's Putter competition, might be said to come a pretty close second. "Just as the beautiful little old town, with its red roofs and huddled houses and cobbled streets, perching on top of a cliff, has a quality of its own, so has the golf," Darwin wrote of Rye in 1925. "It can never be a championship course – and personally I thank goodness for that – because it lies on too narrow a strip of turf and is, therefore, no place for crowds, but it is a battlefield worthy of any champion."

Writing of the club where he was twice captain, he went on: "I know of no course on which it seems to blow so persistently across the player, never helping him or opposing him in a straightforward, open-hearted manner but harassing him by flanking attacks."

In 1954, after the death of his wife, Darwin moved into the Dormy House Club just inside the Landgate in Rye. "The Dormy House Club had been formed in 1896 by sportsmen from London," John Bragg, a director, said. "The visitors' book is full of names like A.E.R. Gilligan, G.O. Allen, Tom and John Blackwell. They would arrive from London on a Friday night, stay the weekend and play golf at Rye. In mid winter, they would come rattling back to the club for tea by the fire, have a drink before going out for dinner and then come back and play slosh, a combination of billiards and snooker, whilst getting sloshed before sloping off to bed."

By the time Darwin moved in, the club contained a number of permanent residents, former diplomats, retired servicemen and the like. He took a room, installed the leather-covered chair that belonged to his grandfather, Sir Charles, author of *On the Origin of Species by Means of Natural Selection,* and made himself comfortable and happy as his life drew to a close. The famous chair now resides in the bar at Rye Golf Club.

"In the evenings at the Dormy [House] Darwin held court beside the splendid seventeenth-century fireplace in the billiard room, and talked to a delighted audience about golf, cricket, his beloved Dickens and the pleasure of late-Victorian England, an enjoyable account of which is to be found in his book, *The World that Fred Made*," John Bruce-Lockhart, a former chairman of the Dormy House Club, wrote.

On Darwin's death, in 1961, many of his possessions were left on display in the Dormy House Club and later sold, realising an appreciable sum. A portion has been spent on establishing the Darwin Salver, a happy suggestion made late last year by John Bradley, a former secretary, who knew of Darwin's interest in junior golf.

The new owner of the Dormy House Club, which will revert to its original name of Tower House, intends to revive the building as a place to stay. She has located all the contents of the billiard room and they will be installed as they were when Darwin held forth after dinner.

Then, perhaps, the winner of the Darwin Salver will be able to immerse himself in the atmosphere that Darwin created 40 or more years ago.

Faulkner's case to be honoured is Open and shut

The Times, April 30, 2001

Fifty years ago this summer, Max Faulkner received a cheque for £500 for winning the Open Championship. Faulkner, who dressed like a peacock and played like an angel, flashed his film star's smile and clasped his massive hands around the trophy. It would be 18 more years before another Briton – Tony Jacklin – won that same trophy again and ushered in a new generation of British golfers such as Sandy Lyle, Nick Faldo and Ian Woosnam, who all went on to win at least one major championship.

"Max had a very good body, a narrow waist, wide shoulders and a wonderful smile," Peter Alliss recalled. "He was very athletic and good-looking and he used to play in plus twos. He was one of the best ball-strikers I have ever seen among British pros. He'd be in my top ten of all time. I remember at Portrush [in 1951] how he held up his cheque and said: 'This'll pay for my children's education.' And he laughed. He had a very distinctive laugh, a cackle almost."

Faulkner, 84, is one of the few remaining links to the highest levels of the game of many years ago. As a boy of 15, he competed in the 1932 Open at Prince's, his prowess boosted by Gus, his father, and the game's authorities turning

Max Faulkner playing a shot at the 1951 Open
Championship at Portrush, Northern Ireland.

a blind eye. A couple of years later, Faulkner played in a tournament with Sandy Herd, who had won the Open in 1902.

"He was 73 and I was 17; I was outdriving him by 100 yards," Faulkner said. "He'd take a spoon [three-wood] or a brassie [two-wood] into the green and I'd be hitting a niblick [five-iron], but you know what? It was my turn to putt first every time. That taught me a lesson, I can tell you. I thought: 'God, I've got to sharpen up my short game.' "

By the summer of 1951, Faulkner had sharpened up to such an extent that, when the Open was held at Royal Portrush, in Northern Ireland, he led by six strokes after 54 holes. He knew he would win and was so confident that he signed a ball "Max Faulkner, 1951 Open champion".

This is the sort of providence-tempting gesture that few others would dare. "Well, I was six ahead," he said on Friday, when he sat in the clubhouse at West Chiltington Golf Club, in Sussex, the course that he and Brian Barnes, his son-in-law, designed and built. "So would you, wouldn't you? An arrogant chap like me, I wasn't going to lose from that position.

"I was kneeling down doing up my shoes and a little boy of 12 and his father came up to me. The little boy said: 'Sir, will you sign my golf ball?' And I said yes. I signed Max Faulkner on it and his father said: 'Would you mind putting Open champion 1951? You're six ahead.' I said: 'Good God, steady on.' I said to myself: 'Yes, I'm six ahead. They'll never catch me.' "

John Jacobs, on leave from the Gezira Sporting Club, in Cairo, had not qualified for the final round of the 1951 Open and followed Faulkner. "Max's swing was something I will always remember," Jacobs said.

"It was majestic with tremendous rhythm, slowish yet hugely powerful, one of the best swings I have seen in my lifetime. It was in the Sam Snead mould in its authority. But he was not hitting the ball at all well in the last round. He was hitting everything out of the heel of the club and Frank Stranahan, the amateur, was hitting it 40 yards past him from every tee. But Max was a very good short putter. He holed everything from three to six feet."

That it is precisely 50 years since Faulkner's success in the Open is one reason why he is topical now. Another is that Faulkner is the only surviving British winner of the Open not to have been rewarded with an honour of any sort.

Jacklin, champion in 1969 at Royal Lytham & St Annes? CBE. Lyle, champion at Royal St George's in 1985, and Faldo, champion in 1987, 1990 and 1992? MBEs. Paul Lawrie, winner of the 1999 Open at Carnoustie? MBE. Not only that, many other British golfers who have not won major championships have been honoured. Jacobs has been appointed OBE. Brian Huggett was appointed MBE, as were Neil Coles, Sam Torrance and Tommy Horton. So why not Faulkner? Henry Cotton, who won the Open in 1934, 1937 and 1948, had to wait almost until to the end of his life. He died on Christmas Day 1987, knowing that in the New Year Honours he would receive a knighthood.

"It's a mystery about Max," Alliss said. "I've written letters, spoken to people and still nothing is done. I cannot understand it." Jacobs added: "It's a shame. At his age it would be nice for him to be remembered."

Old-timers remember that Faulkner was sometimes a bit ripe, that after he had taken part in one of nearly 300 exhibitions that he gave for charity he was not quite as reverential as he should have been. "He was a bit eccentric, but he was not villainous," Alliss said.

Faulkner was a larger-than-life character who used to milk cows to build up strength in his wrists. A physical training instructor, he used to walk on his hands from green to tee to get people talking about him. Recovering from suffering a perforated eardrum during an air raid, he looked round his grey room in a grey hospital and swore to himself that when he got out he would always dress in bright colours.

"His services to golf have been of tremendous benefit at all levels, not only as a winner of the Open Championship but as a tireless worker for charity at the height of his career," Ken Schofield, the executive director of the PGA European Tour, said. "It is a shame that he has been singled out as the only Open champion not to have received an honour for reasons none of us understands."

Faulkner's boat has come in now that he has sold Selsey Golf Club, which he, his father and mother bought just after the war. "That's why I'm worth a few bob now," he said. How appropriate it would be if, in the year of the anniversary of his Open victory, news came that Max Faulkner had received an honour.

Definition of rules is giving an inch

The Times, April 26, 1999

Did you have a good game of golf yesterday? Two down with six to play, yet you won on the 18th green, I understand. And this despite being out-driven and not having played for several weeks, what with having to cut the grass one day, attend your goddaughter's confirmation the next and the heavy rain that fell.

I am sure that there was plenty of banter during your match, because there always is, and I am sure there was not a whiff of cheating. You played the ball as it lay and so did your opponent. You gave him putts of 2ft and less and he did the same to you. He did not walk on your line on the green, you did not cough on his backswing and you beat him. So now you are through to the next round of the club knockout tournament. Bet the drink you had in the clubhouse before driving home tasted good.

Golf is a game of manners. At matchplay, you wish your opponent good luck on the 1st tee and then abide by a set of complicated rules until the time comes to shake hands with your opponent again, you having beaten him or he having vanquished you. At strokeplay, you ask him his score on each hole, if you have not noticed it yourself, you write it down and at the end you exchange cards, sign them and hand them in as accurate and truthful accounts of your game.

That golf is also a game of trust is one of its strengths. It is a game in which it is understood that each player is expected to abide by a set of rules that are framed to make the game as fair as possible. Only the player knows that he has not nudged his ball on a patch of longer grass in the rough while his opponent was across the other side of the fairway. Only the player knows that the ball he found in the bush by the side of the 15th green was his ball – and not one of the same make and markings that had been lost by another golfer.

Golfers are, in other words, both poachers and gamekeepers. Golf does not send out umpires with every match to settle any dispute, nor a referee to blow a whistle when he sees an infringement. You did not win your match yesterday because the referee failed to notice a knock-on, or allowed seven minutes of injury time when he should have allowed only two.

And so, miraculously we arrive at El Prat, near Barcelona, where Severiano Ballesteros was in hot water last week with other professionals competing in the Spanish Open that ended yesterday because of an occurrence in the first round on Thursday. Ballesteros, playing from light rough on the 12th hole, hit his ball into the trees that line this fairway. It was later declared lost and he walked the 200 or so yards back down the fairway to play another ball. So far, so good. The trouble began when Spanish television later broadcast film that showed that Ballesteros played his second ball from nearer the hole. The significance is not so much that the ball was not in the same spot as that it was both nearer the hole and no longer in line with a tree. On the face of it, this seems to be a clear breach of Rule 20-7 Playing from Wrong Place and Ballesteros should have been penalised two strokes.

The chief referee at this tournament was John Paramor, a very good golfer himself and one of the strongest officials in world golf. He has never been known to waive or bend any rule for anyone, not even Ballesteros when in Spain. Indeed.

Paramor has fined Ballesteros for slow play at least once and warned him for slow play at least once.

On another famous occasion at Valderrama in 1994, Paramor denied Ballesteros relief from a tricky position behind a cork tree on the 72nd hole, a ruling that virtually made sure that Ballesteros could not win the tournament. Ballesteros sought relief on the grounds that the place where his ball had ended was amidst some scrapings by a burrowing animal, a plea that Paramor rejected.

On this occasion, however, Paramor ruled that Ballesteros had not committed any breach of the rules. "I asked the player what he had done and what he was trying to do," Paramor said yesterday. "I realised he had replaced his ball closer to the hole, but it comes down to a matter of degree. Was it significantly better? I adjudged it was not because the tree in question was not one that was concerning him. He said that if he was trying to improve his line, he would not have done what he did because this brought other trees into play."

I suspect I am not alone among amateur golfers in suggesting that most times I could return to precisely the spot from which I played a shot. Paramor said that if Ballesteros had not moved from the spot, then he would have been able to replace his ball precisely, but that Ballesteros, having walked 200 yards down the fairway, searched for his ball for a while and then returned, was entitled to get no closer than seven or eight yards to the precise spot in the rough. Paramor cited Rule 20-2b in support of this ruling.

"There has to be some leeway," Paramor said. "Take the rule governing the ball hanging on the edge of the hole on the green. Rule 16-2 says a player has ten seconds for the ball to fall into the hole, but earlier in the rule it says a player is allowed enough time to reach the hole."

As it happened, Paramor had just had to adjudicate on such a situation and he ruled in the player's favour after watching the incident on television and timing the player's walk from the ball to the edge of the hole.

"Golf is not a precise game," Paramor continued. "Supposing a player's ball has gone into a water hazard: he cannot tell precisely where it entered the hazard and so he cannot place his new ball in exactly the correct position. The key to this is that he has used his best endeavours to do it all correctly. I am happy that the player did this."

Ballesteros is the one who has to live with himself after this episode. He has to look himself in the mirror each morning. "The rule is very clear," Ballesteros said. "I spoke to John Paramor and he is happy. The rest is history."

In this situation, most amateurs would not have known the rules well enough to have done anything but replace the ball and, if they were found not to have done so, would either expect disqualification or would have disqualified themselves.

Is the conclusion of this story that amateurs should learn the rules better? It probably is. But another conclusion might be that there is one rule for amateurs and another one for professionals.

MAY

Death came in May for my mother, for Peter Ryde, a predecessor of mine as golf correspondent of *The Times*, and for Severiano Ballesteros, who needs no introduction here. Almost the halfway point of the year, the month of The Players Championship in Jacksonville, the PGA Championship at Wentworth, and once but not now of the Amateur Championship, May is tinged forever for me with the memories of those three.

My mother had been in declining health when I was summoned home in May 1998 to spend the last few days of her life with her. I was sitting in the sun after lunch one day when David Chappell, the sports editor of *The Times*, telephoned to ask me to write a piece about a colleague, Derek Lawrenson, the golf correspondent of *The Sunday Telegraph*, who had holed in one during a pro-am and won a Lamborghini. Chappell sensed an unusual story. It was interesting that a journalist had won a sports car worth nearly £200,000 but much more interesting to see what he, a golf journalist, would do with it. Would he take it and lose his amateur status or would he forgo a prize the like of which he had never had in his life nor likely would again?

"David," I said. "I'm not really concentrating on golf at the moment. You know that my mother is dying?"

There is as much skill and artfulness in persuading a journalist to write a piece they might not want to as there is in the writing of the piece itself. Perhaps more. Chappell wanted it on his pages and this was where his charm came into play. Despite the rather unusual circumstances (my mother would die a few days later) and without much resistance from me because I too sensed the unusual aspect of this story, we agreed that the moral dilemma Lawrenson faced was one that I should and could address. "Thank you very much, John," Chappell said, just before he put the phone down. "Quick as you can."

That was how "Amateur status small price for a Lamborghini" came to fruition.

"Golf mourns passing of Peter Ryde" was the result of another phone call, this time one received while driving down the M4 to the funeral of Chris Lander, a colleague with whom I had covered rugby. It wasn't Chappell on the other end of the phone this time. It was Keith Blackmore, deputy sports editor of *The Times*.

"John," he asked. "Where are you?"

"I'm on the M4 going to Chris Lander's funeral in Somerset," I replied.

"Afraid you're not," he said. "Peter Ryde has died. He was only the second golf correspondent of *The Times*. We need to do something. Can you get on with it, please?"

So I diverted to my parents' home in Gloucestershire, sat in my father's study looking out over the luscious Uley valley and started telephoning and writing. It was a time to make contact with as many people who knew Ryde as possible, both in the US, where Arnold Palmer paid a warm tribute, and in Europe. I was e-mailed the newspaper cuttings and the formal obituary about Ryde. I spoke to members of his family, to colleagues such as Michael McDonnell, formerly of the *Daily Mail*, and Mark Wilson, once of the *Daily Express*, who had recently visited Ryde. Donald Steele, a former golf correspondent of *The Sunday Telegraph*, was helpful.

So were Sir Michael Bonallack, who was that year's captain of the R & A, and Ken Schofield, the executive director of the PGA European Tour. By teatime I had finished. Perhaps 400 words about the man who succeeded the incomparable Bernard Darwin and, as a result, was never given quite the praise he should have been. I could have written 800 but you never have quite as many words as you want, do you?

And then there was Ballesteros. His death wasn't sudden. He had been taken ill with a brain tumour in 2008. There had been more than enough time to prepare both textual and visual tributes, and a formal obituary. The obituary was written to a formula well demonstrated in *The Times*. A tribute to a man I had known for 30 years was not.

Ballesteros was my all-time hero of those golfers about whom I wrote and I was steadfast in my support of the Spaniard. The tribute went through six drafts if it went through one. I crossed out sentences and rewrote them. I changed paragraphs. I showed all or parts of it to some colleagues to check whether they thought I had got anywhere near doing justice to my hero.

I wrote a chunk, then went off to hit some balls or do some shopping. I tried and tried almost as I have never tried before. Finally, some days before his death, I pressed the button and in seconds it was on the screen of an editor at *The Times* who began composing the headline – "Thank you, Seve, the charismatic virtuoso who helped me dream".

That wasn't the end of it. A few days later, while at The Players Championship, I was contacted by *The Last Word*, BBC Radio 4's weekly obituary programme. I went to the radio booth at the back of the press room to be interviewed down a transatlantic line by Matthew Bannister. Without so much as leaving a mark, Bannister deftly squeezed things out of me that I hadn't even thought to mention in my written pieces. I took off the headphones and felt that with what had appeared in the paper and what was about to be transmitted over the airwaves, I had done the best I could. In my mind, Seve was laid to rest.

Thank you, Seve, the charismatic virtuoso who helped me dream

The Times, May 9, 2011

Within minutes of winning the 1979 Open at Royal Lytham & St Annes, Seve Ballesteros had been brought to meet the assembled journalists. He sat on a raised table in front of them and did his best to answer their questions in his broken English.

One came from a reporter on *The Sunday Times*, a man stationed directly beneath Ballesteros so that he was partly unseen by the Open champion and his voice was slightly disembodied. "How are you going to cope with life now that you have won the Open?" this man asked, but somehow, rising up from the floor, it did not come out like that. The questioner had a second go, failing again to make himself comprehensible and when a third attempt also failed, the room broke out in mocking laughter.

At this Ballesteros, all 19 years and three months of him, leant down to pat the reporter on the head. "You no worry my friend," he said. "You speaka da good eeeenglish."

From that moment, I swore fealty to Ballesteros in a way that I have done to no other golfer. When the discussion turns to all-time favourite golfers and the names of Arnold Palmer, Ben Hogan, Jack Nicklaus and Tiger Woods are mentioned, I think of that afternoon in Lytham and reply: "I'm for Ballesteros."

It's not so much his Ryder Cup record, his five major championships, his occasionally wild golf. It is not that he put the pride back into European golf, that no cause was lost when he was around, that he lit up a room when he walked into it. It is all these and others.

Ballesteros hit the greatest golf shot I have seen. It was that famous three-wood from a bunker on the 18th hole of his singles match against Fuzzy Zoeller in the 1983 Ryder Cup. Jack Nicklaus, the captain of the United States team at the time, said recently it was the greatest shot he had ever seen, too.

Jack Nicklaus, now there is a name for Seve to conjure with; a difficult name for Seve to conjure with. He had difficulty with the English pronunciation of the letter J. It came out as a Y or an H, and so to him I was either "Yon" or "Hon". For me this was nothing more than a badge of honour. There was no one in the world by whom I would rather be called "Yon" or "Hon". Whether Nicklaus liked to be referred to as "Yack" or "Hack" is another matter.

So "Yon" or "Hon" I was until one afternoon in New Orleans when we crossed swords over something I had written. "You are a bad man, Mr Hokins," he said (he sometimes forgot his Ps as well), mischievously waving his finger at me, and Mr Hokins (accompanied by a mock finger-wagging) I remained to him for the next few years. In 2006, he proved to me that he could say his Js when he could be bothered. He was on the 12th fairway during a practice round for the Open, the last one he would play, and I was out there, too. "Hello, John," he said briskly as he walked past me, his mind on other things.

Ballesteros was the most charismatic golfer I have met. Woods does not have charisma the way that Seve did. His eyes don't smoulder as Seve's did and his walk is not instantly recognisable as Seve's was. Nor is his swing so graceful as Seve's was at its best: a combination of elegance and power that was unrivalled.

Woods intimidates people with the aura of mystery that surrounds him. He works out in the middle of the night, if necessary. He travels by himself, eating and staying with his people. He deliberately keeps himself to himself. Ballesteros was the opposite. He fed off the reaction of his followers. He engaged with them. He was not so aloof nor, well, so frightening as Woods is and can be.

Ballesteros was charismatic; Woods is intimidating. Arnold Palmer, everyone's friend, was charismatic; Nicklaus was intimidating. Rafael Nadal is charismatic; Roger Federer, with his self-control, is intimidating.

Some people are born to sing or dance, some to play the piano. Ballesteros was born to play golf. When he took up the address position, he made the club look as much a part of his body as an arm or a leg. Even the way he placed his hands on the grip of a club was beautiful, well-positioned, yet soft. In Ballesteros's hands the club was an injured bird or a cracked egg, not the axe that it is in the hands of others.

In July 2007, Ballesteros and Nick Faldo were at Carnoustie to promote the Seve Trophy to take place later that year and a colleague and I interviewed them together just after breakfast one damp morning. To say it was an eye-opener as to what had happened to Seve would be an understatement. The man I held to be the most charismatic golfer in the world wasn't even the most charismatic man at the table, never mind the room. Faldo completely overshadowed Ballesteros. Seve's eyes were sunken. His body was crumpled, his voice soft. He seemed a shadow of himself and an hour later I knew why. He had decided to retire. He would put his fans through torture no more.

I am a member of Royal Porthcawl Golf Club and occasionally hit balls on the practice ground, up above the old, wooden clubhouse. I was there one afternoon last week, working on some delicate chips to a flag set a few feet the other side of a greenside bunker. As I pondered the challenge I was facing, I suddenly found myself wondering: "What would Seve do?"

What am I describing here? A poor golfer with ideas above his station on a windy practice ground where no one can see him? Certainly. But that is why Ballesteros meant so much to me. I have never found myself in a similar situation and thought, "What would Tiger do here – or Nicklaus or Palmer?"

But Ballesteros engaged me with his consummate talent, his genius at the short game. He engaged me by making me imagine that by thinking of him I might play a better shot than I would otherwise. He helped me dream. He gave me hope. For that I say, "Thank you, Seve."

Bigger is not better in Britain

The Times, May 7, 1997

To The Oxfordshire, then, the venue for the International Open, which starts tomorrow. Oxfordshire is a county of honey-coloured houses, of tranquil pubs, the county of *that* university. In the *Wind in the Willows*, Kenneth Grahame wrote:

"The clever men at Oxford
know all that there is to be knowed
But they none of them know one half as much
As intelligent Mr Toad."

And yet I shall set off this morning with no more enthusiasm than a student attending an early tutorial with a particularly bilious professor. The Oxfordshire does not welcome me as Wentworth and Sunningdale do. Send me to Swinley Forest, to Ganton, to Woodhall Spa and my spirits will soar. But nothing similar happens, sadly, when duty requires my presence at The Oxfordshire.

The course and the clubhouse seem unsympathetic to their surroundings. To come upon the club at the base of the Chilterns is as surprising as coming upon a pine tree in the desert. The Oxfordshire has acres of water. It has that dun-coloured grass that one associates with the seaside. It has many artificial spectator mounds, cart paths, massive bunkers. Both its clubhouse and its golf course shriek at you, grab your attention with their muscularity. I am a minimalist not a maximalist and I feel that The Oxfordshire has as much subtlety as a Tiger Woods drive.

It is a big course, well over 7,000 yards, covering a huge acreage. I am unable to warm to it for the same reason I do not like big noisy people. It is overstated. It leaps up and down in front of me saying: "Here I am, aren't I big and strong?" Much the same applies to Chart Hills, to East Sussex National, and did, once upon a time, to The Belfry.

In the matter of designing and building golf courses in many parts of Britain, I am unconvinced that bigger is better. Why on such courses are there so many bunkers and why are so many so big? Why are inland courses built to include characteristics normally associated with seaside courses? Water is needed for irrigation but does it need to be brought into play on seven of the 18 holes?

Water per se is not offensive. Look at the Swilcan Burn at St Andrews, the Suez Canal at Royal St George's and the Barry Burn at Carnoustie. "Water," wrote the late Peter Dobereiner, "creates neuroses in golfers. The very thought of this harmless fluid robs them of the normal powers of rational thought, turns their legs to jelly and produces a palsy of the upper limbs."

For this reason it is a legitimate weapon for a golf course architect in the continual struggle for supremacy over the golfer. Bobby Jones said that the difference between a bunker and a water hazard is the difference between a car crash and a plane crash – "you have some chance of recovering from a car crash".

In Florida, where the water table is only a few feet below the surface, to move earth is to reveal water. At The Oxfordshire, however, as at other similar-style courses, such huge expanses of water merely look out of place and artificial. This is not an attack upon the work of Rees Jones, who designed The Oxfordshire, Bob Cupp, at East Sussex National, and Robert Trent Jones, at Celtic Manor, all of whom are rightly praised. No one can match Jones for the sympathetic manner in which he restores great courses that have become tired.

Rather, it is a plea that if new courses are to be built in Britain they should complement their surroundings, not challenge them. Why should golf courses in Britain resemble those in Florida? Is it forgotten that the challenges posed by 25 strategically placed bunkers can be as great as by 75, that some water hazards are acceptable but that water on too many holes becomes tedious and time-wasting? The Oxfordshire and its ilk sit in Britain as sympathetically as Ganton would in southern California.

Cherry tomatoes, Fig Newtons and the King's English
Golf Illustrated, May 1988

It was getting late when the English Visitor (EV) to the US PGA Tour arrived at Phoenix airport after a long transatlantic flight and a change of aeroplane in New York City. He had been travelling for more than 18 hours and needed badly to find himself an hotel. He picked his luggage off the carousel and was loading it onto a trolley when he noticed a cardboard sign Sellotaped to a wall: "Phoenix Welcomes PGA Tour. Inquire Here." A middle-aged lady wearing spectacles was sitting beneath the sign reading a paper. She looked tired, too.

"I wonder if you can help me?" the EV asked diffidently of the lady behind the desk. "I'm a journalist from England and I've come over to cover your tournament. I've just arrived after a long flight from London and need a hotel room."

"Well, I never," she replied with a smile. "I was over in London last summer. We went on business and had a wonderful time." She shot a glance at the EV. "I didn't see you there." She picked up a phone and as she dialled said: "How long do you want the room for?"

"You're in," she said after a minute. "It's called the Camelback Inn. It's nice. I'm sure you'll like it. The rate is $80 a night. It's normally $110 but we've got you a reduction because you're with the golf."

The EV smiled gratefully. He wasn't so tired that he couldn't appreciate helpfulness when it was given to him. Over the coming years covering golf in the United States he was to experience much more of the same, but now, a stranger in a strange airport in a country he hardly knew, he was especially touched.

The lady pointed towards a glass door. "Go to that exit and there'll be a white Lincoln Continental waiting. It'll take you to the hotel. Here's the number of the tournament office. Call us in the morning and we'll send a car to pick you up. Have a nice night."

The EV smiled again. "Have a nice night." How often he would hear that phrase in the coming years. It seemed that you couldn't do anything in America, not buy a paper or have a drink without the checkout assistant or waitress or bartender saying, "Have a nice day now". In time, the EV would have to grit his teeth to stop himself from muttering under his breath. Now, he was bowled over.

Nothing in America seemed too much trouble. He settled back in the car. If this was the way Sandy Lyle, Nick Faldo, Bernhard Langer and Peter Oosterhuis were being treated, then it was no wonder they liked it so much over here, he thought, as the car sped silently to his hotel.

The EV walked towards the locker room. A burly man in a blue uniform with a peaked cap stood outside the door. A badge identified him as a Pinkerton guard. In England the EV knew he might be stopped from going in. "Players only," a guard would mutter, holding up a hand. But here, in a country club in Phoenix, when he wore a badge identifying him as a member of the media, he was not only allowed in but the door was held open for him. Inside, the size and comfort of the locker room quite took his breath away. The previous weekend he had played golf at his club in north London, changing his shoes while sitting on an old wooden bench.

There were lockers here in Phoenix, but there the similarities ended with the EV's own club. Easy chairs were dotted around the large room next to tables with bowls of fruit on them. Some lockers had messages taped on them, pink pieces of paper headed "While You Were Out".

A man came into the locker room carrying boxes of new golf balls. The EV had never seen so many boxes of balls before. He watched wide-eyed as the man went from locker to locker, peering at the names stuck onto the outside of each and then opening them and putting three or six boxes of balls inside. Sometimes he would put new golf gloves in the lockers as well. All the while, attendants in white jackets bustled about picking up pairs of shoes and taking them off to a distant room from which there came a continuous hum.

A player sprawled in a chair talking on the telephone. The EV was captivated by the length of the phone's cord. It seemed endless, so long that the player could get up, walk to his locker, get some papers out and return to his chair, all the while with the telephone clamped to his ear. The EV rounded a locker and found his eye caught by what stood on a glass shelf above the four washbasins – as many bottles, potions, tubes and aerosols as the EV would expect to see in a chemist's shop back home. On a similar shelf at his own club there might be an old comb with most of its teeth missing. Here there were so many items that he jotted down the make and purpose of each:

- A can of Pinaud shave cream.
- A can of Palm Beach Skin Saver Lotion.
- Brut Deodorant Spray.
- Lime Sec Eau de Cologne.
- Vitalis V-7.
- Aqua Velva After Shave.
- York mouthwash gargle.
- New Image professional ph-balance hair spray.
- Four razors.
- Two tall jugs the size of cafetieres filled with a murky green liquid in which stood six black combs, fully teethed.

Piles of fluffy white towels were placed at each end of each washbasin. There were four showers, and by the entrance to each were paper slippers to put over your feet.

As the weeks passed the EV found himself aggravated by the Americans' sloppiness with the English language. He had spent 14 years studying his mother tongue at school. Each day he had to conjugate nouns and decline verbs and each night he pored over his *Kennedy's Latin Primer* learning the present, future, imperfect, future perfect and pluperfect tenses of verbs. Now he was offended when, after asking a player how he had got on, the player replied, "I done all right. I played pretty good."

The EV found his ears being bombarded with jarring phrases that mixed verbs and adverbs, present and past tenses, split infinitives. He began to note the most extreme cases:

- A courtesy car driver taking him to a tournament in Florida said: "We had a fairly serious fatality on this road last night."

- A sign over a bar read: "We have live recorded music."
- Another sign, somewhere, read: "The most unique offer you'll ever get."
- A player, shocked after a round at the TPC at Jacksonville, Florida, told the EV: "This is unquestionably possibly the toughest course I've ever played. There is absolutely no doubt about that."

In time the EV learned to smile at these nonsenses. He remembered what George Bernard Shaw had said, that "the British and the Americans are two peoples separated by a common language". He indulged himself in food that he liked so much – Peppermint Patties, cherry tomatoes, Thousand Island dressing and chefs' salads, not to mention the Fig Newton biscuits that kindly press room officials would place in little baskets for the journalists to help themselves to as they walked past. Even so, words like "crossanwich" and "Dunkin' Donuts" jarred slightly.

The EV arrived at Augusta, Georgia, for his first Masters and presented his entry card to the policeman at the gate. It was the time of the Falkland Islands crisis, and Britain was at war with Argentina. Seeing the EV's affiliation as being from London, the guard removed an enormous cigar from his mouth, clapped the EV warmly on the shoulder and sent him on his way with the ringing words: "Don't you let them Argies give you no shit, man."

The EV walked to the green quonset hut to get his green credentials and then took his green seat at a green bench. When he felt hungry he ate an egg salad sandwich that came wrapped in green paper and served by a lady wearing green. It was the best egg salad sandwich he had ever eaten, he decided.

He looked at the scoreboard. The players were listed in alphabetical order. What an odd way of doing it, the EV thought. How on earth do you keep track of the leaders? One minute you'd be looking at a score away to the right of the board, directly beneath a (green) clock showing the time in Tokyo; the next you'd have to swing your gaze 20 yards to the left, to a score posted beneath a clock showing Pacific time. The EV noticed that the scores were slow in being posted, and often were incorrect.

As he travelled to more events in the US, the EV found that the system at Augusta was good by the standards of other tournaments. At the US Open, scoreboards out on the course contained names that had no bearing to their position in the tournament. Nick Faldo might have been four under par leading David Frost and Ben Crenshaw, with Dan Pohl and Paul Azinger tied in third place. But the boards would show things like Jack Nicklaus, plus five, and Tom Watson, plus seven.

The worst scoreboard he ever saw was at the US PGA Championship at Palm Beach in 1987, when the scores were filled in only after nine holes and were often as much as an hour late. When the EV was trying to shout his story down the telephone to London, he found it frustrating that players who had finished an hour earlier still didn't have their scores completed on the press-room scoreboard. In this respect, he decided that golf in Europe was light years ahead of the US. At every pro tournament the scores of each player were posted on a huge board within seconds of that player leaving a green. They were accurate, easy to read and after the first two rounds were positioned according to the player's standing in the field. The EV was disappointed to come to the country that had put a man on the moon and find that their scoring systems were outdated.

The EV returned to the US annually for Walker, Curtis and Ryder Cup matches, US Opens and Masters. It was a life he wouldn't exchange for the world. One March morning while covering the TPC at Jacksonville, he saw that the leaders had not begun their rounds and so he was able to sneak away to a nearby driving range. In the warm Florida sun he cracked some good iron shots off lovely, firm turf. When he tired of hitting long irons he took out his pitching wedge and chipped to a practice green for a half hour. A friend, meanwhile, did some repair work on his bunker play from a practice bunker. And when they both tired of that they moved to the putting green, where they putted until their backs became sore.

How nice it would be to have just some of these facilities back home, the EV thought to himself as he walked into the locker room to change. What would he give for a decent putting green, or practice ground with good range balls provided – not to mention Peppermint Patties and Fig Newtons. He'd swap those for any number of split infinitives, ungrammatical sentences and poor scoreboards.

World of golf falls into the hands of a girl with a Wimbledon name

The Sunday Times, May 29, 1988

A surname like Wade could be a handicap in Britain on the eve of the Lawn Tennis Championships, but it doesn't seem anything less than a blessing to Julie Wade, the newly crowned English amateur golf champion.

For Wade, everything is coming up roses these days. She got engaged in March, the month of her 21st birthday, and was selected for the team that will defend the Curtis Cup against the Americans on June 9 and 10. Then, last week-end, came that exciting extra-time victory at the Birmingham course, Little Aston.

"I was a bit fortunate in the English," she says with the hindsight of a week to give her perspective. "I wasn't very confident at the start. I felt there was a lot of pressure on me as a Curtis Cup player, and I was conscious of what people might say if I didn't do well. But then I thought to myself, 'It doesn't matter what they think. Just go out and enjoy it.' And so I did."

"Enjoy it" might almost be a maxim of Wade's. She refuses to take herself or her golf too seriously, pricking incipient balloons of pomposity with a tart line in self-deprecation. And, at a time when almost every other promising amateur can't wait to turn professional, Wade won't consider doing so.

"Playing day after day is not my idea of fun," she says. Her idea of fun, she explains after a thoughtful pause and with a slow smile, is: "Amateur golf, team golf, weekend golf, playing for other people. Professional golf just doesn't inter-est me."

The formation of the women's professional tour in Britain nine years ago was the making of Wade and others. The family of amateur golf, its best silver disappearing to the pro ranks, had to recruit talent. It did, with more coaching schemes and improved competitions and, as a result, a new breed of more skilful players soon began to emerge.

Laura Davies, the reigning US Open champion, who is four years older than Wade, is the standard-bearer of these Young Turks, whose ranks also include Trish Johnson, a heroine at the last Curtis Cup, and Susan Shapcott, Wade's victim at Little Aston.

"It's very evident that there is a new generation of outstanding young golfers, and Julie is in it," says Diane Bailey, captain of the Curtis Cup team. "There's a lot of thinking time in golf, so the mental approach is very import-ant. Julie's mental attitude is outstanding. She's calm, very positive and has a super temperament."

You might not have thought so had you seen Wade hack her way up the 18th hole last Friday morning while competing in the Critchley Salver at Sunningdale, in which she was later to tie for first place. She was three under par at that point, but a bad drive, a poor bunker shot (in the hitting of which she broke her club) and three putts gave her a seven on an easy par-five hole.

"That was pathetic, absolutely pathetic," she said, her face red with anger and embarrassment. At that moment one remembered what Vivien Saunders had said about her erstwhile pupil: "She's very composed ... for a redhead!"

It was in a county match between Essex and Suffolk six years ago that the

15-year-old Wade came to the notice of Elizabeth Boatman, now the vice-captain of the Curtis Cup team.

"She was very bouncy, and she hit the occasional shot quite wrong, but she had something," Boatman recalls. "I can't describe what it was, it was just something special. Even then she looked pretty good all through the game, and she made me feel strongly that she could be very good."

By then Wade was playing to a handicap of six; at 17 she was down to two, and last year she was playing off plus-three.

Does she remember the day she became scratch? "No, not really. It was just another day." She pauses, and then adds: "I do remember my first competition, though. I was 11, and had just got a handicap, 36. I went round in 128. I thought it was wonderful. I was on top of the world."

There is one other occasion she won't forget. "That was when I took a 10 at the 17th at Felixstowe," she says, laughing and running a hand through her short-cropped hair. "I thought that was brilliant, too, and I rushed home to tell mum."

In 1986 she represented England in the European junior team championships in Hamburg, the first time she had been on an aeroplane, the first time out of England. In 1987 she ran away with the English strokeplay title at Gosforth Park.

"When I first saw her she was very scrappy," recalls Saunders, who coaches England's women golfers. "But we sorted that out in a weekend, and now she has a very solid swing and an outstanding short game."

Ian McPherson, the pro at Felixstowe Ferry, has taught Wade since she took up golf as an 11-year-old. "She has so much natural ability, all I have had to do is to guide her," he says. "It's nothing for her to hit a three-iron or a three-wood to within a foot."

There seems little to prevent Wade dominating European amateur golf. Perhaps, I thought, that isn't a true measure of her ability. "Never mind Europe, I think she could become the best amateur in the world," says Vivien Saunders.

Olazábal, driven by loyalty and pride

The Times, May 31, 1999

Last Wednesday, José María Olazábal captivated an audience of 150 when he spoke at the annual dinner of the European Tour at Wentworth. Never mind that the thoughts of most of the guests had been on the tumultuous football match in Barcelona. On that hot summer's evening, you could have heard a pin drop as the Masters champion, speaking without a note, managed to be graceful, self-deprecating and amusing, gently poking fun at Colin Montgomerie, the guest of honour. All this was done in English, at best his second language.

He urged Montgomerie to "truly believe what a gifted player you are" before mischievously reproaching the Scot for not rewarding Eimear, his wife, after winning a tournament two weeks ago. In repose, the shape of Olazábal's face is oval and when he flashes a smile it appears to slice his face wide open. It did now as he mischievously taunted his Ryder Cup colleague: "Come on, Monty, buy Eimear a present – what a good Scotchman you are."

Watch Olazábal play golf and you see an intense man with dark smouldering eyes and a quick walk who spends an age preparing for the stroke. He waggles his club this way and that and you wonder if he will ever hit it. "What are you thinking about when you address the ball?" Olazábal was asked. "I am talking to the ball," he replied. "I am saying to it: 'I don't know where you went last time. Where the hell are you going this time?' "

Olazábal, who won the Masters in April after recovering from a debilitating illness that was first diagnosed as rheumatoid arthritis and was later discovered to be nerve pressure on his lower back, has dazzling skills, chief among them his short game. No one who saw the way that he conducted himself at Augusta will forget his courage on the course and his innate dignity and graciousness in the hours that followed.

He is egalitarian, socially aware, intensely loyal and fanatically private. Though he is a millionaire several times over, he owns two modest cars, a Volvo and a Nissan four-wheel drive. When some other stars of the game go off in search of appearance money at the end of the season, Olazábal goes hunting. No amount of appearance money would have persuaded him to compete in Germany, when vast sums were paid to Tiger Woods, Mark O'Meara and Nick Price. He was recently asked to give a coaching clinic for junior golfers. His fee? A sausage sandwich and a glass of milk.

"Money is of no importance to José María," Sergio Gomez, his manager, said. "He knows he will never carry his money to the grave. Other golfers have their objective in life to build a financial empire or gain respectability through the supposed power you get through money. That is not the way José María feels about things.

"He has enough to have built a very nice house, to buy a car when he wants to, to buy cartridges for his guns and change his hunting ground every four or five years, and enough to buy his friends dinner two or three times a year.

José María Olazábal chips to the second hole during the third round of the Masters golf tournament at Augusta National Golf Club in Augusta, Georgia, 1999.

He could do many company days at $50,000 or $60,000, but he does not want to. For him, money is an instrument, not a target."

Gomez described Olazábal as a modern socialist. "He has no time for politics. He does not understand the need for politicians. He wants a world without frontiers, no passports, one union."

Olazábal's world is small and tight-knit. Severiano Ballesteros is in it, so are Gomez and Maite, his wife. "If anyone says anything to another, it counts," Gomez said. "When Maite feels she has to tell him she does not like his attitude or the way he is facing a problem, she tells him. José María is a very, very good hearer. He attends to things that are said to him. There is no conflict with his parents. We step aside when his mum comes to a tournament. We have no kids of our own and I am as proud of him as if he was my own. He has described me as his dad, out of home.

"We lived together during the Masters in 1985 and he and I found that my vocation was babysitter, nurse, driver, caddie, manager. An hour ago, I was holding a meeting in our hotel. 'Sergio,' he said. 'Remember at 11.15 we are leaving.' I could tell him to take the car and I would get another courtesy car, but to him it is not thinkable. At 11.15, I am the driver so I have to finish my meeting. That is the spirit of our relationship."

John Jacobs, the eminent golf teacher, has known Olazábal for years and been the Spaniard's only teacher. Their closeness is obvious. "John Jacobs is the nicest man in golf and I thank him for coping with me for so long," Olazábal said. "I am a very, very stubborn pupil."

Jacobs was flattered when he heard these words. "We are very, very comfortable with each other, though often we are a bit firm with one another," Jacobs said. "He has supreme dedication and total self-control and is at his best on the big occasions. Once he got a three at the 10th in the last round of the Masters, I was certain he would win. The back nine is easier than the front nine for him because he hits his shots so precisely and you have to do so on those holes – the tee shot on the 12th, the pitch on the 15th, the tee shot on the 16th, for example.

"José María has a tendency to tee the ball too low and I have to try and get him to tee it up, otherwise it leads to a sequence of faults that make him push some shots, hook others. We had a difficult hour when we met in Spain last January. Seven times he teed the ball up low and each time I bent down to tee it up higher. Finally, I had to say to him: 'Look, I'm in my seventieth year. I can't keep bending. You tee the flipping thing up.' When I saw him tee the ball high on the 17th tee in the Masters and set up for a draw, I knew it would be all right. The course is perfect for him."

Spain's contribution to golf has been enormous, starting with Ballesteros, continuing with Olazábal. Now, it seems, Sergio Garcia is the emerging phenomenon. These three – and their lesser-known countrymen – are proud men, worthy of admiration, who have brought great distinction to their country and their sport. Europe is lucky to have them.

Days of wine, roses and records for McEvoy
The Sunday Times, May 13, 1990

The records continue to pile up for Peter McEvoy. At Morfontaine, 35 miles north of Paris, yesterday morning in the international match between England and France, McEvoy, the last of the great amateur golfers, played his 140th match for England, a mark that may never be broken.

In the morning foursomes McEvoy and Ricky Willison were three up at the turn against Alexis Godillot, the 46-year-old Frenchman whose own international career began in 1964, and Jérôme Descamps, a tall 27-year-old making his debut. Godillot and Descamps staved off defeat until the 17th green, but then McEvoy calmly laid a putt close and the French conceded.

"I didn't play very well," McEvoy said as he strolled back up the 18th fairway and, indeed, he had hit a number of uncharacteristic shots. "But a point. That's my 97th victory for England."

Since his first cap in 1976, McEvoy has lost only five of the 70 singles he has played. No one has played as often and arguably no one has played as well, not even the great Michael Bonallack, whose record of 131 appearances and 86½ points McEvoy surpassed last season.

"He's the best amateur golfer in the world," Bonallack said. "He hits the ball better than I did. He's a better striker, a very good short pitcher. I was much riskier than he was. I wish I had a swing like his. If I had I might have won the Open."

McEvoy was 37 last March. His international playing career is drawing to a close as he devotes more time to work and to his family. "I'm starting to look longingly at the barbecues that everyone who leads a normal life has," he said. "My son, Cameron, is just starting to play. I'd rather take one club, shove it in his bag and go out and play with him."

These are the days of wine and roses for McEvoy. Last week was typical, the combination of time spent at home, competing against Nick Faldo in a charity match (he and Ted Dexter beat the Masters champion and Jimmy Tarbuck) and ending the week in France.

He has lived, and lived for, the life of the amateur, although, if only he could have come to terms with its rather boring lifestyle, he could have made a comfortable living as a professional.

Outside, one or two team-mates half his age were practising their chipping and putting. "For those young lads amateur golf is a stepping stone to a professional career," McEvoy said. "They're not as likely to die for it as I am. For me, amateur golf is a way of life. The most important thing to me is to play international golf."

He's a team man through and through, and in time will undoubtedly make a brilliant captain. He has loved team games since the day the under-13 rugby team for which he played stand-off unexpectedly drew with a local school.

For McEvoy nothing transcends a team victory, not even his two victories in the Amateur or his fantastic performance in the Eisenhower Trophy in 1988, when his last round of 71, played under intense pressure, brought victory to Great Britain and Ireland.

He thinks of that event not in terms of his own play, which won him the individual title as well, but as a team performance. Thus it is something much more memorable. "I'm old-fashioned," he said. "Putting on an England jersey is very important to me. It still gives me a big thrill. Playing for my country is a bigger motivation for me than playing for myself. I win a few things, go home and tell my wife and kids, and after ten minutes that's it. A team success will never be forgotten."

McEvoy has seen international golf undergo a quantum change since he made his debut. "When I started nobody practised before a round. In those days it was glamorous to be the gifted amateur, and you were thought a sissy if you practised.

"Now it has become glamorous to work all day, to hit balls before the round, after the round and finish off with chipping and putting. People are better coached now, and the equipment is better, though I think that metal woods and square grooves on irons have equalised the good players and not identified the best ones.

"My strengths are my concentration and my workrate. I'm quite good at being dogged. I feel I can worry a point out of my opponents." Geoff Marks, the captain of last year's triumphant Walker Cup team, said: "Peter's never doubted his own ability. He's got an aura about him. Opponents look at him and think, 'I can't beat him.'"

Never was this better demonstrated than in yesterday afternoon's singles when McEvoy, near to his best, was five up at the turn and coasted to a 5 and 4 victory over 17-year-old Frédéric Duger, helping England to lead 7½-4½ after the first day.

He was content as he drank a beer in the clubhouse, a central figure among the group of his team-mates gathered around a television to watch the Cup Final.

The words of Bonallack came to mind: "We may not see his like again."

Schofield prepares to step into European background

The Times, May 22, 2004

The tributes have been rung out this week for Ken Schofield, who retires as executive director of the European Tour at the end of December. Tim Finchem, commissioner of the US PGA Tour, made a flying visit to Wentworth to speak of Schofield's leadership of international golf. George O'Grady, who will become the next executive director, cited Schofield's vision of trying to unite the world of golf and his lifelong fight to get the maximum playing opportunities for his members.

"The thing about Ken," John Paramor, the European Tour's chief referee, said, "is that he is passionate about sport and consumed by golf." Peter Dawson, secretary of the Royal and Ancient Golf Club, said: "It's his determination to see the Tour grow that is so striking. He is never one to take no for an answer. When obstacles present themselves, he won't lie down. He just goes through, round or over them."

There is so much talk of Tony Blair's alleged agreement to hand over the leadership of the Labour Party to Gordon Brown that, when Schofield made his announcement, some wondered whether he and O'Grady had had their equivalent of lunch at the Granita restaurant in Islington and made a concord of their own. "No," Schofield said, laughing. "George was never that sort of person. Most people, including George, probably thought I would go on until the Ryder Cup in Ireland [in 2006], but my plans are to step down one month short of my 59th birthday.

"I have asked myself, given that I do not want to do this job for ever, do I want to do other things? The answer is yes. I don't want to walk away and put my feet up. They have asked me to do a serious consultancy for the Tour and I will do that."

Continued references to O'Grady are appropriate because, while Schofield has been the boss for three decades, O'Grady has been his right-hand man during all that time. Although both are prolix conversationalists, they are like chalk and cheese. O'Grady, 55, is the taller, a quiet, often inscrutable Englishman with a cerebral air, who captained Reading University at rugby. Schofield, a Scot, is noisy, pugnacious and a terrier for what he wants, a passionate fan of St Johnstone FC and a man who plays golf with six metal woods (1, 3, 5, 7, 9 and 11) in his bag.

In negotiations with prospective sponsors, Schofield paints the broad picture while O'Grady concentrates on the details. Theirs is a relationship that is based on mutual respect rather than an obvious closeness. "There is no way you could live your life if you saw Ken Schofield every day," O'Grady said. "We think similarly, but when the going gets tough I like to think I have him on my side and I would like to think that he thinks the same about me."

Those who have done business with Schofield talk of occasional, powerful disagreements. "He is very opinionated and he doesn't like criticism, though over the years he has accepted it," Jimmy Patiño, the owner of Valderrama, where the season-ending Volvo Masters is staged, said. "He has upset certain people, but, overall, the European Tour and European golf owe him a great debt of gratitude. Ken Schofield has brought the European Tour to the forefront of world golf."

In the early 1980s, Schofield faced the biggest test of his leadership when a row about appearance money erupted with Severiano Ballesteros, then the biggest name in the sport in Europe. "Seve had an agent who basically wanted to hold European golf sponsors to ransom," Schofield said. "We felt that was not right and we had an impasse for the whole of that summer. It was a bad time."

Not, however, as bad as the "Gang of Four" episode in 2000 in which Ballesteros, Nick Faldo, Bernhard Langer and José María Olazábal accused the European Tour of secrecy in its business matters, questioned the business arrangements with Sky television and suggested the Tour was too cosy with the International Management Group (IMG), founded by Mark McCormack. An extraordinary general meeting was called for.

"It wasn't what we wanted to happen and it wasn't the best time of my life," Schofield said. "What they were asking was not and is not the case. TV, I submit, is one of the successes of our time. The game is covered wall to wall on a dedicated sports channel. If you want the European Tour as a golf watcher to be *Coronation Street* or *Emmerdale* you've got it. It's called Sky."

In October, IMG will organise a strokeplay tournament at Woburn called the Heritage. It is named in tribute to Schofield, which struck some as odd considering that not many years ago Schofield had a well-documented outburst against IMG. "I had a real rant," Schofield said. "I blackballed one of his [McCormack's] championship dinners. I gave him the silent treatment as opposed to the hair-dryer treatment."

Schofield is at present defending the selection system for the Europe Ryder Cup team, as well as fending off continued mutterings about the British nature of his organisation. In an ideal world he would rather his last Volvo PGA Championship was not marked by yesterday's announcement that Volvo is to withdraw its sponsorship. But to a man who has dealt with scenarios such as these for 30 years, what else is new?

Westwood enriched by strong family values
The Times, May 25, 2001

At a dinner in the Wentworth clubhouse on Wednesday night, Lee Westwood was handed the Vardon Trophy by none other than Colin Montgomerie. In a speech notable for its felicitous phrases and decorous jokes, Montgomerie lionised the man who had succeeded him as the winner of the Order of Merit and as Europe's leading golfer.

Then the floor was Westwood's and, momentarily, the 28-year-old who is so sure-footed on the golf course was exposed. For a few seconds he was as uncertain of himself as many amateurs are when they play alongside him in pro-ams.

"One of the things I learnt was to try and stay ahead of Colin on the golf course," Westwood said, "and now" – and here he paused as he searched for the right words – "I have just realised I want to speak before he does, too."

It was an understandable reaction, but then Westwood came through with a winning line. "Anyway, thank you for this," he concluded, gesticulating at the trophy. "I'm off now to do a feed and a nappy change."

Westwood has had his share of these family duties since the birth of Samuel Bevan, the first-born child of he and Laurae, last month. Yesterday morning, Westwood wheeled a buggy containing a sleeping Samuel out on to the practice ground before beginning an intensive session under the eye of Pete Cowen, his coach, and John, his father.

As the cavalcade arrived and caddies and coaches and glad-handers gathered round to coo, the thought occurred: is Westwood going for Father of the Year or Player of the Year?

In 2000 there was no doubt. It was his most successful year since he turned professional in 1993. He won five tournaments on the European Tour, as well as the World Match Play Championship, which is an approved special event. In January, he and his father won a celebrity pro-am in South Africa; in December, Westwood lost to Ernie Els only in a play-off for the $2 million first prize in what was once known as the Million Dollar Challenge. By then Westwood had won his first Order of Merit, which had been Montgomerie's province for the previous seven years.

It is a commonplace to talk of Westwood as a yeoman of England. It has something to do with Worksop, his birthplace, being near the heart of England and his forbears having done their duty for their country. Westwood is so attached to Worksop and to his parents that he has never lived anywhere other than in that Nottinghamshire town and never more than 1½ miles from them.

Such a description is also permissible because Westwood demonstrates what are often seen as English virtues of solidity, calmness and equanimity. For all that he won £2.1 million in prize money last year, and probably as much again from endorsements, and has now moved to a 400-year-old house in 55 acres and flies around in a leased Learjet, Westwood is about the least likely person to get above himself.

If he did, then either his father or mother would be the first to tell him so. If it was not one of them, it might be the grandmother, who once ticked him off forcibly after she had watched him on television bashing a bush in anger. "I have it [equanimity] and Trish [Lee's mother] does as well and the parents did," John Westwood said.

"When you come from working-class backgrounds, which we do – my father was a builder and my wife's father was a bus driver – you realise the value of money. Sometimes when he gets a little bit down on himself and you say to him 'you've won £10,000 this week and that's nearly a year's wage for a lot of people', that soon brings him back down to earth."

Westwood's peers cite his attitude as being one of the most crucial factors in his success. Montgomerie calls it Westwood's fifteenth club in the bag. Thomas Björn admires Westwood's ability not to worry, to put things behind him quickly.

"I'd like to have his driving game too," Bjorn said. Darren Clarke, Westwood's stablemate and rival, talks of Westwood's patience, Paul McGinley of the excellence of Westwood's putting, noting that with 28.4 Westwood topped the average number of putts per round category and with 1.7 the number of putts per green category last year.

Most significant of all is the observation of Cowen, who has taught Westwood for five years and whose shrewd instruction in the techniques of the game have turned Westwood from a short and wild golfer into a long and straight hitter.

Lee Westwood on the 18th hole during the first round of the Benson &
Hedges International Open played at The Belfry, Birmingham, 2001.

"To me," Cowen said, "he has the best attitude of anyone I have ever taught. He loves being in the thick of things. He wants to be where it hurts."

"My attitude is my attitude," Westwood said. "I can't explain it. I've just got it. It is just the way I am." At this his father butted in. "It's to do with years and years of dealing with him with a firm hand when he was growing up."

"Steady on now," Lee said. "You could get into trouble here."

John Westwood continued: "One of the things that makes him a good golfer is that he is very, very competitive. We made everything into a competition, balancing the old threepence pieces on their edges on top of one another. If you got to nine you had done well. He'd work hard to win and very rarely would do so. I'd never let him win, so when he did he had done well. Now he never lets me win, so if we play snooker I get 30 start and still lose." Lee, standing nearby, snorted: "30? 50, more like."

Westwood's swing would earn high marks for efficiency but low marks for aesthetics. At first glance it looks slightly agricultural. "There are 200 men on the tour and not one swings like Lee," Tim Barter, the TV analyst and coach of Andrew Coltart, pointed out. "He tilts at the start of it and his left arm is bent, but the significant thing is that at impact he is impeccable and that is where it matters. He rotates beautifully through the ball and this is what gives him such stability of shot."

Stability of shot, consistency, a repetitive swing. These are the words Westwood's peers use to explain the success of the man who, in sixth, one place ahead of Montgomerie, is the leading European in the world rankings. "His line of attack into the ball is superb," Sam Torrance said. "His bad shots are not that bad. He is a great driver, long and straight."

At that Torrance, Europe's captain in the Ryder Cup match at The Belfry in September, stroked another putt into the hole before looking up with a wicked smile on his roguish face.

"When I think of Lee I think 'what a lovely life this young man has ahead of him. He has a great attitude. Nothing worries him. He is very much in control of his emotions. He has a wonderful family. Life is very rosy for him.' If I had one wish for him," he said, "it would be for him to hole the winning putt in the 2001 Ryder Cup."

The dominant figures in European golf before Westwood were Nick Faldo in the late eighties and early nineties, followed by Montgomerie. Westwood has to wrestle with the legacy left by two big men who cast such long shadows. Faldo's single-mindedness may have contributed to the end of two marriages but it did bring him six major championships. Montgomerie has said that, of his seven successive victories in the Order of Merit, the first three were won by his skill and the next four by his mental strength, his character and cussedness.

To whom of these will Westwood be compared? He intends to play more in the United States between February and April next year. Will it be sufficient to give him the sharpness necessary to win a major championship, in which he has so far challenged only once significantly? Or will he be dominant in Europe, as Montgomerie was before him, and, in the eyes of some, be demeaned for not having one or more of the game's four big prizes?

Amateur status small price for a Lamborghini

The Times, May 21, 1998

Amateur golfers the world over will sympathise with Derek Lawrenson, who had to make the biggest decision of his golfing life yesterday afternoon after he had won a Lamborghini Diablo for holing in one during a pro-am. Should he take the £189,000 car, make a fast getaway – it can reach a speed of 208mph – and say goodbye to competitive amateur golf? Or should he forgo this enormous prize in order to continue to enjoy the pleasures of membership at Moor Hall, his club in Birmingham, and of competitions with his fellow golf writers?

For Lawrenson, it was the stuff of dreams. He arrived on the tee of the 198-yard 15th hole at Mill Ride Golf Club, swung a three-iron and holed out. The world, on a glorious summer's day, took on an even rosier hue.

I got my first hole in one two months ago, after 45 years of trying. I won nothing and was happy to pay for three magnums of Bollinger to be consumed by my friends. Lawrenson, for his sixth hole in one, won a vastly expensive car. Some people have all the luck. Lawrenson is a left-hander who holed in one when we played together in the Canary Islands ten years ago. His handicap, once one, is now seven, but there are times when the fluency of his swing and the purity of his striking reveal that he was once good enough to compete in the Lytham Trophy and to have hit balls on a practice ground alongside Sandy Lyle and Mark James.

Yesterday Lawrenson, the golf correspondent of *The Sunday Telegraph,* was not only playing with footballers – he was playing with Steve McManaman and Paul Ince, two stars of Liverpool, the club at which he holds season tickets. To have played with them on a summer's day, and to have played well, would have been more than enough. To hole in one and win such a prize – his cup was surely running over.

But should he take the car? If he did so, according to Grant Moir, assistant secretary (rules) of the Royal and Ancient Golf Club of St Andrews, he would forfeit his amateur status and it could take ten years for him to regain it.

In this time Lawrenson, now known as a non-amateur, would be able to compete only in events at which the organisers were prepared to grant him a temporary handicap.

Moor Hall might be prepared to do so for internal club competitions as might P.G. Wodehouse's Wrecking Crew, otherwise known as the Association of Golf Writers, but equally, they might not.

If Lawrenson was worried at missing out on some of the competitive camaraderie of golf he could, so long as he did not handle the car, immediately hand it over to charity. He could decline to receive the car and accept instead a sum of money to commemorate his feat. But this sum would be a maximum of £200.

A hard decision? Not really. Croesus might walk away from the car because he had a bob or two, as might Jimmy Patiño who has one golden rule down at Valderrama – he has the gold so he makes the rules. But the opportunity to receive a payment – greater, just, than his salary from *The Sunday Telegraph* – is surely one that Lawrenson and almost any other amateur put in a similar position would leap at.

I often said jokingly when we played together that he was a lucky golfer, and particularly when he had narrowly beaten me, by 5 and 4, say. Now he has proved it. Good luck to him.

Golf mourns passing of Peter Ryde

The Times, May 17, 2000

Peter Ryde, whose death was announced yesterday, was only the second golf correspondent in the history of *The Times* and it was his misfortune to suffer comparison with the first. One school of thought believes that if Ryde had succeeded someone other than Bernard Darwin, then his writing talents, his enthusiasm for golf and his wisdom about matters inside and outside the game would have been appreciated more. As it was he became one of the few non-American writers to be honoured for his contributions to golf journalism last year.

"I first met Peter in 1960," Arnold Palmer recalled yesterday. "He stood out not only for his height but also for the quality of his writing." There began a friendship, continued around the bridge table, that lasted for four decades.

Palmer was touched earlier this year to receive a handwritten note from Ryde, commiserating with the death of Winnie, Palmer's wife, from cancer. Cancer claimed Ryde, too, but the fact that he had 18 months' knowledge of it enabled him to prepare himself. "It gives one time to pack one's bags," he remarked drily.

Ryde took over from Darwin in 1953, reportedly because the editor had spotted him whirling through the revolving door of the *Times* building with a bag of clubs over his shoulder. His first appearance, at the English Amateur at Royal Birkdale, was almost as dramatic as Gerald Micklem's unexpected victory over Ronnie White, a local hero. Ryde wore a blue suit, carried a rolled umbrella and wore a beret. "He was never a great golfer but he cared passionately about the traditions of the game and the people in it," Sir Michael Bonallack, the captain of the Royal and Ancient Golf Club, said. "He was very quiet, very authoritative and never spoke ill of anyone."

It was some time before the name of Peter Ryde appeared at the head of golf articles and that was the way he liked it. Even when writing for *Country Life*, he called himself "Water Hazard". He had an infectious giggle and one would guess that he giggled when *Country Life* misprinted his byline as "Waiter Hazard". Ryde's precise and elegant writing was not always matched by the accuracy of his memory. "Life for Peter continues to be a game of hunt the thimble," Geoffrey Green once wrote of the colleague who collected walking sticks and, more unusually, different types of plastic bags, of which he had 200. "Whenever a presentation was made to him of a walking stick," a colleague recalled, "it was made in the knowledge that it would find a new home somewhere else quite soon."

One of Ryde's greatest achievements came in the early seventies, during the dispute between the body of playing professionals who wanted to break away from the Professional Golfers' Association and form what would become the European Tour. "The wise and calm words of advice Peter wrote proved invaluable," Ken Schofield, executive director of the European Tour, said. "His message then – do it but think it through and do it right – still stands good today in our approach to new issues."

Landscape art – the spirit of the amateur

The Sunday Times, May 31, 1981

In the sky high above the ruins of St Andrews Cathedral, a plover soared and swooped over the grave of young Tom Morris, son of the legendary Old Tom. In the town centre, shoppers scurrying through the drizzle passed the Holy Trinity Church where nine years ago a memorial service for Bobby Jones was held. Away to the west, four golfers were swinging nervously as they prepared to drive on the 1st hole of the hallowed Old Course.

St Andrews, a picturesque grey town built on a promontory jutting into the North Sea, has, as well as the cathedral, a medieval castle and Scotland's oldest university. Yet for the thousands who flock to the Fife seaport, it is most famous as being the spiritual home of amateur golf. Last year 41,478 rounds were played over the Old Course alone. As the American, R.F. Murray, has written:

"Would you like to see a city given over
Soul and body to a tyrannising game?"

For six days starting tomorrow, the city will be given over to the best unpaid players while the Royal and Ancient Golf Club stages the Amateur Championship at St Andrews for the fifteenth time since 1885. There will be 256 competitors from 21 different countries competing for the title held by Welshman Duncan Evans.

In his office high above the 1st tee Keith McKenzie, secretary of the R & A, twirled his gin and tonic around in a glass bearing the Tory-blue crest of the club and remarked with an air of satisfaction: "It's a super field. We had a total entry of 394, and we had to ballot out all the two-handicap players and 81 of the ones."

It wasn't always so for, beginning in the fifteenth century, the parliaments of three successive Scottish kings prohibited golf. Nonetheless, James IV became a golfer, and Mary, Queen of Scots, so the story goes, even played at St Andrews. Today St Andrews has four courses that lie side by side like the fingers of a hand between the A91 and the sea. An average of 100,000 rounds are played over the New, Eden and Jubilee courses, which, like the Old Course, are always open, except for one month of the year – and every Sunday, when maintenance work is done.

One morning recently, four men gathered on the 1st tee of the Old Course. Two were locals, one was from Glasgow and the other, up from London, was playing his first round at St Andrews. The talk was of money. The green fees of £6 had been paid, and now the bets were being struck. "We'll play for 10, 10 and 30," said Bill, looking at his partner. He paused, ever the canny Scot: "Pence, that is."

Soon they were tangling with the whins that blazed with colour in the early morning light. On some of the vast double greens, introduced in 1832, they often found themselves squinting down the line of 30-yard putts that had the undulations of a rumpled eiderdown quilt. The course looks wide open because it doesn't have a single tree and some of the fearsome bunkers can go unseen. But how their names ring out: Hell and High, Principal's Nose and the Beardies, Strath and Cockle, Scholars and Road, Shell and Admiral Benson.

At the 13th, an eerie haar swept in from the sea, engulfing the combatants. One of them, who had read the spectral book, *Golf in the Kingdom*, was reminded that Seamus MacDuff, one of the book's central figures, lived in a cave in a ravine hereabouts. The memory caused him to shiver apprehensively in the cool air.

The haar lifted, wafting away as quickly as it has fallen, and soon they were all crossing the arched bridge over the Swilcan Burn and heading towards the huge expanse of fairway spreading out in front of Tom Morris's 18th green. The feeling at that moment was overwhelming. Shivers of nervous excitement raced up and down the spine.

In 1930, when Bobby Jones won the Amateur Championship at St Andrews, the first leg of what is now known as his grand slam, he was acclaimed by 15,000 spectators, and had to be rescued from the crowd encircling the 12th green by a squad of Scottish policemen. Subsequently, Jones was made a Freeman of the Burgh, the first American since Benjamin Franklin to be so honoured, and the 10th hole on the Old Course was named after him.

This week's Amateur Champion won't receive similar canonisation, but he will still experience aspects of St Andrews that Jones would have relished. He might well be woken by a kilted bagpiper playing outside his hotel room. In the clubhouse, he'll find there's always fresh fish on the menu and, something of a surprise, that there is a handsome jockey scales, complete with brass weights, in the men's lavatory. What he might not want to see, lest it should put him off his game, is the cartoon that hangs near the men's locker room downstairs. It is a Bateman original – "The Man Who Missed the Ball on the First Tee at St Andrews".

JUNE

One night in June 1990 while having dinner in Chicago with Nick Faldo, we noticed that there was a book entitled *It's Possible* on a shelf above his head. In those days I had a friendship with Faldo that exceeded, just, the normal relationship between a golfer and a journalist.

It had survived my 1985 biography of him and was nourished by occasional meals such as this. I got on well with Gill, his then wife, and I detected her hand in my invitation after he had won the 1989 Masters, his first green jacket, to a celebration party at a restaurant in Egham at which Max Boyce roughed him up mercilessly. If it is very unusual now for there to be a closeness between a player and a journalist so that they can have dinner as friends, it wasn't quite so unusual then.

He had retained his Masters crown a few months before. Now, after three victories and a second place in the previous 11 major championships, he was the outstanding figure in world golf. The question was whether he could win the US Open at Medinah, a monstrous course just down the road. I looked at the bookshelf again. The words "It's Possible" seemed to be getting bigger and bigger. "Do you really think you can win this week?" I asked. Faldo smiled.

June means the Amateur Championship, perhaps the Curtis Cup, probably a couple of top-ranking European Tour events and a trip to the US. I cross the Atlantic at least four times each year. I go for the Masters, The Players, the

US PGA, two of the Ryder, Walker, Curtis and Solheim Cups and certainly for the jewel of June, the US Open.

Covering the USGA's premier event has taken me from Shinnecock Hills at the east end of Long Island to Pebble Beach on the rocky coast of California south of San Francisco; from Hazeltine National in Minnesota where Tony Jacklin ran away with the 1970 US Open, to Merion in Pennsylvania where the championship was staged in 1981 and again in 2013, in what turned out to be Justin Rose's breakthrough major title.

And from the steamy heat of Oakmont, outside Pittsburgh, where Colin Montgomerie was beaten by Ernie Els in a play-off in 1994, to the steamy heat of Congressional CC, near Washington DC, where Montgomerie once more finished second to Els, this time in 1997. The East Coast is big and brash, the West Coast more flaky and the Midwest is America's breadbasket, the agricultural empire that feeds a nation.

Minnesota is a golfer's paradise, a state that has more golfers per head of population than any other. Golf in Minnesota is not like golf in Musselburgh or Manchester. The harsh winters limit play to a few months each year and consequently Minnesota's golfers are fully focused on enjoying their sport. "They come out in hordes in April," Dick Yates, owner of a public course in Minneapolis, told me. "It's like letting cattle out of the barn."

There was no shortage of spectators at Formby Golf Club in 2004 when Michelle Wie was the star attraction of the US Curtis Cup team and we discovered that she was named after that Beatles song. There were some spectators, but not so many, at the Amateur Championship at Nairn in 1994 where fish leaped past the dining room window and gorse and broom lined the fairways. And there were none at all at The Greenbrier in West Virginia, where I stayed for a few days before the 1999 US Open at Pinehurst while writing a piece about Sam Snead. June is a confection of golf, men's and women's, amateur and professional, and all the better for that.

So there we were, Faldo and I that night, a couple of Limeys in the heart of the US, a few miles from the course where the 2012 Ryder Cup would be won so spectacularly by Europe. We weren't that far from Louisville, Kentucky, where Faldo would captain Europe in the 2008 Ryder Cup, and lose, nor that far from Rochester, New York, where his remarkably doughty play over the closing holes of the 1995 Ryder Cup set up Europe's victory. I knew the dinner in June 1990 might, probably would, yield a story for *The Sunday Times* but I had no idea how accurate it would make me seem.

In *The Sunday Times* a few days later I wrote that "It's not just possible, it's probable, that Faldo…will win this week's US Open." In fact he finished third, one stroke out of joining a play-off between Mike Donald and Hale Irwin, the eventual winner. Irwin got into the play-off by holing a 45-foot putt on the last green and then doing a lap of honour while blowing kisses to the crowd. That June day was Irwin's but it might so easily have been Faldo's.

Snead swings easily to passing of time
The Times, June 14, 1999

Sam Snead is one of the last links to golf in the 1930s and 1940s. He knew Bobby Jones, was never beaten by Gene Sarazen, competed against Ben Hogan. Snead's first Open was in 1937 at Carnoustie, which Sir Henry Cotton won. Talking to him is like turning the pages of golf's history, a task made all the more pleasant because Snead is plus four into talking.

Snead's left shoulder was dislocated in a car accident a few years ago but it has not stopped him from hitting balls every day, drawing crowds of spectators who marvel at his striking and the repetitiveness of his swing. And when he is not playing or practising, he tells stories as long as one of his drives and as slow-moving as a goods train through the Virginia hills. As he tells them he stops frequently and smiles lopsidedly and winks, particularly if pretty ladies are among the listeners.

Snead was 87 last month and these days is ambassador for golf at The Greenbrier resort in the Allegheny Mountains, a few miles from where he was born. There, he eats in Sam Snead's restaurant, crammed with Snead memorabilia, including letters from past presidents Nixon, Ford, Reagan and Bush, as well as President Clinton. There, Snead drinks in Slammin' Sammy's Bar, wipes his mouth on napkins with his signature woven on an edge, parks in a spot marked "Reserved for Sam Snead" and signs autographs and tells stories while sitting in the Sam Snead Collection Shop in the hotel.

Last Thursday, Snead was eating lunch and talking golf when suddenly he took his arms back, brought them down in a graceful swoop over his bowl of cream of asparagus soup and followed past his left shoulder. "Golf is a game of rhythm and timing," he said. "That's all. Some say you've got to thrash it, but you ain't. It's a simple game but people make it so hard."

No one made the game look as easy as Snead, who started caddying when he was seven and received a thrashing from his mother the first time he did so because she did not know where he had been. At 17, he ran the 100 yards in ten seconds. He was nearly 53 when he won his last Tour event. When he was 67 he went round in the same score as his age in a seniors' event, and he was supple enough into his 80s to kick a leg to the top of a door. Driven by arms that are an inch longer than normal, Snead's fluid swing, considered by many to be the best the game has seen, helped him to win 81 tournaments, more than any American in history, to capture three of the game's four major championships at least once, to set a tournament scoring record of 69.2 that still stands and to win tournaments in six decades.

Snead's eyes light up at the memory of Carnoustie 62 years ago. "That was a good course. Remember the traps they had out in the middle of the fairways? I was knockin' it over those traps. I never used a putter in the third round, otherwise I would have won the championship. There was so much rain I had to pitch and chip, 'cos the ball wouldn't roll." Snead returned to Scotland seven years later for the Open at St Andrews. "I win the tournament and at the end they said to me, 'Are you coming back to defend next year?', and I said: 'It's cost me $2,000 to come over here and I've won $600 – are you kidding?"

Snead partnered Hogan and competed against him but never got close to understanding the Texan. "Hogan was an individual. He never talked. I played with him as a partner and he never said one word to me. He was a dealer in cards. He learnt to keep his face expressionless. In 1950, I won 11 tournaments and I beat Hogan in a play-off for the Los Angeles Open and had 96 straight rounds and averaged 69. He won one tournament and got Golfer of the Year."

In his glittering career Snead failed to win only one major championship, the US Open. "I once figured out that if I shot 69 in my final round I would have won nine Opens. I could have won 12 of 'em but something always happened."

There are as many stories about Snead's thrift, which is so great he is said to have won $1 million and saved $2 million, as there are about his gambling at golf, at which he once won $10,000 in one day in the late 1930s.

Snead, the story goes, has buried his money in tin cans in the soil of his native Virginia. The man himself gives the impression that he likes these stories by referring to money constantly. "I charged $600 for a lesson and $2,000 if it is followed by dinner." Snead extended our hour-long appointment to nearer two, followed by lunch in which he scarcely drew breath. He asked whether I played golf. I nodded. "I am a hooker," I said. He had a surprise up his sleeve. "We'd better get a look at this hook."

"You're not going to charge me $600?"

"Probably not, but don't tell on me."

Unprepared as I was, I needed golf shoes. "What size are you?" Sam asked. "Eight and a half."

He paused for a moment before asking: "You got smelly feet?"

"No."

Moments later I slipped my feet into a pair of his white golf shoes. Not fit to lace his shoes, I was suddenly wearing them. Now all I needed were some clubs. "Don't worry," Snead said to the assistant who was trying to help us. "He'll use mine."

In my brief lesson, Snead checked the position of the club handle in my left hand. He told me to pick up the club head more quickly on my back swing, to grip more firmly with the last two fingers of the left hand, to turn my body more and to make sure I pulled the club head down with my left hand. "Don't forget, you can pull a golf club but you can't push it."

Finally, he said: "Boy, I don't see no hook."

The next morning, Snead was signing more autographs in the hotel. Two matronly ladies perched on the arms of his chair, one on either side of him, to have their picture taken with him. "Now girls, you look after yourselves," he said, grinning. It made their day – and it made mine, too.

Woods revels in his role as leading man

The Times, June 19, 2000

On Saturday night in one of the bars in Monterey that may have been familiar to Robert Louis Stevenson and John Steinbeck when they were in these parts, an animated discussion about Tiger Woods was taking place.

Similar discussions were going on all over the United States as golfers came to terms with the fact that Woods had spread-eagled the field in the hundredth US Open. Ten strokes ahead after 54 holes, a tournament record at three better than Jim Barnes, a Cornishman, in 1921, the winning margin was to be fifteen strokes, the largest in a US Open.

The argument started like this: "Is Tiger the best ever?"

"Not yet, he's not," came the reply. "He has not achieved what Ben Hogan did in 1953 when he won the Masters, the US Open and the Open in one glorious summer – and he will not this year either, because Vijay Singh won the

Masters – and has not matched the record of Robert Tyre Jones, the great Bobby Jones, who won the Open and Amateur championships of Britain and the US in 1930.

"Jones's feat, aptly if rather clumsily named the Impregnable Quadrilateral, was the forerunner of the modern grand slam, which now comprises the four major championships, the Masters, the US Open, the Open and the US PGA. And then there was Jack Nicklaus, who won 18 major championships and finished second in a further 19. I think that puts Tiger's achievements into perspective, don't you?"

"But he has won four of the ten PGA Tour events he has entered in the US this year and finished in the top ten in nine of the ten, hasn't he?"

"Yes."

"And he hits the ball farther than anyone ever has?"

"Perhaps."

"But if you compared him with Hogan and he struck the ball better, hit it farther, holed more putts and made more audacious recoveries than Hogan, surely that makes him better than Hogan?"

"Not until he has had a year such as Hogan's in 1953."

What is unarguable is that Woods's consistency has been astonishing. Victory in Pebble Beach, which looked assured last night, would be his 26th worldwide since he turned professional in 1996 and in the 100 tournaments he has competed in as a professional, he would have finished in the top ten on 71 occasions. This is a rate of success that far exceeds Nicklaus's, although it does not approach Byron Nelson's 11 consecutive tournament victories in 1945.

It is also unarguable that Woods has become one of the best-known sportsmen in the world. Because of his parentage – his father is American, his mother Thai – Woods crosses ethnic barriers. He has made golf cool to millions of people around the world.

There the discussion petered out. No one dared mention the unmentionable: that Woods might not win. When the best player in the world holds a lead of ten strokes, then surely that is inviolate? You would think so, but these men knew, as did Woods, that there were precedents for failure in the US Open, albeit smaller ones.

In 1920, Harry Vardon led by four strokes after 63 holes and took 42 on his homeward nine. Arnold Palmer led Billy Casper by seven strokes with nine to play in the 1966 US Open – and Casper caught him by the 72nd hole and beat him in a play-off the next day.

Jones once remarked that Nicklaus played a game with which he, Jones, was not familiar. Nicklaus said something similar about Woods in 1997. Few, if any, of Woods's rivals can understand the magnificence of his play here.

He does not appear to have any weaknesses. He is an enormously long, straight hitter, for whom par-fives are more often than not par-fours. His drives averaged 300 yards in the first three rounds and he was two under par for the par-fives. His iron play is impeccable, his short game, although not quite as magical as, say, Phil Mickelson's, is better than almost everybody else's.

His extraordinary strength enabled him to club a seven-iron out of thick rough and more than 200 yards uphill at the 6th hole on Friday. Then he two-putted for a quintessential Woods birdie.

Then there is his mental strength. Woods himself believes he owes more of his success to his mind than to his body. A demonstration came on Saturday afternoon, when he took a seven on the par-four 3rd hole, one of the shortest par-fours at Pebble Beach, his second shot having plunged into thick grass short of the 3rd green. Woods sought relief on the grounds that his ball was plugged, but Sir Michael Bonallack, the rules official, would have none of it. Woods tried to play out sideways and could move the ball only a few feet and his next went only halfway to the green. Then he chipped and two-putted.

I know exactly what Woods's reaction to this was because I was a few feet from where his second shot landed. I saw clearly that as he walked back to his bag Woods was smiling. No point getting cross, get even, he was thinking. Then he birdied two of his next four holes.

I have covered professional golf for nearly a quarter of a century. I have seen Tom Watson, Severiano Ballesteros, Nick Faldo and Greg Norman dominate the game either briefly or for sustained spells. I never saw Hogan play and caught only occasional glimpses of Nicklaus when he was in his prime. Woods is the best I have seen.

What I watched last week out on this rocky headland above what Stevenson called the greatest confluence of land and sea, was a form of golf with which I, and millions of others, am unfamiliar.

Vivid tale of golfer who lived life to the full

The Times, June 7, 2003

Some book, this. Within the first ten pages it is revealed that the hero was adopted when he was ten days old and that his wife died one night after becoming sick and inhaling her vomit. This may be par for the course for a penny dreadful, but it is the biography of Joe Carr, a significant figure in amateur golf. If the opening revelations do not make you want to read on, nothing will.

Earlier this week, four men who know the present golf scene were eating dinner at a pub near Royal Troon, where they had been attending the Amateur Championship. When Carr's name was mentioned, it evoked hardly any response. The man who competed in 11 successive Walker Cups, ten of them as a player, and was arguably the best amateur golfer in these islands from the end of the war to the mid 1960s, during which time he won the Amateur three times, is forgotten. A shame.

Of how many others can it be said that they were the first non-American citizen to be presented with the Bob Jones award for sportsmanship, the first Irishman to play in the Masters – and who outscored his playing partners, Jack Nicklaus and Arnold Palmer, on his first two visits – and the first Irish captain of the Royal and Ancient Golf Club of St Andrews?

For years, Suncroft, the Carr home opposite the 6th green at Sutton Golf Club in Dublin, was open house. The daily milk delivery was 26 bottles. It is said that John O'Leary, a Ryder Cup player in 1975, went there for a weekend and stayed for two years. That was not true, but there is evidence that several golfers, having played at Sutton, adjourned to Suncroft, where they were royally entertained, when they thought they were adjourning to the clubhouse.

While Carr's swing was not the eccentric thing that his countryman Jimmy Bruen's was, purists would not call it classical. Norman von Nida, the Australian professional, described it thus: "He set up for a draw, hits a fade and smashes the f****** thing a country mile."

What Carr did was work at golf as few had worked before him and not many since. He would go for a two-mile run and hit 200 balls before breakfast. Lunch was taken at Royal Dublin Golf Club, after which he would spend a further 1½ hours practising. And after returning from work in the clothing business, at a gentlemanly time in the afternoon, he would practise his putting on a carpet before moving outside to hit some chips and bunker shots. On dark nights, he turned on two 1,000-watt lights fixed to the roof of Suncroft to help him to see what he was doing. Before he left to compete in the Amateur at St Andrews in 1958, Carr wore out the blades of his eight and nine-irons and, he had estimated, hit 47,000 tee shots in preparation.

There used to be an advertisement that suggested that behind every famous man was a woman. Never was this more true than in the case of Carr.

Roddy Carr, the second son of six children, says that Dorothy's "*raison d'être* was to make him [Joe] a champion, just as Vivienne Player, Barbara Nicklaus, Valerie Hogan, Toots Cotton, Vivien Jacklin and Winnie Palmer had done for the men they married". Which is why her death in 1976, aged 52, may have been given a fuller explanation.

If the measure of a book is the sweep it gives of a man's life, then this does that very well. It is an unexpected pleasure, like coming upon your ball sitting up in the rough.

Breaking 80… The life and times of Joe Carr, Dermot Gilleece (Poolbeg Press Ltd, 2002)

Cruellest cut of the one that refused to get in the hole

The Times, June 19, 2001

Every regular golfer knows the routine when facing an important putt. Take a deep breath. Stand behind the ball and look down the line. Imagine the ball slowly leaving the clubface and disappearing into the hole. Swing smoothly.

These were the thoughts in the mind of Retief Goosen when he looked at his putt on the 18th green at Southern Hills here on Sunday as the sun was beginning to set on a glorious Oklahoma day. Goosen knew what to do at the climax of the 101st US Open. He had holed thousands of putts in his time. Stick to your routine, he told himself. Trust yourself. Do as the pros say and put a good roll on the ball. These were his watchwords.

The prize was riches beyond compare as a result of winning one of golf's four annual major championships. Hole the putt and Goosen would become an instant millionaire, one of the celebrated men in the game he plays for a living. He would earn £5 million from endorsements, from potential revenue from major championships and personal appearances. He would become the second man from South Africa to win the national championship of the United States in seven years, the third in all.

We know now what happened. Goosen missed the first putt that would have given him victory by two strokes and then missed the second as well. There was a gasp when the first, from 12 feet, bolted past the hole, stopping 2½ feet away. There was a roar when Goosen's second putt appeared to be pushed and finished three feet away. Viewers on television saw the way that his putter blade appeared

Retief Goosen holds his head after missing the winning putt on
the 18th hole during the final round of the 2001 US Open at
Southern Hills Country Club in Tulsa, Oklahoma.

to be open at impact, as a cricketer's bat is opened to hit a cover drive, and thus sent his ball to the right of the hole.

As a boy in South Africa, Goosen would spend hours on the practice ground. Often he would line up a short putt and say to himself: "This for the Open." As he stood over the putt, an imaginary voice inside his head would be doing the commentary. "Goosen is crouched over the ball. It's in." And he would straighten up and wave, a grin on his face. If he missed he would make himself hole another five putts of that length before he could go home.

How come then that he managed one of the most calamitous misses with the putter in the history of championship golf? The answer is partly physical and partly mental. The playing of a golf hole can resemble the playing of a piece of music that starts at double fortissimo and quietens to a whisper at the end in the way that the hurly-burly of a thunderous drive is followed by a carefully flighted second, the deftness of a chip by the gentleness of a short putt, the hands holding the putter as if cradling an injured bird.

Putting is golf's black art and the greater the prize for holing a putt, the greater the pressure. At such times, a complicated process is set in motion during which it seems that the senses are required to go in opposite directions. The pulse is racing yet the brain must be ice-cool. There is a dryness in the mouth, yet beads of perspiration are forming on the forehead. Part of the brain is shrieking "you've done it, think of what you are going to say in your victory speech" while another part is shouting out "be quiet, concentrate, keep your mind on the job".

These were the pressures that Goosen faced on Sunday afternoon, pressures that overcame him. These were the pressures that Willie Park Jr faced in 1898 when, needing to hole a three-foot putt to tie with Harry Vardon for the Open Championship, Park yanked his putt wide. And this from a man who practised his putting for 12 hours at a time until his back was so stiff he could hardly straighten up. Park did this because, as he used to say in words that are as true in June 2001 as they were in the nineteenth century: "The man who can putt is a match for anyone."

Even though Goosen triumphed in yesterday's play-off, he will live with his wretched memory for the rest of his life, as will Doug Sanders, who missed a putt of 3½ feet on the 72nd green of the Open at St Andrews in 1970 and lost to Jack Nicklaus in a play-off the next day. Craig Stadler won the 1982 Masters, but for many in Europe the dominant memory of the burly man with the moustache that froths over his top lip is the way he missed a two-foot putt to beat Sandy Lyle and Bernhard Langer on the second day's four-balls of the 1985 Ryder Cup. Europe went on to a famous first victory for 28 years.

Three steps to danger – the sting in Merion's tail

The Sunday Times, June 21, 1981

They had been saying all week that the finishing holes at Merion's famous East Course would hold the key to the 81st US Open Golf Championship. It mattered less how well anyone played for the first 13 holes, said the experts. What really counted was how they dealt with the fearsome last five, and particularly the quarries, small greens and difficult tee shots that characterise the 16th, 17th and 18th holes of this course west of Philadelphia.

Tom Watson and David Graham dropped one stroke each, and Bill Rogers and Jack Nicklaus both lost two shots on one hole as they fought the par-four 16th and the 224-yard 17th with its two-tiered green, and then turned into a freshening south-east wind to tackle the difficult 458-yard 18th. Then, in the cool of the evening and in leisurely, measured strides, came George Burns, a beefy-looking man who will be 32 next month.

He had had four birdies going out, and three more coming in, and now he was clearly in the lead. His 66 was the day's best round. It gave him a total of 135, five under par, and lifted him ahead of Graham and Tommy Valentine – the only other player among the leaders to get to grips with those closing holes – and defending champion Nicklaus.

The pace was hot, even if not so hot as some irreverent players had predicted, and Burns couldn't afford to falter at all. Lurking in a group three strokes behind him was Australian Greg Norman, whose length and accuracy are suited to the course, and one stroke further back were, among others, the 1976 champion, Jerry Pate, and Tom Watson.

Before the tournament began, some players were predicting there would be scores in the low to mid 60s and, for the first time at a Merion Open, par would be broken. Heavy rain at the start of the week had left the greens slower and more yielding than the US Golf Association really wanted.

So much for predictions. Only 15 of the field of 156 beat par in the opening round, and at halfway that was still the total. "It's tough out there, it was windy today," said Nicklaus on Friday night. "And it's going to get harder. Merion is holding her own."

"Merion's own" you might define as charm and character. The 1st tee is set beneath spreading trees and alongside the clubhouse veranda, and is an appropriately graceful setting for the time-honoured ceremony of starting competitors in a US Open.

The USGA official who does the honours is John Laupheimer, a courtly, grey-haired man, and he had alongside him, as he went about his task last Thursday morning, a table on which rested dozens of white tee-pegs, boxes of wooden pencils and charts of each green showing the pin placements. Every eight minutes or so, he would smooth down his tie and announce in soft, grave tones: "Now on the tee…" And, to light applause, another trio would be sent on their way.

That ceremony was accorded to Sandy Lyle, who missed the halfway cut-off after a pair of 74s, as well as to Lee Trevino, winner at Merion in 1971, who was similarly eliminated, and to Seve Ballesteros, still a man seemingly in conflict with most of the rest of the world, who played a sprightly second round of 69 for a 142.

It happened also to "unknown" professional Bob Ackerman, one of the very first group to drive off in bright sunshine at seven o'clock precisely on Thursday morning. Four hours or so later he returned a 68 to lead the field for all of 15 minutes. In fact, it happened to every one of the 19 amateurs and 137 professionals who teed off on the first two days.

There was nothing so ceremonious about the treatment the players received when they arrived on the 16th tee. Perhaps the last three holes on the East Course are so distinctive because it was here in 1910, when he was designing the course, that the architect, Hugh Wilson, had the least promising land on which to work. The ground was covered with clay, and the area also contained a huge rock quarry.

These days the quarry is overgrown by thick, tousled grass, flanked by tall trees, and frogs croak endlessly in part of it. It's just the place for a game of hide-and-seek with the children. The golfers have to play over it on each of the last three holes. Arnold Palmer twice failed to do so, running up one seven on the 18th in the first round, and another on the 16th in the second. He missed the cut. Terry Dill had nines on the 16th and 18th respectively in the first two rounds. He missed the cut too.

And just to show he is human, Nicklaus played one of the soul-destroying holes like a rank bad amateur. On the 16th on Friday he drove into the left rough, and then pushed a four-iron out to the right, deep into the undergrowth and 20 yards off line. From there he could only chip sideways. A second chip shot trickled feebly through the green, and a third pulled up six feet from the pin. In the end it took a good putt to get him off the hook with a six.

If that was reminiscent of the way most of us play, then the rest of the champion's round was not. Helped by his son Jack, who was caddying for him, Nicklaus hit 17 greens in regulation figures in his second round. If anyone is going to stop him gaining his fifth US Open, his twentieth major event and, incidentally, his first win of the year, then they're going to have to play very well, particularly over Merion's last three holes.

Miracle at the 17th

The Sunday Times, June 27, 1982

It is a paradox of golf that one extraordinary moment can outweigh years of hard-won triumphs. Tom Watson, already winner of three Opens and two Masters, had such a moment at Pebble Beach, California, last Sunday, when he chipped in on the penultimate hole of the US Open.

It was a stroke that neither he, nor anyone who saw it, will ever forget. One to rank with Bobby Jones's 175-yard bunker shot on the 17th at Lytham in 1926, and with Gene Sarazen's albatross two on the 15th in the 1935 Masters. "That shot of mine at 17 meant more to me than any golf shot I ever made," Watson said after his triumph.

To get the measure of the audacity and skill of Watson's shot, it's necessary to recreate what went on at Pebble Beach that day. Watson was playing with Bill Rogers, the Open champion, and just ahead of them was Jack Nicklaus who, sniffing a record fifth victory in this historic championship, made a typically courageous last-round charge. He reeled off a string of five birdies to go into a one-shot lead before he fell back. His final round was 69, and his four-under-par total of 284 was a considerable target for Watson to achieve.

What's more, it was Watson's eleventh attempt to win the US Open since he turned pro in 1971, and the fact that he hadn't yet succeeded, despite winning five major titles in seven years, was beginning to get on his nerves. In his pursuit of Nicklaus last Sunday, Watson holed brave long putts on the 10th, 11th and 14th, only to drop a shot on the 16th after a rare wayward drive.

Standing on the 17th tee, Watson glanced up at a scoreboard and saw that he needed to play the last two treacherous holes – a 210-yard par-three, and a par-five of 518 yards – in eight strokes to tie with Nicklaus and force a play-off, or in seven or less to defeat him. His two-iron tee shot was hit slightly off course, and the ball ended left of, and above, the saucer-shaped green. It came to rest in a two-foot wide patch of thick tousled rough, four inches high. Between it and the flag lay another two-foot-wide band of shorter rough, perhaps two inches tall, and the green itself was protected by an 18-inch fringe. According to Dan Hoos of the USGA, the flagstick was 15 feet from the edge of the green nearest Watson.

While Rogers putted, Watson crouched, studying the line and lie of his chip.

Caddie Bruce Edwards cautioned him to play safe, but Watson seized his sand wedge and said defiantly: "I'm going to hole it." He addressed the ball, opened his stance, took two brief practice swings and hit it. The ball pitched 18 inches on to the putting surface and ran on as if drawn magnetically towards its target before plopping into the hole and causing the normally undemonstrative Watson to set off on a celebratory jig.

Nicklaus, watching on a portable television set by the side of the 18th green, was stunned. Seeing his younger rival attempt the shot, Nicklaus had thought to himself: "That's all right, he can't get it close from there." He was so unconcerned that he turned away, and only swung back to look at the screen when he heard the roar. Buoyed by this birdie, Watson calmly birdied the last hole as well to finish two strokes ahead of Nicklaus.

Closer analysis of Watson's shot reveals just how deft it was. He had to lob the ball on to the green, and then stop it quickly on a downslope. To make it more difficult, the green was one of the fastest on the course. Watson's main concern, though, was to make sure that in caressing the shot he didn't mishit it and leave it in the rough, as the defending champion, David Graham, had on the 13th. He also had to guard against taking too much time.

Was Watson really going for the hole? "Yes," says Nick Faldo. "Why lay up? If you're good enough to stop it within a few feet, then you're good enough to hole it. It must have scared the living daylights out of him but, yes, he meant to try and hole it."

Tony Jacklin knows about thunderbolts that come out of the blue. He was hit by one on the 71st hole of the Open at Muirfield in 1972, when Lee Trevino chipped in and, consequently, snatched victory from Jacklin. Watson's chip, says Jacklin, was "one helluva shot, and if he never ever does one again, it doesn't matter. He has done it once, and that's enough."

Nairn tests amateur aspirations
The Times, June 1, 1994

From the silver birches of Wentworth to the stately beaches of Nairn is more than 600 miles, a journey from the Volvo PGA Championship on Monday to the Amateur Championship, which, after two qualifying rounds, starts today. From the Surrey club where José María Olazábal played so gloriously to the Moray Firth. From strokeplay to matchplay.

Nairn is one of those solid, Scottish towns, full of probity, its streets lined with sturdy, grey, no-nonsense buildings, some with turrets. It was here, on its gorse-lined links, that two young men learnt how to wield clubs. Ludovic Kennedy was one; Lord Whitelaw the other. Lord Whitelaw, a past captain of the Royal and Ancient Golf Club of St Andrews, is president of Nairn.

Nairn is the sort of place that captures the heart. Charlie Yates, the venerable American amateur who won the Amateur at Royal Troon in 1938, called in on his way to Royal Dornoch in 1966 and has revisited nearly 20 times.

A 20 to 25-knot south-west wind whistled in from the Moray Firth yesterday. In the distance, Ben Wyvis, a mountain of more than 3,000ft, stood out clear and snowcapped. The flags on the poles were like starched sheets, the flags on the greens snapped and rippled in the wind.

Stephen Gallacher's two-round total of 145, a 71 at Nairn Dunbar on Monday followed by a 74 at Nairn, was about as good a score as was possible. Almost as good a score was the 70 by Gary Harris at Nairn Dunbar, which equalled the course record. Harris is quite a player: in the Brabazon Trophy, the English amateur strokeplay, at Little Aston recently, he recorded a 64, which broke the professional record by four strokes and the amateur record by two. He is not yet 19.

Seaside golf without a wind would be unreal, like a golf course without a clubhouse or a clubhouse without a bar. Dai Rees and Max Faulkner were once invited to play at Nairn on a day when the tiles were rattling on roofs.

"Play in a wind like that?" Rees said, his voice indicating he had no intention of doing so. "I wouldn't play in a wind like that for all the whisky on Speyside," Faulkner said.

Yet, for the 288 competitors who began on Monday to try and qualify for the matchplay stage of the Amateur that begins today, there was no choice. In seaside golf, the degree of glorious uncertainty is high. One day, a par-four of less than 400 yards is barely in reach in two; the next, it is no more than a swish from the tee and a flick with a wedge.

The line on the opening hole at Nairn appears to be straightforward. It runs like an index finger along the Moray Firth, one pointing away from the clubhouse. The hole is as straight as a Colin Montgomerie drive and the green is visible from the tee.

Local lore has it, nevertheless, that it is best to aim at a mountain, the left hand of the Five Sisters of Kintail, some 75 miles away. They did not have anything like that at Wentworth on Monday. Amateur golf is different, particularly when played at a venue such as this. It is all the more welcome for being so.

Wie ready to make name for herself in city of Fab Four

The Times, June 11, 2004

We thought we knew everything there was to know about the Beatles but, soon after lunch yesterday afternoon, we discovered that there was one fact that had escaped our attention. At Formby Golf Club, a few miles north of Liverpool, Michelle Wie, the prodigy who will compete for the United States in this weekend's Curtis Cup against a team from Great Britain and Ireland, revealed that she is named after a Beatles song: "Michelle, ma belle, These are words that go together well, My Michelle."

The words that were sung by Paul McCartney resonated so strongly with B.J., Wie's father, and Bo, her mother, that they chose the name for their only child. Knowing this, you might have thought that Wie would be keen to visit the Beatles Museum in Liverpool but, in fact, it was the Great Britain and Ireland team that went to the Beatles Magical Mystery Tour.

Wie and her team-mates arrived in Britain last Saturday morning to defend the trophy they won at Fox Chapel Golf Club, outside Pittsburgh, two years ago. Indeed, the United States have won 23 out of the 32 times the Curtis Cup has been played. Wie's first thought was to get a look at a pot bunker, one shaped rather like a teacup in that it is round and steep-sided.

She said that there are not any of these in the US, which is more a tribute to the accuracy of her golf, in that she rarely hits into such places, rather than an accurate statement of fact. When the US team practised at Royal Liverpool last Sunday, Wie got her wish. She landed her ball in one such bunker. "Having done so, I never want to see one again," she said.

Wie is arguably the most talented 14-year-old golfer, male or female, there has ever been, as well as the youngest to be selected for the Curtis Cup, which was first held at Wentworth in 1932. In January, she beat or tied with 64 male professionals, including 25 who had won on the US tour, in failing by only one stroke to play all four rounds of the Sony Open in Hawaii, her home state. Wherever Wie goes, she creates what can only be described as a sensation. She hits 300-yard drives and recently caused crowds ten deep to form on the practice ground at a tournament that she was competing in.

Despite this, there is much about her that is refreshingly normal. She giggles, her sentences tail off and she is slightly gawky. Yet, at the same time, she seems

Michelle Wie reacts to a putt on the seventh hole during her
singles match against Anna Highgate of the Great Britain and
Ireland team at the 2004 Curtis Cup in Formby, England.

wise beyond her years in the way that she limits her responses to questions to the minimum to lessen the possibility of putting her foot in it, and she bears the burden of being regarded as a prodigy with a maturity that defies her age. "I never try to cope with [my celebrity status]," Wie said. "I am coping with it by not even thinking about it." How she will avoid thinking about it when thousands of spectators are tramping along behind her at Formby, some cheering for her and some for her opponents, remains to be seen.

Wie could scarcely wait to go to Chester yesterday afternoon to try to buy "something that we can not find in the US". Whatever this item is, it is likely to be an item of fashion. Paula Creamer, Wie's team-mate, who is 17, revealed that she had discovered that there is a television channel in this country that is devoted to shopping. "You go into my room or hers and this is the channel that is always on," Creamer said.

It was a lovely sunny afternoon at Formby yesterday with little wind. It would be unusual if it did not blow harder on one or possibly both of the two days of the competition. Though Wie may not have seen a pot bunker before, she knows all about the wind. She grew up in Hawaii, which is not always calm, and, furthermore, David Leadbetter, her coach, had her practising wind shots in Florida recently. "I've played in winds of 40mph," Wie said. "I'm confident that if a wind blows I can handle it."

All in all, Wie's first public appearance in Britain passed off much as have most of her public appearances in the US. She was cool and slightly tongue-tied, a phenomenon. And few have seen her hit a golf ball in competition yet.

Midwest farm cultivates a passion for the greens
Weekend FT, June 16, 1991

In his best-selling book *Lake Wobegon Days*, which is set in a fictitious town in Minnesota, Garrison Keillor tells the story of how Jack Krueger worked all spring and summer to build a golf course. He paced off 200 yards in a pasture owned by a local character known as Old Man Tollerud, put a can in a hole, mowed the grass and built three bunkers. Then he sat back and waited.

It was a hard struggle to convince the straight-laced Lutherans to take up golf, in part because Old Man Tollerud refused to remove his Holstein cows from the pasture and once Clarence Bunsen's ball hit one amidships and another time the cows trampled over the hole.

In the end Krueger gave up. "It's hard to get people interested," he said. "You set off the fire alarm and they just get up and go to lunch."

Not if they're real golf fans, they don't. And in Minnesota there are only real golf fans. The state has more golfers per head of population than any other – 18 per cent of the population plays golf and most of them, it seems, have been at the US Open this week.

The first shot in the US Open was hit at seven o'clock on Thursday morning. At 6am on Monday, three days earlier, 6,000 spectators passed through the gates the moment they opened. On Wednesday nearly 50,000 spectators thronged the course. A new US Open attendance record is bound to be set.

Golf in Minnesota is not like golf in Manchester or Musselburgh. For one thing, the harsh winters limit it to a few months each year and consequently Minnesota's golfers have their minds concentrated wonderfully on the job in hand. Most courses only open in April.

In October and November, they use windscreen scrapers to clear a putting path through the frost on the greens. A golfer in western Minnesota hit his approach shot from an ice floe in a small lake and then waded back to the green.

"People up here know golf is in a kind of restricted zone because of the short season," Dick Yates, owner of a public course in Minneapolis, said. "They come out in hordes in April. It's like letting cattle out of the barn."

The first-time visitor walking around Hazeltine National Golf Club last week could not have failed to be moved by the sheer beauty of the place. It has more than 26 different species of tree and 1,600 trees in all. If you knew where to look and what to look for you could see more than 100 types of birds and animals ranging from the pileated woodpecker, the northern oriole and the belted kingfisher to the mink, raccoon, jack-rabbit, fox squirrel and white-tail deer.

And if on your travels around the course you came across a barn, well, it's old Fred Molnau's and he's a founder member and it adds to the appeal, so there. This is the Midwest after all.

The courtesy and knowledge of the fans were just as striking. No one cheered when an unpopular player's ball rolled into a bunker, or clicked a camera at the top of a backswing. No one taunted Greg Norman as happened at Shinnecock in 1986 or tried to antagonise Ian Woosnam as happened at the Masters. In their devotion to and knowledge of the game the Minnesota fans may rival the Scots.

In a state where golf is pursued so enthusiastically, it is appropriate that Hazeltine National is a monument to the game. Some US Open venues such as The Country Club at Brookline in Boston and Medinah Country Club outside

Chicago are sporting emporia that offer tennis, swimming pools and everything else from canasta to curling.

The clubhouse at Hazeltine is a modest two-storey model, which is a change because Medinah's last year was only slightly smaller than Buckingham Palace. It was built in an ornate architectural style best described as being a cross between Louis XV and Cecil B. deMille. Hazeltine does not have a swimming pool and its four tennis courts are used mainly by a local school.

The 270 members pay an entrance fee of $16,000 and monthly fees of $265. The club has only 30 carts and they are hardly used. It's a matter of honour at the club that members carry their clubs and walk, as much an anachronism in the US as riding in a golf cart is in Britain. "If we see someone riding a cart we wonder if they're ill," says Dorothy Sprau, a member.

Dave Dokmo runs the club's caddie programme. He is a Lutheran minister in St Paul, which with Minneapolis comprises the Twin Cities. He admits he gets some strange looks when he appears at the club on a Sunday morning. "We may be the only Lutheran Church to hold our services on a Saturday night," he explains.

That's golf in Minnesota for you. Jack Krueger would have been surprised.

Faldo ready to take next step towards elusive grand slam

The Sunday Times, June 10, 1990

Nick Faldo is too much of a realist to be unduly swayed by portents, but even he saw some significance in the title of a book he selected at random while waiting to eat dinner one night last week. The book was called *It's Possible*, and Faldo permitted himself a slight smile at the symbolism of it.

It's not just possible, it's probable, that Faldo, the Masters champion, will win this week's US Open at Medinah Country Club, outside Chicago, as well. Thus he will remain on course for golf's supreme challenge – winning the game's grand slam, its four major championships, in one year.

Traditionally, Europeans don't win the US Open. There have been so few of them eligible to play over the years that Tony Jacklin's historic triumph in 1970 was the first by a Briton for a half-century.

Faldo will break with tradition again this week, as he did with his successful defence at Augusta last April, for a number of reasons. The chief is, simply, that after three victories and a second place in the past 11 major championships he is the outstanding contemporary golfer in the world.

As he prepares to meet Medinah, Faldo is happy and relaxed, unconcerned by the news from home that his son Matthew has mumps. Not normally one to tempt providence, Faldo allowed that his golf was "90 per cent there", which was precisely where he wanted it to be with the Western Open still to be completed.

The news that put him in the best humour was the announcement that as a non-member of the US tour he would not need a sponsor's exemption to compete in next year's Players Championship. Faldo saw this as a significant victory for the Europeans, golf's free traders, over some of the isolationist Americans.

"That means we can play ten tournaments over here without exemptions and that's very nearly what we wanted last year," Faldo said. "It's a complete climbdown by the US tour."

Unlike Tom Watson, who sneaked a visit to Medinah's No 3 course last Monday afternoon, Faldo has yet to set eyes on the 7,195-yard behemoth, the longest ever used for a US Open. Faldo knows, however, that if ever a course was designed to bring out the strengths of one golfer, then it's Medinah for him. Faldo, like the defending champion Curtis Strange, is steady, perhaps the steadiest golfer in the world today.

"Nick and I are grinders," Strange said. "We're not aggressive types like Mark Calcavecchia and Greg Norman. We're on the fairway, on the green, putt, putt types. Not many birdies but not many bogeys either."

In the land of hucksters and hyperbole it is acceptable to say that on all US Open courses the fairways are so narrow the players have to walk in single file, and the rough is so long the competitors daren't fall over lest they go missing. Medinah is no exception.

One fairway narrows to 19 yards at one point and to the fierce, clinging rough is added many trees – 3,700 of them. "Miss the fairway and you're not just in long rough. You're behind two or three trees as well," Watson said. Just as well, then, that Faldo is a straight hitter, if not quite in the class of Calvin Peete, of whom it was once said that he hadn't missed a fairway since the Korean War.

Faldo has the patience on a golf course to make Job seem impetuous. He is the supreme example of the man who coolly plots his way from tee to fairway to green, never allowing himself to get flustered and safe in the knowledge that his rebuilt swing is so steady and secure that it will continue to function satisfactorily when the pressure has burned off almost everyone else. Since he did this impeccably at the Masters, there is every reason to believe he can do it this week at Medinah.

"Nick controls the ball so well now," Tony Jacklin said. "He was like a machine in the Masters, the way he kept putting the ball in the correct place. I believe he is doing this better than anybody else in the world at the moment."

Jacklin also believes Faldo is the best putter Britain has ever produced. If Faldo had putted halfway decently he'd have won the 1988 US Open in a cake-walk instead of losing in a play-off. He was far superior to Strange from tee to green. These days Faldo's putting stroke has been redesigned and he looks entirely at ease on the greens. He uses a 34-inch putter, one that is an inch shorter than most, to make him stretch his long arms and thus induce more of a pendulum motion. He is as well-suited as anyone to the contoured and lightning-fast greens of Medinah.

Most of all, Faldo is a man for the majors. He regards them as the supreme challenge and has built his life and his game around them. There are times when he gives the impression he simply won't be denied no matter what is required nor how long it takes. The play-off at Augusta was one such example; this week could be another.

Herbert Warren Wind

The Times, June 16, 2005

As well as having one of the most distinctive names in golf, Herbert Warren Wind was the game's most elegant chronicler and America's finest golf writer.

Wind made his name with his seminal book, *The Story of American Golf* (1948), which he wrote while he was on the staff of *The New Yorker*. Despite its modest sales, it became a classic and established Wind as a golf writer. He was the man who named the 11th, 12th and 13th holes at Augusta National Golf Club, the scene of the annual Masters tournament, Amen Corner.

Herbert Warren Wind was born in Brockton, Massachusetts, in 1916, and learnt to play golf at Thorney Lea, a club in Brockton, during school holidays. In the summers he went to Camp Zakelo in Maine, where he and his friend John Horne Burns, who would go on to win the Pulitzer Prize for fiction, published a camp newspaper. At Yale, Wind covered sports for the *Yale Daily News* and wrote about jazz for the *Yale Record*.

But it was when Wind came to Jesus College, Cambridge, where he played rugby and took a degree in English literature, that he met the men who would change his life. Sir Arthur Quiller-Couch, the editor of *The Oxford Book of English Verse* and a Shakespeare scholar, was his tutor. While at Cambridge Wind met Bernard Darwin, grandson of Charles Darwin. Bernard Darwin was the eminent essayist and golf writer for *The Times*, and, having fallen under his spell, Wind determined to become a golf writer.

When he returned from active service in China during the war, he settled in New York and was a staff writer for *The New Yorker* from 1947 until 1954. Then he joined a new weekly magazine called *Sports Illustrated* and served as its golf editor until 1959. In 1960 he helped to launch *Shell's Wonderful World of Golf*, a successful television series, and wrote all the scripts.

In 1962 he returned to *The New Yorker* and became its golf and tennis writer until he retired in 1989. He also wrote about squash rackets, polo, real tennis, American football, track and field, basketball, ice hockey, skiing and pelota. But it was his long, ruminative essays on golf that made him famous. He gave his readers not only a vivid description of the tournament being covered but a lengthy discussion on the players, the history of the game, golf course architecture, the rules, the clubs and anything he felt a golfer needed to know to be able to appreciate the game.

He worshipped Bobby Jones, the US amateur golfer who had won the Open and Amateur Championships of the US and Great Britain in 1930, a feat nicknamed "the Impregnable Quadrilateral", and soon after this started the Masters tournament. Wind helped to create the impression that the Masters was a major tournament. He also established the concept of measuring golf greatness by the number of major championships a player had won.

In person Wind was as fastidious in his manners and dress as he was in his writing, which he did painstakingly in pencil. He was only rarely seen on a golf course without a jacket and tie and he quite often wore spats. He usually carried a neatly folded mackintosh, and a shooting stick on which he would sit and make notes. He never married. Like a monk to his religion he devoted his life to his writing – and he liked best to write about golf.

Herbert Warren Wind, writer, was born on August 11, 1916. He died on May 30, 2005, aged 88.

JULY

If it's July, it's the Open. This is the month when the oldest of the four major championships is held in England or Scotland and the month takes its cue from it – whether in anticipation, in reportage or in subsequent dissection. Because the Open is in Britain, because I know the courses, because it's in my time zone, and because it's the oldest and the one at which I feel the most comfortable, it is my favourite major championship.

I've been to 35 of them, starting with the centenary Open at St Andrews in 1970, and for ten or so I was working for *The Sunday Times*. There is no doubt in my mind that the task of previewing the Open for a weekly paper gave me some of the most enjoyable stories to write and some of the most unusual. I spent two days in Sandwich, seven months before the 1981 Open would be staged at Royal St George's for the first time in 32 years, and reported that the manager of the Bell Hotel was receiving dozens of telephone calls from people who wanted to stay during Open week. "I tell them to try somewhere north of Marble Arch," he said crisply.

The next spring I played Royal St George's and wrote afterwards in the paper that: "I tugged at my sodden shoes and tried to decide whether I felt as though I'd spent a sleepless night with Candice Bergen (yes please) or gone a few rounds with Joe Louis (no thanks)." My observation about the course's length that year makes interesting reading now. I described it as "a monster at 6,829 yards" and noted it had only three par-fours that were fewer than 415 yards. There is little more to add here except that today championship courses of 1,000 yards longer with at least one par-four of more than 500 yards are not unheard of.

In 1987 I interviewed Mac O'Grady in the men's locker room at the Olympic Club where he was competing in the US Open and asked him about Severiano Ballesteros and Greg Norman, two of the fiercest rivals in the game. "These guys have gone through their apprenticeship and *are* the game today," O'Grady said. "They are the modern living giants, the Michelangelos, the Picassos, the da Vincis working together sculpting their own works of art out there. We are lucky to have them."

The Open at Royal Troon in 1989 provided the opportunity to write in detail about the Postage Stamp, and for my preview I spent time in Ayrshire, haunting the famous short hole and asking as many people as I could find about it. The next year the Open was at St Andrews and so I gave the same treatment to the par-four Road Hole as I had the previous year to the Postage Stamp. The golf journalist Malcolm Campbell, then editor of the local paper, once scored birdie threes on the Road Hole on successive days.

More often the most famous hole in golf, which contains the most famous bunker in golf, has wrought havoc. Michael Bonallack once went 10, 9, 3 on successive days. In the 1978 Open, the year that Tommy Nakajima took a 9 there, only one player of 80 in the third round could birdie the hole and only 19 managed par.

Open weeks are long, hard work and fun. For much of a golf journalist's year you're competing for space in the paper with football, cricket, tennis and rugby stories. The week of the Open, the sports pages are all yours, which generates excitement and creates pressure. The understandable journalistic tendency to enjoy oneself at the end of a day, no matter how long a day it has been, seems more pronounced at Opens than any other event.

The Times's team pondered making an excursion to France for dinner one night during Open week in 2011 and ended up eating on the side of an English cliff overlooking the Channel, noting that for a couple of hours our telephones worked – or more often didn't – courtesy of a French provider. We stayed in a castle with a waterfall in the garden plus a suit of armour and a couple of snooker tables near the front door for one Open, and in a building of Scandinavian origin shaped like a toast rack for another.

There are two Open champions I consider I knew better than any of their peers. Writing a biography of Nick Faldo that was published in 1985, I noted that July was a good month for him. He was born on July 18, his mother on July 22.

He received his first set of golf clubs, won the English Amateur, recorded his lowest competitive round in Europe all in July. His then father-in-law and his then manager had both been born in July – as had Faldo's friend Tony Jacklin. In my book about Faldo I predicted he would win the Open by the time he was 30. I was wrong. He won the 1987 Open at Muirfield the day after his 30th birthday.

On the Saturday evening of the 2011 Open at Sandwich I was heading back to my car when a Range Rover came towards me with Darren Clarke at the wheel and Chubby Chandler, his manager, alongside. I liked Clarke and had been pleased when I covered a World Golf Championship event in Ohio in 2003 that he won from a field that included almost all the best players in the world, including Tiger Woods, then the best. "Darren Clarke," I wrote, "knows the outside of a cigar, the inside of a Ferrari and the bottom of a glass of Guinness."

At Sandwich I had followed Clarke for most of a round that was played in difficult conditions and as he slowed the vehicle and wound down the window I said to him: "I haven't trudged through the mud and rain today for you to throw it away tomorrow. Make sure you bloody well win." Fortunately he did.

The inclusion of a paean of praise to amateurs in a chapter otherwise devoted almost exclusively to the Open might be seen as odd. After all, the Amateur is a month earlier, the Walker Cup a month later. But amateurs are a part of the Open, albeit a small part. Amateurs are my heroes. And most professionals, even the ones who compete at the Open, were once amateurs. Regard this piece as a reminder that professionals, however highly ranked they are, should not forget their roots.

Senior statesman with record that leaves him clear of the field

The Times, July 17, 1993

A moment of symmetry occurred at Sandwich on Tuesday. Jack Nicklaus, who achieved his first victory in Britain on the Royal St George's course in 1959, returned for what will surely be his last competitive event at the famous Kent links, the 122nd Open.

Enter the sturdy, two-storey clubhouse less than one mile from the ancient Cinque Port of Sandwich and, on the wall just to the right beyond the inner door, you will see a big brown honours board. It is headed "The St George's Grand Gold Challenge Cup". At the bottom is the legend: "Presented by Mrs W.R. Anderson 1888".

There, scored in gold lettering, are the dozens of winners of this amateur competition, led by John Ball Jr, in 1888. The entry for 1959 reads: J. Nicklaus 73 + 76 = 149.

If Nicklaus has a hallmark to put on his career, it is that he is competitive. It is not sufficient that he has won twenty major championships – six Masters, five US PGA championships, four US Opens, three Opens and the US Amateur championships of 1959 and 1961 – a record far beyond that of anybody else. In the history of the game nobody has played so well for so long. He has not missed a major championship since he turned professional in 1961 and he has won more major titles than most golfers have won tournaments.

He has achieved 16 holes in one (Seve Ballesteros has not scored one competitively) and he has won 96 tournaments around the world, the most recent being the US Senior Open last Sunday.

Almost as remarkable is that in the 124 major championships in which he has competed as a professional he has come second in 18, third in nine and in the top ten in a further 20. The consistency of the man, not to mention his longevity, beggars belief. Nicklaus is not just the best player the game has seen, but, given the way the game is changing and spreading around the world, his record will stand unrivalled well into the next century.

The remarkable drive for victory, which has served him so well for more than 30 years, is at the root of a dilemma Nicklaus faces, namely how much longer should he continue playing? How long can he continue to play golf worthy of his name? The demands on his time are considerable – so considerable that he has his own plane, with the call sign Air Bear, to speed his passage from appointment to appointment.

Golden Bear Enterprises includes a thriving business designing golf courses; the hundredth will open next week. It is possible to play golf on Nicklaus-designed courses on most continents. There is a management company and a club manufacturing company. And, of course, there is his family, his wife Barbara and their five grown-up children, Jack II, Steven, Nancy Jean, Gary and Michael.

Today, at 53, Jack William Nicklaus is certainly not always as good as he once was. He has been unable to see far enough to follow the flight of his golf ball for years. His back is weak, he has a pain in his hip and this week he has been talking of a stiffness in his left shoulder. But, on occasion, Nicklaus is as good as he was.

He could hardly have demonstrated this better than in his opening rounds in two of the major championships this year. First there was a 67, five under par, in the Masters in April, good enough for him to share the lead with four men young enough to be his sons. In a nation where ageism is as much a topic of conversation as sexism, this was news to hold the front page for. After all, Nicklaus is older than the president of the United States and he was competing in his 35th successive Masters.

Then came Thursday at Sandwich, the opening day of his 32nd successive Open. Nicklaus, notching two birdies in his first three holes, recorded a 69, one of a host of players to be under par. First rounds, then, are no problem. It is the later ones in which Nicklaus struggles and his 75 yesterday was no exception.

Golf has a habit of bringing almost everybody into line, making them observe the sanctity of the rules and cherish the honourable spirit of the game. Nicklaus has spoken of what golf has taught him. "A kid who plays golf is different from a lot of other athletes because he hasn't always had his own way. He's had to get along with older people and if he won't play by their rules he can't play at all."

Nicklaus believes the source of his enormous power was his physical strength. His only teacher, Jack Grout, encouraged him to hit the ball as hard as he could from the start. Nicklaus, underpinned by what you might call a sturdy undercarriage (he has massive thighs and a sprinter's calf muscles), became a prodigious hitter.

This enabled him to go for the green even when his ball was in the rough and to reach almost any par-five in two. As an indication of his strength and power when he was at his best, he reached the green of the 528-yard 17th hole in the final round of the 1966 Open at Muirfield, which he won, with a three-iron and a five-iron.

Before Nicklaus, nobody had prepared so intensely for every championship. He was the first leading player to start measuring distances instead of relying on eyesight. In practice, he would hit one drive to the middle of the fairway, one to the left and one to the right. Sometimes he would drop balls in the rough and play them all to the green. He would hit putts to every possible pin position. He left nothing to chance. By the start of play he could practically play each hole blindfold.

The nearest equivalent to Nicklaus among today's generation of professionals is Bernhard Langer, who measures from the front and back of sprinkler heads – in yards and metres.

Nicklaus was born into middle-class surroundings on January 21, 1940, in

Columbus, Ohio, the son of a chemist. He had a comfortable upbringing. He wanted for nothing that could be bought on his father's credit card at the Scioto Golf Club, a wonderful Donald Ross-designed course in Columbus.

It was at the 1960 US Open at Cherry Hills, in Denver, Colorado, that Nicklaus burst to national prominence. He was then a student at Ohio State University and a golf prodigy who had won 29 out of 30 matches against the world's best amateurs the previous year. Nicklaus was 5ft 11in and weighed nearly 15 stone. His imposing physical presence was not diminished by a spiky crew cut and a high-pitched voice. His nickname at university was Blob-o.

That June, Blob-o, the 20-year-old sensation, played the last two rounds with Ben Hogan, then aged 47. With six holes remaining Nicklaus led and history was in the making. But he was overtaken by Arnold Palmer, then 30, and Nicklaus finished second, setting a record for an amateur in the tournament.

Last Sunday Nicklaus thrilled his supporters with victory in the US Senior Open at the same Denver course where he had almost unseated Palmer 33 years earlier. On Thursday Nicklaus delighted the burghers of Kent with his play on the course he had first competed on 34 years ago. The wheel has surely turned its allotted circle. Even Nicklaus, the golfer of the century, cannot go on forever.

In praise of the amateur
www.globalgolfpost.com, July 9, 2012

A herogram is a message of congratulation sent by a boss to an employee for a well-executed piece of work. "Good job, well done" are the words that are often used in such circumstances. The same four words are just as applicable in the following herogram to amateurs in golf, to almost everyone, male or female, who isn't a professional. "Good job, well done. You are the heroes of golf."

Amateurs are a misunderstood, unappreciated, slightly downtrodden race who play golf because they adore it and believe that dark thoughts of redundancies, rising inflation, soaring food and fuel costs, can probably be blasted away by a quick game of golf and certainly by a quick good one. Amateurs, then, are the backbone of the game and what follows is a paean of praise to them, to you. Without amateur golf there would be few if any professionals and no pro-ams.

Without amateurs pros would make a lot less money because there would be nobody to buy the stuff they endorse. Without amateurs who would pay to go and watch a tournament? Without amateurs there would be no golf clubs.

Let's see now, who among us has not dashed home after work and gulped down a quick supper before racing down to our golf club to spend two hours talking about the irregularities in the surfaces of the 3rd and 9th greens or the slipperiness of the floor in the men's changing room or the difficulties of finding a new steward or the bad behaviour of a junior in a recent club match. Exciting stuff, eh? But somebody has to do it and that somebody is an amateur.

The real amateur is the sort of golfer who gets up at 4am to drive 25 miles to a municipal course to stand in a queue to get a tee-off time four hours after first light. The sort of golfer who puts on his thermals, several sweaters, a bobble hat and ski gloves to play golf on a crisp winter's day when the ground is white with frost and so hard it is impossible to stick a tee into it.

Have you heard the anecdote about the golfers who stood recently on a windswept tee? It was midsummer in Britain so, naturally, the rain hammered down and there was a mischievous gusting wind. Keeping the ball on a high tee was difficult and hitting into the wind required skills that were beyond them. One turned to the other and said: "Aren't we lucky? We could be playing golf in 100 degrees in southern Spain?" That's the spirit of the true amateur.

Amateurs are anything but amateur. The USGA are amateurs. The R&A are amateurs. Peter Dawson is an amateur. Mike Davis is an amateur. But no one would call their work amateur, work that governs the rules of the game, stages major championships on both sides of the Atlantic, distributes millions of pounds and dollars throughout the game. The amateurs of the R&A organise the Amateur as professionally as they organise the Open, just as the amateurs of Far Hills organise the US Amateur as professionally as they organise the US Open.

Amateurs pay to play golf when they can. While there are occasional games that are etched in the memory because of the larksong overhead, the softness of the grass underfoot and the click of an exceptional drive from that difficult tee, so there are memories of games when all common sense is yelling: "Stay inside. It's warmer. It's drier." Yet such siren voices are ignored because amateurs have three hours in which to play, have looked forward to their game for days and, damn it, are going to play.

Amateurs inconvenience themselves again and again to administer their golf club, to play their own games. They do it because they love golf. When you're in love with a game and it does not represent your livelihood, you're an amateur. You don't whinge about the sponginess of some of the greens or moan that there is too much sand in most of the bunkers and too little in others.

Amateurs get on with it. Why waste time moaning when they could be playing? They understand the intricacies of a game that can appear very intricate. Amateurs love golf's lasting appeal, that it can be played by someone of 7 and someone of 97. It may have taken them time to learn one of the game's eternal verities, namely that golf's challenge is not only to strike the ball crisply and cleanly as often as possible but to learn how to deal with the breaks that come along during a four-hour game that involves hitting a ball over four miles of undulating terrain and putting on greens trodden on by 500 pairs of shoes.

Amateurs play golf because it is an accompaniment to their daily rituals, helping them to achieve a sense of fulfilment and perspective. They come back to it again and again. It enhances their lives. Amateurs adore golf and amateurs adorn golf.

And that is what makes them, you, our heroes.

Donald taking in quiet views of life from his position on top of the world

The Times, July 9, 2011

Luke Donald will arrive for the Open Championship at Royal St George's next week ranked the world's best golfer. He is not the most famous, though. He is not even the second most famous. Tiger Woods is more renowned than Donald and so is the heart-throb kid, Rory McIlroy, the runaway winner of last month's US Open.

There is no sign, however, that Donald, a naturally quiet and reserved man with an accurate, unthunderous style of play founded on a magnificent short game, is discontent with this status. He knows that, as that rare combination of a man of artistic bent who also has a Stakhanovite appetite for work, he has deserved his success.

"Luke has the ability to use both sides of the brain," Jim Fannin, the performance coach, said in 2005. "He is highly creative, but there is a discipline about him that most creative people do not have."

Donald's rise to the top of his game has not been without criticism. His ability to earn huge prize money without winning many tournaments was once described as "a disease" that many other professionals suffered from. More recently, Lee Trevino cackled with indignation that Donald could be the world's No 1 golfer "without winning a major championship".

It is because he is so obviously at ease with himself that Donald is capable of dealing with the twin challenges he faces – continuing the run of form that has brought him two victories and eight top-ten finishes in the 12 tournaments he has played this year and not being affected by the criticism of a mathematical formula that happens to name him the world's best player.

His wife, Diane, an exuberant American of Greek descent, and their new, first-born daughter, Elle, have given him confidence. Never mind that he has his own wine label, wears shrieking trousers and shirts on behalf of Ralph Lauren, a sponsor, that he takes so many clothes to tournaments that he hogs all the coat hangers in his hotel room and his wife has to beg to get more than one from him.

Never mind, either, that this supposedly reserved Englishman tweets voraciously. The really heart-warming thing for Donald, 33, is that he understands his style of play and is supreme at making sure that it is in first-class working order.

"If you have the game of Luke Donald, there is no point in trying to become like Tiger Woods," Thomas Levet, the winner of last week's Alstom French Open, said. "If you are Tiger Woods, you overpower a golf course. You go for par-fives in two. You have to play irons off the tee because you are not that straight. That is not the way Luke Donald plays. Luke has realised where his strengths are and he sticks to them. That is very, very intelligent."

Ah, intelligence. Donald is the only one of the three boys and one girl of Colin and Ann Donald who went to a grammar school, where it was thought that his academic ability would be better served. "He didn't like school much and couldn't see the point of much of what he did there," Colin wrote in 2007.

Just as Luke may not be your conventional golf professional, so Colin was far from a conventional golf father. "Most golf fathers you see are dressed in golf gear swinging a club," Paul Casey, a direct contemporary of Luke, said. "You see way too much of the hands-on approach. I never saw Luke's dad out there with a club in his hand. I don't know if he even plays. When Christian [Luke's brother] was my caddie I'd get texts from Mr Donald saying, 'Oh, you're looking strong. You're looking fit.' He'd talk about a lot of stuff other than golf. I really liked him."

Other aspects of Luke Donald's character were moulded by his father and Ann, his mother, and Eve, Andrew and Christian, his older siblings, who were born within four years of one another. "We were physically very close," Colin said. "I don't know whether I should tell you this but Luke was breastfed for a year. We would give each other head massages and back scratches. It was our custom to eat together in the evenings. No snacking from the fridge or disappearing into our room to watch TV or play on the computer as there was no bedroom TV or computer."

Meals were noisy, enjoyable family occasions. Ann, of whom it has been said did a very good job of making sure that Luke was brought up to be just like her other three children, might be telling a joke or Christian might be explaining what he had done in school that day.

"Suddenly someone would say, 'Where's Luke?'" Christian said. "He had a remarkable knack of disappearing without anyone noticing. He would sneak under the table and scurry out of the door. He didn't want to talk. That's Luke.

"He is getting better at talking now, but he has always been very quiet. Some people take it the wrong way. They think he is being rude, but it is just the way it is. I am more open than Luke. If I have a problem, I will talk to my parents, whereas Luke always wants to keep things very much to himself. I'd say to Mum, 'Bet you can never guess what happened to me at school today.' She would say to Luke, 'Did you have a good day at school?' and he'd just reply, 'Not bad.'

"Even now you wish to yourself sometimes, 'Come on, Luke. Give me something. Give me a little bit.' Yet to interpret this quietness as a lack of determination would be wrong. I remember when Luke was 9 he did something wrong. Dad tried to teach him a lesson by not talking to him. After five days Dad had to give up. Luke aged 9 had broken my dad."

Donald's fellow pros agree on the secret of his swing. "It's his rhythm, timing," Casey said. "Even when he is not swinging it right, he can get by because he times it beautifully. He also has the world's best short game. From 100 yards in there is nobody better right now."

Or as David Howell puts it: "Good shot or bad shot, Luke's rhythm is always the same. In today's 'bash it and find it' culture that is a lost art."

The Royal and Ancient game has always had talented golfers. It has not had many who are also prepared to practise. "I don't see anyone working harder than Luke," Jack Nicklaus said recently. Denis Pugh, who coaches Eduardo and Francesco Molinari, said: "You are on the range, you usually see Luke. If you are on the putting green, you usually see Luke. If you are doing your short-game stuff, ah, there's Luke Donald. Wherever you are, you see Luke Donald working hard."

When he was taking a liberal arts course at Northwestern University in Chicago, Donald's nickname was "Cool Hand Luke", but Pete Cowan, the leading coach, has come up with a better one. "When I think of Luke, the words 'silent assassin' come to mind," he said. "Luke's golf swing is all about good mechanical movements that can be trusted under the gun. That is what elite players do – demonstrate that they are very comfortable in very uncomfortable situations."

Good as he is at strokeplay, Donald is devastating at matchplay because his relatively error-free style is compounded by his betrayal of nothing facially or physically to his opponents. This unusual combination of attributes has helped him to compile a remarkable record in amateur and professional golf. In 19 matches for Great Britain & Ireland in the Walker Cup, and Europe in the Ryder Cup, he has lost only three – one singles, one foursomes and one four-ball. Every Walker and Ryder Cup team he has been in has won.

Lee Westwood may have been the engine of the Europe team at Celtic Manor last year, the man to whom everyone else looked up, but it was Donald, with three victories out of four, who delivered the points, just as he had in 2006, when he won his three matches, and on his debut in 2004, when he won two and halved one of his four matches. "He is a great guy to play with in a Ryder Cup because he is so solid," Ian Poulter, Donald's team-mate in 2004 and 2010, said. "There is something about him that is entirely at ease. I found him easy to play with in a Ryder Cup because he always had one frame of mind and that was a 'he is going to beat you' frame of mind."

Early last year Robert Ellis, Donald's brother-in-law, set up a meeting with Dave Alred, the performance coach. Ellis had unearthed a newspaper article that listed the five greatest one-on-one coaches in sport. "They were Tim Gullikson with Pete Sampras, David Leadbetter with Nick Faldo, Peter Coe with Sebastian Coe, Angelo Dundee with Muhammad Ali and Dave Alred with Jonny Wilkinson," Ellis said. "I knew Dave a little from training with him in the same gym in Bristol and one day I plucked up the courage to ask if Luke could call him. They got together in February 2010."

Alred's input has included getting Donald to keep a diary of his aims. This, together with Donald's improved fitness regime and contentment at fatherhood, has contributed significantly to his success. "It has certainly unlocked something in Luke," Ellis said.

Eighteen months ago Donald was clearly not as good as he knew he could be. Now he is No 1, the world matchplay champion, a Dead Eye Dick, an automatic favourite in every tournament in which he competes.

Watson: I never want to see that putt again

The Times, July 24, 2009

There was the standing ovation Tom Watson received when he boarded the flight to London on Monday and the computer of his that received so many e-mails after his astonishing performance in last weekend's Open, it simply shut down and wiped everything off. "I had quite a few e-mails in there but there's nothing there now," Watson said, smiling.

There was the practice round for the Senior Open at Sunningdale, when he had lost £10 to Bob Gilder, and the dinner at the club on Wednesday at which he said he wasn't going to call Nick Faldo "Sir Nick". Watson said: "I'll call him Snick. That'll do."

There was the bad news he received yesterday that a childhood friend had died of brain cancer in Kansas City, Missouri, and a missed eight-foot putt on the 13th hole in the first round of the Senior Open. "I'm not very good at eight-foot putts right now," Watson said with another smile.

Watson has said a lot and done a lot and not slept much since he sized up the putt of that distance at Turnberry late on Sunday afternoon and had the chance to complete the greatest golf story in history, one in which a man of 59, the oldest in the field, beat every other competitor to win a record-equalling sixth Open.

But now he had to get past the man wearing a tweed cap standing near the tee on the 11th at the Old Course at Sunningdale, pressing the rope forward to get closer to Watson. He may have been a captain of industry, a peer of the realm even. For him, at this moment, the most important thing was to get a nod from the man walking towards him, who was on his way to a three-under-par round of 67.

Tweed Cap nodded at Watson – several times, in fact – and got the nod back he coveted. Thus in the time it took for Watson to move his head up and down, Tweed Cap became another of the thousands who have been captivated by the performance of the American in the past few days.

Yet do not think that this is a one-sided affair. Watson, it is fair to say, has fallen for us. Twenty-five years ago he described Britain as the last civilised country. He believes it still is.

"The kids here still have the manners and the respect that you really love to see," Watson said. "I love the kids here because they are polite and they ask you for things in the right way. America has gotten what I call 'casual Friday'. In fact, some businesses had a casual dress code for a while, but it didn't work. So they went back to a more formal code and things started getting better.

"I give respect to my elders. I was brought up that way. Which is why I love Japan so much. There is a wonderful respect for the elders there. It is right to give that respect to people who have lived a longer life than you. They presumably have more wisdom."

He was asked if any part of him felt British. After all, it is where he has spent time most summers since 1975, when he won his first Open. The smile widened and the voice roared: "No. I'm a Yank." But a Yank who feels so at home on this side of the Atlantic that he has no fear of driving on the other side of the road and has queued for fish and chips.

"I haven't driven over here for a few years, but I feel comfortable doing it," Watson said. "I love fish and chips. I love haggis, too. But grouse? That is a different story."

If no grouse ever appears on a plate in front of Watson, there is no grousing in him. He has not bothered to see replays of last Sunday's putt because it is over. "I don't want to see that again. That was a big story for me last week," he said. "But it's a different story this week. I've got to write it. Let's get on with it."

He said he felt sorry for Stewart Cink, the champion no one wanted to become champion. "Stewart is a good man," Watson said. "He's got a great family. He won the Open. I hit two perfect shots on the last hole. I couldn't hit the eight-iron any better. I could have hit my putt better. That was the ugliest stroke in the world. I don't want to relive that thing."

Play by the rules. Play quickly. Acknowledge your rivals but try like hell to beat them. These are Watson's mantras. Success came early to him. "When I was a kid, 14 years old, I won the Kansas City men's matchplay," he said. "That was really a watershed event for me. There I was, a kid, beating all the men. I liked getting the congratulations for beating the men. That feeling of beating men has never left me. I still like the feeling of being congratulated."

Watson may be the best player of links courses the world has seen. He has won five Opens and three Senior Opens on links courses. "Clearly I love links golf," he said. "I've always enjoyed playing links golf with people who love it. Sandy Tatum really got me started on how to enjoy links golf back in 1981, just before the Open at Sandwich. We played Ballybunion for the first time. Then we went to Prestwick and Troon and up to Royal Dornoch. Playing those courses was the beginning of me understanding what it was all about.

"I wasn't playing particularly well, but it gave me a new appreciation. Seeing links golf through Sandy's eyes was a learning experience for me."

He was asked if he could conceive of life without golf and if so what he would have done? Again there came that wide smile and firm answer. "Sure, I can conceive of life without golf," he said. "Who knows what I'd do? I would like to have been a doctor or a surgeon."

Those who have watched him can only say how lucky they are that Watson chose the career he did. Without him, golf these past nearly 40 years would have been immeasurably poorer – last Sunday and those last few minutes notwithstanding.

Cink steals the spotlight with
late charge to victory

The Times, July 20, 2009

On Saturday night, less than an hour after he had taken a one-stroke lead in the Open, Tom Watson, dressed in a check shirt and grey trousers, took his seat with Hilary, his wife, at a window table in the restaurant of the Turnberry Hotel. Adjoining the Watsons was a table containing Miguel Angel Jiménez and his two children.

The course where Watson had made history that afternoon – where he could possibly make history the next day – was eerily quiet as Watson, nursing a glass of water, looked out over it.

Suddenly a shaft of sunlight burst through the fluffy clouds. Ailsa Craig was lit up and it looked as though a carpet of sunlight had been unrolled from the Isle of Arran up to the hotel window. Watson was illuminated. A waiter, sensing that this was proving a distraction to a diner at another table, asked if he should close the curtains. "No, no," the man replied. "I don't want to be the man who takes Tom Watson out of the spotlight."

In time, Stewart Cink would do that. The tall, lanky American would win the Open in a play-off and deny Watson a sixth Open, at the age of 59, 34 years after his first victory.

Cink, 36, is tall and gawky, as well-known for his appearances in the past four Ryder Cup teams as for being one of the first pros in the US on Twitter. He does not look particularly amusing but his eye is keen and his humour is wry. Consider this tweet, sent from Turnberry: "This vending machine at Turnberry locker room can meet ANY need that arises. 2nd to last [option] is condoms."

Little wonder that the American has a following of several hundred thousand: a number that will surely increase as they wait to hear the latest musings of the 138th Open champion. "There is always one person who feels an inner calm the week of a major championship," Cink said. "This week I was that man. I did not feel nervous in situations where I have felt nervous in the past."

Cink, who is ranked 33rd in the world, is quietly spoken, and thoughtful. It is not an insult to say that he was not the man most spectators were cheering for as the Open reached its climax yesterday.

Stewart Cink during the play-off on the final day of
the Open Championship 2009, Turnberry, Scotland.

They weren't cheering for Lee Westwood and Ross Fisher, either, the Englishmen, who had, at one time during a thrilling afternoon's play, held the lead in this most venerable of championships.

Most spectators had eyes only for Watson, the ginger-haired, freckle-faced American, a man some spectators had first set eyes on at Carnoustie in 1975 when he won his first Open and his first major championship before going on to win three more Opens in Scotland and one in England. Watson, almost an honorary Scotsman, once said that Britain was the last civilised country in the world.

And how they cheered for him on the 1st tee, on the 10th and on the 18th. They cheered him on to make a par four at the 18th that would have given him an immortal place in golfing history.

They wanted him to make light of his age and the new left hip, inserted eight months earlier. They wanted him to become the oldest man by a decade to win a major championship and thereby defy his world ranking of 1,373. They wanted him to do the impossible, the unbelievable.

But then Watson's second to the 72nd green trickled over into the short grass at the back of the green and his putt ran past the hole. Now Watson was facing an eight-foot putt to remain three under par and win by one stroke from Cink.

Watson's penultimate putt in regulation play was limp, pushed, and after he had hit it he grimaced, slightly embarrassed at how poor an effort it was. How ironic that the department of his game that had undone him in the fourth round of the 1994 Open should have been a strength in this Open – until the end.

The denouement, the play-off between the gawky American in the green cap and the gap-toothed American in blue, was as clinical as the previous 72 holes had been thrilling. Cink won comfortably, the finest victory in a career that has not been littered with them. At the end he bent his head and embraced his family while Watson took the cheers of the crowd.

Even in victory, Cink seemed to be the loser. Even when he cradles the famous old trophy he will know that he won it from under the nose of the one man whom almost everyone here wanted to win.

"That's all right," he said later. "I knew what to expect. I had played with Lee on Saturday and the crowds cheered for him, quite rightly. I am often the guy the crowds appreciate but are not 100 per cent behind."

We thought the Open at Hoylake, making a belated welcome return to the Open rota [in 2006], was good. Carnoustie in 2007 was thrilling, producing the first all-European play-off for the Open in modern times. The way Padraig

Harrington's five-wood bored through the wind to within a few feet of the flag-stick on the 17th green is likely to be scored into the consciousness of anyone who saw it. It was as good a shot as anyone had ever seen.

Could anything be better? Then along came Turnberry in 2009. To cap this Open we will need Old Tom Morris, Ben Hogan and Sir Henry Cotton to fight out a play-off refereed jointly by Arnold Palmer and Jack Nicklaus over the Old Course at St Andrews next July. If you think that is impossible, then think about what almost happened here.

Carnoustie comedy turns out to be no laughing matter

The Times, July 20, 1999

It gives me no pleasure to write the following words: the Open Championship at Carnoustie on Sunday was spoilt by its ending and the blame for this should be laid at the door of the Royal and Ancient Golf Club. It has, rightly, taken credit for the success of past Opens and it must shoulder the blame for this one, whose ending was bizarre, at best, and laughable, at worst.

Down the years, I have supported the R & A in its conduct of golf and the Open, in particular, against all-comers. It seemed to be an admirable organisation in the way that it was prepared to serve up a stern test to the most skilled players in the world. Indeed, in these columns yesterday, I advanced what I hoped was a temperate argument against all the criticisms that had been made of Carnoustie by players competing in the Open.

My mind was changed, however, by the last few hours of play on Sunday, a time when the meticulous arrangements made by the R & A seemed to dissolve into near-pandemonium. In the last 100 minutes of the 128th Open, two journeymen professionals and one former winner were reduced to something approaching nervous wrecks until, thankfully, one held his nerve long enough to play some brilliant strokes and, as a result, became the champion.

Sadly, the sixth Open to be held at Carnoustie, the most demanding of venues, does not bear comparison with any of the previous five. Jean Van de Velde's struggle on the 72nd hole, so tragic and so public, was a vivid demonstration of just how hard it is to win a major championship. That the 1999 Open should have been won by a player who was ranked No 159 in the world at the start of the week is not so much a case of all praise to Paul Lawrie for winning, as a time to suggest that the difficulties that the course presented were such that the levels of skills were reduced and thus the list of potential winners went from 15 to, say, 159.

Distort a golf course, as Peter Thomson would say, and there is a real possibility of a fluke winner. This is what happened. A consequence of this is that Lawrie, who may become one of the great talents of European golf over the next ten years – but equally may not – has won himself a place in the Europe team that will face the United States in the Ryder Cup two months from now.

If he remains as he was, then he will be merely one of many professionals struggling to lever themselves out of the margins of the game. A further consequence is that Van de Velde, whose nerve was so obviously wanting on the 72nd hole, might also be in that same team and might find himself playing the last hole of an important match in the Ryder Cup. Given his performance at Carnoustie, is this what supporters of European golf – and of Europe – really want?

What a shame it was for Sir Michael Bonallack, the retiring secretary of the R & A, that his last Open should be remembered as the one that Van de Velde lost when he should have won, that Lawrie won when he should have lost and that Justin Leonard, the only world-class player among the three men in the play-off, should have made two mistakes on the same hole and cast himself out of contention.

The Open at Royal Birkdale in 1998 was an Open fit for a knight, one to mark the honour that had so appropriately been given to Bonallack one month earlier. The 1999 Open was a blot on the escutcheon of the R & A.

Fate beckons on the most fearsome hole of them all

The Sunday Times, July 15, 1990

If the Old Course is the most famous course in the world, the 17th is its most famous hole. The Road Hole has broken more hearts than a gigolo and sent the scores soaring of both humble and mighty alike.

Tommy Nakajima, who took a nine in 1978 and J.H. Taylor, five times Open champion, who once took 13, are the best known and most extreme examples of men who have come to grief somewhere along its 461 trouble-strewn yards.

"The reason the Road Hole is the greatest par-four in the world is because it's a par-five," Ben Crenshaw said, a view with which Michael Bonallack, now the secretary of the Royal and Ancient Golf Club, would agree. He once went ten, nine, three at the Road Hole in successive rounds.

You can drive out of bounds from the tee and end in the grounds of the Old Course Hotel. The second shot is threatened by the newly refaced and deepened Road bunker eating into the green on the left, and the metalled road, from which the hole gets its name, running just behind and a few feet below the right edge of the diagonal green.

Thus an approach shot hit slightly to the right can end on, or over, the road and an approach shot hit to the left will be gathered by the Road bunker. And if that is not enough, the kidney-shaped green is guarded by a rise that acts as a doorstep to the green.

Fail to carry this rise when you are putting and your ball will be swept as if by some unseen hand into the Road bunker, as happened to Nakajima who was on in two, in the bunker in three and not back on the green until he had played seven.

"It has been more praised and more abused probably than any other hole in the world," the late Bernard Darwin, the former golf correspondent of *The Times*, wrote soon after the turn of the century. "It has caused champions with a predilection for pitching rather than running to tear their hair; it has certainly ruined an infinite number of scores. Many like it, most respect it, and all fear it."

It induces fear into even the strongest heart, in part because it is the penultimate hole after which there is only one hole in which to recoup any lost strokes, and in part because the slightest wind can make it nigh on impossible to achieve a par.

It sets three specific tasks to the golfer: an accurate drive, a pinpoint second and a deft putt. And if one of these tasks is performed less than adequately all can be lost. It certainly was for many competitors in the third round of the 1978 Open.

That day only one man from a field of 80 birdied the hole and only 19 matched par. For the remaining 60 it was a horror show: 47 bogeys, 11 double-bogeys, two treble-bogeys and Nakajima's nine.

In the 1984 Open, when played into a slight breeze, the hole was even more difficult and yielded only 11 birdies all week. The field played it in a staggering total of 355 over par.

It is not as if it is the creation of some inventive architect. Like the other holes on the Old Course, it has been more or less unchanged since the time, 150 years ago, when the land available for fairways was widened and the greens enlarged to form the famous seven double greens. Only the 1st, 9th, 17th and 18th holes have their own greens.

Peter Thomson, the four-times Open champion, says it is just as well the hole was laid out so long ago. "As a planner and builder of holes worldwide I have no hesitation in admitting that if one built such a hole today you would be sued for incompetence," he said.

One of the most significant episodes at the Road Hole came 60 years ago when Bobby Jones reached the penultimate hole all square with Cyril Tolley in the fourth round of the Amateur championship. Jones's approach landed on the putting surface, bounded forward and struck a spectator on the chest from where it rebounded to ten feet from the hole.

Jones snatched a half. He went on to defeat Tolley on the 19th and kept alive his hopes, ultimately realised, of a grand slam in the 1930 Open and Amateur championships of the US and Britain.

One thing is certain this week. The Road Hole will play as crucial a part in the 24th Open at St Andrews as it has in the previous 23.

The stamp of tradition

The Sunday Times, July 11, 1982

The two members banged their putters back in their golf bags and, chortling with pleasure, made their separate ways to the 8th tee at Royal Troon, the famous golf course thirty miles south-west of Glasgow. "Ah, the Postage Stamp," said one, lifting his white cap and wiping his brow and looking over the wild scrub to the small narrow green in the distance. "It may look easy but believe me it's not. I brought an Indian friend here once and he just wouldn't give up. In the end he took a 20."

They each teed up and drove off into the calm air. "I've had a hole in one here," recalled the member in the white cap as he replaced his eight-iron. "I hit a seven-iron on to the green, it took two bumps and disappeared. I'll never forget it. It was a Dunlop 63 No 5 and I've still got it at home though it's a bit yellow now."

Everyone remembers the Postage Stamp. One of the shortest holes in British championship golf, it's a maddeningly difficult par-three that has caused cards to be torn up in anger, scores to rocket to double figures and, once, the elderly American Gene Sarazen to do a jig of joy on the tee when he holed in one during the 1973 Open.

"It can be a vicious hole," says Brian Huggett, who finished third behind the runaway Arnold Palmer at Troon in 1963. "And if anyone had offered me four

The 8th hole at Royal Troon, popularly known as the Postage Stamp, the shortest hole in Open Championship golf at 123 yards.

par-threes after leaving the 7th green in each round then I would have taken them and gone straight to the 9th tee."

On a still day the 8th can look benign. The green, dominated by the 20ft sand-hill on the left, is due west and of the five bunkers that guard it – two on the left, two on the right and one in front – only three are visible from the L-shaped tee.

At 123 yards, it's very short. "Some of the world's great short holes are very short," says Michael Bonallack. "The 7th at Pebble Beach and the 10th at Pine Valley for example. It's a lesson to golf course architects that a short hole needn't be 200 yards long. However, if the wind doesn't blow it's an easy hole."

But at Troon, set on the edge of the Firth of Clyde, it nearly always does blow. The prevailing wind is from the south-west, sweeping in from the sea and helping on the opening holes.

On the 8th tee, which is marked by a red ball-washer, a stone-framed seat and a wire litter basket, the wind blows over a golfer's left shoulder. Peter McEvoy remembers that on this hole he always placed a five-iron with the clubface hooded to keep the ball low as he retained his British amateur title.

Furthermore, the hole's reputation seems to mock players as they stand on the tee: "It's what happens if you miss the green that makes you feel nervous," says the home pro Brian Anderson. "It's all in the head." It's hard to forget that in the 1950 Open a West German amateur, Herman Tissies, put his tee shot into the bunker on the left, took 13 more to reach the green, and one-putted for a 15. There's a verse in a book in the clubhouse that seems appropriate:

> Oh the dirty little pill
> Went rolling down the hill
> And rolled right into a bunker
> From there to the green
> I took thirteen
> And then, by God, I sunk her!

The pear-shaped green is 30 yards long. At its narrowest it closes to a mere nine yards before swelling out at the front to a welcoming 15 yards. The green is the smallest on the course, a mere 20 square yards, little more than one third the size of the 18th green.

A few years ago greenkeeper Norman Fergusson would hear bangs from beneath his feet when he worked on this green. Soon the green began to subside, the result of mine-working from a nearby colliery. The cure, according to Fergusson, a tall, weather-beaten man whose father was greenkeeper at Troon before him, was to raise the back of the green by three feet so that now it tilts down, discernibly, from back to front.

Though it is more welcoming to high tee shots than it used to be, the green remains an object to be handled with extreme caution. "It's a defensive green," points out John Beharrell, amateur champion in 1956. "You can't attack on it because it's so small that you might roll off into a bunker."

In 1950 when he won the Open at Troon, South African Bobby Locke didn't once three-putt. Even he, arguably one of the world's finest putters, was forced to treat the hole with reverence. "I made sure that I put my tee shot onto the apron so that I was playing for a four," he recalled last week. "Luckily, on the last day when we had to play two rounds, I managed to get two threes."

After it was redesigned in 1909–10 the hole was named Ailsa after the view across to the Ailsa Craig. Then the professional Willie Park described the hole as "having a surface skimmed down to the size of a postage stamp", thus giving the hole its contemporary name.

"It was a soggy green a few years ago," recalls Fergusson with a slight shake of his head. "The drainage wasn't good, so we had to drill some holes in and fill them with rubble. That did the trick." If trick you call it.

"I don't know what brand of hair tonic you use but you'd better douse it on well because the Postage Stamp will make your hair stand on end," Sarazen once wrote to a friend. "It's one of the world's greatest short holes," Sarazen reiterated last week.

"There are more tragedies on that hole than on the 7th at Pebble Beach. Hit it on the 7th at Pebble and the ball will roll towards the pin. When the wind blows at Troon and you stand up on the tee anything can happen, believe me, I tell you it's frightening."

Turning Tiger cub into golf's younger Master

The Times, July 14, 1997

If there is no more important task for a parent than overseeing and directing the upbringing of their offspring, then Earl Woods can sit back now and pat himself on the back for a job well done.

Tiger Woods, the only child of his second marriage, is acclaimed as a golfing prodigy who, at the age of 21, is the Masters champion, has won seven tournaments in his first 11 months as a professional and has sent ripples through sport in the way that only the likes of Pelé and Cassius Clay have done in the past.

Tiger has been the subject of a carefully thought-out strategy by his parents from long before he was born. Earl and Tida Woods decided that Tiger would come first in their relationship from the moment he was born and, since then, the planning and carrying out of predetermined ideas has never stopped.

Earl Woods, for example, loves jazz. "It is so creative, so melodic," he said last week from the offices of the Tiger Woods Foundation in California. "I wanted Tiger to hear it at the earliest possible moment and so I made sure that music from the local jazz station was playing on the radio when Tiger was brought home from the hospital. I wanted him to hear it straightaway."

In his book, *Training a Tiger*, Earl Woods recounts how, when Tiger was asleep in his cot, he would stand over him and talk gently to him, while stroking Tiger's cheek with his left finger. "The bond between us is very powerful now," Earl Woods repeated last week. "For example, Tiger was in Chicago two weeks ago. I was in the same hotel as he was, but I did not go to his room and he did not come to mine. We met only once, and briefly at that. That was sufficient. Tiger wanted me there. It made him feel comfortable.

"Same at Troon. Unfortunately, I shall be there – unfortunately, because I have a foot-high pile of administration to do here, but, if Tiger wants me to be there because he says it makes him feel comfortable, then I shall be there."

Woods is open to accusations of attempting genetic engineering instead of allowing his offspring to develop naturally. "There was no grand plan that he would be a golfer," Woods said. "He could be a fireman for all I care, so long as he was the best fireman it was possible to be. It was simply to make sure he was a good person."

Then why was such an elaborate plan thought up with Tiger and not with the children of his first marriage? "With Tiger I had time," Woods said. "I was around Tiger from the time he was born. With the other children, I was away. I was in Vietnam, Thailand. There were gaps in their development."

The moment that Earl Woods realised Tiger was exceptional came early in their son's life. Before Tiger could walk properly, he would sit in a chair in the garage and watch his father swing a golf club. Then he would try to copy what he had seen. Because he was facing his father, he swung in a mirror image, swinging left-handed in other words. "One day, he stopped in mid-swing and changed from swinging left-handed to right-handed," his father recalled. "At the same time, he changed his grip to that of a right-hander. He did that when he was ten months old. That was when I knew I had a special son.

"I never had to punish him. I never restricted him. I never put a hand on him. I never had to admonish him. He always did his homework. He was a self-starter.

He drove me, not me him. He was an almost perfect child. An almost ungodly perfection exists in this child.

"I taught him to analyse so that he could control things. I said to him: 'Whose responsibility is it when you bang your club on the ground in temper? Is it that crow in the big tree over there? Is it his responsibility? Or is it the sound of the wind whistling – through those trees over there? Whose responsibility was it?' I asked. He would say: 'Mine.' I always tried to tie the lessons of golf into lessons of life.

"The first time he wanted to stay out, we had to establish a curfew. I did not tell him what I had in mind. I said to him: 'What do you think? Talk to your friends. Let me know.' He came up with a time that was an hour earlier than the time I had in mind."

Yet even Tiger, this paragon, was not spared the traditional rebellion of adolescence. It came about over a girl. "It was his first relationship and he fell head over heels with a girl," Earl said. "He was about 15 at the time and it lasted for 3½ years.

"He would not listen to anyone. He was Mr Know-it-All. I told him he was too young to be in with one person 100 per cent. It took him a long time to realise, but, when he did, he severed the relationship. It was time to move on, he said."

There is an air of certainty about Earl Woods and the way he talks that is as striking as some of the achievements of his son. Surely, he and Tida must have had some doubts as to the regime they imposed on their son? "I never had any self-doubts, or reservations," Woods replied. "I had raised three children before who had become adults. I had experience in parenting."

As important as bringing children up is allowing them to leave home, both literally and metaphorically. Woods knew about that, too. "I said to my wife that, when Tiger walks out of that door to go to college, he ceases to live here. She said: 'But he's only 18.'" Woods replied: "That's it, he's gone. He only comes home for laundry and to see his friends."

And so it is now. Tiger, besieged by his popularity, lives on a guarded estate in Florida, as far from his parents as it is possible to go and remain in the United States – but the bonding has been done. He will always be Tida and Earl's son.

"I have let him go," Earl Woods said. "You know all these public relations *faux pas* he has made and the trouble he has been in with the press? I could have prevented all that, but I wanted him to fumble and bumble his own way so he would learn, grow and mature. And it has worked.

"Two weeks ago, he called me and said he had been doing some soul-searching. He thanked me for allowing him to make the mistakes that had made him grow. He was truly grateful."

AUGUST

I have a favourite four weeks of the year. They start with a trip out west for the US PGA Championship in mid August and continue into the first weeks of September when the Walker Cup is often staged. Within these 28 days come a major championship annually and a Walker Cup biennially. Not many similar periods of time can match the excitement of one of the game's four major championships and a terrific amateur team event; none can beat it.

With their preference for promotion over syntax, for years the Americans called the PGA "Glory's Last Shot" when they meant Last Shot at Glory – because it is the last major championship of the year – but that is being pedantic. The winner is elevated to rather exalted company: think of past winners Paul Azinger and Davis Love III, who both went on to become US Ryder Cup captains.

The year's final major was once staged on sub-standard golf courses for reasons that were not immediately obvious, but probably were to do with money. For the past 20 years, though, the PGA has been held at Baltusrol, Oak Hill, Winged Foot, Southern Hills, Medinah and Hazeltine National, all cracking US Open venues where the combination of excellent courses set up to reward attacking golf and the world's best players is a bit like paraffin and matches. Good golf and drama are practically guaranteed.

Remember Shaun Micheel's seven-iron to within two inches of the flagstick on the 72nd hole of the 2003 PGA? Remember the rainbow that appeared in the sky as Love walked towards victory at Winged Foot in 1997? Remember Azinger's play-off victory in the 1993 PGA over Greg Norman, Norman's fourth play-off in major championships and the fourth he had lost? Remember Sergio Garcia's remarkable shot from the base of a tree on the 70th hole in the 1999 PGA, when he skipped like a frolicking lamb up the fairway to see where the ball had landed?

In 2008 Azinger captained the US team in the Ryder Cup in Louisville. He and I had had an extraordinary spat in the months before. At a press conference I had asked him a question I quite often ask captains, namely, "Is there anything that can be said for coming second?" It seems to me to be a worthwhile consideration for a captain who, much as he might not want to admit it, must have thought how he would react to captaining a losing team.

Azinger bridled at the question and threw it back to me. Maybe he thought I was a Fleet Street veteran trying to trick him into a controversial answer. Come to think of it, he was right. I was trying to get him to admit that he had thought about losing and what his conclusion was.

"What do you think?" he asked. I said it didn't matter what I thought. I wanted to know what he thought. We got nowhere. A similarly crisp exchange took place in a later telephone conference call. Azinger intoned "uh, uh" when he heard my name mentioned before I came on the line and we had another flare-up.

Odd he may have been in his reaction to my not-very-penetrating questioning, but there was nothing odd about his brilliant captaincy. He completely outthought Nick Faldo, whom I and others had predicted would be meticulous in his preparation. He was not. In certain areas, such as knowing the names of his players and which country they came from, Faldo was unprepared. He didn't seem to have written a speech of an appropriate length for the opening ceremony. Azinger was a clear winner.

The Walker Cup is matchplay for amateurs, a competition I adore and one that has brought off the difficult trick of remaining as popular in 2013 as it was in 1991 – and in 1971, for that matter. It doesn't attract as many column inches as it did in 1991 and certainly not in 1971 but it has many more minutes on television. It is played in front of small but knowledgeable crowds and the fairways are not properly roped so you can walk down them and watch the players at close quarters.

The Walker Cup is unlike any other team match and this might be because the teams are selected by the two governing bodies of the game. It is an event in which the traditions of the amateur game are maintained, sometimes in contravention of the match agreement or the rules of the game.

At the 2011 event at Royal Aberdeen, a Great Britain and Ireland competitor used a professional caddie in the first morning's session. This was a breach of the match agreement and the US could have made a fuss, but Jim Holtgrieve declined to do so. In the 1953 Walker Cup at Kittansett in Massachusetts, a US player was found to have two extra clubs in his bag. "We haven't come three thousand miles to win a 36-hole match by default on the 2nd hole…" Tony Duncan, the GB & I captain, said, and did nothing. The next morning the local paper story carried the headline: "Britannia waives the rules". Things like this are what make the Walker Cup so special.

The Walker Cup is my fifth or sixth transatlantic crossing of the year and often the last. After the best part of 300 flights to and from the US I have established a routine. When I leave Britain I have my car collected from the departure terminal and cope with the lengthy plane journey by sleeping or reading, knowing that going west offers the bonus of a night's sleep when you get there.

When I begin my homeward journey the last thing I do is to head for a newsagent to buy *The New Yorker* magazine. Then I search out a shoeshine stall to have the undisguised pleasure of seeing someone turn my scuffed shoes into not just clean but gleaming objects. Finally, I have a cup of coffee before getting on the plane. This now is not so much a practice as a ritual and on the ensuing days and weeks when I wear the recently polished shoes, I look at them and am reminded of where they were done – always in the US and sometime in August or early September. My favourite four weeks.

With just one shot, Garcia joins greats

The Times, **August 23, 1999**

On the Sunday of the US PGA Championship, eight days ago, Severiano Ballesteros did not stray far from the television set in his home in northern Spain. This was, in part, out of a professional interest to follow the fortunes of his peers, but rather more out of sheer pride at the play and behaviour of Sergio Garcia, Ballesteros's countryman, whom Ballesteros rightly regards as a protégé.

No one was more pleased than Ballesteros when Garcia finished second and no one was less surprised than Ballesteros at the bravery and skill Garcia demonstrated in playing that famous stroke from the base of a tree on the 16th hole.

"Everybody was happy for Sergio and so was I," Ballesteros said last week. "I am a great fan of Sergio's. When I saw the ball and how it lay against the tree, I enjoyed listening to the commentators saying he would have to play it out sideways. I knew he was capable of playing that shot. Most people would look for the fairway. That would be their first choice. That would not be mine. I would look for the green and Sergio is the same as me."

For most of last week, Garcia's remarkable shot was *the* subject of conversation among golfers and on Thursday evening I started jotting down a list of the most memorable strokes of the twentieth century, the ones that were courageous, skilful, influential in winning a championship. Did Garcia's deserve to be among them? The more I wondered about it, the more I thought it did. So here, in order of importance, are my ten most memorable golf strokes of the century. The best letter I receive that convinces me that my selections are wrong will receive a jeroboam of champagne.

1. Ballesteros's three-wood from a bunker in the 1983 Ryder Cup at Palm Beach. Ballesteros, who had been three up with six to play against Fuzzy Zoeller, was all square playing the last hole and had hit his second shot into a fairway bunker no more than 200 yards from the tee. For sheer audacity, this is my golf stroke of the century. Ballesteros had to aim his ball out of the left side of the bunker and fade it perhaps 20 yards in the air back to its target, 230 yards away. He did this to perfection, his ball ending pin-high a few feet from the edge of the green. From there he chipped and one-putted to halve the hole and his match.

2. Sandy Lyle's seven-iron in the 1988 Masters. Lyle's shot from the fairway bunker nearer the tee on the 72nd hole was hit so cleanly and accurately it reached the upper level of the green and spun back to leave him a 12-foot putt. This stroke was described by Herbert Warren Wind, the famous chronicler of golf, as the second-greatest shot from a sandy lie in the game's history, Bobby Jones's being the greatest (see below). It gave Lyle a chance of birdying the hole, which he did, to beat Mark Calcavecchia by one stroke.

3. Bobby Jones's mashie iron in the 1926 Open at Royal Lytham. Using the equivalent of a four-iron, Jones, an amateur, hit his second shot from a sandy lie to the left of the fairway on to the 71st green. The significance of this stroke was that it so surprised Al Watrous, his playing partner, who was tied with Jones, that Watrous three-putted the 17th and dropped a stroke on the 18th as well, so that Jones won his first Open by two strokes.

Sergio Garcia during the first round of the 81st PGA Championship
held at Medinah Country Club in Illinois, 1999.

4. Gene Sarazen's holed four-wood in the 1935 Masters. After sinking this shot on the 69th hole for an albatross two, Sarazen went on to tie with Craig Wood, whom he beat in an 18-hole play-off the next day. This is the shot that established the Masters, which even then was known in newspapers as the Masters, although the event was still officially known as the Augusta National Invitational.

5. Tom Watson's chip-in in the 1982 US Open at Pebble Beach. Watson tried to repeat this remarkable shot from rough grass 20 feet left of the flag on the 71st green. He took 100 balls and failed to sink one. This was another in the duels between Watson, who had not won a US Open, and Jack Nicklaus, who was watching on a television by the side of the 18th green. Until this moment, Nicklaus had appeared to be about to win his fifth US Open. Instead, Watson won his first and only one.

6. Garcia's six-iron at Medinah Country Club in the 1999 US PGA Championship. It was not only the degree of skill required to play this shot, but the fact that danger was involved that makes this stroke so special. Had Garcia mishit his iron from the base of a tree, he might have broken the shaft on the tree trunk or caused a piece of bark to fly up into his eye. Instead, the ball flew out cleanly, moved from left to right in the air and reached the green 190 yards away. Its significance was that the stroke played on the 70th hole was played at the last major championship in the twentieth century and watched by a huge television audience around the world. It thrilled the predominantly American spectators who were there, captivated the audience watching on television and launched a rivalry with Tiger Woods that could start a huge growth in golf around the world. The only thing it did not do was win Garcia the championship.

7. Arnold Palmer's six-iron in the third round of the 1961 Open at Royal Birkdale. From fierce rough on the right of what is now the 16th hole but was then the 15th, and 145 yards from the flagstick, Palmer took an enormous heave and extricated his ball from grass so thick he could hardly see it and on to the green, from where he two-putted. Palmer went on to beat Dai Rees by one stroke.

8. Ben Hogan's one-iron at Merion in the 1950 US Open. Immortalised in a photograph, this was the stroke that gave Hogan his second victory in a US Open. Hogan needed four shots to tie with Lloyd Mangrum and George Fazio, whom he beat in a play-off the next day, and this shot to the

72nd green finished 40 feet from the flagstick. Hogan's victory was the more poignant because it came 16 months after he had nearly been killed in a car crash in Texas.

9. Ballesteros's nine-iron chip and run in the 1976 Open at Royal Birkdale. Lee Trevino watched on television at home in Texas and whooped in delight when he saw Ballesteros bring off a dextrous shot to the 72nd green, a stroke that required accuracy to squeeze between the bunkers as well as pinpoint precision to stop near the flag. The brilliance of this shot enabled Ballesteros, then 19, to par the hole and tie with Nicklaus for second place.

10. Jack Nicklaus's one-iron at the 1972 US Open. Ten years later, Nicklaus would lose the US Open to a brilliant stroke on this green, but now, on a windy day by the seaside at Pebble Beach, his tee shot on the 71st hole hit the flagstick and guaranteed him victory in the US Open, his third, and the second leg of the grand slam after his triumph at Augusta, two months earlier.

Reasons behind those tales of the unexpected
The Times, August 19, 2003

In professional golf, there has not been a year like the one that has just ended, for nearly half a century. The last time the year's four major championships were won by men who had never won before was in 1969. George Archer won the Masters, Orville Moody the US Open, Tony Jacklin the Open and Ray Floyd the US PGA. That was a season of surprises.

So, too, has been the one that ended in Rochester, New York, on Sunday night. When Mike Weir won the Masters four months ago, it seemed appropriate since he was one of the most in-form players at that time. Likewise the victory at the US Open in June by Jim Furyk was no real surprise. Furyk is among the straightest drivers in the world and has been a world-class golfer for many years.

But Ben Curtis, ranked No 396 in the world, winning the Open at Sandwich and then Shaun Micheel, ranked No 169 in the world, triumphing at Oak Hill to become the fifth consecutive first-time winner of a major? What is happening in the old game?

One reason behind the trend is that Tiger Woods is not the dominant player he was. Woods won his first major championship in 1997, won three in 2000 and the Masters in 2001 to hold all four and has won eight in all. He has not, however, won one major since the US Open last year and, this year, his average finishing position in the majors was nineteenth. Coming 39th equal in the US PGA was his worst in a major as a professional. He bogeyed on average every fourth hole.

A second reason is that advances in technology have made it easier for older players to maintain their skills or even improve them. Thus the number of potential winners has increased. Kenny Perry, for example, is having his best season at the age of 42. Having won three tournaments in the previous 15 years, he has won three this year and finished third, eighth and tenth in the past three majors.

As a result of players hitting the ball farther, the officials have made their courses a harder test. All courses have been lengthened and the fairways often narrowed. At Oak Hill, nutrients were added to the wispy rough one month before the US PGA and this, combined with rain, produced four-inch deep rough that was very hard to hit out of.

"This was the hardest, fairest golf course I've ever played," Woods said. Hal Sutton, the captain of the United States Ryder Cup team next year, added: "We're hitting the ball farther and straighter. They're making courses longer and fairways tighter."

What also has to be considered is that there is greater depth in golf. Standards are higher in most countries, there is a boom in the Far East and golfers are achieving success younger.

Last January, Michelle Wie, the extraordinarily talented 13-year-old from Hawaii, went round in 73 on a 7,200-yard course and beat 40 male professionals in an attempt to qualify for a men's US tour event. The attraction of Woods's name, the amount of money that he earns and the increasing interest in sport in general has prompted this surge.

The final reason is that golf, like the seasons, is cyclical. It happened in 1969. It happened in 2003. It will happen again.

Ian plays a straight drive

The Sunday Times, August 25, 1985

The 10th hole at The Belfry will be a most exacting test for the best golfers of Europe and the United States when they meet there next month. It is fully 300 yards long, and the green is tucked inside a fringe of trees. Anyone who dares to go straight for the flag must first clear the lake lapping the foot of the green which narrows into a menacing stream running along one side of it.

It will be a desperate player indeed who cuts the corner and attempts to land on the green to emulate Seve Ballesteros, who seven years ago became the first man to reach the green. Much more likely is that his ball will end in the trees or the water – or anywhere other than on the putting surface, and every convention demands the "par-four route" – a medium iron and a straightforward chip over the stream.

So it was that when the Australia captain, Allan Border, reached the 10th last Sunday, he cautioned his partner, Ian Botham, to take the safe option and hit an iron down the fairway. "Bugger that," said Botham, his competitive instincts fully aroused, "I'm going for it." And go for it he did. With one massive shot, which landed 25ft from the pin, Botham earned himself a place in golfing history, not to mention a plaque by the tee to go alongside the one marking Ballesteros's drive.

But Botham did more than that. He showed that he, an occasional golfer with a handicap of 10, can hit the ball further than almost any amateur – and further than most of the best pros in Europe.

Cricketers, of course, have long had an affinity with golf and, as you would expect, batsmen are often prodigious hitters. "You don't get the feeling that the earth is about to shake when he tees up," says Vic Marks of Botham, his Somerset colleague. "His knuckles aren't white, nor are his forearms bulging like Popeye's. It's just that when he hits the ball it goes an awfully long way, 80 or 100 yards further than my best effort."

Technically, the best golfing cricketer is Ted Dexter, who was once considered good enough to have made a living as a pro golfer. In his heyday, Dexter dispatched the ball vast distances and now, at age 50, he has the distinction of having holed in one on the 9th at Sunningdale recently, a distance of 260 yards. But whereas Dexter was a classical stylist, as elegant with a golf club as he was with his bat, Botham is a slogger.

Brian Rose, formerly his captain, has this to say of Botham's style: "Ian's got a short backswing, and a long follow-through. When he's hitting sixes, he lets the bat go straight through. You have to if you want the power, and most cricketers do that when they play golf. They tend to swing straight through the ball, and that's why so many of them tend to push their shots. But Ian's follow-through in golf is more like that of a golfer's. He gets his hands up and around, and that's one reason why he hits the ball so far."

If Botham can hit the ball so far in the rain, how far could he hit it on a still, sunny day? The longest recorded drive in a contest is 392 yards, by the Irishman

Tommy Campbell, a tiny figure at 5ft 8½in and 10½st when compared with Botham at more than 6ft and 14st-plus. "My ball carried 325 yards," Campbell recalled last week, fully 21 years after he had set the record. "So you could add at least 50 yards to Ian's shot to take into account the roll of the ball. Believe me, if Ian used an ordinary ball [he did, a Wilson Staff, 100 compression] and it was raining, then that's a helluva dig. He must have superb timing."

We told Botham about a challenge currently being thrown out by the American magazine, *Golf.* Their man, Mike Dunaway, who claims to drive more than 350 yards regularly, is willing to take on all-comers at $10,000 a shot. The light of competition burned in Botham's eyes. "I don't care if he hits it 400 yards, I don't think I'd have much trouble handling him."

McEvoy full of praise for Britain's bond theme

The Times, August 14, 2001

Late on Sunday night, as the shadows began to lengthen from the tall trees at the Ocean Forest golf course at Sea Island, Georgia, Peter McEvoy was being lionised by those who wanted to congratulate the captain of the first team from Great Britain and Ireland to retain the Walker Cup. Spectators with faces that bore the marks of having been out too long in the powerful sunshine of the preceding days milled around him as he spoke quietly. "This was good, wasn't it?" said the man who, in 1989, had been in the only other Great Britain and Ireland team to win a Walker Cup in the United States.

"This is a really good team and they played so well," McEvoy said. "This is not an easy course. In fact it is a very hard course."

It was going to be a long night for McEvoy and it was some time before he was able to address two key questions. The first was why and how had this team made history in such an emphatic way? The 15-9 margin equalled the record margin set at Nairn two years ago. The second was what had happened to amateur golf in the United States that in the past two matches they had won only two victories on the second day's singles? Played 16, won two are not your conventional United States figures.

"Our players are better [than they used to be]," McEvoy said. "They are physically stronger, more experienced, better coached and they travel more. It is a talent thing and it is cyclical. At the moment, we have a thick stream of talent and I would say that at the top end, our players are better than those in the US."

McEvoy could have mentioned the benefits of the team's preparation in Spain last month, when they experienced the heat and were counselled by the English Golf Union's fitness and health adviser. He could, too, have emphasised the way that the team arrived in the United States four days before they got to Ocean Forest. This prevented them from playing too much golf at the scene of the match and helped to build team spirit.

"When we went out to play those extra holes [Michael Hoey against Lucas Glover] they all came out to the 17th tee where Michael was playing. You get ten people together and they pull for each other," McEvoy said. "With ten other people it might not have been the same. Going to Spain was part of that, so was going to Hilton Head. This group was not only very accomplished but they did bond remarkably well."

The team's success reflected an increased commitment to coaching in England, Scotland, Wales and Ireland. More money has been diverted to send players abroad to let them discover how different the game is on another continent. Gary Wolstenholme won an amateur event in China a few years ago and was in the team that won the World Amateur Team Championship in Chile in 1998.

Nick Dougherty has won competitions on four continents. Hoey has won in Dubai and Argentina. As well-coached young players came through in Europe, so some went to the United States on golf scholarships. Graeme McDowell and Jamie Elson are good examples but the best is Luke Donald. The 23-year-old has competed on the United States college circuit for four years and won 13 events.

The conjunction of all these factors enabled McEvoy to claim that his team was the best to represent Great Britain and Ireland, adding that three or four of them would soon be good enough to play in the Ryder Cup.

Lastly, there was McEvoy's captaincy. Beneath his thick red hair, which always seems to be threatening to overflow its territory, lies an astute brain. Having played in five Walker Cup matches himself, he knows what does and does not cut the mustard.

McEvoy is one of the most obtrusive captains in history in the way he would appear alongside a player at a moment of crisis. His greatest strength is his ability to get the best out of his men. To achieve this, he adopts different approaches.

At Nairn in 1999 he was cocksure, trumpeting for weeks in advance that his team would win. Last week he was more subtle, saying only that his team could win if they played very well. He knew they had to be at their best and that some of the United States players needed to be off form. He suspected that some of the older Americans would struggle in the heat. This is exactly what happened. Jeff

Quinney, the US Amateur champion, was so out of sorts that he was dropped from the second day's play and John Harris, 49, and Danny Green, 44, each played and lost three times.

On Saturday night, when Great Britain and Ireland trailed by one point, McEvoy spoke bluntly to his team. They had let themselves down by playing poorly on the first day, he said, and he wanted them to experience the full extent of his disappointment. The next day, the team won nine of the 12 matches and the clamour for McEvoy to remain as captain for the 2003 Walker Cup at Ganton began.

That, surely, is a foregone conclusion. Modesty prevented McEvoy from saying anything publicly, though privately he hinted that he might be persuaded. It is inconceivable that having achieved so much, British amateur golf will allow its most successful captain to retire.

Matthew makes her own history with the mother of all victories
The Times, August 3, 2009

Catriona Matthew became the first Scot to win the Ricoh Women's British Open yesterday and thereby added another piece of history to the storied Royal Lytham & St Annes Golf Club on the Lancashire coast where so much has happened already. It was here that Bobby Jones, the great American amateur, won the first of his three Opens in 1926 and here that Tony Jacklin triumphed in the Open 40 years ago.

The spectators gave Matthew a rousing welcome as she approached the 72nd green, forming a semicircle behind her, their faces infused with excitement. Sweeping her visor off her head and smiling in that rather bashful way she has, looking, in fact, as if she was embarrassed to have done what she had done, Matthew became only the third mother to win a major title in golf in the past half-century, following in the footsteps of Nancy Lopez in 1985 and Juli Inkster in 1999.

The extent of the reception was a hint of the wider significance of the Scot's remarkable performance: she had won her first major title less than one month before her 40th birthday and 11 weeks after giving birth to her second child. Super Mum indeed.

After the startling performance of Tom Watson, 59, in the Open at Turnberry last month, comes a startling victory in the women's equivalent event by a most understated, placid woman at an age when many golfers feel they are past their best. "I know 39 sounds old but I don't feel that old," Matthew said. "I feel as though I am playing as well as I have ever played."

Words like serene are too animated for Matthew. A wide smile is about the most she can produce to show her excitement. "It was unbelievable," she said. "I never imagined I would win. I just wanted to make the cut."

Her last round was a 73, one over par, good enough for her to win by three strokes from Karrie Webb, the Australian who won this title in 1999 and 2002, and four from Ai Miyazato. Matthew finished on three under par.

There had been a hint that Matthew was in inspired form as long ago as last Thursday when she played the inward nine holes in 30, a better total in a championship than any man or any woman has ever scored. She had an eagle on the 11th and followed it with a hole in one on the 12th. Clearly something was up.

For a while, though, yesterday her nerves looked rather frayed on a gloriously sunny afternoon when what wind there was began to die down from 3.30pm onwards. Matthew missed a putt of six feet for a par on the 1st, dropped another stroke on the 3rd, failed to hole a putt of six feet for a birdie on the 5th, hooked a shot from the fairway on the 6th and pushed one from the fairway on the next hole.

Since both these are par-fives and she could do no better than pars she was not exactly pulling away from the field. When she hit into a gorse bush on the 10th and had to take a penalty drop out of it, Matthew, who had led by three strokes overnight, had fallen back to level with Miyazato.

Two of this year's men's major championships have gone to play-offs but there was no need for extra time in this, the fourth of the women's annual major championships. From the moment that Matthew holed from 18 feet at the 13th for her first birdie of the day, she seemed to announce to all her rivals that the title was hers.

This was confirmed when she birdied the next two holes as well and now she had a lead of three strokes. "When I holed the putt on the 14th, I thought: 'This is mine for the taking now'," Matthew said.

Only Paula Creamer, Miss Pink herself, was near and the American's challenge ended when she drove into a bunker on the 18th and took a six. Matthew dropped a stroke on the 17th, where her failing of hooking the ball came to light once again, but to play the last eight holes of a major championship in two under par while enduring all the pressure attendant on being the tournament leader makes her thoroughly deserving of the title.

Matthew clearly finds it beneficial to her golf to have children. She finished second, third and second in the three tournaments she competed in after the birth of Katie, her first daughter, in December 2006. Now she has won the second event she has played in since Sophie was born. Was she planning any more children? "I don't think so," Matthew replied. "Two is enough. Maybe I should have started earlier."

She will now lead the Europe team against the United States in the Solheim Cup in Illinois, a huge task if ever there was one. But if this past week here in a fold of the Fylde coast was anything to go by, Matthew is up to the task. She is some golfer and some mother.

Princely Price approaches perfection

The Times, August 16, 1994

When Nick Price rolled in his final putt at Southern Hills here on Sunday evening, he did more than win $350,000 for becoming US PGA champion for the second time in three years. He announced that, without fear of contradiction, he is the best player in the world.

It is not just because of this victory, nor just because of his win in the Open Championship at Turnberry a month ago. It is because, for the best part of two years, nobody has played so often and so well. His total of 269 here, the lowest score at a major championship in the United States, brought his fifth victory this year (including two majors) and, in all, his sixteenth since his success in the US PGA Championship at Bellerive, St Louis, 24 months ago.

His prize money during this golden spell is $5.6 million. He has had 39 top-ten finishes in 59 tournaments. Nobody can come within a bull's roar of such a record. He is the game's dominant player, the man golf has been searching for since Nick Faldo won five major championships between 1987 and 1992 and, before him, Tom Watson headed the US PGA Tour money list for the fifth time in 1985, by which time he had won eight major championships.

It is easy to be magnanimous in victory. Everyone is nice to you and you feel as though you are walking on air. Price, 37, was magnanimous in defeat, too, in the aftermath of his loss to Watson in the Open at Royal Troon in 1982. Later that week, I tracked Price down on the telephone. He sounded as though he had come to terms with the loss. He was not filled with self-pity. He was pragmatic. Then, and subsequently, he was charming. "How's it?" is his usual greeting, with an occasional "how is it, man?" thrown in for good measure. In a sport that has more than its share of gentlemen, he is a prince.

On Sunday night, after his six-stroke victory and before he was encircled by backslappers, autograph-seekers and people who just wanted to say hello, Price spoke eloquently of his place in the game. No, he said, he did not bear comparison with Jack Nicklaus, even though Nicklaus hardly had such a 24 months as Price has had. "I'm 16 major championships behind Jack Nicklaus," Price said. "I don't think I'll ever class myself in his league until I win that many."

Yes, he said, he admired Arnold Palmer for the love of the game that Palmer had. No, he said, it was unfair to the Americans to emphasise the sudden dominance of non-American players. "Look at Greg [Norman] and me for example," he said. "You can't classify us as total foreigners, even though we are not American-born. We are not total foreigners. We have learnt so much of our golf here and in Europe." And because he is unbiased on this subject, his words rang true.

Price is a product of the David Leadbetter teaching school, as is Faldo. Price and Leadbetter were playing golf together in Zimbabwe (then Rhodesia) when they were eight years old. After Severiano Ballesteros won the Open at Royal Lytham in 1988 and Price finished second for the second time in six years, it was Leadbetter who pointed out to Price that his short game, particularly his putting, was not good enough.

To Price, that was enough. He went away, practised hard and turned himself into the complete player he is today. He attributed his victory last week to his short game. "My round-the-green play was flawless this week," he said.

"God, he's magnificent to watch," Ben Crenshaw, the player-cum-historian, said. "He's a man in full flight. He knows his game as well as anyone else knows theirs. He's so strong. That is one thing that is often overlooked. And he is so confident in the way he is playing. His putting comes and goes along with everybody else's, but I'd say, striking the ball, he's as good as anyone since Ben Hogan."

Will Price last? The odds are that he can, even if he cannot quite continue this pell-mell run of success. He came to success late, serving an apprenticeship on the PGA European Tour when his quick and rather flicky swing let him down in the moments of greatest stress.

By the time he was 34 and a regular on the US tour, he had won one tournament. By the same age, Watson had won 28. Price seems at peace with himself. Setting up his own management company to look after himself (and now Ernie Els) was the last step. He has a supportive wife, a growing family, his own plane. We have not seen the last of Nicholas Raymond Leige Price.

Elementary Dear Watson

Golf International, **August 2011**

Tom Watson may not have known it would come to this. The popular American may not have realised that at the same time as he was preparing for his annual love-in with golf courses and the public in Britain, an occasion also known as his trip to Britain for the Open, so the R&A were preparing for his appearance in their championship. The R&A clearly think that Watson, after winning the Open five times and considering his remarkable standing in the game, has become such a good role model, such a wonderful ambassador for golf that they wanted to give him an appropriate young man with whom to play in the Open.

It was not an entirely selfless thought by the R&A. They realised it would be a bonus for whichever competitor was chosen in that he would be mentored by Watson for two rounds and be able to study one of the greatest golfers of all time at close quarters. And it would possibly, perhaps probably, guarantee press attention and TV coverage if either Watson himself or the prodigy did something special.

At Turnberry in 2009 it was Matteo Manassero, at 16 almost one quarter Watson's age and the youngest competitor in the field, who had the pleasure of competing alongside the American, the oldest. At Sandwich this year it was Tom Lewis, at 20 one third as old as Watson, who played with the five-times champion. Though Watson outscored both Manassero and Lewis, finishing second in 2009 and 22nd in 2011, he spurred his young companions on to good play, too. Manassero won the silver medal for coming leading amateur in 2009 and Lewis, who started with a 65 to share the lead with Thomas Björn, just kept ahead of Peter Uihlein to win the same prize at Sandwich.

Manassero and Lewis were proud of themselves as they relished the chance to learn from one of the greatest in the game, to see him magic his golf ball around difficult courses, sometimes in foul conditions, and to observe how he never seems to stop thinking and often eschews the obvious in favour of the unusual.

For his part, Watson was pleased, clearly enjoying his role as the wise old man and clearly relishing the popularity he still enjoys in Britain. And the R&A were delighted. Their efforts had paid off handsomely. Watson is entirely comfortable about this role of mentoring highly promising young amateurs from Europe.

"I love it," he says with a smile. "I get real pleasure out of playing with these

Tom Watson on the 8th hole at the Open Championship 2009, Turnberry, Scotland.

youngsters. I get some vicarious pleasure out of watching these youngsters play on the golf course, watch their eyes, see how they do it. They remind me of me and what my passions were at their age.

"I wasn't that good at that age as these kids but I certainly had the same passion as they do. I wasn't as good at 20 as Tom Lewis and I wasn't as good at 16 as Matteo. Not even close. Not nearly. It took me a while to be a golfer. If I had to give one piece of advice to Tom, and I said the same thing to Matteo, it would be 'Don't get too complicated in your life. Keep it simple. Keep your mind uncluttered.' That is not meant to mean don't prepare properly. But clutter is what we don't need."

Watson is a great and proud American. Asked if any part of him felt British after the seven months he has spent in Britain attending the Open on 34 occasions, as well as the Senior Open and occasional private visits, he replied firmly: "Hell, no. I'm a Yank." But at the same time he is as British as can be, a hero in this country, a welcome visitor to our shores each year. He is a Yank who is an Anglophile and there aren't many of those. Few Americans in recent memory have become so accepted by the ordinary bloke in Britain.

There is a special warmth in the voices of British spectators when they shout "Come on, Tom!"

Not many Americans seem so at home in this country and are so curious to learn its rhythms and rituals. Not many Americans are so tolerant of what other Americans regard as Britain's vicissitudes. Without a hint of a frown passing over his freckled face, Watson copes with driving on the left-hand side of the road, does not mind queueing, eats fish and chips and when he drank beer he did not mind a pint or two of best bitter. Oh yes, and he once admitted that "Britain was the last civilised country".

"The attraction is the love of the game everybody has here," Watson said during the Senior Open. "You see people out today and they're following in the rain and [at Sandwich] last week it was the people who made it. Filling the stands when it was blowing 25mph and raining sideways. That's why I like it over here.

"This country still has a marvellous flavour to it. Getting to know the country better over the years has been fun. It's different to the country in which I live. The politics are different. The education is different here. Sport is different. It's football and cricket and golf here. It is all to the good. I love the kids here because they are so polite and they ask you for things in the right way. The kids here still have the manners and the respect that you really love to see.

"I give respect to my elders. I was brought up that way. Which is why I love

Japan so much. There is a wonderful respect for their elders there. It is right to give respect to people who have lived a longer life than you. They presumably have more wisdom.

"America has got what I call 'Casual Friday'. In fact, some businesses had a casual dress code for a while but it didn't work. So they went back to a more formal code and things started getting better."

Watson even has a workmanlike grasp of cricket, which to most Americans is as mysterious and impenetrable as Ancient Greek. "I know that they hit the ball," Watson said. "I know how they score. There are six pitches to an over. I know how they get out. I know how the batters are put out. It has a little to do with American baseball as far as spinning and making the ball move. They make the ball move off the ground rather than through the air, which is different, but that's all."

Then there's his surname, Watson. Byron Nelson bears the surname of a great British admiral – Horatio Nelson, the man who defeated the Franco-Spanish fleet at the Battle of Trafalgar in 1805. The square in central London is named after the battle. Tom Watson bears the surname of one of the characters in British crime literature. Dr Watson was the amanuensis of Sherlock Holmes, the great British detective, the pair having been created by Arthur Conan Doyle. One of Holmes's catchphrases, which he uses when Watson seems a little slow in understanding something, is "Elementary, my dear Watson".

It was pointed out to Watson that Conan Doyle was a golfer and that his name is still on a locker at the New Zealand club, near Woking, though it has a line through it to signify he is dead. "I did not know that," Watson said, interest in his voice. "Sherlock Holmes was a big character when I was growing up in the 50s and 60s. Sherlock Holmes came in the form of TV and movies, too. I read one of his [Conan Doyle's] books when I was about ten. It was pure pleasure. It wasn't a book I had to read. They should have an icon on that locker of the up and down hat [Holmes's deerstalker] and the pipe."

At times in the Open at Sandwich and the following week's Senior Open at Walton Heath, Watson indeed made golf look elementary. That's his secret. An uncomplicated swing, a rhythm that shows no sign of disappearing, and a curious and shrewd brain. Watson's length has shrivelled now as he approaches his 62nd birthday but course management enables him to cope with men half his age who can blast their drives 50 yards past his. When he holed in one on the 6th in the first round at Sandwich, he used a four-iron. Tom Lewis used a six-iron.

Watson may be the best player of links courses the world has seen. He has won five Opens and three Senior Opens on links courses. "Clearly I love links golf," he said. "I've always enjoyed playing links golf with people who love it. Sandy [Tatum, a past president of the United States Golf Association and close friend] really got me started on how to enjoy links golf back in 1981 before the Open at Sandwich. We played Ballybunion for the first time and then we went to Prestwick and Royal Troon and up to Royal Dornoch.

"Playing those courses was the beginning of an understanding of what it was all about. I wasn't playing particularly well but it gave me a new appreciation. Seeing links golf through Sandy's eyes was a learning experience for me."

If Watson has had a love affair with golf courses and golfers in these islands these past nearly 40 years, it is fair to say his feelings have been reciprocated. After his remarkable performance at Turnberry in 2009, when he had an eight-foot putt on the 72nd green to win a record-equalling sixth Open at the age of 59, Watson flew down from Glasgow to London. Boarding the plane he received a standing ovation from his fellow passengers. His computer received so many e-mails that week that it shut down completely.

Before this year's visit to Britain Watson, Hilary, his wife, and some British friends went to visit the Second World War beaches in France. It was typical of the curiosity of this unusual man that he would take the trouble to do something like that. "I had no relatives who fought in this part of the world," Watson said. "My father was in the Pacific theatre and survived it. But I just wanted to stand on the beaches and see what Allied soldiers saw.

"It was an undertaking the like of which the world had never seen. The Canadians hit Juno beach. Gold beach was British and then the Americans hit both Omaha and Utah beaches. Some of the things I read about were remarkable. They constructed an oil pipeline across the Channel. They moved 160,000 men on to the beaches the first day and I think it was over a million and a half men the first week. The mistakes that were made from a logistical standpoint, the luck that happened as always happens in battle ... and it was all supremely accented by the cemeteries, specially the US cemetery just outside of Bayeux.

"The manner in which they keep that cemetery shows the respect they have for those 9,000-plus crosses in the cemetery. I just wanted to physically stand there and see. War is awful. It was really moving. One of the things that was lovely was to see the American flag flying in people's homes near the beaches. That was moving as well."

The time is going to come when Watson, this most British of Americans, is not going to compete in the Open. "Bound to be," Watson, who will be 62 in September, said. "You don't get out of this life alive and whenever I hang my clubs up, I hope it will be for the reason that I can't hit it far enough to be competitive and not a health reason. I will be here for next year's Open and the Senior Open at Turnberry. But that is as far as I am prepared to go."

It is hard to imagine a time when Watson will not visit Britain annually and light up golf on these shores. He is as much a part of the game in these islands as green fees and foursomes, Labradors and plus fours. Long may Thomas Sturges Watson make it all seem so elementary.

Alfredsson counts her blessings rather than her score

The Times, August 2, 2001

Helen Alfredsson was sitting at a table in a marquee next to the clubhouse of Sunningdale Golf Club, where today she will play in the Weetabix Women's British Open. She had a pile of letters in her hands and her face was suffused with pleasure. Her blue eyes were all the more penetrating for peering out of a tanned face, on top of which was a bob of ginger hair swept back in a bun and kept in place by a pair of sunglasses.

"Look at this," Alfredsson said excitedly, waving a letter. "It's from Frank Prescott," she said, stumbling over the pronunciation of the name of the secretary of Royal Porthcawl Golf Club, where she won the WPGA Championship of Europe on Sunday. "It says here: 'It was a momentous occasion and the fact that you made yourself available to speak to the members after the prize-giving was very much appreciated. It would be an honour to have you as a member.'"

Porthcawl, the leading club in Wales, and Alfredsson, its newest honorary member, is a love match. As much as the members took to their hearts the gregarious Swede who revels in cocking a snook at convention, Alfredsson was lost for words – a rare experience – when she first saw the course in all its sun-blessed majesty.

"As we drove in I thought, 'Oh my God.' It is amazing that this place has never been a big part of Great Britain golf because it is as good a golf course as I can think of. There was not a cart path in sight. It was so beautiful. We sat around talking on Sunday evening with a bottle of champagne. It's funny I was the one who was least Swedish when a group of us went to the US [to attend university] and now I have become the one who is the most European."

As a way of positioning Alfredsson in contemporary women's golf, and of describing her character, the events at Royal Porthcawl suffice well. Her undoubted skill was demonstrated by her victory, her eighteenth since turning pro in 1989 and her first since June 1998. The fact that she played the last round alongside Suzann Pettersen, of Norway, who is 20, and Karine Icher, of France, who is 22, was a reminder that while these two have the world of golf at their feet, there are tournaments when Alfredsson's nous, experience and length are unbeatable. At 36, she has been a key member of the Europe team in all six Solheim Cups.

"I think it's great there are so many young ones coming through but, you know, there is life in the old bag yet," she said. "It was such a treat to play Porthcawl. The greens were not perfect but we didn't grow up in perfect conditions. Everything needs to be so perfect for so many of them today. I say make the best of things. It can be hard to have one suitcase for three months when you are all over the place, but I don't know why we complain because you always run into someone who has it 100 times worse. We are so lucky. I don't care how bad the greens are, we are still a very, very fortunate bunch."

Throughout the week in South Wales there were demonstrations of Alfredsson's exuberant nature, manifested on the course in repeated exclamations in English, one of the four languages she speaks. "Oh, that's good," she said loudly as her tee shot on the short 14th flew left of the green. "What on earth are you thinking of?" She swears and curses in Swedish.

It was typical of Alfredsson that she should pause and socialise with the members last Sunday rather than jump into a car and head on to the next tournament. Life is for living for Alfredsson: for meeting people, hearing and telling stories, exchanging addresses. "A lot of them today think it is a time to make money and they think it is all going to happen for them. It's not," she said. "You have to make an effort. A lot of them are extremely scheduled. It's like they feel they lose control if they do something out of the ordinary. I don't care. It's their lives that get messed up, not mine."

Alfredsson was born in Gothenburg, the elder of two girls. Her childhood was happy, noisy, full of laughter and with lots of parties. Her parents were strict "but crazy" and disliked mediocrity.

Her father began to play golf in 1974 and now, aged 62, plays off four, his lowest handicap. "His knees are not very good right now so I have given him one of those battery-driven things," Alfredsson said. "He's got this slow swing, very efficient, nothing much happens." And her mother? "She's hopeless. Everything she hits goes off at right angles. I say, 'Mummy, don't hit it so hard.' She's trying to kill it. We've tried everything so we just let her go now."

Alfredsson's birthdate of April 9 is significant because it is the same as Severiano Ballesteros's and Hugh Hefner's. Alfredsson is an admirer of the artistry and guile of the Spaniard, while there are those who would proclaim similarities between Alfredsson's colourful lifestyle – she modelled for six months in Paris when she was 18, drank too much and later lived for 12 years with a man 13 years her senior – and that of the founder of the *Playboy* empire.

"A Swedish newspaper once described me as being like an Italian race car driver in rush-hour traffic," she said. "I find it funny. Just because you speak your mind or have an opinion, that makes you a radical. To me it's about standing up for what you believe. I am pretty opinionated, I think. I think that my soul would die if I were told to do things against my will."

She recounted a story about Oscar, her 8-year-old nephew. "He has problems at school with his teacher and he says: 'I don't like the way she is always nice when the parents are there and she is so different when it is just us.'" There is an echo here of Alfredsson's brushes with authority when she was at school. She had to sit at the front of the class because there she was least able to disrupt her classmates. Tall, heavy for her age and with bright red hair, she was described as a skyscraper on fire by her peers. She turned to golf and sport as a way of getting their acceptance and an end to being teased.

She picked up her baseball cap, her mobile telephone, the letters and a purse from the table. She had worn the cap conventionally throughout her practice round but now, the imp of mischief that is never far from the surface of Alfredsson made her put it on back to front. That's Alfredsson: wise yet youthful, fun yet respectful, reluctant to grow up. Most of all she is a breath of fresh air.

Tough test awaits on faux links in middle of nowhere

The Times, August 11, 2004

The US PGA are staging their annual championship in a place so remote and small it makes villages such as Maidens near Turnberry and Worth near Royal St George's appear to be metropolises.

Haven, 60 miles from Milwaukee, consists of a fire station, a church, a couple of houses, a bar and that's it. Oh, and Whistling Straits, the remarkable faux links positioned on two miles of land on the edge of Lake Michigan over which the fourth of the year's major championships begins on Thursday.

Pete Dye, the designer of Whistling Straits, has set the course on what was once a US Army anti-aircraft training facility, full of concrete runways and missile silos. After the army moved out they left behind 80 waste dumps where local people deposited their refrigerators, tyres, old cars. For a while, this place was also a haunt of drug dealers.

All signs of that have gone now. In their place is a remarkable course with fescue fairways, grassy dunes, 1,400 bunkers of which 1,200 are cosmetic and, here and there, Scottish Blackface sheep, heads down, grazing. To come upon all this artifice amidst all the rolling flat agricultural land dotted with the small farms prevalent in these parts is as much of a shock as would be discovering a parkland course complete with trees and lush fairways between Royal Troon and Prestwick.

Dye's nickname is not "Diabolical" for nothing. He is 78, yet still has the invention and imagination for which he is famous. The joke here is that he has created a course that looks like Ballybunion yet is about as far from the sea as it is possible to be in the United States.

At 7,514 yards it is long and hard, too. Lee Westwood's remark after his first round will live long in the memory. "I had been told before I got here there were ten really difficult holes and eight impossible ones," Westwood said. "I'm trying to work out which the ten difficult holes were."

There are going to be a few players come Friday evening when the halfway cut is made who will feel that their stay this week may have been in a haven but not a heaven. If the wind blows as strongly as it did yesterday, then an over-par winning total is possible. If it does not, then there are bound to be players who will go round in 67 and 66, five and six under par, because there always are and the winning total is likely to be in the region of ten under par, as it was at Royal Troon.

What the blackface sheep will make of it all remains to be seen.

The Mr Masterclass of golf

The Independent on Sunday, August 23, 1992

If you watch Nick Faldo in practice before a major golf championship, you will soon notice David Leadbetter, a tall man with a clipped voice and a quiet yet authoritative manner who appears to be exerting considerable influence on the proceedings. He is dressed like a professional golfer: short-sleeved shirt, plain trousers and golf shoes. When it's hot, as it was in St Louis for last weekend's US PGA Championship, Leadbetter will be wearing a wide-brimmed straw hat and dark glasses secured around his neck by a string.

While Faldo prepares to hit a golf ball, Leadbetter takes up station a few feet away. He stands with his legs wide apart, as if bracing himself to withstand some sudden burst of wind, and folds his arms. For a moment his face is impassive. He could be an art lover looking at a Picasso or a painter standing back from his easel to assess his work.

Every so often he will step forward and say something quietly. He might touch Faldo's right elbow, adjust the position of Faldo's right hip, move Faldo's left shoulder almost imperceptibly. Then he will step back and watch as Faldo strikes another ball towards its target.

Leadbetter had a serious conversation with Faldo for the first time when they met at a tournament in South Africa in December 1984. Leadbetter was a relatively unheralded teaching professional in Florida. Faldo, despite being the leading player in Europe the previous year, wanted to become the world's best.

The eight years since this meeting have been good to them. Using techniques developed and taught to him by Leadbetter, Faldo is now No 1 in the world, winning five major victories starting in July 1987. No other player has won more than two in this time.

With Faldo as his client and best possible advertisement, Leadbetter has become the pre-eminent golf teacher. From Seve Ballesteros to Tom Watson there is hardly a leading golfer who has not asked Leadbetter for help at one time or another. One of his first pupils was Nick Price, who won the US PGA Championship last Sunday. Faldo finished second.

It is a fact of life that teachers are made by their pupils, despite the opposite appearing to be the case. Who would have heard of Jack Grout if it were not for Jack Nicklaus, his prodigiously gifted pupil at the Scioto Country Club in Columbus, Ohio? In time, Nicklaus became the greatest golfer ever, and he never forgot the debt he owed to Grout. When Grout died in 1989, Nicklaus said: "Jack was a friend to everybody. I don't think he had an enemy in the world. He was part of the family. We all loved him. Farewell, my teacher and my guide."

Similarly, the name of Stewart Maiden only rang around the world 70 years ago because it was he who first taught a six-year-old, tousle-headed boy at the East Lake golf club in suburban Atlanta, in Georgia. In 1930, that boy, by now 28, set a record that will never be equalled when he won the Amateur and Open championships of Britain and the US in one dizzy summer. Bobby Jones's feat became known as the Impregnable Quadrilateral and was the forerunner of the modern-day grand slam.

In the matter of fame, however, Leadbetter is giving Faldo a run for his money. At championships in the United States, Leadbetter receives almost as much recognition as Faldo. Spectators thrust their programmes at him as he hurries between green and tee. "Leadbetter, sign this," they demand. He does as he is told.

Walking behind the ropes while following one of his players, Leadbetter was startled when a man leapt in front of him, assumed the position of a golfer addressing the ball, and said: "David, how does this look?" "Great," Leadbetter replied. "You should be on the tour."

He recently graced the covers of *Golf Digest* in the US and *Golf World* in Britain, the leading golf magazines, certainly the first teacher ever to do that. At the US PGA Championship he was commentating for the Turner Broadcasting System television network. Last week he flew to Japan to give clinics, part of a contract he has with Dunlop in Japan. He has teaching schools bearing his name around the world. His two instructional videos are among the all-time bestsellers, and his first book, *The Golf Swing*, which has been printed in six languages, has sold more than 250,000 copies worldwide.

These days Leadbetter can't lose, seemingly. His life is a helter-skelter round of travelling. In return, everything he touches turns to gold, though at the cost of some home life. He and his wife Kelly, a competitor on the women's tour in the US, have one son, Andrew, and are expecting a second child in two months.

If this suggests a man who is stretched to the tension of piano wire, drawn in one direction by the need to attend to Faldo's errant iron play or Watson's flinches on the putting green, and the other by his television or book demands, then that is wrong. Leadbetter remains the same purveyor of slightly chauvinist stories and practical jokes he always was. He is easy to talk to, apparently unaffected by his recent success. Perhaps it is because he is a rotten timekeeper. "There's Eastern, Central, Pacific, Rocky Mountain and God knows how many other time zones in the US," John Huggan, Leadbetter's collaborator on *The Golf Swing*, says. "And then there's Leadbetter time. He's always late."

Leadbetter was born in England in June 1952 and brought up in Zimbabwe where the family moved when he was young. For a while he tried to compete as a professional on the European Tour. He couldn't cut it. His analytical mind, soon to become a source of strength, condemned him to endless analyses of his own swing and its multitude of moving parts instead of learning how to become a better player. Once other players started turning to him for advice, his move to teaching was inevitable.

Leadbetter bases his teaching methods on the fact that no two players are identical. "You can't just say there is only one way to do it," he says. "You've got to blend. A guy like Scott Hoch has an idiosyncratic swing, whereas Nick Faldo came to me with a very complex swing. You tailor your instruction to the player."

Nevertheless, he has his basic beliefs about the golf swing, and in this he is like many other teachers. John Jacobs declares that the flight of the ball reveals how it was struck. Sir Henry Cotton swore by the importance of the hands and encouraged his pupils to attack a car tyre with a club, rapping it firmly until their forearms screamed with pain. Bob Torrance, Sam's father, swears that the legs are the engine of the swing.

Leadbetter's litany is that golf is a game not of the hands but of muscles, and that big muscles are more important than the smaller ones. "He believes that the smaller muscles are unreliable under pressure," Huggan, who is *Golf Digest's* instruction editor, says. "A golfer who uses the small muscles of his hands a lot might look terrific on the practice ground but when it comes down to the closing holes of a championship it's a different matter."

Faldo, pre and post-Leadbetter, is a perfect example of his teacher's theories. The Englishman had a wonderfully rhythmical, if somewhat loose and sloppy swing when he first went to Leadbetter. It looked good but with it Faldo hit the ball high so he had less control than he wanted in a wind, and it was always liable to cave in under pressure, as it had done in two of the major tournaments in 1984. On a scale of one to ten Leadbetter rated it no better than six.

Faldo was ordered to rebuild his swing, concentrating more on turning the big muscles of his torso. "The first three or four feet of Faldo's backswing these days are a combination of hand and body movements," Huggan, a scratch golfer, notes. "Thereafter the body alone takes the club to the top of the backswing. This means there is a smaller margin for error than there was before, and this is why Faldo has become so consistent."

Still, Leadbetter's greatest gift may be in communicating to a player what is required. "David doesn't say 'do this, do that'," Bob Tway, US PGA champion in 1986, says. "He explains as he goes along. That gives me a much clearer picture of both my swing and what I need to work on."

"David is a very introspective person, which may be to his detriment," Price says. "But if you disagree with something he encourages you to bring it up, to give him your opinion. He listens to you, tries to understand what you're saying and then guides you into an understanding of what he is talking about."

Faldo cites Leadbetter's ingenuity in making practising more interesting. After his third round in the US PGA, a disastrous 76 that put him out of the running, he and Leadbetter repaired to the practice ground. Then they took it in turns to put a small blue dot on each ball. The purpose was to make Faldo concentrate on the dot as he hit each shot and forget about everything else.

"That round of Nick's was just one that happens sometimes," explains Leadbetter. "In essence he was hitting the ball beautifully. There was nothing wrong at all. The one thing I did not want was to spend time going over it shot by shot."

Another Leadbetter technique requires him to stand alongside and to the left of Faldo and dangle a towel like a curtain. Unable to see where the ball is going, Faldo has to concentrate on the moment of impact.

"I try to make practising more interesting," Leadbetter says. "So now we are working on certain shots. For example, Nick can play a shot known as the chicken wing and another known as the bunt. That second shot to the 15th in the last round of the Open, a five-iron that rolled to within a few feet of the hole, that was a chicken wing."

Leadbetter is endlessly inventive in finding devices to help his pupils understand what he is trying to get them to achieve. He was working with Faldo on the practice ground at Wentworth two years ago when a passer-by did a double-take at what he saw – Faldo with a child's water wings on his arms.

"Nick was having trouble keeping his right arm in the correct place," explains Leadbetter. "They worked beautifully. Not only did they help him get his arms into the positions I wanted but they gave him the feeling I wanted him to have when his arms were in the right positions.

"I try to help players by getting inside their mind to see what they're thinking," Leadbetter says. "Once you have established the ways in which you can help, the key is to explain them, give them concepts. But I always listen. I learn from these players. They are the greatest players in the world doing it under pressure. I want to know what works and what doesn't work."

SEPTEMBER

No one needs reminding of the date. September 11, 2001 is scored into my mind in a way that no golfing date is, not Europe winning the Ryder Cup in the United States for the first time, nor Nick Faldo's 18 pars for victory in the Open at Muirfield, nor Tiger Woods's stupendous golf at Pebble Beach in the 2000 US Open nor Rory McIlroy's remarkable performance in the 2012 PGA at Kiawah Island. I remember no date in golf so clearly as that Tuesday morning in New York City when terrorists inflicted on the US its worst peacetime tragedy.

Two days later, the American Express Championship, a World Golf Championship event, was due to get under way in St Louis. It was postponed; then cancelled. Discussions about the 2001 Ryder Cup, due to take place a little over two weeks later, went on and on between the respective bodies on either side of the Atlantic before it was announced that the event would be held at The Belfry one year later with both continents fielding the same teams.

I had arrived in St Louis on the Sunday afternoon, not knowing how grateful I would be for my tendency to arrive early. I rented a car, checked in to my hotel and got myself ready to go to Bellerive Country Club the next day. Monday was quiet. I found that the media car park was close to the media tent, had my usual engagement with the guards outside the locker room ("Who are you looking for, Sir?" they asked. "No one in particular. I am just looking," I replied), inspected the practice ground, nosed around the clubhouse and went back to my hotel.

As I was driving to the course the next morning I heard the first faint reports of what was happening a few hundred miles to the north-east. The car radio was tuned to a local university station and an uncertain young voice got the message out. An aeroplane had crashed into a building in New York. By the time I got to the course, word had leaked out that it was terrorism.

It was eerie being in St Louis when some competitors had not arrived and many journalists and officials were stopped en route. I was near the centre of the action but not in it. Professionally, I wanted to get to New York and do some reporting. I don't mean to sound ghoulish but I regard myself as a reporter first and foremost. The office, however, told me to stay put in St Louis.

Some of the players voiced their feelings very articulately. "You can't hide your head in the sand and cry all day. But I felt like it," Bernhard Langer said. "This was not an attack on America," Colin Montgomerie said. "This was an attack on the free world. It could just as easily have happened in London. We must support the Americans."

For the best part of a week I read, kept the television on in my room and wrote. A group of us went up the St Louis arch. Nothing could rid me of the feeling that though I was a lot nearer to Ground Zero than my colleagues at *The Times* in London and useful to them for that, I remained an insect on the perimeter of a spider's web.

Two weeks later, when the Ryder Cup should have been about to begin, I visited The Belfry and wrote a piece about what I found: a couple from Sioux Falls, South Dakota, and a couple from Houston, Texas, four Americans who had never met before, who had travelled around the world to be united on a golf course in Britain on a day when they expected to be watching some of the world's best golfers prepare for the Ryder Cup.

When I think of September now, I remember that once in that month I accompanied Jack Nicklaus on a whistle-stop tour of the golf courses he was designing in Britain, Ireland and France and how one night, while Nicklaus sat in shorts in his suite looking at drawings of the courses, I was transfixed by the size of his thighs and calves. They're enormous, I thought to myself. That's where he gets his power from.

I remember the sight of Tom Watson leading the Americans at The Belfry in the 1993 Ryder Cup, and of Justin Leonard holing that huge putt and the ensuing green invasion before José María Olazábal could putt in the 1999 Ryder Cup at Brookline. The Americans have apologised and more than made up for it but it lingers in the memory.

I still think of magnificent Walker Cups, of interviewing Tiger Woods while he sat on a canvas chair in a field in Ireland just after Europe's crushing victory over the US in the 2004 Ryder Cup and called for changes to the US qualification system. I remember the Solheim Cup at Barsebäck, Sweden, in 2003, itself conducted in the aftermath of the death of that country's foreign minister. This victory in Sweden came, incidentally, a week after Great Britain and Ireland's victory over the US at Ganton, Yorkshire, in the Walker Cup.

But as I do so I find myself harking back to September 11, 2001. I remember a nation's disbelief at what had happened, the intense dignity of the National Prayer Service in Washington Cathedral, the sight of Americans clutching one another and waving their national flags, big and small. "The sound then was of a nation recoiling in horror, catching its breath," I wrote in *The Times* on the day after my visit to The Belfry.

September, a wonderful month for matchplay golf, with Ryder, Walker and Solheim Cups all being contested within its 30 days, would never be the same – at least not for a long time. Nor should it be.

Woods states his case for turning US into winners once more

The Times, September 29, 2004

Tiger Woods has called for a number of changes to the selection process for the United States Ryder Cup team that will face Europe at the K Club, near Dublin, in 2006. Woods believes that his proposed reforms will improve his team's chances of winning and put an end to Europe's recent run of success that has seen them win four of the past five events.

Woods said that he would like to be named as a playing vice-captain of the US team for the match in Ireland to help with the selection of pairings and team strategy and assist in bringing the players together. The former world No 1 also believes that the PGA of America should alter the two-year selection period for the team and adopt the system used by Europe.

Woods also said that he was puzzled as to why Phil Mickelson, his playing partner, did not use a driver on the 18th tee of their Friday foursomes match against Darren Clarke and Lee Westwood. Mickelson hit such a wild shot with a three-wood that he and Woods lost the hole and with it the match.

Speaking on the eve of the American Express Championship, a World Golf Championship event, at Mount Juliet in Kilkenny, Woods looked relaxed and interacted well with those friends and clients of Nike, his sponsor, who had been invited to what had been billed as a clinic. He positively charmed two young Irish boys by patiently answering their questions on all aspects of his life and his sport.

Woods has believed for some time that the 24-month selection period for the US Ryder Cup team is too long. "I have never been happy with that," he said. "To get the true team that's playing the best we're going to have to go to a one-year period, like the Europeans do. If you go back to Kiawah [Island, and the 1991 Ryder Cup], Wayne Levi won four tournaments in 1990 and could barely make a cut in 1991 and he was on the team. I don't think that's the way to send your 12 best players out. I think what the Europeans do with the one-year period is certainly the best way."

The idea that Woods be made a playing vice-captain of the next US team was one of a number of changes I suggested in these pages immediately after the US had been beaten 18½-9½ at Oakland Hills. Woods jumped at that idea when it was put to him yesterday.

"What I would like is to work with the captain on the pairings and team strategy and working on the whole concept of bringing the team together and doing what I can to make our team successful at the end of the week," he said. "I basically kind of do that now, but if I were a vice-captain it would have an official role."

Had Woods been a playing vice-captain at Oakland Hills two weeks ago, would he have agreed to play with Mickelson? "I think I would have because we were excited about playing together," he said. "We were both playing well going into the event. We were up in the second match and got beat and in the first match we got boat-raced, but we almost pulled that out so we were so close to winning both matches, but we just didn't get it done. It happens."

Woods's diplomatic answer rather ducked the obvious, which is that he and Mickelson are not particularly good friends and there was such an obvious lack of chemistry between them from the halfway point of their Friday afternoon foursomes that it was later publicly remarked on by Hal Sutton, the US team captain. What was missing between Woods and Mickelson was the obvious camaraderie that was evident between Woods and Chris Riley when they played together in the Saturday morning four-balls.

But Woods was less diplomatic about Mickelson's club selection on the 18th tee in the match against Clarke and Westwood. As Mickelson's drive flew perhaps 40 yards off-line, television showed a stony-faced Woods staring impassively for perhaps ten seconds and slightly shaking his head.

"What I was looking at was whether the ball was in or out [of bounds], because we never got a signal," Woods said. "It looked like it was out and I didn't feel like walking all the way down there and having to walk all the way back. No marshal came out to signal what was going on. So we asked one of the rules officials, 'Can you radio down there and find out? Do I have to play our third from the tee or is it down there in play?' And they said, 'It's in play.' That is one of the reasons why you see that look on my face. I am trying to figure whether the ball is in or not."

Reminded that he looked astonished at the result of this shot, Woods replied: "I was very interested in why he [Phil] didn't hit driver. It was 490 [yards] into the wind and a normal three-wood would go 280 and that would leave us 215 to the front. I thought that was a long way to leave us."

Toiling McGinley still talks good game

The Times, September 17, 2002

Looking for an enjoyable dinner companion among the men gathered to fight Europe's cause in the forthcoming Ryder Cup? Want someone whose restless mind will make him ask as many questions of you as you ask of him? At the end of a long day's golf, do you want someone who has put golf far from his mind and talks about Tony Parsons's latest novel, the Woody Harrelson play on in the West End at the moment and the plunging stock market? One answer might be to buttonhole Colin Montgomerie, but the right answer is to search out Paul McGinley, one of the most rounded of today's professionals.

Amid the rows of slightly cynical and cautious golfers, who exist within their own parameters and seem defensive when they are away from them, McGinley stands out. He does so because of the way his dark face, which can seem to be brooding one minute, can light up dramatically the next and his easy manner, which is stereotypically Irish. Another McGinley characteristic: the speed of his walk. It is as if he is permanently late for a train.

Think of McGinley in these past few days before he makes his debut in one of the biggest sporting events of this or any other year. Think of how he grew up in Dublin within a few miles of Padraig Harrington, went to the same school as Harrington, played in the same football team and the same Gaelic football team as Harrington, has named a room in his house after Harrington, played as an amateur in the Walker Cup with Harrington, won the World Cup as a

Paul McGinley during the final round of the Linde German Masters
at Gut Lärchenhof in Cologne, Germany, September 2002.

professional with Harrington. If ever Sam Torrance, the Europe captain, had a natural pairing for the first foursomes, it is the Dubliners.

"I enjoy his company on and off the course," McGinley said of Harrington. "We have similar backgrounds, upbringings. He is even-tempered, whereas I can be a bit fiery. I have never seen him lose his temper. He is the same off the course as on it. He is a sound guy with a strong family. He is extremely focused on his golf and Caroline [his wife] is with him completely in that. He won't let you down."

Harrington won't let Europe down; the worry is that McGinley might. He got into the team when he reached No 39 in the world rankings last September (and rose to No 35 in November), after a memorable year. A year later, he has fallen to No 67, as a result of which he has not qualified to play in this week's American Express event at Mount Juliet, Co Kilkenny, where seven of his team-mates are putting the finishing touches to their preparations for the Ryder Cup.

"I am anxious, not hugely, but I am not as confident with my game as I'd like," McGinley said. "This time last year I was buzzing and I am not now. On the other hand, I am more experienced a year on. I am better equipped to deal with it. There is a lot of adrenalin around. It is a huge challenge. I am going into an arena I have never been into before. It will be interesting to see how I cope, how I play, how I feel."

In Germany last week, McGinley was reading Roy Keane's autobiography and he shakes his head at the memory of the confrontation between the Ireland captain and Mick McCarthy, the coach, at the World Cup finals. "I understand Roy and I understand Mick McCarthy. It was very unfortunate," he said. But he was also reading *Man and Wife* and enjoying it as much as he, the father of two children with another on the way, had enjoyed *Man and Boy*, both books by Parsons.

It is unusual to find a man so obviously Irish, who will return there to live one day, so comfortable in London. McGinley's present home is in Sunningdale, convenient for Heathrow, next door to Darren Clarke. There, he devours the Irish papers, which he drives to London to get, has Gaelic games broadcast into the house on a Sunday and restlessly monitors the business channels. "I get bored easily," he said. "There is too much going on in my head. I keep in touch with Irish politics and music. I miss Ireland, I really do."

McGinley is 35. He has a trophy wife, trophy cars outside the house and dresses like a trophy golfer. What he lacks are trophies from competition. He has won three events on the European Tour, a record that stands in stark contrast to his world ranking this time last year. Next week's Ryder Cup could be the making of him, demonstrating that this most likeable of men belongs in the company he keeps.

Europe's single currency pays dividend in stunning finale

The Times, September 30, 2002

Europe, led by a supreme performance by Colin Montgomerie, regained a Ryder Cup that had been lost in Boston three years ago on a stunning afternoon here at The Belfry yesterday. Astonishing feats, including a holed bunker shot by Paul Azinger, of the United States, at the 18th and remarkable displays by Europe's lesser-known players in the singles, contributed to a memorable afternoon's golf and placed the 34th Ryder Cup among the most exciting there has been.

Inspired by a rampant Montgomerie, who played 82 holes without being behind in any of his five matches, Europe inched towards the points total that would secure victory. For every step forward they made, though, the Americans countered so that progress was slow and nerve-racking.

There were moments when a 14-14 tie, as it finished here in 1989, looked to be on the cards, or even that the experienced campaigners in the US team led by Tiger Woods would pull off another victory. In the end, the final impetus for a famous victory by 15½-12½ was achieved by Phillip Price and Paul McGinley, who have been out of form for most of this year and yet performed heroically against their highly fancied American opponents. If, on the eve of this event, you had been asked to name the men who would secure a thrilling win for Europe, you would not have come up with these two, both of whom were appearing in the Ryder Cup for the first time.

Price was Pontypridd's Man of the Year in 1994. What will they name the world No 119 after he defeated Phil Mickelson, the world's No 2 golfer, who had not been beaten before in three Ryder Cup singles matches?

Price holed a 30-foot putt on the 16th to put Europe to within half a point of their third win in the past ten years. The putt, and where it occurred in the match, was an echo of the enormous one on the 17th that Justin Leonard sank against José María Olazábal in the last Ryder Cup that prompted an invasion of the green by his team-mates.

McGinley struck two important putts to win the half a point that took Europe to the necessary total of 14½ to ensure victory. Down from the 2nd hole, McGinley sank a 15-footer on the 17th to level the match and then, amid extraordinary tension, holed an uphill putt of nine feet to halve the 18th and with it his match against Jim Furyk.

Sam Torrance, the Europe captain, had gone for a high-risk strategy in selecting the order of his team. Torrance sent out his best men one after the other, expecting the first seven or eight to have secured the Cup before the match came down to its most tense moments. Curtis Strange, the US captain, decided on a different tactic, leaving Woods and Mickelson, the top two players in the world, to go out last.

This was a Ryder Cup for the fans, who showed considerable restraint for the first two days as a mark of respect for an event that was postponed and rescheduled after the tragedies of September 11 last year. Their decorum helped to re-establish it as a true sporting contest, even if there were moments yesterday when their exuberance ran away with them. And it was a Cup that belonged as much to men such as Montgomerie, who was heroic all week long, as to Europe's lesser fry.

To be at The Belfry yesterday was eerily similar to being at Brookline, outside Boston, three years ago. Then one side stormed towards victory, one colour dominated the scoreboard and yells and cheers came from every point of the compass. If anything, the drama was heightened yesterday by the layout of The Belfry, where holes are clustered together in loops. No matter where you stood, whether it was by the 3rd green, down the fairway between the 5th and 6th or squeezed in among thousands in the stand that cups the 9th green, the noise was regular and relentless.

Montgomerie, first European out, was the first home, bringing his total of points in the match to 4½, soon followed by Padraig Harrington, who beat Mark Calcavecchia, and Bernhard Langer with his defeat of Hal Sutton. "When we saw Sam's line-up, we never said 'he should win, he should lose'," Langer, who was playing in his tenth Ryder Cup, said. "With 21 of the best players in the world, anyone can beat anyone on any given day, but we felt confident."

Sergio Garcia's defeat by David Toms was a blow to Europe, but then Thomas Björn won on the 17th against Stewart Cink and although Lee Westwood lost to Scott Verplank, Niclas Fasth was leading Azinger and Price always had the measure of Mickelson. The 6th was a hole that demonstrated how form can be stood on its head. Price played a miraculous second shot with the ball well above his feet and then holed for a birdie after which Mickelson, considered to be one of the world's best putters, missed from little more than two feet.

It looked as though Fasth would deliver the half-point for Torrance to become the fourth captain to win at his first attempt, but Azinger holed for a miraculous birdie three from a greenside bunker on the 18th to steal the hole and halve the match. And so the stage was set for Price's heroics, followed by McGinley's bravery. "All I did was lead them to the water. They drank copiously," Torrance said.

Americans grab tainted triumph

The Times, September 27, 1999

The United States regained the Ryder Cup at The Country Club in Brookline, Massachusetts, last night after mounting a comeback of the sort normally only seen on celluloid and peddled by Hollywood. Their victory, by 14½ points to 13½, at this stately and historic venue brought scenes of relief such as have never before been seen in US golf, but was achieved only after a display of bad manners by many of the US team and its followers.

After Justin Leonard had holed a 45-foot putt for a birdie on the 17th, his team-mates invaded the green before José María Olazábal could putt. This is the kind of breach of etiquette that golf has always prided itself on avoiding and Sam Torrance, a vice-captain of the Europe team, was almost beside himself with anger as he claimed that Tom Lehman had run across the line of Olazábal's putt.

Later, Colin Montgomerie and Olazábal both emphasised that the incident had not affected the result of the match and Ben Crenshaw, the US captain, began the process of mending fences when he described his regret and apologised profusely to the Europeans. "There was no call for it," Crenshaw said. "Celebrating started spilling over and for this we are truly sorry." Leonard said: "Blame me. I should not have left the green after I holed the putt. It was my fault."

This did not diminish the fact that it was an extraordinary thing for competitors to do to a rival, because not only did Olazábal still have a chance to halve the hole, but had he done so both his match with Leonard and the destiny of the Ryder Cup would also have still been in the balance when they went down the 18th. The only plausible explanation for the Americans' behaviour is that they mistakenly believed that Leonard had at least halved with Olazábal and that therefore they had wrested the trophy away from Europe.

In some ways this was an entirely appropriate way to bring down the curtain on a pulsating match, in which the fortunes of Europe had waxed strongly over the first two days only to wane when the US performed to the full extent of their ability in the 12 singles.

Inspired by the criticism of their performance, and particularly of the attitude of some of them to the vexed matter of being paid to compete in the Ryder Cup, they were as dazzling in their play as the spectators were throaty and loud in their support. Another significant factor that contributed to their success was an emotional speech given by David Duval, the world's No 2 player, in the team room on Saturday night.

Europe, holding a 10-6 lead at the start of the day, needed only four points from the singles to retain the trophy that they won at Valderrama, but the leafy acres that had proved to be such a happy hunting ground for Mark James's Europe team on Friday and Saturday were transformed into stony ground yesterday.

Suddenly, all the putts that had gone Europe's way on the first two days were sliding past the hole and the Americans had rediscovered the touch on the greens that had previously deserted them. As the roars for the US rang out from every quarter, The Country Club was a very unwelcoming place indeed for the Europeans.

The US players were a collective 38 under par for the day, 28 shots better than Europe. "I am stunned," Crenshaw said, as he cradled the gold trophy. "I have never seen such an indomitable spirit about any group of guys. They knew what they were doing and they never lost sight of what they were doing."

It was Lehman who set the US on their way with a resounding victory over Lee Westwood. Lehman was an approximate four under par when he beat Westwood on the 16th green and can rarely have played better on such an occasion. Hal Sutton polished off Darren Clarke on the same green and then Europe's three sacrificial lambs – Jarmo Sandelin, Jean Van de Velde and Andrew Coltart – were all swept aside, Coltart without winning a hole against Tiger Woods.

The American dominance was such that not even Jesper Parnevik, perhaps the outstanding player for Europe on the first two days, could do anything against Duval, who was at last playing like the second-best player in the world. Neither could Sergio Garcia, who had hitherto seemed capable of almost anything, repeat his earlier form in his match, against Jim Furyk, who was an approximate four under par when he won.

After the one-sidedness of the top six matches it became clear that it required four Europeans to win their matches for their continent to retain the trophy. Paul Lawrie, the Open champion, was never in any difficulty against Jeff Maggert and won a match that attracted hardly any attention, and Padraig Harrington, encouraged by almost every Irishman in Boston, did well to overcome Mark O'Meara, even though the American was clearly out of form. O'Meara managed to save himself three times on the inward nine before hitting twice into bunkers on the 18th and capitulating.

There was both symmetry and justice in the way that Colin Montgomerie was never behind against Payne Stewart, and as it became evident that he had to win his match for Europe to stand any chance, the Scot demonstrated both the remarkable resolve and skill that he had shown all week.

He was rewarded by being conceded the 18th by Stewart, who told

Montgomerie, in a gesture of apology for the raucous crowd scenes and for the occasional heckling he had had to endure, that he could not possibly be expected to putt out now the match was over.

And so a wonderful match was spoilt almost at the very end. "That was no way to behave," Olazábal, who had been four up with seven holes to play against Leonard, said of the Americans. "I think that kind of behaviour is not the one everybody expects.

"It was very sad to see. You should all take a look at the picture and be the judges. Showing emotions is fine, but we are trying to show respect to one another. Those players should have realised the situation we were in and I call for respect from fellow professionals to make sure this doesn't happen again."

It was not the first time that Olazábal has been capable of summoning the right words for a situation. Nor had he finished. He then went on to emphasise, as had Montgomerie, that the episode had made no difference to the result. "We are not making excuses," Olazábal said, "but it will be for the benefit of golf if we all manage to behave a little better at The Belfry."

Norman: the long and the straight and the tall

The Sunday Times, September 23, 1984

All seems to be orderly in golf at present. The right men are at the head of the game. Tom Watson has won more money that anyone else this year, Ben Crenshaw, Fuzzy Zoeller and Lee Trevino were each rapturously received as they won, respectively, the Masters, US Open and US PGA. And to mark the growing influence of European golf, Seve Ballesteros took his second Open Championship and his fourth major victory.

But don't overlook the boundlessly confident, long-hitting Australian, Greg Norman, who has leapt to prominence this year, and will be battling with Gary Player, Crenshaw and Ballesteros, among others, when he defends his World Match Play title at Wentworth this week. Norman's performances since last autumn and his thrilling play in the US Open have raised him to membership of that small group of heirs apparent who jostle in the wake of Watson and Ballesteros.

Norman is a sight worth seeing on a golf course, and not only for his guardsman's walk, his parchment-coloured hair and a voice that echoes around fairways. He hits the ball as if his life depends on it. From the top of his backswing, when his powerful shoulders are fully turned, he brings his club down at high speed, often grunting with the effort, and swinging so hard that his hands are swept through, up and around his head until his body position resembles a reverse C.

When his dander is up, he creates such an impression of power that you wince as he makes contact, and you half expect the ball to burst under the onslaught. I wasn't at St Cloud a few years ago when Norman reduced the par-fives to a drive and a nine-iron. I did, however, see him in the 1982 Dunlop Masters when he took his three-wood and drove the 15th green at St Pierre, Chepstow – a trifling 375 yards. Not for the first time we rubbed our eyes to make sure we weren't seeing things.

Norman may not be the longest hitter of all on the American tour. Zoeller is as long, and so is Dan Pohl; Fred Couples may be even longer. Norman, though, is more accurate than most. "Some people may be longer, and some may be straighter, but day after day he is very long and very straight," says Hale Irwin. "I'd say he is the longest *and* the straightest."

In his early days, Norman's chipping and putting didn't approach his prodigious long game. He could reach most of the par-fives in two, and hit the par-four holes in regulation figures as often as anyone. But he would often take 33 or 34 putts in each round. Hard work these past two years has improved his short game beyond recognition, and it was only a matter of time before he took the world of golf by storm.

Since last autumn he has won seven events around the world (in two more he was runner-up), and amassed over $300,000 in the United States alone. There was a time in midsummer when it seemed that Norman won, or came second every week. Towards the end of that run he was asked how difficult the game was. "Difficult?" he replied querulously. "It's easy. At the moment I feel I can do anything, I'm so confident." In that glory time, only one prize eluded him – victory in a major championship.

Lack of confidence has never been a weakness of Norman's. Nothing seems to stop him from being noisy, talkative, irrepressible. Photos often reveal a person's true nature, a haunted look can be caught, or tenseness in the eyes frozen. Photos of Norman at 6 and 16 reveal him to be as confident and cocky then as he is now, approaching his 30th birthday. Significantly, he has no superstitions, which is rare among professional golfers. "It doesn't bother me what ball I use, what colour trousers I wear or what I ate the night before. How can that sort of stuff have any effect on your game?" he asks, with genuine puzzlement in his voice.

His outspoken belief in his own ability doesn't always endear Norman to his peers. At dinner one night a British pro asked me about Norman: "Was his head touching the walls of the room?" I can't help feeling that Jack Newton's nickname for Norman – the Great White Fishfinger – is only partly a joke. Perhaps Newton felt that it was about time Norman's golf lived up to the noise being made about it.

A man whose golf and attitudes are far removed from Norman's, Hale Irwin is well placed to pass judgment on the Australian. "If you want to talk about loud guys who hit it a long way, then you had a perfect pairing in the US Open with Fuzzy and Greg," he said. "There are two sides to every story and for those who like Greg and Fuzzy and their mannerisms, there are other people who would rather see the ball-strikers and the purists." Irwin paused thoughtfully before adding: "The acid test is on the golf course. If he's to make it, he has *got* to win a major. He just has to."

Forging links in a Russian revolution
The Times, September 6, 1994

Ivan Ivanovich was delighted. A huge smile wreathed his face and beneath his bushy eyebrows, his eyes danced. Ivan was about to speak the words he had wanted to utter for more than 20 years. "Good afternoon, ladies, gentlemen and comrades. Welcome to the Moscow Country Club." A red ribbon was cut, champagne was drunk and, on a sunny September afternoon, Russia's first 18-hole golf course was opened for play. The working classes will hardly be rushing out from Moscow, 40 kilometres to the east. Basic annual membership is US$1,500 and the dachas that can be glimpsed from the fairways average $10,000 each month.

Built at a cost of $3 million and paid for, owned and administered by the Russian government as an incentive to attract Western investment, the country club is aimed at the international businessman in Moscow.

That a capitalist game has a toehold in what was once the capital of communism is just one of the surprises that make up modern-day Moscow. Moscow is not the lightly trafficked capital the visitor remembers from 18 years ago, when there were no bath plugs or soap in his state-approved hotel.

Now red traffic lights in Moscow mean go and green mean go faster as a growing automobile population jostles for space. These days the cassette player in the hotel bar is Japanese, the brandy French, the cigarettes American, the language English and the currency US dollars.

The story of the Moscow Country Club, designed by Bobby Trent Jones, an

American, and built by Antti Peltoniemi, a Finnish construction engineer, mirrors the rise and fall in the tensions between the world's great superpowers these past two decades. For Jones, words such as SALT talks, summits, détente, the Cold War, the Moscow coup, perestroika and glasnost have become as relevant as birdie and bogey.

It began when Dr Armand Hammer, of Occidental Petroleum, an American with a voracious entrepreneurial spirit, visited Leonid Brezhnev, the Soviet leader, to discuss trading between the two countries. "What is golf?" Brezhnev asked and, having heard the answer, agreed it was an appropriate pastime for the USSR.

In 1974, Bobby Trent Jones and his father were members of a small delegation that visited the mayor of Moscow. Bobby brought a golf bag – red of course – as a gift and soon they were all chipping balls on the parquet floor of Moscow's town hall. The talk turned to the rules of golf and Vladimir Kuznetzov, a Russian diplomat and golf enthusiast, whispered to Jones: "Why are they talking about rules? Everyone knows we Russians make up our own rules anyway."

Much later, when he saw the design of the course, Kuznetzov summoned Jones. "Jones," he said, "you cannot have these dog-leg holes to the right."

"Why not, Ambassador?"

"Because they are ideologically incorrect – they must go to the left."

Moments of humour were rare and cherished all the more as the project seemed fated to die with each worsening of relations between East and West. In 1976 the Russians pulled out of the Montreal Olympics. In 1979 Jones twice travelled to Moscow in search of land but a few months later, Russia invaded Afghanistan. In 1980 the Americans boycotted the Moscow Olympics.

At the 1988 summit in Moscow, George Shultz spoke to Eduard Shevardnadze about the golf course. Soon work began again. Jones completed the course and once Russians had cleared the forest, he brought in Finnish contractors.

In character, the course resembles The Berkshire, although a couple of holes are dominated by a marsh and others play around a man-made lake. "It's Russia's first course so I want it to be worthy of the country," Jones said. "I want it to be a treasure hunt of golf course architecture. I want to give the guys who play this a feel of what they'll see elsewhere in the world. Here, look." He pointed to a row of bunkers marching horizontally up the fairway of the 14th hole.

"These are my Church Pews," he said, referring to the famous bunkers at Oakmont Country Club in Pittsburgh. "Only here they're Russian Orthodox."

The doggedness shown by Jones, a lifelong Democrat, borders on the heroic. It is just as well that his other passion in life is politics, which has brought him the sobriquet "FOB", which stands for Friend Of Bill's (President Clinton). But for him and Peltoniemi, the course might not yet have been completed.

Yet a curious spirit has sprung up among these disparate men. The Russian who cleared the forest, a man as strong as a bull who once wrapped a club around his neck, was formerly an aviation expert. One of the construction workers, an honest, law-abiding communist, trained in the aerospace industry. He could never have dreamt that, in his forties, he would change from building communist rockets to labouring in a capitalist sporting playground. Later he would spend six months at a Jones-designed golf course in Florida and cry when he had to return from the US.

The spirit that bonded all these men was present all through last week's inaugural Russian Open. It was fuelled by Finnish drinking toasts, American knowledge, Russian humour. "Did you know they call a putt that stops on the lip of the cup a Russian putt?" Jones asked during the first round of the 54-hole competition.

"No, why?"

"Because it needs one more revolution."

Europe sweep to Solheim Cup landslide

The Times, September 15, 2003

The grieving in Sweden was suspended yesterday. The candles that had been lit last week in memory of Anna Lindh, the murdered Foreign Minister, were temporarily extinguished by the celebrations marking victory in the Solheim Cup and the Straits of Öresund echoed to the rhythmical clapping with which Swedes express their pleasure. A smile was back on the face of a nation that is bearing its sorrow with dignity.

Yesterday was the day the Swedes voted in their referendum on the euro and Catrin Nilsmark, who captained the Europe team so successfully to victory over the United States, was only one person from that country to express her doubt as to what to do. But if there was uncertainty throughout the country there was none at Barsebäck Golf and Country Club, where Europe swept to their biggest triumph in the series of matches that started in 1990.

"What a fantastic day this has been, what a fantastic week," Nilsmark, a broad smile on her face as she leaned on the crutches that have been her constant companion for the past six days, said. "I am proud of Sweden for what they did for us this week."

Annika Sorenstam of Europe celebrates winning her match during the singles matches of the 2003 Solheim Cup at Barsebäck Golf and Country Club, Sweden.

Nilsmark should have been as proud of the way that her team of three Swedes, three Scots, a Dane, a Norwegian, a German, an Englishwoman, a Frenchwoman and a Spaniard united to carry out their task with such *élan*. From the moment that Catriona Matthew and Janice Moodie won the second foursomes match on the opening day, Europe were never behind and though there were some limp concessions on both sides once the match was decided, something that goes against the spirit of international matchplay golf, there was no doubt that Europe had delivered a thumping defeat to the US.

For the second week in succession an American team had crossed the Atlantic and had to return home having been beaten. Yesterday's 17½-10½ victory gave Europe their third triumph in the eight contests and it followed Great Britain and Ireland's success over the male amateur golfers in a thrilling Walker Cup match at Ganton the previous weekend.

Golf enthusiasts from these islands went for years waiting to see repeated victories over the US in Ryder, Walker, Curtis and Solheim Cups and now two have come within the space of eight days. Having won last September's Ryder Cup, three of golf's leading team trophies now reside on this side of the Atlantic. Only the Curtis Cup is in the hands of the Americans.

The conclusion to an exciting and well-fought match came soon after noon on a day of brilliant sunshine. It began with Moodie, a controversial selection by Nilsmark, birdying the 1st hole on her way to defeating Kelli Kuehne, whose brother was a member of the vanquished Walker Cup team. The way the day unfolded could only have been bettered from a Swedish point of view if Annika Sorenstam, the world's leading player, had delivered the point that took Europe to the 14½ needed to regain the trophy.

Sorenstam's win against Angela Stanford, during which she was an approximate three under par, righted a wrong. Last spring Stanford wrote an article in an American magazine saying that Sorenstam should not compete in the Colonial tournament, a men's event. "I never thought about Colonial and what she said," Sorenstam said as she basked in the applause after her victory by 3 and 2. "The Colonial was one of the best experiences I have ever had. Today was a new match. This has been a first-class tournament and a first-class week."

Sorenstam was perhaps the single most important member of the victorious team. She played all five matches, won four points and late on Saturday evening engineered a victory in her four-ball match that may well be regarded as one of the most exciting ever played and gave her and her team some momentum for the final day. It was right and proper that the Swedes were as proud of Sorenstam as they were.

It was left to Matthew to deliver the *coup de grâce*. The Scot has a distinctive walk, taking long, measured strides, and is rarely to be seen without a serene smile. If her smile after she had beaten Rosie Jones was wider than ever, it was because she had not only come from being two down after two holes, but had also secured a win that gave her 3½ points out of five. Not bad for a golfer who was not considered good enough to be selected for the 2000 or 2002 teams.

There was a touching moment soon after Matthew had sunk the putt that won the match. Helen Alfredsson, a Swede who had captained the junior Solheim Cup side to triumph over the US at a nearby club earlier in the week, wrapped her arms in a tearful embrace around Nilsmark. Two Swedes in Sweden united in victory over the US. Never did a country deserve it more.

Europe's man of the people searching for his uncommon touch

The Times, September 16, 1995

Among the six winners of golf's major championships who reside and ply some of their trade on this side of the Atlantic, Ian Woosnam is immediately recognisable. Put him among a group consisting of Severiano Ballesteros and José María Olazábal, the Spaniards, Bernhard Langer, from Germany, the Englishman Nick Faldo, and Sandy Lyle, who was born in Shrewsbury but has pledged his allegiance to Scotland, and it is immediately clear that the 1991 Masters champion is distinctive.

Among these men, Woosnam is the one who smokes and drinks, the titch, fully ten inches shorter than Faldo. The others rent planes. Woosnam owns one. They were prodigies while Woosnam was still being prodigal. At three, Lyle could hit a ball 100 yards. At 18, Faldo won ten events in his last season as an amateur. At 19, Ballesteros thrilled the world by leading the Open. Until he turned professional at 18, Woosnam was remembered as a small figure with a roundhouse hook, unable even to reach the semi-final of the Welsh boys' championship.

Whether it is Langer's impassive stare or Faldo's hauteur, Olazábal's burning eyes or Ballesteros's brooding charisma, not one of them could stand comfortably at the bar, one hand clasped around a pint of beer, the other cupping a cigarette, its smoke curling lazily towards the ceiling, in the way that Woosnam can. This is, perhaps, Woosnam's greatest attribute. The others are heroes, he is the anti-hero.

They are stars, he is a man of the people. They seem comfortable with the trappings of fame, Woosnam seems ill at ease.

Again and again it is Woosnam, 37, who demands our attention, whether it is for drink-driving and losing his licence, for taking his wife, Glendryth, and three children from Oswestry to live in the tax haven of Jersey, for having such an oily swing or being called up, as he was last Monday, to replace Olazábal in the Europe Ryder Cup team that will play the United States in Rochester, New York, next week.

There are two anecdotes about Woosnam that are revealing of his character and standing in the professional game. While he was competing in the recent German Open, attempting to win his way into the Ryder Cup team as an automatic choice, his greatest supporters were the other players and the caddies. Not only his caddie but most caddies. "Go on, Woosie, bloody do it," they urged him as he set out each day to avoid having to rely on being selected by Bernard Gallacher, the captain, in order to compete in his seventh successive Ryder Cup.

That same tournament was notable for providing a rare sighting of Woosnam attempting to behave as his peers among the major championship winners would. One night he took himself off to bed early, scarcely a drop of liquid having passed his lips, the better to concentrate on the task in hand. He hardly slept a wink. The next morning he said he had spent half the time looking at the walls of his room, wondering what the hell he was doing.

The next night he was back at the bar and, as some of his friends and colleagues wandered out into the warm Stuttgart air in search of a restaurant for dinner, Woosnam was to be seen helping Mark Davis, a fellow professional, get his hands in the right position at the top of the backswing.

In an episode of *Blackadder*, Rowan Atkinson characterised the Welsh as "small, dark people running round the countryside terrorising the population with their close-harmony singing". Woosnam, who is small and dark, though not known to have any talent for singing, is driven by the demons that are attributed to those who come from the other side of Offa's Dyke. He can be broody and moody. In the real dark night of his soul, it can always be three o'clock in the morning, as F. Scott Fitzgerald once wrote.

Like many a Welshman, Woosnam probably cannot do more than mutter the opening verse of *Hen Wlad fy Nhadau,* the national anthem, but he can swing from being in a brown study to a mood of genial benevolence almost as quickly as he addresses and hits his golf ball.

Though Lyle may be perceived as a carpetbagger in choosing to represent

Scotland rather than England, Woosnam is proud to proclaim his Welshness. "Although I was born in the village of St Martin's, near Oswestry, on the English side of the border between England and Wales, that does not make me English," Woosnam wrote in the foreword to *Golf in Wales: The Centenary*, published to mark the first 100 years of the Welsh Golfing Union.

"Nor does the fact that I grew up playing golf at Llanymynech, where three holes are in England and 15 in Wales, take away from the pride I have in pulling on the red sweater of Wales. I regard myself as a Welshman through and through, as did David Lloyd George, the Liberal prime minister, who was born in Manchester."

More and more these days, there is a wary look on Woosnam's face, something that is partially explained by the fact that he has become rather tired of patronising remarks along the lines of "What's the weather like down there, Ian?" or "Howdy, titch". It was Ronnie Corbett, who manages the unusual distinction of being even keener on golf than Woosnam and is several inches shorter, who noted, wryly: "Life's not much fun when you're only five foot one." Well, as Woosnam demonstrates, the level of fun is not necessarily more when you are only five foot four.

What casts a dark cloud over Woosnam's face is his putting. It is a department of the game that he has completely failed to master. He might as well be asked to explain Archimedes' principle in French as to read a short putt. The frustration is magnified by the fact that, from tee to green, Woosnam's swing delivers the ball considerable distances with a simplicity that suggests it would be a model for an instructional film. Ballesteros has publicly marvelled at how easy Woosnam makes it all seem. If only it would apply to his putting. He missed a putt of little more than 14 inches in the first round of the British Masters at Collingtree Park on Thursday.

Tweak a tiger's tail, if you dare, and you get what you deserve. Tweak Woosnam's tail and the reaction is much the same. He gets angry. His friend, D.J. Russell, has noted that Woosnam is at his best when he perceives himself to have been insulted. In this he is not alone. He cannot rise above such slights and the same could be said of Ballesteros, much of whose early success was prompted by an overwhelming urge to get back at those he felt to be hindering him.

The calmness Woosnam demonstrated in the closing holes of the 1991 Masters sprang from a determination to prove wrong those supporters who had shouted insults at him. Perhaps Gallacher could arrange for Woosnam to be insulted late on Thursday of this week.

That might spur him to play the sort of golf that is necessary for Europe to win the Ryder Cup and, who knows, perhaps even ensure that he wins his singles match on Sunday for the first time in all those Ryder Cup appearances. It would be about time.

Clubs unite to celebrate the legacy of Frank Stableford

The Times, September 30, 1998

One of golf's heroes will be celebrated in Penarth, South Wales, today when a ceremony will unite Wallasey Golf Club, from the Wirral, and The Glamorganshire, the distinguished Welsh golf club. Representatives from these two clubs and others are coming together to commemorate a man whose name resounds throughout the sport.

Frank Stableford is as important in golf as W.G. Grace is in cricket. On September 30, 1898, a South Wales newspaper carried a report of a competition that used a scoring system that he had devised while he was a member at The Glamorganshire. It was not dissimilar to that known as the Stableford system throughout the world today.

Frank Barney Gorton Stableford was born in the Midlands in 1870 within a few months of Harry Vardon, James Braid and J.H. Taylor, golf's Great Triumvirate. He was not in the same class as any of them, but he could play a bit. At Royal Porthcawl, he had a handicap of plus one in 1907, when he won the club championship, and reached the semi-final of the Welsh Amateur championship. While in the Royal Army Medical Corps, he served as a surgeon in the Boer War and the First World War. After returning to Great Britain, he moved to the Wirrall, where he established a medical practice and joined the Wallasey club.

Descriptions of him in middle age suggest that he must have cut quite a dash. He is portrayed as a tall man with a military bearing, who favoured spotted bow ties. Though he had little hair on his head, his moustache was luxuriant and his eyes, peering out from beneath bushy outcrops, were said to be a penetrating sparkling blue. He drove a yellow Rolls Royce.

However, it was the points-scoring system that he thought of while in South Wales and his later refinement of the same system when he was a member at Wallasey for which he is chiefly remembered. "A special prize was given by Dr Stableford … the method of scoring being as follows," the account reads of a competition at The Glamorganshire in the *South Wales Daily News* on September 30, 1898.

"Each competitor plays against bogey [par in those days] level. If the hole is lost by one stroke only, the player scores one point; if it is halved, the player scores two; if it is won by one stroke, the player scores three and if by two strokes the player scores four. To the score thus made, one third of the player's medal handicap is added."

The first Stableford scoring system had one obvious advantage over other forms of scoring, namely that one bad hole did not ruin a score. It also had one flaw. The higher handicap player was favoured – and there it all rested for more than 30 years until another version was tried out, this time at Wallasey.

Stableford, it is said, was frustrated at being unable to reach some of the long par-fours in the required number of strokes when playing into westerly winds. "I was practising on the 2nd fairway at Wallasey when the thought ran through my mind that many players in competitions got very little fun since they tore up their cards after playing only a few holes and I wondered if anything could be done about it."

Stableford's second attempt allowed players to add their full handicap to the points they had gained. That autumn, he added a further alteration when severe gales made him aware that if no player scored any points, the player with the highest handicap would win. He decided that instead of adding the handicap allowance at the end, the allowance should be taken at the relevant holes, these holes to be determined by the stroke index, an option that was not available to him in 1898 since there was no stroke index at that time.

Thus was born the system that, with minor variation, is used today. For years, Wallasey described itself as the club where the Stableford system was invented, but then Peter Corrigan, while researching the history of The Glamorganshire for the club's centenary in 1990, unearthed the yellowing newspaper cutting that told of the experiment in the last years of the nineteenth century.

"There can be no dispute that Wallasey Golf Club can boast as being the home of Stableford as it was there that the system was refined and flourished," Bob Edwards said. He was the captain of The Glamorganshire in 1995, when he commissioned a painting of Stableford to hang in the club lounge and a plaque to be placed in the doctor's memory alongside the 18th green. "Nevertheless, there can be no doubting the fact that it was on September 30, 1898 that the Stableford point-scoring system was conceived and first saw the light of day."

Many a drink will be sunk at The Glamorganshire this evening in memory of Stableford. Perhaps a thought will be spared for the end of his life, which was less convivial than this evening will be. In his eighties, Stableford's eyesight began to fail and, at the age of 88, he was told he was going blind. He took to his study and shot himself.

Ryder Cup in doubt as players come to terms with events

The Times, September 13, 2001

In days gone by they gathered around the parish pump on the village green to hear the news, to spread the stories. In ports around the coast of Britain, houses have railings around the upper storey and it was to there, to what is known as widows' walks, that the womenfolk ran to see when their menfolk returned – and how many of them had survived.

In golf, the practice ground is the community meeting place where everybody goes to exchange views, to gossip, to tell jokes. And it was on the practice ground here at the Bellerive Country Club in St Louis yesterday, before the American Express Championship was cancelled, that the world's best players began to come to terms with the scale of the atrocities that had befallen the United States.

The atmosphere was subdued. Manufacturers' representatives moved among the players, talking club specifications. Spectators held out cushions to be autographed, but there was none of the usual shrieking out of players' names. The click, click, click of balls leaving the clubface is normally drowned in the buzz of laughter and talk. Now you could hear each one as it was launched into the blue sky.

In an anteroom off the locker room, a television flickered with its doleful news, pictures of pundits trying to assess the damage and the implications for the Ryder Cup, due to start in England two weeks tomorrow.

To be in St Louis now is to be present while a nation wrestles with its conscience. All Major League baseball was cancelled yesterday, as it had been on Tuesday. Many college games planned for the weekend were called off but the commissioners of the National Football League (NFL) said they would announce a decision within 24 hours on their scheduled weekend matches. Theirs is an important decision. Everyone remembers how the NFL played a full programme two days after the assassination of President Kennedy in November 1963. It was the wrong decision and it left a mark of shame on the heads of sports administrators that has not disappeared to this day.

Tiger Woods was due to fly to Paris next week to play in the Lancôme Trophy and has already expressed doubt about the trip. "As for the Ryder Cup, I really don't know," he said. "We will be talking to our US tour officials about all the different scenarios. It's difficult for anyone to come out strongly either way."

In Britain, Mark James, the Europe captain in 1999, said that he thought the Ryder Cup could not be rescheduled for later in the year. He suggested that if it did not go ahead, both sides would simply look to the next match in 2003. Somehow, his voice was all the clearer for coming from so far away.

Here in the US, nobody knows, least of all the players. Golfers feel comfortable playing in front of thousands of fans but they do not when asked to make decisions about other matters. They are no more gifted in this situation than politicians are when they compete in a pro-am.

On Tuesday Bernhard Langer had said: "You can't hide your head in the sand and cry all day, but I felt like it." A day later he was still confused. "You don't know what to do," he said. "Do you give blood, do you give money? You want to do what is best for the people who are suffering."

Niclas Fasth's face, as he made his way to the 10th tee for a practice round, told a story. The Swede kept his eyes groundwards. "It is a terrible thing," he said. "It is hard to know what to think."

On the practice ground, the mind went back to David Duval's heartfelt words after his victory in the Open two months ago. Duval said how much he was looking forward to returning to Britain and being announced as the Open champion on the 1st tee at the Ryder Cup.

Now he stopped his practice and looked up quizzically. How does he feel about that now, he was asked? He answered the question with a question. "Are you asking whether the Ryder Cup should go ahead or not?" he said. "It depends on the response over the next few days," he replied.

"The prospect of the Ryder Cup is still exciting. Certainly some of the drama and excitement and some of the importance that has been placed on the matches has gone. Maybe some of the animosity of the participants has disappeared."

Would he support any decision that was made? "Yes, based upon what happened yesterday, we have to see what the reaction is going to be this week. It is not so much the match that concerns me, it's the travel."

Colin Montgomerie took up a position a few feet away from Duval. On Tuesday, he had declined to comment. He had not been able to come to grips with what had happened. Now, his mind was clear. "This was not an attack on America, this was an attack on the free world," he said. "It could just as easily have happened in London. We must support the Americans.

"Tim Finchem spoke very well in helping us to decide whether or not to cancel the American Express event. He said Friday to Sunday will be days of mourning and you can't play golf at that time."

Finchem, commissioner of the US PGA Tour, gave no guidance, however, about the Ryder Cup. "The decision is not ours to make," Montgomerie added. "It must be made by the PGAs, the relevant bodies, but it must be the American voice that comes out loudest and is heard. If the Americans do come over, it could be unreal. They will not be able to concentrate on golf, I am sure of that."

Ryder Cup decision on hold as Europe awaits guidance from Americans
The Times, September 14, 2001

In the United States this morning, the nation is riddled with questions. It is 72 hours after the start of its worst peacetime tragedy and no one seems any nearer to providing answers.

One of the most important questions in sport is whether or not the Ryder Cup should go ahead at the end of the month. It is due to start at The Belfry two weeks this morning. More importantly, the US team, defending the trophy they won at The Country Club, Boston, in 1999, are due to leave for Britain in nine days' time.

"Our invitation remains open for the US team to come here for the match," Sandy Jones, executive director of the Professional Golfers' Association, said yesterday. "We are so advanced in staging, everything is in position. We are ready to go. All the security is being reviewed."

He had just put the telephone down after talking to Ken Schofield, the executive director of the PGA Tour, who was stranded in New Brunswick, Canada. He said that there would be another conference call to officials at the US PGA last night.

Jones said there were two possible courses of action. "One is to cancel the whole thing and run the risk of being accused of being cowardly," he said. "The other is that by playing the Ryder Cup, we are demonstrating that life must continue. There are supporters and critics of both views." The PGAs of Britain and the US and the Ryder Cup committee, which must make the decision, are in a "damned if you do, damned if you don't" position.

"We are reassessing every logistic connected with the matches, a process which will take a number of days and which will require input from our government," Jim Autrey, chief executive officer of the US PGA, said. "When our assessment is complete we will make further announcements as appropriate."

Paul McGinley, who with Phillip Price and Padraig Harrington, his fellow Europe team members, spent yesterday morning practising at the Bellerive Country Club, spoke of the difficulty of the decision facing the golfing authorities.

"The decision to cancel the American Express Championship [which was due to start at Bellerive yesterday] was taken democratically and the overwhelming opinion was not to play," McGinley said. "It is the same with the Ryder Cup. The decision must be made democratically and I think you're going to have Americans not wanting to come. The problem will be that we are going to have some kind of retaliation from the Americans in the next two weeks. That will be the biggest problem for the Ryder Cup. It is a horrible situation and a horrible decision for people to have to make."

Elsewhere in this vast country, sports authorities are divided. College football and women's professional golf will recommence this weekend, Major League baseball will resume on Monday, but other sports have yet to decide. The National Football League has called off the weekend's American football programme and has yet to determine whether the 15 matches will be played at a later date.

In short, no one really knows what do to. "What you want to do is to make the appropriate response," Gary Bettman, commissioner of the National Hockey League, said. "You want to avoid a decision that makes you appear insensitive. You don't want to grandstand, either. You want to strike a balance."

Mark Calcavecchia, a member of the US Ryder Cup team, said: "You have got to move on. If you don't, you're giving in." But then it was pointed out to him that the previous day he had called for the event to be cancelled. "Did I?" he grinned. "If you ask me next week I'll probably say something else.

"Time heals all wounds. Maybe next week it won't seem so bad, but maybe it will. If they play I'll be there, but if they don't, then I will support that decision too."

It is fascinating to be in this country at this time, to see how a nation pulls itself together. There is so much dignity in the US at present. At ten to eight yesterday morning, television broadcast a tribute to America. As a strong female voice sang the national anthem, followed by one minute's silence, I stopped bustling around my hotel room.

Then I did what I knew millions of Americans throughout the country would be doing at that moment. I paid my own tribute. I stood to attention and listened to the words of this powerful song. As I did so, I looked around my hotel room. My golf reference books lay on a desk. I was in the country to cover a golf tournament, an event of little significance outside the sport itself. I did not know what more I could do and, in this, I dare say I was typical of millions of Americans.

What golf has to address today is not simply a question of whether or not the Ryder Cup should be played. There are too many attendant and far greater issues that have to be resolved and the actions that will be taken are likely to determine whether or not the Ryder Cup goes ahead.

As McGinley suggested, there is more to come. The United States is poised. It is experiencing a lull after the storm, a pause before the next step. But which way will it turn and what does it all mean?

"The Americans must take the lead," Colin Montgomerie said on Wednesday. "Their voice must be heard loudest." At times like this, sport seems small and insignificant. The Ryder Cup can wait. It will surely be overtaken in importance anyway.

Pressure is mounting on Europe to call off Ryder Cup

The Times, September 15, 2001

Nine members of the Europe Ryder Cup team, their caddies, European Tour officials and other players were able to board a chartered Boeing 757 in St Louis yesterday evening. They left the city known as "The Gateway to the West" and were due in London at noon today in the country where the Ryder Cup is scheduled to begin in 13 days.

As a traumatic week draws to a close here in the United States, the debate is whether or not sport should have recommenced this weekend. The National Football League and Major League Baseball (MLB) represent the two sports that most Americans hold most dear. "We have decided that our priorities for this weekend are to pause, grieve and reflect," Paul Tagliabue, the commissioner of the NFL, said.

His words were echoed by Bud Selig, the MLB commissioner. "The more I thought about it, I couldn't rationalise starting before Monday," he said. In addition, tennis officials yesterday postponed the Davis Cup tie against India in Winston-Salem, North Carolina, until next month.

Ranged against the Tagliabues and Seligs were those who urged that sport had a duty to resume a more regular pattern. "People do want to get back to life as normal – whatever normal is," a woman said on television. Earlier, Bryant

Gumbel, a national figure of standing because of his daily appearance on a break-fast television show, suggested that starting sport today would be "a relief from the sadness we are working on".

The debate was won by those who wanted a quiet period of reflection. "I don't buy into this 'if we don't play, they win'," Gene Upshaw, a football players' representative, said. "This isn't about terrorists, it's about us – the people who are here, the firemen and rescue workers, the victims, their families and friends. Do you really think the terrorists care if we play?"

In a way, the discussions about sport mirrored smaller discussions that are going on about the Ryder Cup. The PGA in Birmingham and the European Tour at Wentworth and the US PGA from its base in Palm Beach, Florida, have said that they hope the event will go ahead. But it was no more than a hope. At present, the decision is not theirs, unless they decide to abandon the event. At the moment they are waiting for a lead from the US government.

For nearly a quarter of a century I have been privileged to have had a ring-side seat at golf events. I was so close to Severiano Ballesteros when he played a three-wood out of a bunker on the last hole of his match against Fuzzy Zoeller in the 1983 Ryder Cup that the hairs on the back of my neck began to rise at the audacity of what I was seeing. It would have taken me only six or seven paces to reach Bernhard Langer after he had missed that putt in the Ryder Cup at Kiawah Island in 1991.

Sometimes I stand so near to golfers that I can see the number on their golf ball. Two years ago, I sat in an hotel room in Houston and watched on television the moving scenes of the memorial service in honour of Payne Stewart. Now I am in the thick of it again. I sat for a few moments with Paul McGinley in the clubhouse at Bellerive on Thursday. At another table, Padraig Harrington and David McNeilly, his caddie, were working through a plateful of spaghetti. They had been out practising in the morning heat and soon they would go back out and hit more balls. The Ryder Cup was on their mind. They wanted to make sure that, if it goes ahead, their golf is in mint condition.

"It was difficult trying to concentrate here this week," McGinley, an excep-tionally intelligent and perceptive man, said. "It's going to be an unusual two weeks." Then he leant back in his chair, stretching his arms above his head as if he were an animal emerging from a deep sleep. "I shall be so disappointed if it is cancelled."

It is all very well to list the seductive advantages that would accrue if the Ryder Cup went ahead. The Americans would never forget their welcome. Here in the US they were astonished at the ceremony outside Buckingham Palace on

Thursday and late that night a pianist in a bar in St Louis had tears of gratitude as he thanked me for this gesture of friendship to his country – as if I had anything to do with it. "God effing bless you," he said, a phrase of such vivacity I shall remember it for the rest of my life.

It is guaranteed that, if the US team reaches The Belfry, the roars of welcome will spread to every corner of Britain. Playing the match will help life return to normal from now on. It will be a message to those who are responsible for what happened this week that Europe is joined at the hip to the US. All that is undeniable. That is on one side of the ledger. On the other side is this. News has come that Tiger Woods has withdrawn from the Lancôme Trophy to be played next week in Paris. "I don't believe this is an appropriate time to play competitive golf," he said. "I have always felt that I must be fully committed to each and every golf competition I enter, but due to this week's events I am not. I also fear the security risks of travelling overseas at the present time are too great."

I am sitting in my hotel room where the television images change almost as often as I blink. Now it is a studio in Manhattan where a lot of heads are talking. Now it is inside the National Cathedral in Washington DC, where soldiers are playing their violins before the start of the National Prayer Service. Now the congregation is in full voice: "Oh God our help in ages past," they sing. And "God Bless America!" they bellow.

The flickering box in the corner has just shown pictures of a woman receiving a phone call from a person she thinks might be a loved one lost in the rubble in New York City. She cries, a friend consoles her. Who is it? she asked. "It's a caller who got my number from the placard I held up on television. She has never met me but she said she wanted to call and give me support. She said that she, too, had lost someone."

Emotions are running high here and perhaps they are slightly obscuring matters. A hot head is not always a wise one. Perhaps the Ryder Cup should go ahead. But, as I sit here watching the National Prayer Service draw to a close, I have my doubts.

OCTOBER

October, what a month. The Ryder Cup, with all its attendant drama since Europe arrived at the party. A one-legged man forcing me to rub my eyes in disbelief at his ability to play golf at Kingsbarns. Walking down a corridor in the Old Course Hotel with Colin Montgomerie, not with a reporter's notepad in my hand as I would have done on every other occasion but as a fellow competitor in the Dunhill Links Trophy. Despite the notion that golf is slightly out of season – an intrusion into time for football – this is a month with no little charm. (And when, pray, does football not dominate in this modern age?)

It's the unpredictable aspect of things in an otherwise very predictable world that strikes me about many months of my golfing year and particularly about October. At the start of each year I would collect the various calendars, select the events I wanted to cover and put them in my diary. Thus I knew I'd be at the Ryder Cup that ended at the beginning of October, probably the Alfred Dunhill Links Championship, the Portuguese Open when it was staged that late in the year and when I covered the national Opens of the leading golfing countries.

I had no idea that in one October I would barely have returned from the excitement of a Ryder Cup in Boston before I was back on an aeroplane to Houston, Texas. There in the aftermath of the death of Payne Stewart in an air crash, I was chronicling the reaction to his death among his peers who were competing in a PGA tournament. Likewise I had no idea that one crisp autumn morning at Kingsbarns, I would rub my eyes in disbelief, not sure I could believe what I was seeing. I appeared to be watching a man with only one leg hitting the ball a healthy distance from the tee, chipping with finesse and grace, and generally confounding almost all the principles of golf.

On the other hand, I knew that when I went to Paris for the Eisenhower Trophy in October 1994 that I was going to see something special. The Eisenhower Trophy does not get as much prominence these days as it used to. But that year enough had been heard about Tiger Woods to know that a trip to Paris for the men's event in the World Amateur Team Championship would provide good copy. Two months earlier the august *New York Times* had run a front-page story about Woods becoming only the second man to win the US Junior Amateur and then the US Amateur. This was just the second time that golf had been so prominently displayed in this most conservative of papers in the nineties.

Grant Spaeth was the US team's manager and he was justifiably protective of the team's young star. John Harris, known as "the Bishop" for his stately walk and reverential demeanour, was the captain and Allen Doyle another team-mate.

It was still nearly three years before Woods won at Augusta by 12 strokes and almost a year before he was on the losing Walker Cup team at Royal Porthcawl, but there was enough about Woods for him to stand out even among much older, more experienced and some better players. I have always subscribed to the words of Pat Ward-Thomas, the wonderful golf writer on *The Guardian*, who told me: "I always try and set the scene."

When you watch someone extremely promising for the first time, then this instruction becomes doubly important. Birdies and bogeys are relevant but descriptions of his character are more so. What does he look like? How does he hold the club and swing it – with vigour or with a languid air? Is he balanced? What sort of putter does he use, how does he address his ball on the green? All of these I could now see with my own eyes and convey to readers of *The Times*. What I didn't know was how easily we managed to find out about prejudice against the young Woods on account of the colour of his skin.

For possibly the first time and probably the last, Woods recounted how, the only black student in his class, he was tied to a tree and taunted by fellow pupils on starting at a particular school. He revealed that he was studying calculus and battling his way through the 18 books he had been set for his first year at Stanford University. Had he seen any of the sights of Paris, he was asked. "McDonald's," he replied, smiling.

I would like to be able to say that from the moment I first set eyes on him I sensed he was going to be one of the best golfers the world has ever seen. And I can. There was an eerie stillness about him. He seemed astonishingly focused for a young man not yet 19, mature beyond his years. There was a venom about his striking, a steadiness about his scoring that has not always been with him. Though the youngest team member and knowing it might all come down to him, Woods was put out the last of the four Americans. It did come down to him. He did withstand the pressure, compiling a solid round of 16 pars, one birdie and one bogey. The US did win.

"Of the 17 matches that I have seen this was the greatest yet"

The Times, October 1, 2012

Being a sportswriter is a pretty good gig, but being a golf writer and setting off to cover the Ryder Cup, on whichever side of the Atlantic it is taking place, creates levels of envy that should be illegal.

The Ryder Cup are three words that are guaranteed to bring a smile to any golfer. That biennial competition that delivers thrills and skills and has done it once again. Does anything else in sport rival this competition for practically guaranteed excitement?

What an astonishing competition it is. I thought I had seen something special when Jack Nicklaus conceded that putt to Tony Jacklin at Royal Birkdale in 1969, thereby ensuring a tied match. It was the one of greatest acts of sportsmanship ever in a game that can sometimes be a little pious about its sportsmanship.

I knew I had seen something special when Europe won at The Belfry in 1985, the first home victory since Lindrick in 1957. Concorde roared overhead. Paul Way held up a champagne bottle that was almost as big as he was and showered its contents over team-mates and spectators from an hotel balcony.

There had been a sign that this was coming, that changing Great Britain and Ireland into Europe in 1979 and thereby including one Severiano Ballesteros, was about to pay off for Europe. In 1983, Ballesteros bounced around the team

Bernhard Langer chipping in from the side of the 10th green
during the 1987 Ryder Cup tournament played at Muirfield
Village, Ohio, Europe's first victory in the United States.

room and said, inspiringly: "This was not a defeat. This was a victory. We'll win the next one." And Europe did.

And then came Europe's first victory in the United States. It came in that most appropriately named place, Dublin, Ohio. If you saw grown men cry on the verdant fairways of Nicklaus's magnificent course in 1987 then they were Ken Schofield, the executive director of the European Tour, Tony Jacklin, the captain, Ballesteros, who had hit the winning shot, and others.

Eamonn Darcy holed a memorable putt against Ben Crenshaw, who had broken his putter in disgust after the 6th hole and thereafter putted with either a one-iron or a sand wedge. Europe put out some team that year, one that contained six major championship winners present or future: Bernhard Langer, Nick Faldo, Ian Woosnam, Sandy Lyle, José María Olazábal and Ballesteros.

The play by the Europeans in the Saturday four-balls caused the great Nicklaus, the owner of 18 professional major titles, to rub his eyes and say: "I never thought I'd see golf like this."

In 1995 Nick Faldo got down in two from 93 yards on the 18th at Oak Hill to set up victory and said later that doing that "had taken him to his max".

Brookline in 1999 was memorable for one wrong reason – the green invasion by the Americans during Justin Leonard's singles match against Olazábal – and one right one – Ben Crenshaw saying on Saturday night "I have a feeling".

Thereafter came a record Europe victory under Langer's captaincy in 2004, amid a run of success that was American in its dominance and reminiscent of the way the competition ended in the first years of its life.

So where does this one stand in the pantheon? It was the greatest of the 17 I have seen, the most thrilling of all, the most remarkable in the way it went down to the last man on the last hole and that man being Tiger Woods. It equalled the greatest comeback by either side. Even 200 yards away writing in an air-conditioned tent, one shivered. Was it the cold or excitement or both? What a remarkable competition it is.

If I had to pinpoint the moment the competition changed and started to become the spectacle it now is, it would have to be the arrival of Ballesteros. Not so much his first appearance, in 1979, and certainly not in 1981 because he wasn't selected, but in the years thereafter. He quickly became the heartbeat for the team, its never-say-die leader, the man who set the standard for others to try to reach.

Last week's competition, at least in the eyes of Europeans anyway, was a celebration of the memory of the great man and that it was won against all odds made it unbearably poignant.

Prodigy now prowling riskier fairways

The Times, October 11, 1994

No tiger could have burned brighter than Eldrick "Tiger" Woods in Paris last week. From tee-off to teatime, Tiger would have eclipsed even the Sun King at Versailles, where, Sunday morning, he had his photograph taken in front the palace by *Sports Illustrated* magazine, and where, on Sunday afternoon, he anchored the United States to an 11-stroke victory in golf's world amateur team championship.

There have been better golfers than Woods at 18, though not many. And there have been blacks who have played golf, though very, very few. Woods, the son of an American soldier who was a Green Beret in Vietnam, and a Thai mother, is inarguably the best young black golfer to have emerged in the United States. He could not have arrived at a more auspicious time for a game that is trying to shed its whites-only, country club image. "Tiger is the right kid in the right sport at the right time," an American golf official said.

Two months short of his nineteenth birthday, Woods faces twin imposters, a Kipling reference that is as unavoidable as the Blake line about his nickname. He has to cope with the pressures attendant on the first man to win the US Junior Amateur and US Amateur titles, and with the nagging suspicion that some of the publicity is down to the colour of his skin.

Tiger, so nicknamed by his father after a colleague in Vietnam, could have chosen to take up a golf scholarship at any university in the United States. Instead, he selected the academically rigorous Stanford, one of the best in the country, in his home state of California. There will be no easy ride for him because he is a top sportsman. Woods has not yet settled on his degree course. Meanwhile, he is reading calculus, studying Portuguese cultural perspective, and doing his best to read the 18 books he has been set for the academic year.

So the pressure is on him, off the course and on it. The only black student, he was tied to a tree and taunted by fellow pupils on his first day at school. Later, he encountered racism when he played in junior tournaments. Earl Woods taught Tiger how to cope by using psychological techniques he had learned in the US Army.

The message seems to have got through. "My strengths are my mind, my short game and my ability to scramble," Tiger said. "My father had a strong mind. He gave it to me. I was not born with it." He has learnt how to turn racism to his advantage. "It makes me want to play even better," he said.

No golfer has received so much publicity at such an age. It is as if Woods is the man American golf has been waiting for. When he won the US Amateur in August, *The New York Times* ran a story about him on its front page, only the second time that golf has been so prominently displayed this decade.

The signs are that Woods is coping with all the pressures as well as he is playing golf. On Sunday afternoon, he knew it might all come down to him, the last of the four Americans on the course, and he played a solid round of 16 pars.

The one bogey he had was followed immediately by a birdie. Woods seemed immune to the pressure which affected the four Great Britain and Ireland players, for example, all of whom found water on one of the four closing holes. "Tell Tiger it's all set up for him," John Harris, a team-mate, said to Grant Spaeth, the American captain, on the 15th, which was to prove the breaking point for the Scotsman, Gordon Sherry, and Warren Bennett, of England. "The goal is a four." Nobody needed to tell Tiger what the goal was. He got his four.

"Tiger may be 18, but he has the maturity of someone in their late 20s or 30s," Allen Doyle, 46, another team-mate, said before comparing Woods with Phil Mickelson, 24, the previous outstanding American amateur. "Phil had more finesse, Tiger has more power. Phil had the edge as far as his short game, but Tiger has the edge in terms of accuracy off the tee. Tiger can focus better for 18 holes than Phil."

Woods is a phenomenon in a country full of phenomena: articulate, gifted and politically correct. The world of golf is at his feet. He carries a tremendous weight of expectation. "This young man is one of the best players to come out of this country in a long time," Butch Harmon, who has coached Woods as well as Greg Norman, said. "That is the good news. The bad news is that he has to live up to it now."

Game of life has royal seal of approval
The Times, October 2, 2001

Golf, the Duke of York said, late on a summer's afternoon, had made him a better person. It is not often that golf is credited with such properties. A.A. Milne described it as "the best game in the world at which to be bad", and Winston Churchill as "a good walk spoiled". But to talk of the royal and ancient game as one that shapes a character, by smoothing a rough edge here and there, was unusual.

The surroundings in which the remark was made gave it added emphasis. The Duke was talking golf in a room in Buckingham Palace that looked down The Mall and immediately outside it had an arrow-straight corridor as long as a hefty par-three. It did not take long to realise that talking golf was something Prince Andrew was able to do as well as he plays it, which is good enough to hold a handicap of 7.8 at Royal Liverpool.

"I used to get very upset at myself," he said, placing the ends of his fingers together, "and then I thought 'what's the point of shouting and screaming at myself?' so over the years I have become a much calmer person as a result of playing golf, I suspect." Having first become a calmer golfer? "Yes, because you can't affect the outcome." So golf has made you a better person, do you think? "Never thought about it, but probably. Certainly a calmer person because I can vent my frustrations on the practice ground.

"It is almost the same sort of thing as being able to talk about problems, d'you know what I mean? If you can talk to someone about them, then you get things off your chest. Each of us has a way of doing it. I suppose I have done the same thing in golf. Hitting that little white ball and trying to knock the skin off it is really quite useful. You can imagine it being all sorts of things, the head of your photographer…" His voice trailed off. The photographer ducked, nonetheless.

The Duke has lent his name to the Champion of Champions' Trophy, which will be contested by 13 champion junior golfers at Royal Liverpool this week. Among the competitors who will play 54 holes on Thursday and Friday are the boys' champions of England, Scotland, Wales and Ireland, as well as Grigory Bondarenko and Ouliana Rotmistrova, both from Moscow, who are the winners of the Faldo Junior Series for boys and girls respectively, and Pablo Martín, of Guadalhorce, in Spain, the British boys' matchplay champion.

"The idea was to try to get together all the winners of the other events that are held and play it at strokeplay so that they get an idea of where the pinnacle of junior golf is for that year," the Duke explained.

"It is not designed as a junior Open. It is designed as fun but at the same time it is encouraging people to realise that junior golf needs encouragement, particularly encouragement, in some cases, at club level to allow younger people to play and give them the same playing privileges as full members. Some clubs will and some clubs won't.

"There are some excellent golf clubs around that give their juniors a good time and encourage them. It is not that younger members should be given *carte blanche*. I think that younger members should be encouraged by the older members and mentored by them in the folklore and etiquette of the game. Things such as 'you should keep up to the game in front, not keep ahead of the game behind'. When you teach somebody how to play a foursome there should never be more than two people on the tee at any one time. The people out front should behave like forecaddies.

"The thought process behind this event was to encourage juniors into understanding strokeplay and the mentality of strokeplay and the individuality of strokeplay and realising that it is all yourself. You are playing the course and it is up to you either to attack or to defend. Golf is a wonderful game. It does not matter what background you come from. We should be encouraging everyone to have an equal opportunity to play the game."

So golf is a game for gentlemen, then? A long pause and then, slowly: "An interesting way of putting it. I don't think it is necessarily only for gentlemen. It is a game that, although steeped in tradition and gentlemanly behaviour, should have an element of needle and should have an element of excitement.

"You learn more about a playing partner on a golf course in anywhere between two and four hours than in any other discipline, more than you would if they wanted a job and came for an interview. You understand how they operate under pressure, how good they are at being distracted. Can they be a team player? There is so much more to the discipline and the playing of the game."

Is that one of golf's appeals, that it is not just a matter of moving a white ball from a tee to a green, but that it requires one to display so much more of one's character? "At the beginning you don't see that. Then you realise that the more you can deal with those anxieties and bad shots and turn the next one into a good shot, you soon learn how to deal with yourself."

When asked if the competition was one he would have liked to have played in as a junior, the word "yes" was out of the royal mouth before the question had been completed. "I played as a kid with a five-iron at Windsor, but never seriously. Had I started as a junior then I think it would have been a more structured game. I would not have been in control of my destiny and somebody would have had to deliver and take me and so I would jolly well have had to play the competition."

How much competitive golf do you play? "Not much. Don't get a chance," Prince Andrew admitted. "I played in a pro-am last year, playing off seven, and the two other amateurs were off 16 and 18 respectively. They played out of their skins and I didn't really have to play for the front nine. There is a danger that you start to lose interest at times like that – only two scores to count. As it was I came back in two over par having had a jumbo Kit Kat to give me a chocolate intake. I had to play better because these guys were playing so well. I had to compete."

He got up out of his chair and loped across to a side table and returned with a silver urn. "This is the trophy," he said. "It's from the Queen's vaults. It is a George V silver sugar basin made by Benjamin James Smith in Birmingham in 1810." Being the son of the monarch does mean that when you raid your mother's possessions for something to present there is little danger of coming up with a bashed-in pewter mug won at a fete.

After an hour or so of pure golf talk, the Duke suddenly looked at the man from Buckingham Palace who had been designated to sit in on the interview. "It doesn't mean anything to you this, does it?" he asked, a half-smile on his face. The man in question did, indeed, resemble someone who found himself in the middle of something he had neither a clue about nor much interest in. "You're completely bamboozled by this, aren't you?" the Duke guffawed.

The Duke will become captain of the Royal and Ancient Golf Club of St Andrews in September 2003, and his year of office coincides with the 250th anniversary of the R & A. The day he takes office begins at 8am with him driving from the 1st tee of the Old Course, accompanied by the salute of a cannon. Doubtless then he will remember not only to turn off his mobile phone when he plays, but not even to take it on to the course, a habit to which he has admitted.

"I am there [as captain] to celebrate golf and what golf has meant to the country and what it means to the R & A. I am not going to have a campaign against slow play and go out and say 'all you guys who play slowly should be shot'. It is more a celebration of the R & A."

After Ian Woosnam had been penalised for carrying too many clubs at the Open, I wondered what sort of clubs the Duke had in his bag and whether he embraced new technology? The answer came back as a joke. "Fourteen," he replied. Years ago he used to play at Balmoral carrying two clubs and a putter. He would hit two balls and play them both from the worse position. His best rounds are 76s at the Old Course at St Andrews and among his favourite memories are playing golf with, and taking money from, President Gerald Ford.

The future captain of the R & A is less worried than most people in golf about slow play, which may be a by-product of who he is rather than what he knows. It is hard to imagine the Duke and three playing companions being held up by a four-ball the way almost everybody else has been at some time or other.

"I think the speed of play could be improved but again a four-ball should take 3½ hours, I would suggest," he said. "You can do that if there are no delays. To most golfers, spending hours lining up a putt is not going to make a huge difference. That is where time can be saved. Everybody loses a golf ball. Everybody sprays them around. One has to accept those sort of delays. Time on the greens is where the problems are."

When it was pointed out that at many golf clubs 3½ hours for a four-ball would be exceptionally fast, the Duke replied: "Really? I am fortunate in that I play at Swinley Forest early in the morning so there is not usually anybody in front of me and so I can get round in 3½ hours for a four-ball.

"The other thing is, being a single-figure handicapper, I don't tend to spray the ball as far as I used to and because I know the ground I can usually step up to my ball, if I do go off the fairway, reasonably quickly because I know what the ground is like.

"I don't think you will change the speed of play apart from continuously reminding people that it is in the interests of the game to allow as many people to play as possible. It is a ridiculous situation at St Andrews that they have, on a not infrequent basis, four players, four caddies, four wives and four video cameras per four-ball."

Cricket and hockey had come naturally to the young Prince Andrew but, from the age of 13 to 30, he had not played golf at all. Then a naval colleague took him to a driving range at Weymouth in the autumn of 1989. "I hit a golf ball and thought 'uh, uh'. I dragged out a set of golf clubs that Sarah had won at her raffle and played with them. I tried to practise at Windsor.

"Doug McClelland [a teaching professional at Tilgate Forest, in Crawley] has shaped my swing. When I first asked him to come to Windsor to give me a lesson I think he thought it was a joke. He was told to go to Shaw Farm Gate and only when someone met him there did he believe that his assignment was serious."

Some time after this, Prince Andrew rang McClelland at his home. One of McClelland's children answered and asked who was calling. "The Duke of York," the Duke said. "Dad," the child yelled out. "The pub's on the phone."

Sense of loss leaves golf in shock

The Times, October 28, 1999

There is an empty parking space at The Champions Golf Club and 29, not 30, men will compete for the Tour Championship, which begins this morning. David Duval's car is parked on one side of the space and Vijay Singh's on the other. In between, a printed sign rests on a green metal railing and says: "Reserved for Payne Stewart".

But Stewart is dead now, and in Houston, where the US Open champion should have competed in the Tour Championship, and in Orlando, where he lived and left soon after nine o'clock on that fateful Monday morning, people are saddened beyond measure. There has been a death in the family, a sudden one, and it has left them tearful, puzzled and disorientated.

"I keep expecting to see him," Tiger Woods said. "I saw him just the other day. It is hard to believe he is not going to show up." The 72-hole tournament has been altered so that 27 holes will be played both today and Saturday, leaving tomorrow free for everyone to fly to Orlando, to the First Baptist Church of Orlando at which the Stewart family worship, for the memorial service. At 7.45 this morning, Tom Lehman will say a prayer during a service on the 1st tee of the Champions course. A lone piper, on the 1st fairway, will bring the service to an end.

Stewart should have parked the bonnet of his car against the metal railing, where now are six bunches of flowers. The flowers demonstrate the measure of the outpouring for the man whose courtesy towards Colin Montgomerie at the Ryder Cup last month added to his substantial following.

They are smaller than the enormous bunch of yellow roses sent by Shaquille O'Neill, the basketball player, to the Stewart household and they say simple things such as "Gonna miss you, Payne. You always brought joy to the game." "Peace be with you, Payne. Peace be with your family."

But peace is one thing that cannot be with Stewart's wife and family, who are at home in Orlando. Every golfer in Florida, seemingly, has paid a visit to the Stewart household. Alicia O'Meara, Mark's wife, has not left since Monday. Ian Baker-Finch dropped by. The Azingers, the Hochs and the Janzens have visited. This is the caring side of a caring game. "There's been a lot of crying," one person who was there said.

In Houston yesterday, no one was thinking of golf. They thought instead of the golfer who had become so famous because of his dress and earned himself so much popularity. They thought, too, of Tracey Stewart, who watched television on Monday trying to follow the story of the pilotless plane in which her husband had perished.

They thought of Aaron, 10, and Chelsea, 13, the two Stewart children, and of Norman and Shirley Ferguson, Tracey's parents, who had flown from Australia to be with their daughter and son-in-law for a short holiday. It was going to be such a wonderful time. They were going to watch him receive a special tribute from the city in which he lived.

Stewart was to be given the key of Orlando, the first sportsman and only the 52nd person in the city's history to be so honoured. A few weeks earlier, Stewart and Tracey had surprised officials at their church by making a donation of half a million dollars to help the church to build facilities for school athletes. Stewart was like that.

After William Louis Stewart, his father, died of cancer in a Florida hospital in 1987, Stewart handed over the prize of $108,000 that he had won at the Bay Hill Classic in Orlando. "Orlando has lost a treasure," Glenda Hood, the mayor, said. "Payne Stewart had an incredible spirit and a faith that went far beyond the world of golf."

On Monday afternoon, Norman and Shirley Ferguson spent a blissful five hours at a theme park in Florida, somehow managing not to hear the appeals that were made over the public address system every 15 minutes.

Golf has not been spared tragedies such as this one, a real tragedy, and not what is often referred to as a tragedy when a golfer misses a short putt or takes a five when a par-four would have won a title.

In 1966, "Champagne" Tony Lema, who won the Open in 1964, died in a plane crash and in 1988 Davis Love Jr, the father of Davis Love III, lost his life in similar circumstances.

The golfers may be able to perform wonders with clubs in their hands, but at times like this they are clumsy, overwrought, ill at ease, just like everybody else. Woods has assumed the role of leader of, and spokesman for, the men gathered here for this event, and he explained how he had come to terms with Stewart's death in a way that would have benefited others, too. He recounted how he had just met Stuart Appleby, the Australian golfer whose wife died in an accident at a railway station in London last year.

"Stuey said 'he is in a place where Renay has just welcomed him and Renay is going to be there and will take care of him. He is going to be OK.' That was pretty eye-opening and put everything in perspective for me. I am walking down the fairway and occasionally I get a few flashes in my head of Payne and some of the memories I have. It is just a matter of dealing with it and coming to the peace and understanding that he is in a better place right now."

Jeff Sluman was practising alongside Stewart at the tournament last week. "I turned round and there was Payne with Aaron, his son," Sluman said. "They were laughing around, just having a good time. That is my memory of Payne and I will never forget it. He was riding off in a cart to play golf with his son."

Wales celebrates in all manner of ways
The Times, October 1, 2001

It was early yesterday morning when the Falcon 900 private jet taxied to a halt at Cardiff airport, having crossed the Atlantic from Canada. Sir Terry Matthews, its only passenger and travelling on his own plane as he has for nearly 30 years, was back in the country of his birth. The first man he saw as he stepped out of his jet stuck out a hand and said it to him straight and true: "Well done on the Ryder Cup."

The Mabinogion, that reserve of Welsh mythical lore, would have been enhanced if the man who had brought a £100 million-plus prize to his home country at a time of economic stress were larger than life, had got off the plane with a cigar in one hand and a magnum of champagne in the other, and burst into songs of praise.

Matthews, 58, is a big businessman but not someone who puts a lot of store in personal aggrandisement. He had heard that Celtic Manor had won golf's biggest prize in an hotel room in Nashville, Tennessee, where he was making a routine telephone call at lunchtime on Thursday to his sister back in Wales. Midway through the conversation, Kay Dawes interrupted. "Hang on a minute, Terry," she said. "They're saying something about the Ryder Cup on the BBC News. Have a listen." And she put the telephone next to the television, a Heath Robinson way of communicating such important news to a man whose business life and billions of pounds have been devoted to, and come from, developing cutting-edge technology.

Now at Cardiff airport, Matthews adjusted his dark jacket, brushed his thinning hair and said quietly: "This is not for me, Terry Matthews, this is for Wales. The economic spin-off for the country will be enormous, incalculable. It is a monster win for Wales and Wales needed that sort of win to regain some self-confidence and self-respect. There is a monster steelworks closing down and that is a big setback economically. It is uplifting to the spirit of the entire area. This will affect the national spirit. We can say we have just won something."

Even as Matthews spoke, the cries of "foul" and "unfair" that had been raised at the news that his massive resort on the side of the M4 near Newport had won the right to stage the 2010 Ryder Cup had not died away. Fiery Scots had suggested that the bid process was not transparent and that it had not been fair. Indeed, towards the end of last week, there were rumours of legal action being prepared against the PGA and the European Tour, the two bodies that comprised the Ryder Cup Committee that made the decision.

"I wouldn't do that," Matthews said. "I am trying to emulate the Home of Golf in everything I do. You can't beat Scotland for golf. Who do I get to look after my courses? Jim McKenzie, a Scot. I have a large research department outside Glasgow. I bow to no one in my admiration of Scotland but look, they've got the Ryder Cup. They have got four more years in which to market themselves. This is a terrific thing for them."

As the euphoria in Wales began to die down, it became clear that there were two significant events that helped Celtic Manor to beat off the challenges of Scotland, represented by Gleneagles, venue of the 2014 Ryder Cup, Loch Lomond, Turnberry and Carnoustie, to stage the world's third-biggest sporting event. The first was that a bid document was prepared and tenders were called for. Now if there is a man who knows how to shave tens of thousands of pounds from one part of a bid document in order to add hundreds of thousands of pounds to another, then it is Matthews.

"Sandy Jones [chief executive of the PGA] tipped me off that it was going to be a bid process," Matthews said. "That's right up my alley." A few days before bids closed last October, Matthews sat down with his team at Celtic Manor. Wales's bid to stage the 2009 Ryder Cup [as it then was] amounted to £35 million. Matthews thought it was not enough. A couple of hours' brainstorming, with Matthews's gruff, forceful voice leading the discussion, and that figure had been raised to £50 million.

Another factor that contributed to Wales's success was the speed with which they drew in the regional assembly, led by Rhodri Morgan, First Minister, and made it a countrywide bid. This enabled extra funding to be made available to the bid from the start. Of course, it did not harm Wales's chances that objective funding money from the European Union was to be available to parts of Wales between now and 2010, which could be used to help appropriate ventures in the appropriate parts of Wales.

Scots were saying last week that this tipped the scales Wales's way. But it was not because funding can only be used in the parts of the country that are below a certain income per capita figure. Celtic Manor is not in such an area. What won it for Wales was Matthews's considerable personal wealth, his commitment to the cause and his belief that it would mean more for Wales to receive the Ryder Cup than it would Scotland. These, and the well-enunciated admission by Ken Schofield, the executive director of the European Tour, that money makes the world go round; Matthews has been lavish in his support of the Tour.

Late yesterday, Matthews was closeted with his advisers on the sixth floor of Celtic Manor. There was an air of quiet jubilation in the room, even though outside rain was coming down just as it had during the Wales Open in August. Matthews went out onto the balcony in the rain and from there he could have looked across towards the Wentwood Hills course, which requires new holes and a new clubhouse to satisfy the requirements for the Ryder Cup. When he came back in, he appeared to be bone dry. Clearly, the rain was all water off the back of Matthews the billionaire, the miracle man, the man who had secured the Ryder Cup for Wales.

Montgomerie is a Ryder Cup captain true to his words

The Times, October 5, 2010

The interviewer for an American television network leant forward, a microphone in his hand. "So is Monty the split personality he seems to be to us?" he asked. "Yes," I said.

I described him as having two sides to his character. In this, Colin Stuart Montgomerie, though four months past his 47th birthday, resembles the little girl with the curl in the middle of her forehead. "When she is good she is very, very good, but when she is bad she is horrid."

From the time he arrived at Celtic Manor on Friday, September 24, there had been only one side of Montgomerie on show – the determined, intelligent, articulate man, a born leader. He was on a mission to regain the Ryder Cup, a mission he knew would bring financial stability to the European Tour for another few years as well as enormous personal glory.

If Montgomerie does nothing more in his life, he can be assured that the triumph he engineered at Celtic Manor will serve as a perfect coping stone to his career.

On one of the most recent times Montgomerie had been at Celtic Manor, it was to discover that his car had been damaged while it was being parked for him and while it was being repaired he had to be driven back to Scotland with his father. This time, though, there were no crashes. For ten days, from September 24 to yesterday, Montgomerie was faultless.

Montgomerie likes to portray himself as a broad-brush man. In reality he is a controller, a man whose attention to detail can be forensic in its intensity. For example, he wanted his vice-captains to report every shot to him over the team radios. No wonder he went through three batteries by Saturday night.

"I need to know every detail," Montgomerie said, adding and repeating himself as he so often does in what might be termed a nervous tic, "every detail."

Monty, the detail man, had two speeches prepared weeks ago. He knew what he was going to say, win or lose. Thus when he was interviewed at the gala concert he was able to point out not only that he had played in eight Ryder Cups, but also that he had been on the winning side five times. Corey Pavin, the US captain, alongside him, must have smiled inwardly at the smooth way Montgomerie scored that point. He could not match that.

Knowing what he wanted to say at all times ensured Montgomerie did not make the mistake that Pavin had at the opening ceremony of leaving out one of his team – and in Stewart Cink, the tallest at that.

Clearly, Montgomerie had learnt one of the key lessons of Nick Faldo's captaincy at Valhalla in 2008, namely write your speeches, deliver them perfectly and without variation, remember the names of your players. Most of all that he, even he, needed help as he marshalled his 12 men.

Montgomerie appointed four vice-captains and welcomed with open arms José María Olazábal, who arrived at the weekend, to act as a fifth. Sometimes tongue-tied, often repetitive, Montgomerie was word-perfect in public this week.

As Pavin found, the good Monty is a hard man to outwit. Montgomerie saw no need to narrow the fairways at Celtic Manor to disadvantage the longer-hitting Americans, but he did ensure the rough was thick and the greens slower than the Americans were used to.

Then, with no attempt at subtlety, he openly called for the leaderboards to be reconfigured so they showed more of the state of the match, which of course happened to be being dominated by Europe. "I want a sea of blue," Monty said, later thanking "some techie" who had been up all night on Saturday to ensure that this was done.

Montgomerie is also a hard man to outplay. It is arguable that his seven successive victories in the Order of Merit – and also his eighth six years later, by which time he was 42 – should carry at least as much coinage as one major championship.

He is inclined to argue they are. "Oh yes, I would have thought so, wouldn't you?" he says when the subject is raised, that plausible smile spread over his face. At such times it takes a hard man to disagree.

Yet it remains an intriguing question to ask why this man who could so dominate Europe, never chose to base himself in the US and test himself in the hardest school of all. Was it out of a sense of family unity, not wanting to uproot his children, that made him unprepared to move out of an arena in which he was both comfortable and successful? Was it as a result of this decision that he didn't have his game sharpened to a finer pitch and was found wanting when the game's greatest prizes seemed at his mercy? We will never know.

One also doesn't really know who Colin Montgomerie is. He was born in Scotland yet grew up in England. He went to public school in Scotland but only for a year. He is said to be familiar with links golf because of his Scottish background, yet he was moulded much more on Ilkley golf course than Royal Troon. Where is his constituency?

The Scots regard him with a raised eyebrow, thinking him less of a Scot than, say, Sam Torrance. Torrance could do cartwheels down Sauchiehall Street, be found bleary-eyed and comatose in a hedgerow, live in Surrey and vote Conservative and still be referred to as a gallus wee laddie. Not so Montgomerie, who is regarded as Scottish by the English, as part English by the Scots.

Now, though, both countries will unite in hailing him for his captaincy in Wales.

Clearly the Ryder Cup is the summit of his life, as a player and being unbeaten in eight singles, and now in becoming a winning captain at his first attempt. Montgomerie was astute when he had to be, not afraid to dish out a tongue-lashing when he needed to.

He himself described that ticking-off speech as a "bollocking" on radio, a term that was later modified to a "roasting". It worked. From a couple of rather lacklustre sessions of play in which Europe scored half as many birdies as the Americans yet were only two points behind, Montgomerie rallied his men to such effect they went on to be undefeated in the next six matches.

This surge to the front was what underpinned Europe's victory. After arguably the finest session of play by a Europe team in the history of the Ryder Cup, victory still had to be confirmed and there were moments on a magnificently thrilling last afternoon when it looked as though the US might snatch a tie.

As Graeme McDowell and Hunter Mahan teed off on the 17th, Montgomerie was standing with Gaynor, his wife, half the way down the hole and looking, according to one witness, as "near to hyperventilating as anyone could be".

"This was the greatest moment of my golfing career," Montgomerie said. "Personally it means nothing to me. But this [touching the trophy as he spoke] is in Europe and we are delighted that it is. This is a one-hit time and I will not be doing this again I can assure you of that."

Nonetheless, he has created an intriguing question. What does he do for an encore? The Senior Tour? Hardly. Becoming a politician, an ambassador for Scotland? Hardly. In the short term he has personal matters to attend to with Gaynor and his and her children.

But in the long term? Working out how to follow a near-perfect performance in a beautiful valley in Wales is one question to which he, the meticulous man who was not baffled by anyone or anything during his captaincy, has still to find an answer.

Of the hundreds of questions he faced during his captaincy this may be the hardest question of all with which to deal.

Victory that made Europe smile

The Sunday Times, October 4, 1987

To appreciate the full measure of Europe's thrilling victory in the Ryder Cup, we must return to that July day when Tony Jacklin won the Open at Royal Lytham. It was 1969, and in golfing terms the decade had been dominated by Arnold Palmer, Jack Nicklaus and Gary Player. To prove he wasn't a temporary phenomenon, Jacklin won the US Open 11 months later. With his jaunty walk and gleaming smile, he laid the foundations of European golf.

Peter Oosterhuis helped the cause. He wasn't as good as Jacklin, but he came third in the 1973 Masters. John Jacobs made an important contribution, too. In the early 70s the tournament director general of the Professional Golfers' Association saw sooner than most that for golf to grow it had to embrace the Continent.

As soon as it did, events moved fast. Seve Ballesteros burst on to the scene in 1976, and we know what he has achieved. A few years later, Bernhard Langer emerged from West Germany. By the time of the 1983 Ryder Cup, European golf had reached unprecedented heights. The team of four Scots, four Englishmen, two Spaniards, a Welshman and a West German went within one point of an historic first victory on American soil. In 1985, Langer won the Masters, Sandy Lyle the Open and Europe the Ryder Cup. It was all falling into place.

How appropriate, then, that the coping stones of the wall of European golf should have been slipped into position in an American town called Dublin by a European team captained by Jacklin.

In Ohio last Sunday, grown men wept at the conclusion of the most thrilling sports event many of them had seen. For them, the events that led to Europe's win exceeded Australia's victory in the America's Cup, England's triumph in the 1966 World Cup and the 1971 British Lions' defeat of the All Blacks.

Jacklin twice broke down and cried as he tried to explain on American television what victory meant to him. Ken Schofield, boss of the European Tour, went so far as to congratulate me, as if I'd had anything to do with it. Not wishing to appear churlish, I accepted his congratulations – and then burst into tears, too. It may seem an odd way to celebrate the event that put a smile on the face of Europe, but if you'd been there you might have done the same thing.

One memory that will remain forever is of hundreds of fans surrounding Ballesteros in adoration. By then Eamonn Darcy had been lionised with a noisy rendering of *Cockles and Mussels*, and had flexed his muscles in acknowledgement. And Nick Faldo and Ian Woosnam had ripped off their shirts (and that's all, thankfully) and thrown them to the crowd. Then it was the turn of Ballesteros to be hauled up on a trestle table to autograph visors, scorecards, gloves, programmes; anything, in fact, that was thrust at him. Not since the 1984 Open at St Andrews had he looked so happy and carefree in the presence of so many people.

His role had been immense in the preceding days. All week he had been a leading light at the team meetings in Jacklin's villa. We *can* beat them, we *will* beat them, he kept on saying, and he had been saying so privately to friends for months before. In the opening morning's foursomes, he played the finest golf I've ever seen. This poses a question. In shepherding José María Olazábal through the opening days of his first Ryder Cup, did Seve rediscover the joy of golf, something that has been missing from his own game? Lately he has given the impression that golf has become a tedious chore. While playing, he has more often than not looked like a man having a bad day at the office. Some people gain an inner resolve in moments of despair. Has he found himself in victory?

And not only Ballesteros. In the two months since he won the Open, Nick Faldo has shown signs of levity bordering on lightheadedness, which has made him more approachable and sympathetic. Last Sunday evening he frolicked like a pit pony beginning its annual holiday. It was as if he had realised that the Americans would never again represent such an unattainable target. For Faldo, read Woosnam, Lyle, Torrance, Clark, Darcy and Olazábal.

Everyone waits to see how American golf will react to all of this. If past form is anything to go by, then the US PGA will invite all the members of the European team to next year's championship, as they did after 1985. It is also possible that the Europeans will be invited to the Tournament Players' Championship in Florida next March. But what about the Masters? Will traditional policies be bent to accommodate the whole team?

Hord Hardin, chairman of the Masters, was firm. "Let me tell you once and for all that we will not invite the entire team," he said, in a voice that brooked no argument. "Scotch foursomes don't mean a hell of a lot to me. Four-balls don't mean anything, either. That's a different kind of contest. I hope that we can include some players from the team whose records are great aside from Scotch foursomes." But he didn't sound very hopeful.

Tony Jacklin drives off into the sunset
The Sunday Times, October 2, 1983

Tony Jacklin had taken the family dog, an 11-year-old Labrador, to be put down, arranged for the cats to be given to friends and invited his parents-in-law out to dinner. The Rolls had been sold, the BMW too. By Friday, after a last look around the house in Jersey, his home for the last eight years, he caught a mid-morning plane to London en route to Spain and thence into retirement from competitive play.

From now on Jacklin, the best golfer Britain has produced since the war, will be found in a rented house by the side of the 3rd green at Sotogrande Old Course, Spain. He is to become Commissioner of Golf at Las Aves, the new course at Sotogrande, the famous resort just east of Gibraltar.

Jacklin, who is not yet 40, is calling it a day earlier than many golfers. Though the legendary amateur, Bobby Jones, gave up at 28, Arnold Palmer is still competing fiercely at 54. Jack Nicklaus is only a few months from his 44th birthday, and the greybeard of the European Tour, Neil Coles, is 49.

Since he turned pro at 17, Jacklin has reached heights that almost everyone else only dreams of. In one incandescent spell between July 1969 and June 1970, he took the Open at Lytham, and then spread-eagled the field in the US Open, winning by seven shots. For a time his grinning face, with teeth as regular and gleaming as a newly painted picket fence, peered out from advertisements. He commanded £3,000 for a day's clinic, £2,000 in appearance money at tournaments. He was 26, famous and a millionaire.

But Jacklin has also sunk to lower depths than most golfers of recent times. He cracked under the strain of trying to live up to his former achievements; his putting went to pieces. He used to wake up at night sweating with fear at the thought of having to play golf the next day. He consulted doctors, hypnotists, scientists.

Through it all, Jacklin has gained some solace from the loyalty of his supporters. They followed him with the same enthusiasm, faith and even touch of awe that such people had shown for Henry Cooper, and later would accord to Bill Beaumont. Jacklin, they felt, was truly an English sporting hero.

But not until the end of the decade that had begun so gloriously did their hero give them one last opportunity to cheer. That recovery was confirmed when Jacklin won last year's PGA title. "Eeeeee, it's wonderful to be back," he said at the time, puffing out his cheeks and holding up his trophy. But it didn't last.

His seventies experiences had marked him for life, and now he simply doesn't want to spend any more time playing tournament golf. "I'm finding it boring," Jacklin said in a contemplative moment in Jersey last week. "I've learned a terrific amount doing what other people thought I ought to do in certain situations. If doing well means anything in this world, it means the right to suit yourself." Gesticulating towards Spain, he continued: "That is the place of my choosing."

At Sotogrande, Jacklin will oversee the golf shop, and cosset the enthusiastic golfers he hopes will be attracted by his presence. It sounds menial work for a man who was, for a time, one of the world's best golfers.

"Look," said Jacklin forcefully. "McCormack [his manager] could come to me and say 'we've got you half a million dollars over five years to represent a golf complex in Florida,' and that wouldn't stimulate me a bit. It's not even on my chart. I don't need half a million dollars. I need involvement, and that's what I've got."

He ordered another Guinness and the conversation turned to the state of the European golf tour which had been built up around him, at one time its only truly international star. Now, he says, too much emphasis is placed on raising the prize money, and too little on the condition of the courses they play on.

"You don't put some great musician on a goddamn joanna in a pub if he's going to give a recital. You give him a Steinway, and that's the way it ought to be. But with us they've always got some bloody excuse about the courses. Either it's the hot summer, and if it isn't that, then it's the cold winter, and if it isn't that then it's the tsetse fly coming in from Africa."

This sounded like a man who had lived in a glass house throwing stones. For ten years Jacklin had sat on the players' committee, a body that should have concerned itself with such matters. "You're right, we should have done something," he admitted. "I fought like hell for ten years, but I don't care enough any more."

A rueful look came over his face as he realised that two weeks before he captained the European team against the Americans in the Ryder Cup wasn't the most tactful time for such an outburst. But then that's Jacklin.

He headed back towards his car. Back at his house, a lady from the dry-cleaners was waiting with some clothes belonging to his wife, Vivien. The telephone hadn't rung tor hours. Jacklin pointed out the mat from which he practised his wedge shots, chipping over the house. It was clouding over, and fog, which had closed the airport that morning, was threatening once again.

Amputee takes the balanced approach to his game and wins many admirers

The Times, October 2, 2009

At Kingsbarns golf course yesterday morning, I saw one of the most remarkable sights I have come across in 50 years of playing and watching the sport. My eyes widened in admiration at seeing Manuel De Los Santos, 25, a one-legged man who plays without the help of an artificial limb, boom 300-yard drives from a tee and chip with the deftness of Severiano Ballesteros.

Wait until he putts, I thought to myself. He won't be able to stop himself from wobbling. Guess what? Had you not seen with your own eyes that he could hold himself so steady you could not have moved him if you pushed him, you would not have thought it possible that he was balancing nearly 80 kilograms of bodyweight on one leg while swinging his putter in a silky-smooth stroke.

Golf is a game of balance. You transfer your weight to one side on the backswing, to the other on the downswing. It is a game that requires one's base to be stable to allow the moving parts of the upper body to do their stuff. Bob Torrance, the distinguished coach, believes the legs to be the all-important part of the golf swing.

Yet on an exposed course where the wind was present during the first round of the Alfred Dunhill Links Championship, here was a man with the narrowest of bases hitting the ball crisply, powerfully and much more accurately than many two-legged golfers.

"I am not sure about technique; I prefer to watch the ball flight," Gavin Dear, one of De Los Santos's professional playing partners, said. "All I can say is that Manuel is in control of all aspects of his game. He strikes it great, he putts well. Sometimes you see guys who don't rotate on the backswing, he rotates. His ball flight says he is a good golfer. I had heard he was a quality golfer and now I have played with him I can see that he definitely is. I think he may be the best three-handicapper I have ever seen."

Blind men play golf and so do one-armed players. Most one-legged golfers have a prosthesis to help to support themselves. I have seen Ballesteros hit a ball over 200 yards from on his knees and a trick-shot artist drive a ball from a four-foot high tee. But until yesterday I had never seen a man play golf on one leg entirely unaided, and to be honest I would not have thought it possible that it could be done so well by someone who took up the game seven years ago only after losing his leg in a car accident.

Manuel De Los Santos plays an approach shot during the Melbourne Golf Invitational
Pro-Am at Woodlands Golf Club on November 12, 2012 in Melbourne, Australia.

De Los Santos, who was born in the Dominican Republic, was a promising baseball player until that accident. Having moved to France with Elena, his wife, he turned to golf in April 2004.

Now consumed by the old game, he hops to the address position and takes a couple of hops after he has hit the ball to disperse the force with which he has hit it. He easily drops almost to the ground to retrieve his ball from the hole or to push his peg into the ground. He hops around on the greens having handed his crutches to his caddie.

"Many amputees play golf, but with a prosthesis," Elena said. "Manuel has a very, very strong right leg from his baseball and a strong back, too. He has very, very developed arms from walking six or seven miles in a round of golf on a pair of crutches. I think he is resistant to pain. He is mentally as strong as he is physically strong."

Hugo Corvet, a friend from Paris, began golf at the same time as De Los Santos. "I remember one day I saw him practising in a bunker first thing in the morning," he said. "When I left at the end of the day he was still there, still in the same bunker. He has so much will."

His physical strength comes from doing 100 crunches each day to reinforce the core muscles of his body and from walking everywhere on crutches, often carrying his golf bag or another bag. Other than that, he does nothing other than hit balls – 2,000 a day when he started the game, maybe 200 daily now.

He taught himself using Tiger Woods's instruction book to help him. "Tiger Woods is my hero," De Los Santos said. "I love Tiger Woods. I play against him on his PlayStation and I win all the time. When I play golf I don't think about my handicap, I think, 'Punch the ball, punch the ball, punch the ball.' "

Wind is less of a problem for this remarkable man than rain. "Rain is his enemy because it can make him slip," Elena said. Steep downhill lies are difficult, too, because he cannot take up a stance and likewise certain lies in a bunker would be close to unplayable. Yet even today's expected bad weather does not dampen his enthusiasm. "I am so happy to be here in Scotland," he said. "I am very happy when people come to look at me. I can feel their love for golf, the respect they have for the game."

You watch this man and you admire his athleticism and his unyielding spirit, and a part of you is humbled. "He is so strong, his forearms are like thighs," Richard Bland, his professional playing partner, said after the two men had combined to be six under par and in 44th place after the first round, with De Los Santos going round in 76 for four over par. "He is an inspiration."

Am I Popeye or Olive Oyl? It's all about striking the right balance

The Times, October 18, 2001

Sweaters, short sleeve, 2. Sweaters, long sleeve, 4. Sweaters, polo-neck, 3. Socks, thick, 3 pairs. Socks, thin, 6 pairs. Mittens, 1 pair. Gloves, woollen, 1 pair. Hats, peaked, 1. Hats, woollen bobble, 1. At last, enough clothes to survive a winter in Siberia were in my suitcase and I headed north for a week's golf at St Andrews. Just to be safe, George Plimpton's *The Bogey Man*, the definitive work by an amateur golfer participating in professional events, was included in the luggage as well as a copy of *The Mystery of Golf* by Arnold Haultain with an afterword by John Updike. If you can't play the game, you can at least be well-read.

To take part in a pro-am event such as the Dunhill Links Championship is an experience only rarely accorded to golf correspondents. More normally, one's lot is to walk a few holes watching a particular player and hang around to ask searching questions about why he preferred a four-iron for his second shot to the 14th when, surely, a five-iron was the correct club?

Watching from near the ropes is the common currency but now I was to be inside, playing one round each at Kingsbarns, Carnoustie and the Old Course at St Andrews with Tony Johnstone, my professional partner, in the company of David Howell and Trevor Eve, the actor, Howell's amateur partner.

So it was that on Tuesday evening in the St Andrews Old Course Hotel, I shared a lift with Colin Montgomerie, exited the lift with him and walked along the corridor until I discovered my room was almost next to his. "You'll hear the click, click, click from my room," I said.

"What, of you tapping the keys on your computer?" Montgomerie asked. "No, of me putting on the carpet of my room. The click of the putter on the ball will be followed a few seconds later by the thud as the ball hits my bedroom door."

Montgomerie laughed. "Play well," he shouted over his shoulder.

There were two schools of thought as to how I should prepare for the singular honour of competing in an event with a prize fund of $5 million that may determine the outcome of this year's Order of Merit. The hard school was that I should be completely disdainful of practice and waft up to the 1st in a champagne-fuelled haze with a silk scarf loosely tied around my neck. The other was that I had bloody well better not make a fool of myself.

The latter view won and, in mid morning on Tuesday, I collected a bucket of balls on the practice ground at the Old Course and carried them to a position where I hoped I would be able to slice and hook and top golf balls to my heart's content. Bob Torrance took a close look and turned away, then Ernie Els and his retinue came over and started practising next to me.

The best way I can describe how I felt at that moment was if I was an aspiring writer and had just crafted a few clunking sentences on to my computer when Updike sat down next to me and said: "How are you doing, John? Can I have a look at what you've written?"

Bob Torrance saved my blushes. He came over and, in a guttural torrent, some of which I understood, made me stand straighter and quieten down my hands. "Remember, John, the legs are crucial," he growled. "The game goes from the ground up and not from the head down. It's no good having arms like Popeye if you've legs like Olive Oyl."

Torrance had a way with aphoristic instructions. At the draw in the hotel that night, John Nash, a pupil of Torrance's, mentioned another aphorism. "I was swinging a bit quickly one day and Bob said: 'Remember, John, the film doesn't begin until 6.15.'"

On Tuesday afternoon, Michael Lynagh, the Australian rugby union player, and I had played a round at Kingsbarns with Gordon Brand Jr and Marc Farry. On the second green Brand, a Ryder Cup player in 1987 and 1989, could take no more of my putting. "For God's sake, John, everything's moving. Keep still," he said. "You've got more moves than Shakin' Stevens."

It is noticeable that, of the 156 competing amateurs, footballers and cricketers seemed to have the lowest handicaps. Rugby's Zinzan Brooke, playing off 10, cricket's Nasser Hussain, 14, and Lynagh, 12, were somewhat overshadowed by Kapil Dev's 3, Alan Hansen's 2 and the 4.3 of Marco van Basten. Indeed, if the reports of the quality of Kapil's striking and the distance he hits the ball are to be believed, he could turn professional. He began playing only in 1995 but, clearly, has found a synergy between the requirements of cracking a cricket ball through the covers and those of whacking a golf ball from a tee.

Hugh Lewis, the former touring pro, used to say how much more agreeable tournament golf would be if one could play practice rounds, then go home before the pressure of the event was brought to bear. There was no escape for him and there is no escape for me, either.

Armed with my yellow go-farther tees supplied at Wentworth last week by Nick Faldo, my anvil for a driver, my game-improvement irons that have a sweet spot as big as Fife and my Hi-Brid three-piece technology, high-velocity thread-wound golf balls that are less affected by spin and wind and thus fly for ever, I shall take to the tee at Kingsbarns at 9.24 this morning.

Not without considerable trepidation, I might add. Those of a nervous disposition are advised to cover their eyes.

My fondness for Hoylake

Foreword from *Mighty Winds ... Mighty Champions: The Official History of The Royal Liverpool Golf Club* by Joe Pinnington (Guy Woodland, 2006)

"It is a great honour for me, a stranger, to be asked to write some words of introduction to a book about Hoylake. As far as an alien can be a patriot, I am a Hoylake patriot; I love every cop of it and every breeze that blows across it, and I know no sensation more akin to home-coming than that of reaching Hoylake on a spring evening just in time to dash out on the links with a club or two before the darkness falls."

These are not my words but those of Bernard Darwin, a predecessor of mine as the golf correspondent of *The Times*. He wrote them, and many others, in the opening paragraph of his foreword for the first history of Royal Liverpool, one published in 1933. I have a copy beside me as I write. It is green, frayed and with a half-broken spine; just like a very old friend really.

Darwin's words seem to me to express my own feelings as well as if I had written them myself. I have a special fondness for Hoylake. I have been to the course no more than 20 times and played it only half as many, yet I have found myself forming an attachment to it that is as great as if I had been born overlooking it and had played it regularly since.

I cannot explain this affection, other than to say the club has insinuated itself into my heart. Down the years I have found myself thinking of it when I least expected to. For example, I was reading a newspaper at Christmas time and in an article that had nothing to do with golf I came across a reference to Aunt Agatha, one of the larger-than-life characters created by P.G. Wodehouse, a hero of mine. "Aunt Agatha," Wodehouse wrote, "had a voice of one who calls the cattle home across the sands of the Dee."

Hoylake is one of the aristocracy of golf clubs, and one of the most noble of those. Its full measure was first brought home to me at the Amateur Championship in 2000. The day after the final I flew to the US Open at Pebble Beach and as I settled back in my seat on the aeroplane I thought what a shame it was that, while Hoylake had hosted the first-ever international golf match between England and Scotland in 1902, the first match between Great Britain and Ireland and the USA (the forerunner of the Walker Cup) in 1921, and the first English Amateur Championship – as well as holding 10 Open Championships and generally doing more than its share of the initiating and staging of golf events – it had not held an Open since 1967. How disappointing it was that such a wonderful course, clearly in tip-top condition, was not scheduled to host the Open in the foreseeable future.

I wrote as much in both *The Times* and *Golf International*. I said I believed that the game's revered championships should be held on the game's best courses. I felt this way not just because that was how things were years ago, but because those courses provided vivid examinations for the modern players as well as offering a link with the past that should not be cut lightly, if at all. When a course as historically distinguished and good as Hoylake effectively disappears from public view it seems a shame, to say the least. A national treasure is less than half a treasure if it is not fully appreciated. "We are custodians of one of the great golf courses in the world. We have an obligation to share it," Harry McCaw – a past Captain of the Royal and Ancient Golf Club of St Andrews – said of his club, Royal County Down. The words could just as well have applied to Hoylake.

Happily, moves were afoot then to get Royal Liverpool back on to the rota of courses on which the Open could be staged, though I did not know it.

Far-sighted club members had struck up a relationship with far-sighted officials at the R & A and there had been much work going on behind the scenes involving a golf course architect, course changes, the local council, representatives of the railway network, the police and, of course, officials from Royal Liverpool itself. The result was that on February 12, 2001 it was announced that the Open, which had last been held at Hoylake when Roberto de Vicenzo won in 1967, would return there. When it would return was not revealed. No matter. The intent to return was the main thing. And anyway, it did not take long for the due date to become clear, too.

In December 2002 came the further announcement. The 2006 Open would be staged at Hoylake. "Royal Liverpool is a club with a long and distinguished history and we are delighted that we are now able to bring the Open back to this wonderful course…" Peter Dawson, now the chief executive but then the secretary of the R & A, said: "Many people have contributed to the agreements that underpin today's announcement and it is right that Royal Liverpool, which is justly regarded as one of Britain's outstanding links, will again be put to the test by the world's top golfers." Dawson made this announcement personally to the 100 or so members gathered in the clubhouse, who were as pleased at the news as they were at the realisation that 2006 would be the 50th anniversary of Peter Thomson's hat trick of Open victories.

All in all, a circle had been squared and everyone had reason to feel pleased with themselves. One of the most historic of all golf clubs, where John Ball Jnr and Harold Hilton were members and where Bobby Jones, the amateur, had won in 1930, his imperishable year, was back among the aristocracy of the competitive game. How fitting!

These words were begun in an hotel in San Diego, California, just about as far from Hoylake as it is possible to go. As I wrote them, in February 2005, I wondered what Darwin would make of all that was going on at Royal Liverpool at the moment as preparations for the 2006 Open moved on apace? What would he think of the changes to the course brought about by the R & A? What would he say about the caravanserai that will descend on Hoylake for the first Open here for 39 years? Indeed, what would he make of the fact that this foreword was being written on a laptop computer, the size of a briefcase, that shortly would be plugged in to a mobile telephone little bigger than a pack of cigarettes, after which a number would be dialled, a few buttons pressed and in little more time than it took Darwin to take a couple of practice swings, the words would have travelled from California to the Wirral?

I have one other reason for holding Hoylake as high in my esteem as I do. I call it the Turner connection. Other clubs have their credentials; some strong, some overwhelming. None, so far as I know, can count among their admirers one of the best painters produced by this country, namely J.M.W. Turner.

Turner was born in 1775 "… in London to working-class parents" goes the introduction accorded to him at the Turner, Whistler, Monet exhibition held at the Tate Britain gallery in London between February and May 2005. "During a career of over 50 years he produced an enormous range of landscapes in oils, watercolours and prints, collecting material through travels in Britain and Europe, especially Italy. Although his achievement was recognised by the art establishment, he was not admitted to its highest honours. His greatest champion was the critic, John Ruskin. Turner died at the age of 75. The work he bequeathed to the British nation had a profound influence on later painters, including Whistler and Monet."

What has Turner to do with Royal Liverpool? The answer is this: I think Turner acquired his remarkable ability to paint so vividly by spending time on the Wirral peninsula or across in north Wales and seeing the flaming sunsets that are so dramatic in this part of the world. Turner was able to keep the colours in his mind's eye until he came to use these images in his paintings. Think of *Sun Setting Over a Lake* which he painted between 1840 and 1845, for example. Think of *The Scarlet Sunset: a Town on a River*, painted a few years earlier. Look at the colours in his painting entitled *Venice: Looking Across the Lagoon at Sunset* and marvel at the colour in *The Burning of the Houses of Lords and Commons*.

The critic Sam Smiles talks of Turner's ability to produce "sumptuous colour". "The notion of a Turner sky, usually applied to spectacular sunsets, is widely understood, linking the artist with effects of weather which he alone is deemed to have noticed and celebrated in his art," Smiles wrote. I have evidence to support my claim that Turner visited this part of Merseyside. In a guide to the Wirral peninsula, a local author writes: "Local tradition has it that the immortal Turner came here to paint them [his sunsets]." I was told this on one of my first visits and I used it in one of my articles in *The Times*. A reader from the Wirral wrote to me and asked for the evidence to support my claim. "I found this comment fascinating and contacted the Tate gallery in London for clarification of your comments re Turner," he wrote. "However, they assured me that Turner never travelled to Merseyside and could find no trace of any sketches or paintings." I replied that I had not said he had done any sketches or paintings of this part of England, but that he had visited it on his travels and been inspired by what he saw. Turner was a considerable traveller.

Smiles tells us that he visited Bath and Malmesbury in the summer of 1791, Wales in 1792, the Midlands in 1794, south Wales and the Isle of Wight in 1795, the north of England in 1797 and Wales, again, in 1798 and 1799. Am I wrong to believe that on these travels, or at some other time, Turner was on the Wirral peninsula as dusk approached and was able to see the sun setting over Stanley Road with Hilbre Island in the foreground and the Welsh hills and Snowdonia in the background? That is an image I carry in my mind's eye and until someone can prove to me that Turner never went near this end of the Wirral peninsula that is what I shall continue to believe.

"Hoylake golf is never, or so it seems to me, slack or casual; it is the golf of men rigorously brought up, who will always do their best and die if need be in the last of their own sacred ditches. This is a spirit which is often lacking in those trained in softer, less exacting surroundings, and it fills the visitor with admiration and a little awe. To play on such a course must make a man humble so that he wants to learn, and proud so that he determines to be worthy of his school. What better blend of qualities could a golfer desire? What better place is there to instil them than this dear, flat, historic expanse of Hoylake, blown by mighty winds, breeder of mighty champions?"

Those were the words with which Darwin ended his foreword in 1933.

What a noble course it is! How stern a test of skill and strength! It may not at first sight be a beautiful one to the stranger who looks out with disappointed eyes on that expanse only broken here and there by its characteristic cops. To those who know it, it has a beauty of its own and let that suffice.

NOVEMBER

If you were trying to name the most momentous month for Tiger Woods you might go for April, that being when he won the first of three Masters, or July when he won his three Opens, or March because that's when the Arnold Palmer Invitational is held at Bay Hill and this is an event he has won eight times.

November would not be an obvious choice, yet the most extraordinary sequence of events to happen to him, and indeed to any sportsman, began in the early evening (Greenwich Mean Time) on a Friday in that month. An agency report landed in the offices of media outlets around the world saying Woods had been involved in a car crash.

It was one of those "where were you when?" moments. I know where I was the night that Winston Churchill died. I was outside his house in London and had been there for some hours. The day that word reached Britain of President Kennedy's assassination was a Friday and I was standing in the corridor of a packed train from Paddington to Kemble, Gloucestershire, on my way to spend the weekend at my parents' home. Word passed down the corridors and compartments like wildfire and my father confirmed it when I got off the train. When England won the rugby union World Cup in 2003 I was watching on a flickering television in Sea Island, Georgia, one of 100 people among whom were two Australians.

And at 7.35pm on November 27, 2009 I was awaiting the arrival of six dinner guests when the telephone rang. It was the office. "John, we're getting flash reports that Tiger Woods has been involved in an accident," Matt Dickinson, the Saturday sports editor, said. "We don't know how injured he is. Can you make some calls and see what you can find out? By the way, did you ever write an obituary of Tiger? We might need it."

The answer to that last question was no. For an hour or so panic was in the air, but then came word that Woods's accident was less serious than had been thought, which was a relief. However, what followed was a period when golf and Woods was all anyone talked about.

My mind went back to November 1999, the days when I wrote a weekly golf column in *The Times*. "Golfing legends continue to put Woods in the shade" was the headline. That November, I noted, Woods had won ten of his past 14 tournaments and was farther ahead of his rivals in the world rankings than any golfer had been since the rankings started 13 years earlier.

"The way Woods is playing suggests that his challengers are competing for second place. In Houston recently Davis Love III described Woods as being head and shoulders above everyone else. A few days later Colin Montgomerie said the same thing. 'I don't think anyone can catch Tiger in the foreseeable future,' Montgomerie, who had just become Europe's No 1 golfer for a record seventh year in a row, said. 'He has pulled even further ahead.'

"In this dominance of his sport, Woods puts one in mind of some of the great sportsmen and women of the twentieth century. Jahangir Khan, the squash player, went unbeaten for five years and seven months and 500 matches, 485 of them by a margin of 3-0. Herb Elliott, the great Australian middle-distance runner, won every mile and 1,500 metres race in which he competed. For a while Ed Moses was unbeatable over 400 metres hurdles and Martina Navratilova had 74 consecutive victories in 13 tennis tournaments."

I mentioned that Young Tom Morris had won four Opens in a row in the nineteenth century and set scoring records that were not beaten for 30 years. Between 1896 and 1900 there was no one to match Harry Vardon. He, James Braid and J.H. Taylor, golf's Great Triumvirate, dominated the Open for 20 years from 1894. I pointed out that Bobby Jones, the amateur, won half of all the tournaments he entered as well as the four major championships of his era in one four-month spell in 1930. Walter Hagen won five PGA Championships in the US in a row in the 1920s. Ben Hogan's 13 tournament victories in the US in 1946 and ten in 1948 – and Sam Snead's 11 in 1950 – paled into insignificance when compared with Byron Nelson's 11 tournament victories in a row, and 18 in all, in 1945. These were all remarkable achievements by the great and the good in Woods's sport.

"Woods's achievement, however … is to make a highly successful start since he turned professional in the autumn of 1996," I continued, concluding that he was "… good and you should do everything you can to catch sight of him at a tournament. But he is not that good. Not yet anyway."

On the night of November 27, 2009 the millions of words that had been written about Woods, the world's best-known athlete to that date, were soon to be overtaken by the tens of millions that were about to be written about him as his career took one bizarre turn after another.

As it happens, the following week I had been invited to go to the West Indies by officials from the Wentworth Club who were establishing a link with a golf club on Barbados. Normally it would be hard to give up a week in the West Indies in winter but the emerging story concerning Woods made it an obvious choice to remain in Britain and see which way the story went. Like Ben Johnson's disqualification from the 100 metres at the 1988 Seoul Olympics or Lance Armstrong being stripped of his seven Tour de France titles, both for doping, these are the news stories that run at full steam. So too did the Woods saga, from late November through to March. It only started to abate after the 2010 Masters.

Even without the Woods story, November had proved to be a more fruitful time than it might have seemed, whether it was the month when Sandy Lyle heard he had not topped the money list nor been named Player of the Year in the US (1988), when Tom Watson was named Ryder Cup captain of the US for the first time (1991), when Ernie Els returned to South Africa as the Open champion for the first time (2002) or when Nick Faldo was sacked by Fanny Sunesson, his long-time caddie (1999).

November wasn't just the month before Christmas, a time described by Ernie Els as being "the time to get the wheelbarrow out", by which he meant the time when players had one eye on making appearances in tournaments that would pay them a lot of money to participate. It was a good month to be writing about golf, however unlikely that might seem.

World sees new face of Tiger Woods but respect eludes him

The Times, November 27, 2010

Tiger Woods, once one of the most secretive of sportsmen, has authorised a campaign in the print media, on radio and on Twitter to help people to see beyond what occurred 365 days ago today. A calendar year after crashing his car into a fire hydrant and beginning the greatest fall from grace in modern sport, Woods has gone on the offensive.

No longer the No 1 golfer in the world, no longer the advertising symbol for three large companies that paid him an estimated $100 million, no longer the holder of a single golf title, Woods is presenting a different image from the one he projected a year and more ago. One of the most recognisable faces on the planet now portrays a media-conscious figure aware of his standing in the game and showing the responsibilities that go with it.

The man who used to be so secretive, dismissive of so many and resentful of intrusions into his private life has written an essay in *Newsweek*, the weekly current affairs magazine, and authorised Mark Steinberg, his notoriously taciturn manager, to give an interview to CNBC.com.

In an attempt to make himself seem more contemporary, Woods – despite being described by Steinberg as "not a technology geek" – has even started tweeting. "It's a great way of connecting with his fans en masse," Steinberg said.

"I am beginning to appreciate things I overlooked before," Woods wrote in *Newsweek*. "Some victories can mean smiles, not trophies, and life's most ordinary events can bring joy. Giving my son, Charlie, a bath, for example, beats chipping another bucket of balls.

"Making mac and cheese for him and his sister, Sam, is better than any restaurant. Sharing a laugh, watching cartoons or reading a book beats channel-surfing alone. Some nights, it's just me and the kids, an experience that's both trying and rewarding. Probably like the experience a lot of families have every evening around the world."

These words are indicative of a man who is trying to address imbalances in his life. It is understood that an important part of the divorce settlement between Woods and Elin Nordegren, his former wife, was that she would remain close enough in Florida for Woods to have regular access to their children.

Yet there are a number of good reasons why these self-centred manoeuvres may not have the effect that Woods and his advisers would like. The first is the extent of the interest in Woods's fall from grace. Passengers on a recent flight from Heathrow to Dubai were able to view a 50-minute film called *Tiger Woods, the Rise and Fall*, which contained interviews with some of the women who emerged in the weeks and months immediately after his car crash on November 27 last year.

Also interviewed in the programme was Woods's first coach, Rudy Duran, who hinted that some of what he did for Earl, Woods's late father, would suggest that Earl was the father of his son when it came to recreational activities.

A second reason is that because so much of his life has been a tissue of inaccuracies, there are good reasons for doubting the accuracy of this latest phase. We want to imagine that Woods is gaining genuine pleasure from seeing Charlie get soap in his eyes in a bath, from slightly overcooking Sam's burger, from reading the pair of them stories and hearing one or both begging him for one more story before the lights are put out.

But Woods and his agents on one hand, and the truth on the other, have been such distant companions these past months that we are legitimately entitled to ask why should we believe a word he says now.

It is a question one would expect to be asked in a corporate world burnt by association with Woods, but Steinberg has talked about "a society that is about second chances" and predicted that Woods could soon "be back where he was before" in terms of his commercial stature.

"We're close to a deal coming out of Asia and we're in discussions with a number of companies interested in being on his golf bag," he said. "We're definitely being aggressive."

Perhaps the greatest of the challenges facing Woods is to regain a semblance of normal life. There was an interesting contrast between the former world No 1 and the incumbent in Shanghai last month. At a function for the caddies, six of the world's top ten players turned up but Woods did not and Lee Westwood, the new world No 1, treated it as any other function.

At another function in China, Woods put in an appearance but spent most of the time talking to Colin Montgomerie while sheltering behind a rope. "IMG have kept a barrier around him," a manager said. "I am not sure whether it is cotton wool or barbed wire. It's a bit hard under those circumstances to have a bit of craic with your mates, isn't it?"

As he struggles to meet this challenge, Woods will also find that he will have to repel some very talented young men who have emerged in the past months.

Ryo Ishikawa, the Japanese also known as the "Bashful Prince", who turned 19 in September, is one. "He's just a great kid," Woods said. "He just won again recently, which I think was his ninth professional win. When I was his age, I was still playing college golf."

Rory McIlroy, 21, is another. A third is Matteo Manassero, an Italian who at 17 is not old enough to be served at a bar in Britain but who has become the youngest winner on the European Tour, in Spain, and finished second in Hong Kong in his past five tournaments. Then there is Rickie Fowler, the American, who will be 22 next month, 17 days before Woods turns 35.

Woods's life has been devoted to attempting to pass Jack Nicklaus's record of victory in 18 professional major championships. The events of the past year have lengthened the odds on his achieving this.

He might be helped slightly in that Phil Mickelson has health problems. If you think that starting in January 2000, Woods or Mickelson has won 16 of the past 44 major championships, that does not leave many for anyone else. Mickelson's health, never mind that of his wife and mother, might help to explain why three of this year's major champions had not won a major before.

Surely everyone wants to see Woods in full flight once more, to be given further demonstrations of those exceptional skills that carve vivid mental images into the mind's eye: the power of his swing; the uppercuts after a holed putt; the sight of his red shirts on a Sunday; holing out from a fairway; ramming in a 15-foot putt he knew he had to hole. Images and demonstrations of skill such as these come along once in a lifetime. We all want to see them again. But can he deliver?

Much emphasis is being put on Woods's swing reconstruction with Sean Foley, his new coach. "I finally got it going on Sunday, when I played the last six holes six under par and shot 65," Woods wrote on his website after a tournament in Australia. "I can't wait until I can do that for an entire tournament. It just takes time to build. Before, I couldn't even do it on the driving range and now I can. Now, after working with Sean Foley, I can do it on the golf course sporadically, then it becomes more consistent. Eventually, it becomes a full 18 holes and beyond that, a full tournament."

This is to overlook the fact that when Woods was at his most imperious, when he won four major championships in a row in 2000 and 2001, the tendency towards wildness that has always been a striking and puzzling aspect of his game was obscured by his remarkable powers of recovery. Then, Woods was the man you wanted to putt for your life. Do you now?

Montgomerie's opinion that rediscovering this aspect of his game is going to be a greater challenge than learning how to drive more accurately may be prescient.

In his new, media-friendly campaign, Woods seems to be asking for trust. He has tried to demonstrate that there is a degree of normality in his life now that he is tweeting, cooking for his children and bathing them before reading them bedtime stories. This is the dichotomy with Woods. He wants us to like him and applaud him for trying to be normal when he made few attempts to be likeable and normal in the past.

Woods is about to learn that it is not his God-given right to be respected. Nor, for that matter, that he must be trusted. Respect and trust are earned. It is sad but true to say that despite his apparent attempts to humanise himself, Woods does not yet seem worthy of respect or trust. He might in time but he does not now at the end of this, the most tumultuous year of his life.

Driving ambitions turn to sand

The Times, November 19, 2009

In many ways, what is happening in Dubai at the golf tournament that will decide the Race to Dubai – the European Tour's Order of Merit – and the Dubai World Championship is a microcosm of what has happened to this emirate in the past few years.

Everything from the golf course to the prize money is more or less in place and 58 of the top 60 eligible players have gathered, but the recession has ravaged its property-driven economy so much that nothing is what was promised. Dare one say it, there is something approaching a mirage here in the desert.

For example, the two events are taking place on the Earth Course at the Jumeirah Golf Estates, as trumpeted exactly two years ago. Yet Leisurecorp, the original company behind the project, has been subsumed by Nakheel, a larger property company, which is in talks with Dubai World, its parent company that is said to owe $40 billion. As a result of Dubai's economic troubles, the European Tour offered to accept a prize fund reduced by 25 per cent from $20 million for these two events, an offer that was accepted with alacrity.

A further example of not all being what it once seemed is that the Greg Norman-designed course on which the events will unfold over the next four days, while well conditioned, is little more than a resort course that was tweaked to make it more difficult after construction had begun, particularly the last four holes.

Then again, the players are competing for $15 million, which is hardly chicken feed. Yet the clubhouse is temporary, all the houses on the Jumeirah Golf Estates are empty and there is no mains electricity (it is provided by generators).

Dubai's nicknames tell the story of its astonishing rise over the past 20 years from an Arab trading station to its appearance as a massive construction site on which little construction is taking place.

At first, and for years, it could have been known as "Do-buy" for its affluence. Property was cheap, the sun always shone and golfers, who had hitherto gone to Portugal and Spain for golf in winter, could play for 11 hours a day on well-manicured courses in temperatures in the seventies.

Oil drove the economy, and when it became clear that the black gold would run out far sooner than in nearby countries, tourism and property became the focus, with huge housing projects such as the Palm developments and eye-catching hotels such as the 321-metre high, seven-star Burj Al Arab.

But the boom has ended and the cranes have fallen silent. Fewer properties are being built and many of those that have been built are not sold. Perhaps "Du-bye" is more appropriate.

Some claim that there are signs of a recovery. "I've lived here for 20 years," said Nick Tarratt, who works for the European Tour. "My property has doubled in price, then halved and is now on the way back up again. I can feel a sense of improvement. We will get through this."

George O'Grady, the executive director of the European Tour, was asked how confident he was that the Race to Dubai and the Dubai World Championship would be staged at the same venue and for the same prize money next year. "Extremely confident," he said. "As long as everything goes well, the contract is there, they intend to honour it. There's my answer: extremely confident."

For golf, it all began in Dubai in the late 1980s. The Dubai Desert Classic, named after the sponsor, Dubai Aluminium, was the first tournament on the European Tour to be held in the Gulf, in 1989. It was new. It was exciting. It was unusual. Professional golfers from Britain had been used to going to South Africa or the Safari Tour in Kenya, Zambia, Botswana, Ivory Coast and Nigeria for warm-weather golf. Now they could go to the Gulf.

"There was nothing here then," said Norman, who played in some of the early Desert Classics. "The Hard Rock Cafe was the tallest building in this part of the world. I stayed down at the Jebel Ali and what was that, a three-storey hotel?"

David Williams, a tournament director for the European Tour, played in the first event, which was held at the new Emirates course. "All I remember of the journey from the airport to the golf course was sand, sand, sand," he said.

Andrew "Chubby" Chandler was a competitor in the inaugural Desert Classic. "I had never been to America, so the concept of golf in the desert was a new one to me," said Chandler, who manages Andrew Flintoff, the England cricketer, and Ernie Els, who is No 17 in the world golf rankings, among others. "I remember a lot of sand and an amazing clubhouse. I thought, 'Well, this is going to be different because of the perceived oil wealth.' "

Just how different became immediately apparent the moment you set eyes on the Emirates course, a rectangle of grass nourished daily by more than a million gallons of desalinated water. The course was surrounded by sand. That first year, and for a few years afterwards, you could look in any direction and not see any building. Now it would take too long to count how many are visible.

"The Emirates course was nothing but a square piece of land," Pete Cowan, Lee Westwood's coach, said. "But it's what started Dubai. Everybody thought to themselves, 'I'd love to go and see a course in the desert.' "

Tarratt arrived in Dubai in September 1990. "I lived opposite the Trade Centre, the tallest building in the Middle East," he said. "In those days you could go out for a meal and be amazed if you did not see someone you knew. Now when you go out for a meal you are amazed if you do see someone you know."

Soon came the Dubai Creek Course, with a 50-metre high clubhouse shaped like the sails of a dhow, and Nad Al Sheba, where floodlights allowed golf to be played at night. The Dubai Country Club had oil-based greens that were known as browns, and the last person in a group to putt out on each one had to roll it to leave it pristine for the next players.

To be in Dubai this week is to marvel at how much has been done in the past 20 years – and how much appears to have come to a standstill. As players and caddies took part in the pro-am over the Earth Course on Tuesday, bets were taken as to how many of the unoccupied and unfinished villas that lined the fairways were bought. The favourite bet was none. Dubai resembles a mixture of Manhattan and a building site.

"The dream was too big," Cowan said. "I said to them, 'Please don't go too quickly because you have a pearl down here. Spain and Portugal have shown you what not to do. Go slowly. Here should be quality.' "

Norman is confident that things will get better. "Dubai will survive," he said. "It's not going to happen overnight. I don't think the era of the eighties and nineties will return. A lot of people have been hurt big-time and regulations are going to be implemented that are going to change that. There is going to be a lot more overseeing taking place. We are not going to get back to making a lot of money, but we will get back to the good days.

"A lot of wealth has been lost, so there has to be some correction. But don't focus on the fact there's a lot of empty buildings here. Focus on the fact that there's a lot of wisdom and foresight and vision to go ahead. It will take time. Dubai will come back."

Faldo and the female of the species
The Times, November 22, 1999

Golf is a game of contradictions. Two of the more obvious are that to hit a golf ball up in the air, you must hit down on it and to hit it farther you must swing more smoothly. A third is that, whereas Spaniards think of their country in sporting terms only of football and cycling, Britons' perception of sport in Spain is of a country in which to play golf beneath a warm sun.

So it was last week. From the La Manga club came the satisfying sights and sounds of true amateur golfers from Britain hooking and fading their way in the final of *The Times* MeesPierson Corporate Challenge. After a season dominated by the professional game, this was reassuring evidence on the eve of a millennium that golf is a game that incites discipline, manners and good behaviour. From Sotogrande, a few hundred miles to the south-west, came the torturous shrieks from those attending the European Tour's annual qualifying school, a place for would-be touring professionals.

Two questions were continually being asked last week: is Justin Rose going to make it and why did Fanny Sunesson sack Nick Faldo? Rose's popularity is not hard to understand. Young, articulate, self-assured and modest, he could not look more clean-cut and wholesome than he does and the way he caught the mood of excitement in July 1998 when he finished fourth in the Open was something very special indeed. Perhaps the good form he is demonstrating at the qualifying school really will mark the return to form of a prodigiously talented young man who is, let this not be forgotten, four years younger than Tiger Woods.

Sunesson, meanwhile, was on holiday in Australia, just about the farthest point from the place where news that she had downed her golf bag and was looking for another employer was being discussed. "Sunesson trades Faldo for a younger model," was one clever comment I heard, a play on the way that every few years Faldo had tended to do just that with his wives or companions.

Nick Faldo was a top player of his era, having won six major
championships, three Open Championships and three Masters.

Faldo and women are as inextricably linked as his left and right hands on the grip of a golf club. His life has been dominated by women. First came his mother, followed by Melanie, his first wife, and Gill, his second wife. After he left Gill he turned to Brenna Cepelak, and now to Valerie Bercher, whom he plans to marry in 2001.

I have felt for years that Faldo only needs a woman to act as his manager, instead of the estimable John Simpson, and a woman to act as his swing coach, and he would be all of a piece. How many other sportsmen make national head-lines in successive weeks, first because of an announcement that he is to marry for a third time, then because he is sacked by his caddie, a woman?

I had dinner with Faldo at his rented house in Ascot in 1990, just after he had started to employ Sunesson. By then he had won the Masters for a second time and had just failed to get into a play-off for the US Open. Life could scarcely be better and while Gill kindly busied herself making dinner, Faldo talked about his career and why he had taken the surprising step of employing a female caddie.

Faldo admires other self-starters. He grew up in a modest house, the much-loved son and only child of parents who both worked hard and did everything they could to advance him. His mother was a part-time seamstress, his father a book-keeper. Faldo likes people but saves his respect for those who work hard. Faldo has a considerable work ethic.

So, too, does Sunesson, as Faldo explained this midsummer night nine years ago. She was hard-working, unpretentious, dedicated to making herself the best caddie she could be. She was doing in her field what Faldo himself had done in his ten years earlier. She trained, scarcely drank and she was cheery. When Faldo showed signs of becoming morose, she cheered him up. In time, she became a much-valued member of Team Faldo and when Faldo went to Florida to spend time with David Leadbetter, Sunesson, a good golfer herself, went as well in order to learn what Leadbetter was trying to get Faldo to do.

The relationship between a player and his caddie is extraordinary. A player as determined as Faldo can spend all day with his caddie and may see much more of his caddie than his wife. Striking a balance between employee and friend is one that few can manage.

But this is not why Sunesson has dropped Faldo. She has decided to move on because he is no longer good enough for her. Languishing nearly 200 places below the position of world pre-eminence he held when she first joined him, Faldo no longer presents Sunesson with the success he once did, not to mention the income. She is one of the best caddies in the world who can command the highest rates and now needs to be associated with a player of equal standing.

Normally it is Faldo who dismisses the women in his life. Now one had dismissed him. It must have hurt, the more so since Sunesson was probably right and justified in doing so. No man is a hero unto his valet. Not even Nick Faldo. That is a truism, not a contradiction.

Parents' dreams weigh heavy on young shoulders

The Times, November 15, 1999

Earl Woods and Victor Garcia are two men who have guided talented sons past adolescence to a maturity that has enabled them to achieve astonishing success at golf.

At 23, Tiger Woods has already won two major championships and, as unquestionably the world's best player, he is forcing his rivals to raise their games to keep up with him. Sergio Garcia, 19, only turned professional in April but upstaged Woods over the closing holes of the US PGA Championship in August and made a remarkable debut in the Ryder Cup the next month. He is now ranked No 15 in the world.

This week, Ken and Annie Rose will be at Sotogrande, in southern Spain, for the European Tour's torture chamber – the final qualifying school. There they will see whether Justin, their son and oldest child, who stunned the world of golf by finishing fourth in the 1998 Open when he was still 17 and then turned professional, can continue his steady comeback.

At present, Justin Rose would feel uneasy at being mentioned in the same paragraph as Woods and Garcia. Yet when Rose turned professional, the hoopla that surrounded it and his performance in his first tournament as a professional was enormous.

Parenting is never easy and parenting a gifted child is particularly difficult. Earl Woods mapped out Tiger's development from long before his child was born, going to extraordinary lengths to build a bond with him. Jazz was being played when Earl brought Tiger home from the hospital where he had been born. When Tiger was in his cot, Earl would stand over him, talking while gently stroking his son's cheek.

Garcia's ascendancy to the top of the professional game was as well planned as a battle campaign. First, he won junior and then senior events in Spain. At 12, he visited the United States to compete in a junior event and won it by 13 strokes. Thereafter, he was exposed to new challenges year by year, all of which he met, until after more than 70 wins, including the Amateur Championship, and having competed in 27 professional events as an amateur, including winning the silver medal as the leading amateur at the Masters this year, he turned pro.

The nurturing of Rose was never done in a comparable way. "I was the original pushy parent with Brandon," Ken Rose said, referring to Justin's half-brother, who is nine years older. "I had him on the practice tee at 6.30am. I took him to every junior Open in South Africa. I made him work really hard. By the time Justin came along, Brandon was not jealous of what might have been. He knew that what was happening to Justin had happened to him.

"Justin had a talent to play. There was never any doubt about that. At eight, he was beating 14-year-olds and at 12 he was beating 18-year-olds. I had dreams for him, just as Jennifer Capriati's Dad did for her and Earl did for Tiger. Not only were they dreams for my child; they were *my* dreams. I got huge motivation and pleasure from him and I still do.

"Everybody thought I was a golf nut, a maniac, yet when you see what Earl has done and the meticulous preparation the Garcias have made for Sergio, then what we have done by comparison is amateurish."

Earl Woods has spoken about the twofold tasks of a parent: bring up the prodigy and then let them go. "I said to my wife that when Tiger walks out of that door to go to college, he ceases to live here," Earl said. "She said: 'But he's only 18'. I replied: 'That's it, he's gone. He only comes home for laundry and to see his friends.'"

Justin Rose still lives with his parents at Fleet, in Hampshire, travelling with his family at times and occasionally sharing a room with Margaret, his sister, who is two years younger. The normal sibling rivalry in the Rose household has never extended beyond the usual disagreements over music, television programmes, clothes and who takes more time in the bathroom.

"Margaret and Justin are very close," Ken Rose said. "In fact, every time Justin has played well, Margaret has been with us. She is the intellect of the family. She seems to be able to reason things out. Justin is cognisant of the effect the attention he is getting has on her.

"We have tried to involve her in Justin's golf and make her aware that we realise it is a potential problem for her. We have told her that if she feels that way, she must tell us. She has not done so.

"I do not feel that we have had to spend the same amount of money on Margaret as on Justin. In fact, I have avoided that like the plague. In material terms, we have not felt the need to make it up to her and nor have we made it up to her. We have tried to make Justin's success a positive for her."

Earl Woods and Ken Rose share an unshakeable belief that what they were doing for their sons was the right thing and that they were the right people to be doing it. "I believe no one can do with Justin what I envisaged," Ken Rose, who will caddie for Justin this week as he has done from time to time all year, said. "They do not have my technical skill, nor are they sufficiently correctly motivated to take a kid to the highest level of professional golf."

When Woods and Garcia turned professional, it was accepted that they were clearly ready to join the paid ranks. When Justin took the same step, aged 17, there were many who thought he was far too young. "We had decided the previous March [in 1998] that he would turn pro after the Open because he had stopped learning and improving as an amateur," Ken Rose said. "I always looked upon Justin's career as a pro as being one of gradual development. Even David Leadbetter said he would be 21 before he is ready to play.

"Just how much Justin has progressed in the pro ranks is clear from his scores at the qualifying event [that enabled him to progress to Sotogrande]. There were several of his contemporaries from his amateur days there and the best was Graham Rankin. Justin, playing over a more difficult course, beat him by eight strokes, others by 16 and still others by 24. That is a measure of Justin's improvement as a professional."

Long may this improvement continue.

And so, four million words later...

The Sunday Times, November 8, 1981

One wintry day in 1949 a struggling freelance writer named Pat Ward-Thomas met the then sports editor of *The Manchester Guardian*, Larry Montague, over tea in the Old Rectory Club in Manchester. They talked of this and that and Montague read a hitherto unpublished account by Ward-Thomas of the 1949 Ryder Cup. Tossing back the 1,500-word manuscript, Montague remarked, "I like golf written like that."

Soon he appointed Ward-Thomas golf correspondent. It wasn't the casual, shot-in-the-dark choice it might have seemed. Not only had Montague read that one story but he knew that Ward-Thomas had been a founder of the Sagan Golf Club in Stalag Luft III PoW camp a few years earlier. (Stalag Luft III subsequently became famous for the famous Wooden Horse escape.)

Indeed, using a ball that he manufactured by winding cotton and wool around a piece of pine and then covering it with cloth, and wielding an old hickory-shafted lady's mashie, Ward-Thomas became the first Open champion of Sagan. The course on which he won this title included tree stumps, poles, an incinerator door and an 18-inch-high fir tree as holes.

Following that meeting with Montague, Ward-Thomas was the golf correspondent of *The Guardian* for 28 years until his retirement in 1978. He also produced 46 articles each year for *Country Life* and wrote five books. A sixth, *Not Only Golf*, will go on sale tomorrow.

At home in Norfolk last week Ward-Thomas settled into a chair in his study and did some calculations. "There are 270 books about golf up here," he said, pointing to the shelves behind him. "And 172 magazines come into this house each year."

He walked to a filing cabinet in a corner of the room, opened the bottom drawer and pointed to a row of scrapbooks: "That's all my *Guardian* stuff. I reckon I wrote four million words for them." He shut the drawer with his foot, and moved across to a cupboard built into a wall opposite. Thrusting his head inside, he pulled out a folder from beneath a dressing gown. "This is where I keep my *Country Life* articles."

Ward-Thomas's style is languid and elegant, and inclined to the purple. "I have always tried to set the scene," he said. "I felt it was important to explain where the wind was coming from, whether it was behind or against on the long 8th."

But a weakness of his is that he is rarely able to lighten his writing with humour in the way, for instance, that his former colleague Henry Longhurst could. "I'd like to be more amusing," he said. "I wish I had a little of Henry's gift for seeing the absurd side of almost every situation, but I'm afraid I haven't." Across the table his wife Jean observed quietly: "I think you lack imagination." "Quite true," muttered Ward-Thomas. "I do."

His words and phrases are those of Edwardian England. Jones was "grievously stricken"; an ocean was "ever-changing in its hue"; golf shots "stream through the morning sunshine" and "bore through the greying twilight".

His great friend, the American golf writer Herb Warren Wind, recalls a day they spent together nearly 30 years ago. "We played a round on my course in the morning, and then headed into New York intending to hear some jazz in the Village," Wind said last week. "Pat had asked me in that way of his: 'Would it be possible for you to take us somewhere where some tied-up, emotional black trumpet player is blowing his aches to the ceiling?' "

Returning from the Walker Cup last August, Ward-Thomas calculated he was making his 92nd Atlantic crossing. He knows the Palmers well enough to stay with them. Byron Nelson is both "a celestial striker" and an old friend. Ben Hogan calls him Ward. And Jack Nicklaus, one senses, is probably his greatest hero. A close friendship that began in 1959 was marked this year when Nicklaus chose Ward-Thomas to deliver the tribute to Harry Vardon at the memorial tournament honouring Vardon in Columbus, Ohio.

Approaching the status of the Oldest Member, Ward-Thomas might reflect that since the war he has avoided the Wodehousian Hell Bunkers on Earth and passed his time instead in life's Elysian Fields. He has taken his readers there in his writing, setting the scene, and not forgetting which way the wind was blowing on the 8th.

He will be 69 in May next year. His handicap, which once was four, is now 16. He is tortured by his bad temper and, following a bad drive on the first hole, is likely to explode: "Oh God, that's it, the match is over, finished, gone."

Perhaps it is because of his own failing that he usually writes so sympathetically of others. "There is no such thing as an easy three-foot putt in golf," he says firmly. "Not for me, not for Tom Watson. Believe me, if you've felt the hurt of golf you don't forget it."

Foreword

Green Memories by Bernard Darwin (Flagstick Books, 1998)

At home in Norfolk I have a bookcase that stretches the length of one wall and is half as high again as I am. One shelf is devoted entirely to books by Bernard Darwin. I have many of the old favourites but what I did not have was a copy of *Green Memories*.

That arrived, courtesy of Robert Macdonald, one day in November 1997. I resisted the temptation to fall upon it, like a wolf on the fold, and read it from cover to cover, and for several months it lay on an empty shelf, face up, silently reproaching me for ignoring it. Not until March of this year when I went to Rye to cover the annual match between Oxford and Cambridge, a match in which Darwin played in 1895, '96, and '97, did I pick it up again. On something of a whim I packed it in my briefcase. That night I lay in my bed in my room in Mermaid Street in Rye, the window open and half an ear registering the baas of sheep out on the marshes, reading *Green Memories*. I was entranced. In the 30 minutes before my eyes closed and the book slipped from my hands, I was reminded once more why Darwin is regarded so highly.

Darwin is important for any number of reasons, but one of the chief ones, in my view, is that no one chronicled life so well as he did. If you want to gain an insight into the life of a golfer in those days, then Darwin does it best. What he also did well was summon up words that remain appropriate and fitting as much as 80 years later.

It was at Rye that I read Darwin's chapter on the Oxford and Cambridge Golfing Society. Its closing sentence gave me the opening words for my report of the first day's play, namely: "It is enough to say that the Society has warmed both hands before the fire of Rye". In *Green Memories* there are many examples of Darwin's ability to come up with precisely the right phrase. Has anyone captained a team and not felt as Darwin did years ago: "as to our tail, I felt prayerful rather than positively hopeful."

I grew up in Gloucestershire, 100 miles due west of London. Each August our family would strike out for our summer holidays to north Wales, to Morfa Nefyn and Nefyn, seaside resorts with a magnificent cliff-top course 40 miles north of Aberdovey, which is in a county called Merionethshire. Darwin on Merioneth and Aberdovey is simply unbeatable because so often he seems to be describing places, occurrences, people that are strikingly similar to those I met on our family holidays.

I, too, have stayed in houses like Pantlludw with flagged stone floors ("very cold for bare toes") with "a huge verandah, perched on a hillside in a great wilderness of garden and woods, a cottage at the end of the garden". "It always seems to me to have been raining at such times," Darwin wrote of those rare days when he could not play golf and sat with his grandmother on the verandah. One of my memories of our family holidays is of the rain teeming down unceasingly. And if it was not raining then it could be windy and cold. I remember sitting on the terrace one afternoon listening on the radio to the transmission of a cricket match. I was wrapped in several sweaters and a thick rug. How true were Darwin's words: "The dripping is always in my ears as I think of the verandah and indeed it does rain in the Welsh hills".

Writing predominantly for an American audience, I am pleased to report that of the 27 chapters in *Green Memories*, Mr Ouimet Makes History may be the one that most caught my imagination because it taught me so well about those historic days in golf when Ouimet, an amateur, tied with Vardon and Ray, two of the greatest professionals in the game, in the 1913 US Open and then defeated them both the next day.

This is how Darwin described Ouimet over the closing holes of the final round when he needed to take ten strokes for the last three holes and the par figures were 3, 3, 4. "The clearest picture that remains to me is of the youthful Ouimet here playing all the last crucial shots just as if he had been playing an ordinary game. He did not hurry; he did not linger; there was a briskness and decisiveness about every movement, and whatever he may have felt he did not betray it by as much as the movement of an eyelash."

Better was to come for Darwin was Ouimet's marker in the 18-hole play-off the next day. "The day of the play-off was damp and horrible," Darwin wrote. "The ground was a sop." Again, there is one passage that not only perfectly captures the day's play but could appear in the columns of *The Times* in 1998 just as happily as it had 85 years earlier. It goes as follows: "I cannot remember exactly when I began to feel thoroughly uneasy about the Englishmen's chances, but it was fairly soon. Mr Ouimet was so obviously master of himself and never looked like breaking down. He was driving right up to his competitors; he was doing everything as well as they could do it, and he was a better putter than either of them."

The final reason why Darwin has taken a place so deep in my heart is a surprising one. I did not know until reading *Green Memories* that he possessed one human frailty that I, and many journalists, possess, indeed seem to have been born with. As we hurtle toward the millennium, journalists work on laptop computers, which they can hardly begin to understand, which are then connected via modems, a word they scarcely know the meaning of, to telephones, which baffle them, and then somehow, on to their offices. They will understand immediately Darwin's feelings of uncertainty and wonder as he explained it nearly 100 years ago: "Though I have sent off many press telegrams I am still a little alarmed at doing so, conscious how helpless I should be if some emergency arose. In short, I know next to nothing about the technical part of the job."

I am an unreconstructed Darwinian. I do not think it is over-egging the cake to suggest that *Green Memories* is the best of Darwin's books, which, in turn, makes it the best book on golf. Read it and I hope you will enjoy it as much as I did.

A beguiling champion wins on merit

The Sunday Times, November 27, 1988

If you want conclusive evidence of the spread of golf outward from Britain to mainland Europe then look at the two golfers who topped their respective orders of merit after the 1988 season. The name of Seve Ballesteros is no surprise on the men's tour. It's the fifth time he's done it since he turned pro in 1974.

But Marie-Laure de Lorenzi de Taya is the first French woman, not to mention the first non-Briton, to win the Order of Merit since women's professional golf began in Britain in 1979.

After seven victories on the European Tour, de Taya now stands comparison with England's Laura Davies, the 1987 US Open champion, and Liselotte Neumann, the Swede who won this year's US Open. No one player has ever won seven events in one season before, at least not in Europe. Davies jointly held the previous record of four victories.

At 27, de Taya is the only one of the three to be married, the only mother and also the most senior, two years older than Davies, five more than Neumann. Because she remained an amateur until 1986, she is also the newest professional of the three, not that you would notice after nine victories and winnings of nearly £150,000 in her two seasons as a pro.

Once before, France threw up a great female golfer. Catherine de Prado, née Lacoste, is a daughter of the great tennis player René, and 21 years ago last summer she stunned the world of golf by becoming the first, and so far the only, amateur to win the US Open. By 1970 she had married a Spaniard, retired and moved to Spain.

For Lacoste read de Taya. The young Marie-Laure was on a sports scholarship at the University of Southern California when she met Roman de Taya, a Spanish amateur international who even then, at 30, had played amateur golf for Spain for 14 years. Soon after, she abandoned her studies, married de Taya and moved to Barcelona where they live with their four-year old daughter Laura.

No other player came close to de Taya on the European Tour in 1988. She entered 22 events and won seven of them, eight if you include a team event with Mark McNulty. She came second four times and even in her worst tournament she finished 36th. Not only did she win the most money (£99,360) and compile the lowest stroke average (72.3), she won twice as many events as her nearest rivals, Alison Nicholas and Laura Davies.

"She's the nearest thing to Laura in terms of striking ability and power," says Nicholas graciously. "She is difficult to play against because she is so calm and steady. Occasionally she has a brainstorm on the greens, missing short putts and misjudging the pace of her longer putts. But apart from that she's a force to be reckoned with."

This would be enough for any one person but, just to put the cap on it, it seems that no one has a harsh word to say about the tall, elegant Basque, the daughter of a coffee importer in Bayonne, who is a fashion plate on and off the golf course.

"She's intelligent, articulate, attractive and a very well-rounded individual, a very sensible lady," says Joe Flanagan, the head of the Women Professional Golfers' European Tour. "She is calm, can play well under pressure. She is a role model."

Flanagan paused after this fulsome praise, as if aware that the picture he was painting might be dismissed as Irish blarney. "I'm making her out to be a paragon, aren't I?" he asked. He paused again, realising that further lavish praise could devalue his comments.

"Let me put it like this. When she won the Spanish Open, the final event of the year, some of the girls went down to the last hole and chaired her off the green. That speaks for itself, doesn't it?"

Few sportswomen can combine the role of mother and competitor. De Taya has, or has so far, thanks to an understanding husband and caring grandparents and nannies. She is determined to combine motherhood and golf, a determination that may be harder to honour when she has a second child. "My family comes first," de Taya says, firmly and clearly. "I am first a mother and second a professional golfer." This is why de Taya will not compete on the women's circuit in the US. It would be too disruptive to her family life although she has not ruled it out for all time.

She is also a hot property financially. Six companies, including Lacoste, already sponsor her, giving her an off-course income conservatively estimated at £200,000 annually. Other sponsors are forming a queue from the left. "I don't think that France has produced a lady sportswoman of Marie-Laure's calibre – ever," says Neil Hobday, her manager, who can't be accused of total disinterest.

For the burgeoning women's tour, which next season will be longer and richer than ever before, and for the spread of golf throughout France, where 70,000 women and 130,000 men play the game, there is only one thing to say: "Vive Marie-Laure."

1912: A very good year

www.globalgolfpost.com, November 19, 2012

Were they still alive, Ben Hogan would have been 100 last August, Sam Snead the same age last May and Byron Nelson the same last February. It was a good year for golf, 1912. As Martin Davis, the historian, says with authority in *The American Triumvirate*, the made-for-TV film on Golf Channel: "Hogan, Snead and Nelson were truly the American Dream."

Those years just before the First World War were the dying embers of a high old time in Britain. The end of the Edwardian Britain meant an end to ladies in tight bodices and long skirts. The *Titanic* went down in 1912. You might remember that year for these events alone. I remember 1912 because that was the year after my father was born.

My father had two sporting loves in his life: golf and rugby. As a teenager more than 80 years ago, he had played on the wing for Tredegar County School on Saturday mornings and in the same position for Tredegar RFC in the afternoon.

Remembering those days as if they were yesterday, he often talked of a game in which the players were so disenchanted with the referee that they threw him into a nearby canal. He recalled being sent off for rough play – he always said it was a case of mistaken identity – and how he had played for the weeks of his suspension under an assumed name – A.N. Other.

When he turned to golf, he pursued it with vigour, playing most Saturdays and Sundays. He had a smooth swing with a pronounced in to out movement. "That's the secret, John," he would say to me. "In to out." Even his putts, hit from a closed stance, went from in to out. He must have modelled himself on Bobby Locke.

Little did I know how this instruction to take the club back so that it practically brushed my right ankle (and thus was miles offline at the top) would hobble me for years. Meant as a gem of fatherly wisdom, it became a piece of nightmarish advice as my swing created first a loop as I got it back on plane at the top, and later, a pronounced hook.

Nonetheless, my father communicated his enthusiasm for golf to me and I shared it. I remember as a child he took me with him to watch a *Shell Wonderful World of Golf* programme when it was shown at Stinchcombe Hill, my father's golf club in Gloucestershire.

He once took part in a competition to beat Hogan's score on a given day and the certificate that he had done so – his net score against Hogan's gross – was kept with pride in his wardrobe.

Years later, I watched Nelson and Snead at Augusta, and in 1999, when Snead was 87, I interviewed him at The Greenbrier where he had just been appointed professional emeritus. Expecting him to be talkative, I found him garrulous. The interview over, he invited me for lunch and posed a question: "Do you play, kid?"

I said, "Yes, but I'm a hooker. I can't hit the ball straight." He paused, twirled his knife and fork, and said, "Come outside. I'll have a look at you."

Not only didn't I have any clubs, I didn't have any footwear. Snead lent me a pair of his. Not fit to tie his shoelaces, I was now wearing his shoes.

The lesson was not a success. After watching me hit a few poorly hit strokes, he moved to his cart and drove away, reluctant, perhaps, to intrude any longer on private grief.

My father's amateur golfing idol was Albert Evans, the farmer who played for Wales for years and was rightly described as the "Granddaddy" of Welsh golf. When Ross Golf Club, Albert's club, played a friendly against Stinchcombe Hill, we would invite him to our house on the course for tea and crumpets and Welsh cakes.

My father's professional idol was Sir Henry Cotton, the public-school-educated Englishman who won the Opens of 1934, 1937 and 1948. He was to British golf what Hogan was to American golf, and my father never swung his woods with such pride as the day he bought a set of woods, a driver, a brassie, a spoon and a four-wood, with the name Henry Cotton stamped on the top of each shining piece of persimmon.

The American Triumvirate is a gem, based on Jim Dodson's book of the same name. It is full of crackly footage of one or all of the three heroes swinging their clubs or putting on a green that did not look as smooth as some of today's fairways. Hogan dug the dirt, hitting ball after ball in his relentless pursuit for perfection; Snead told the stories; Nelson demonstrated the grace and humility of a gentle man and a gentleman.

They are dead now, God bless them. But their memory lives on, in part, because of Dodson's book and the Golf Channel film. My father lives on, too, creating elderly mayhem in a village in Gloucestershire. Born on January 28 1911, he will be 102 next January. God bless him.

The Ballesteros ban – golf's split widens

The Sunday Times, November 10, 1985

It has been ten days since the banning of Seve Ballesteros from the US tour, a wretched time for supporters of international golf which is souring the end of the most exciting year in European golf since the 1920s. All last week the lines of communication between Britain, the headquarters of the European Tour, Spain and the US tour in Florida were blazing as explanations were sought and compromises suggested.

But by yesterday there were signs that the American professional golf authorities were becoming even more isolationist. Indeed, one day last week there was a rumour, mercifully later denied, that foreign players would have to renounce their home tours altogether in order to compete in the US in 1987.

At this moment, in golfing terms, the Atlantic seems wider than at any time in memory. From a European viewpoint, the ban on Ballesteros seems a deliberate slapdown for the world's leading golfer who, unusually, happens to be European, at a time when European golf has never been stronger.

At best it means the temporary exclusion of the brilliant Spaniard from all but four tournaments in the US in 1986. After that Ballesteros could, in theory, rejoin the tour, abide by their rules, play the required 15 tournaments, which he didn't do this year, and harmony would reign. But if you believe that you'll believe anything.

More likely the Americans are going to cut up rough with overseas players. They are fed up with the disrespectful tactics of golfers such as Ballesteros who sweep in, grab large sums of money (Ballesteros won more than $200,000 from a mere nine events in 1985) then sweep back to their own tour. "They want players to be members of the US PGA Tour and to regard themselves simply as that; they put low priority on whether that guy happens to be Spanish, Scottish, Mexican or anything else," says Ken Schofield, the executive director of the European Tour.

If any proof of their growing isolationism were needed, it came last week when the Americans announced that next year no one who is not a full member of the US tour may play more than six events. This rule change followed the recent announcement of a $4 million sponsorship deal designed solely to deter the leading Americans from deserting tournaments in their country in September and October.

There are 41 tournaments in the US tour, each one financed by a sponsor. Last week even the sponsors were beginning to complain that the ban on Ballesteros and the growing protectionism were bad for the game. "Seve Ballesteros is the best player in the world and should be able to play wherever he wants," maintains Sandel Pavic, tournament director of Jack Nicklaus's Memorial event in Columbus, Ohio. "The tour is not complete without him."

Charles McCabe, of Manufacturers Hanover Trust, is on the executive committee of the Westchester Classic sponsored by his bank. He will suggest a compromise when the sponsors gather in Dallas tomorrow for a three-day meeting. "Ballesteros adds stature to our tournament and gives fans more value for

Seve Ballesteros plays out of a bunker during the 1985
Ryder Cup at The Belfry in Sutton Coldfield, England.

money," suggests McCabe. "Why can't he be allowed to play in all the tournaments he has won, for example?"

While all this was going on, Ballesteros was at home in Pedreña, in northern Spain. He had been, according to a friend, "cut up, infuriated, disappointed and disgusted". But slowly his anger turned to resignation. He walked on the beach, brooded in his new house just up the hill from his parents' home and began work with Schofield on an appeal which will be presented to the Americans at their tournament policy board meeting early in December.

To try to defuse the situation Ballesteros telephoned Deane Beman, the boss of the American tour. Ballesteros received short shrift for his pains.

Perhaps Beman should heed the words of the American magazine *Sports Illustrated*, which said: "In essence the PGA Tour has told the best golfer in the world to get lost, and we agree with Ballesteros who says 'it was a thoughtless decision that can only harm international golf'."

This year the European Tour welcomed Lee Trevino, Curtis Strange, Craig Stadler and other Americans without any hint of resentment. Thousands of American golf enthusiasts who have warmed to Ballesteros over the years must now be hoping that the US authorities will have a change of heart towards the game's greatest star.

How the chosen one soon buckled under the pressure

The Times, November 30, 2009

Although he is still only 33, Tiger Woods has gone through enough to know more than most about the ages of Man. At birth, his father described him as the Chosen One, a person who in time would be bigger than Buddha and have as much influence as Mahatma Gandhi or Nelson Mandela. When he was 2, Woods putted on *The Bob Hope Show* on US television.

Then there was the Age of Success. Having had a stellar career as an amateur, Woods turned pro in August 1996; in April 1997 he won the Masters by 12 strokes, setting off in pursuit of Jack Nicklaus's record of victories in 18 professional major championships, his avowed aim. Woods, who now has 14 such titles, won all four in succession starting with the US Open in June 2001 and finishing at the Masters the following April.

Yet he was already in the Age of Disillusionment with the media. In 1997 an article had appeared in *GQ* magazine in the course of which the writer reported that Woods told dirty and racist jokes.

This was followed by the Age of Contentment, when he met and married Elin, a Swedish model, and fathered two children. Woods has been the world's highest-paid sportsman since 2002 when he overtook Michael Schumacher, the former Formula One racing driver. *Forbes* magazine recently reported that Woods's total career earnings topped $1 billion.

Now, though, Woods is in the Age of Mystery and Scrutiny. The mystery surrounds his marriage, which is rumoured to have been in trouble for some months. There have been stories of confrontations when Elin has tackled her husband. The most recent, it is being suggested, came after Thursday's publication in the *National Enquirer*, a US tabloid newspaper, of a story alleging that Woods had been seeing a New York nightclub hostess. The story has been denied by both parties.

Woods has never appeared publicly at ease in the Age of Parenthood, either. He has never been a prominent father, as was Nicklaus, who was known to fly home from a tournament to attend a baseball game in which one of his children was playing.

In 2007, Woods did not attend the christening in Sweden of Sam, his first child. Instead he hosted a function that raised $500,000 for a school learning programme and Elin's friends were reportedly "surprised" at his absence.

Assessing Woods now, you notice how much he has talked about the influences of his own parents. Woods has always shown great respect towards Kultida, his mother, wearing a red shirt on the Sunday of a tournament because she told him it was "a power colour".

He spoke often of the influence on him of Earl, his father. "He was an amazing dad, coach, mentor, soldier, husband and friend," Woods said after Earl died in 2006.

Perhaps it is the twin pressures of a year without winning a major championship and the difficulties in his marriage that have made Woods more sour this year than before.

Sandy Lyle remains the quintessential British hero

The Times, November 6, 1988

Goodness knows, European golfers have pulled up enough trees in the United States lately. The Ryder Cup a little over a year ago, Sandy Lyle's thrilling annexation of the Masters in April and then Nick Faldo's brave fight in the US Open at Brookline in June. Yet one tree remains firmly rooted: the US money list.

For a European to earn more money in the US than any other player would be a stupendous achievement. Only a handful of men from this side of the Atlantic play regularly on the US tour, and two of them, Bernhard Langer and Sandy Lyle, barely more than the minimum number of events necessary to retain their playing privileges, while at the same time conducting a campaign on their home tour.

So it was very much against the odds that Lyle led the US money list for four months earlier this year and currently lies third with earnings of $653,334. It's also against the odds that this week he will top the money list and be named US Player of the Year. Lyle must earn at least $130,000 more than Chip Beck, the current leader, in this week's Nabisco Championship at Pebble Beach, California, and to be realistic this means he must take the $360,000 first prize.

But if he did, what an achievement that would be. He would become the first Briton, the first European and only the second non-American since 1934 to do it, and he would have done it having played only 17 events compared with Beck's 24 and the 30 of Joey Sindelar, the player in second place. "Yes," said Lyle quietly last week, showing all his well-known animation. "Yes, it would be nice."

Lyle will have to play better at Pebble Beach than he did at Valderrama, in Spain a week ago. Lyle is an enthralling player to watch – long, powerful, sometimes wild, always unpredictable. For him to play a round without a birdie is as rare as a Ben Hogan smile. But Lyle played his last 39 holes in Spain without a birdie, and nobody can remember the last time that happened. "Not since God were a lad," suggests his caddie, Dave Musgrove, helpfully.

Nothing should surprise us about a man who hit his first shot 110 yards when he was three years old, and has now become one of the most popular and respected golfers in the world. Spectators see him ambling down the fairways and like his ordinariness, his big feet, his unglamorous style of dress and unaffected manner, his honest forthrightness. There is something about Lyle that suggests he will change in character and values when Nelson's column topples.

Alexander Walter Barr Lyle is archetypically British, an understated hero to whom people naturally warm. They have even come to relish his occasional sporting malapropisms.

Lyle's career can be divided into parcels, wrapped with red ribbon and labelled. There was the Gifted Amateur, followed by the Journeyman Pro.

He became the Great Home Hope, and the European Star Who Couldn't Win in America. His victory in the 1985 Open at Sandwich turned him into the European Star Who Can Win in the US, and success at Augusta last spring showed him in full fig, unarguably one of the three best golfers in the world.

"They always say, don't they, that golfers mature at 30," says Musgrove, who has humped Lyle's bag since the autumn of 1981. Lyle was 30 last February. "Sandy reminds me of Roberto de Vicenzo. Some players change when they get on to a golf course. Faldo never speaks, for instance. Some others lose their temper. Not Sandy. His life is the same off the course as on it. His natural habitat is a golf course."

Much is made of Lyle's apparently placid temperament. Musgrove even suggested that Lyle manages to remain so calm because of a slow pulse rate. One evening last week Lyle's pulse rate was measured and found to be a conventional 79. "I can get worked up if I'm stuck in traffic or behind a bad driver," he says. It comes from his mother, who is rather more fiery than his easy-going father. What else comes from his mother? "A long back and a big bum," he says with a laugh.

The point about Lyle is that his life runs the way he wants it. No one tells him where or where not to play golf – witness his refusal to play in the US PGA.

There's the way everyone else prepares before a round. And then there's Lyle's routine. He'll spend 30 minutes helping colleagues on the practice ground, followed by a few quick hits, some chips and hurried putts of his own. On the 1st tee of the last round at Valderrama, Lyle even spent time giving instruction to a golf photographer.

Lyle plays well when he has played a lot, and his natural strength is put to good use. This is one reason why he does so well in the World Match Play. His win at Augusta was in his sixth successive event, and he came thirteenth the next week as well. He plays well when he putts well. At Augusta his total of 81 putts after three rounds was the lowest in the field, 11 fewer than Ben Crenshaw, who was then lying second.

Lyle also plays well when he is happy and in a comfortable environment. It's significant that all but one of his American successes have come at Greensboro (1986, 1988), where he stays with an English family, at Phoenix (1988), where he stays with a close American friend, and at Augusta when his parents were visiting. "It's nice to be in a house with English people, whose company I enjoy," Lyle says. "I can relax, make myself a cup of tea when I want it. It may be coincidence, but it's nice to be able to do it to break the routine up."

Calm, collected, capable, courteous and confident, Sandy Lyle has the world of golf at his feet. And it's nothing less than he deserves.

"He prowled Royal Aberdeen ceaselessly"

Golf Quarterly, **November 2011**

The Walker Cup is the best event in golf. That has been my view since I watched Great Britain and Ireland win it at St Andrews in 1971, and nothing that has happened in the 14 contests I have attended since has given me cause to reconsider.

I love watching the dynamics among individual competitors when they have to play as a team, and I like the way spectators can flock down the fairways – it creates a special atmosphere. The Walker Cup is just as good as the Ryder Cup but better-mannered and on a smaller, more manageable scale. It reduces competitors to knee-knocking, palm-sweating, hand-trembling individuals, exposing them to unfamiliar pressures and putting them in a sometimes harsh spotlight.

Why was it that Great Britain and Ireland won the 43rd Walker Cup at Royal Aberdeen in September when all known form suggested they would not? The stormy weather helped, forcing the Americans to cope with conditions they had not previously experienced. And Rhys Pugh, for one, played the golf of his life. Watching him hit iron after iron into the wind, none rising more than 30 feet in the air, was to be given a lesson in wind play. Pugh, who had returned from university in Tennessee for this match, was 17 then, looked 27 and behaved as if he was 37.

Ryder, Walker and Solheim Cups are often won by the team that putts better and this was again true at Royal Aberdeen. In addition to putting on greens of different constitution and speed, both sides had to gauge the effect of the wind on the ball. The Americans found this harder than the home side because they had far less experience. How else to explain Patrick Cantlay, ranked the best amateur in the world, and Chris Williams, ranked not far behind Cantlay, three-putting their first three holes in Sunday morning's foursomes?

The captaincy of Nigel Edwards, 43, was crucial. Just as Colin Montgomerie's attention to detail helped Europe over the line in the 2010 Ryder Cup last autumn so, arguably, it was Nigel Edwards's leadership that made the difference in this year's Walker Cup.

Edwards, 43, a small man with large self-belief, instilled this characteristic into his team at Royal Aberdeen. He refused to accept the Americans as favourites, despite the presence of six of the US team in the top ten of the world rankings, and he made sure that his men were as well prepared as they could possibly have been. That said, he did not go to quite the same lengths as Montgomerie who, at the eleventh hour, had bigger beds installed for his players and humps in the road put in to slow the traffic and reduce noise near the team's hotel.

Edwards prowled Royal Aberdeen ceaselessly, a radio in one ear, a look of complete concentration on his face. He had the same routine for each player when they arrived on the 1st tee. He would remove his cap, extend his right hand and give them a quiet word of encouragement. He knew when to speak and when to keep quiet. When he addressed his players at lunchtime on Sunday, with Great Britain and Ireland leading 10½-5½ , he knew that the US would be highly motivated for the ten afternoon singles. "It's not over yet, boys," he said in his soft voice, his eyes burning with Welsh fervour. "The Americans are great players. They have a lot of passion. They will come back at us."

Edwards was a combination of the control freak that was Colin Montgomerie at Celtic Manor and the tactician that was the Great Britain and Ireland Walker Cup captain Peter McEvoy at Nairn in 1999 and Sea Island in 2001. He also avoided the mistakes that Nick Faldo made in the 2008 Ryder Cup at Valhalla, paying close attention to the length as well as the content of his speeches.

When he leads the team to the US in two years' time, however, he may find it a harder task to retain the trophy than it was to regain it.

The spirit of the Walker Cup was much discussed after Great Britain and Ireland had unwittingly broken a rule of the competition by allowing Jack Senior's brother Joe, a professional, to caddie for him in the first morning's foursomes. Professionals are not allowed to caddie in this event. The error was pointed out by BBC TV and brought to the players' and officials' notice after play had finished on Saturday morning. To his credit the American captain could not have cared less and had no interest in seeking retribution.

In this he was reminiscent of Tony Duncan, the Welshman who captained the 1953 Great Britain and Ireland side at Kittansett in the US. When Duncan was informed that an American player had broken a rule by having 16 clubs in his bag and therefore Great Britain and Ireland were eligible for some redress, he said magnanimously: "We haven't come three thousand miles to win a 36-hole match by default on the 2nd hole..."

The headline in the local paper the next morning was "Britannia waives the rules".

DECEMBER

December always gave me time and scope to write features. There wasn't usually much else to write about, although the row between the "Gang of Four" and the European Tour that came to a head in December 2000 put golf on the news agenda. Severiano Ballesteros, Nick Faldo, Bernhard Langer and José María Olazábal, who had won 15 major championships between them, were unhappy at the way the Tour was being run on their behalf. They wanted the Tour to open their books, either to the four of them or to their accountants.

They felt that the Tour should have been making more money than it was, that it was too dominated by the British and Irish, that there was no pension fund for players, that the Ryder Cup was not generating as much money as it should, that there were extravagances towards Tour officials. It was a spicy list of criticisms.

Ken Schofield and officials at Wentworth went into overdrive at this challenge. When two resolutions were put to an ensuing meeting, the Tour won them both. The first, that the Gang of Four should have access to all accounts, books and documents of the Tour, was defeated, with 61 in favour and 122 against. The second, proposed by the Tour, was that an independent firm of auditors should be able to examine the financial affairs of the European Tour and report back to members. This was carried by a greater majority, 139-53.

"We were a little outgunned," Faldo said. "They mounted a major campaign to get players on their side. It was a bit like the opening scene of *Zulu*, with

20,000 coming over the hill at us. I hope we can all get the full story. We are trying to represent the players. It looks like the four of us are trying to upset the apple cart but that is not the case."

Olazábal added: "In the long term the members should be happier because they will get more information than they are getting now." Clearly there were few lingering hard feelings because Langer (2004), Faldo (2008) and Olazábal (2012) all went on to captain Europe in the Ryder Cup, the German and the Spaniard's teams both winning.

One brisk day not long before Christmas 2004 I parked in a multistorey car park in Bracknell and made my way to Ottakar's bookshop to watch Peter Alliss give a singular demonstration of why he remained so popular. He was signing copies of his latest book and it reminded me of Alliss's popularity and that while we might be a nation of shopkeepers, we are also a nation of book buyers.

Alliss divides golfers and television watchers. One group, by far the smaller, is against him for being old, stereotypical and for waffling, for wearing a cardigan or for being the sort who might wear a cardigan, for his commentary on the closing stages of the 1999 Open. The other, the larger, likes the quirkiness of his commentaries, believes he has done a huge amount to promote golf and wonders who on earth can succeed him?

I am in the latter camp. I judge the famous people I interview by the interest they show in me when we have finished our interview and are whiling away the time. Alliss does talk, very well and amusingly and sometimes for a long time. But he also questions and listens. He would be a good man with whom to be stuck at a bus stop.

Alliss's likely reaction to the extravagance of Loch Lomond Golf Club and East Sussex National Golf Club can safely be guessed at. These two clubs, which were said to have cost £52 million and £32.5 million respectively, opened in the heady days of the late 1980s when everyone seemed to think that lavish golf clubs were the thing of the future and rushed to build them. By December 1990 I reported that Loch Lomond was in the hands of the receiver and East Sussex National was close to being in that situation too.

It is said that there aren't many stories in a sport as calm and gentlemanly as golf. There was little that was calm, even if it was gentlemanly, about the one that blew up in December 2002 when it was discovered that The Links Trust in St Andrews, the body that oversees all the St Andrews golf courses, was in the process of making changes to the Road Hole bunker, the most famous bunker on the most famous hole in golf. Golfers around the world were said to be raising their sand wedges in anger at this apparent desecration.

That was as nothing compared to the frenzy surrounding Tiger Woods in December 2009. I wrote something about Woods on most days of the first three weeks of December, not all of these stories on the sports pages. *The Times*'s Miami correspondent was just as busy, if not busier. The stories reprinted here give a flavour of the intensity of Tiger mania in this month.

December should be the last golfing month of the year as it is the last of the calendar year. But it isn't in the European Tour's current schedule: it is the first. The Race to Dubai starts in December one year and ends in November the next. Much the same sort of thing is happening in the US where the PGA Tour recently announced it was splitting its season into parts. There is no longer reference to a calendar year on the PGA Tour. Instead the years are joined together, as in the 2013–14 PGA Tour season.

One thing has not changed, however, and that is that from December 20 or so, competitive golf comes to a halt and everyone heads for home. Whether December is the first month of the European Tour's year or has almost been done away with on the PGA Tour in the US, it remains the month in which Christmas falls. And we all know what happens then.

Tempered praise for Montgomerie
The Times, December 22, 1993

Let us first praise Colin Montgomerie, the leading money-winner in Europe in the golf season that has just ended. We shall consider later whether or not to bury him.

Montgomerie has come so far so fast it is a surprise to discover that in 1986 he was still a student at Baptist University in Houston, Texas, where he got a degree in business management and law. After he had turned professional in the autumn of 1987 he handed out business cards that read: "Colin S Montgomerie BA, European Tour Golf Professional".

To have become No 1 in Europe in only his sixth full season is quick. It took Nick Faldo seven years to reach that position, Bernhard Langer, nine, and Ian Woosnam, 11, though José María Olazábal did it in his first season as a professional. Montgomerie, who was 30 last June, is ranked fourteenth in the world.

"What impresses me about Colin is that he drives the ball so well," Dave Marr, the former US PGA champion who is now a golf commentator for BBC television, said.

"It is easy to say that he is a left-to-right hitter, which he is. But I am impressed at how well he draws the ball from the tee when he wants to. In the three years I have been watching him he has improved so much. He is in his prime now. The years between 30 and 38 are when he should have a feast."

Montgomerie's year to end all years began slowly, though he was second in the Johnnie Walker Asian Classic behind his hero, Faldo, and in the Volvo PGA behind Bernhard Langer. In between these events he was second in the Scottish PGA, a minor tournament.

When he finished 50th in the Bell's Scottish Open and missed the cut in the Open the following week, Montgomerie, never one to avoid basking in self-pity, began to sulk to himself at his lack of success.

Not for long, though. Seven days after Norman's conquest of Sandwich, Montgomerie achieved his third victory as a professional. Helped by powerful driving that was so straight he missed only one fairway in his last two rounds, he took the Dutch Open by one stroke.

More good performances followed as his confidence rose, including a fine Ryder Cup, when he and Faldo won 2½ points out of a possible four and he beat Lee Janzen in the singles. Montgomerie was dominant and dogged in winning the Volvo Masters in October and his record-breaking season was concluded last Sunday when he came fourth in the Johnnie Walker world championship in Jamaica.

Montgomerie, then, can play a bit. It is relevant to ask whether he can also behave. P.G. Wodehouse observed that he had no difficulty in distinguishing between a ray of sunshine and a Scotsman with a grievance. He might have been talking of Montgomerie who, on golf courses around the world, often appears to harbour not just one, but half a dozen grievances.

Just when you want to like Montgomerie, to admire his velvet touch on the greens, be swayed by his articulate charm, he sends these good intentions to all points of the compass with a display of petulance that might normally be demonstrated by a small child. It was a colleague on these pages who wrote mischievously of Montgomerie before the Ryder Cup: "…no longer the baby of the family since his wife, Eimear, gave birth last March".

The demonstrations of Montgomerie's temper have been thick and fast. He verbally abused a woman ball-spotter in the Toyota World Match Play Championship at Wentworth. The previous week he had hardly been a paragon

Colin Montgomerie plays a shot during
the Johnnie Walker Championship in Jamaica, 1993.

after Scotland's defeat by Paraguay in the Dunhill Cup. In the fourth round in Jamaica, where he plummeted from three strokes behind Larry Mize, the eventual winner, to 12 strokes behind after his worst round of the week, there was a lot of tutting and strutting, growling and glaring.

"We've all got pressures in our work," John Simpson, Montgomerie's manager, said in an attempt to explain his client's behaviour. "We all have our flashpoints, whether it's a telephone not working or a hotel booking that should have been made but hasn't been. We've talked to Monty about this and he is aware of it. He is trying. He wrote a letter to that lady at Wentworth, for example, and Bernard Gallacher told me the other day that she has become one of his greatest supporters."

Perhaps it has all come too quickly and too easily for Montgomerie, who has improved his position in the European money list every year. He needs a grain of humility to enter his soul, a smile to brighten his features, an equanimity and politeness to be evident in his manner on the golf course. Then one will recognise him for being the talented golfer on the fringe of true international stardom that he is.

The world of golf is at Montgomerie's feet. A prospect that exceeds, just, the size of his shoes. "He should be licking his chops for '94," Marr said. Some of us, though, are ducking for cover fearing that Montgomerie's exposure next year as Europe's leading money-winner will be accompanied by more of the tantrums of which we have become so heartily fed up. Would that he will prove us wrong.

The beloved country shows off its welcome new face

The Times, December 4, 2000

An ambition has been realised. Last week I flew to Johannesburg and was driven in a rattling car over the wide open stretches of the high veld. My destination was Sun City, where I was able to report from the Million Dollar Challenge golf event. It has taken me 20 years to achieve this, as long as the event has been in existence.

When this competition began in 1981 the purse was a million rand (about £40,000 in those days) and the five men who competed for it were Johnnie Miller, who won, Jack Nicklaus, Lee Trevino, Severiano Ballesteros and Gary Player, who had designed the course.

That was the year I first attempted to cover this extravaganza. In those days South Africa was gripped by apartheid and the uncompromising authorities who ran the country had taken exception to some articles I had written the previous year when covering the rugby tour of South Africa by the British Isles rugby team, known as the Lions.

I was banned from the Republic and later realised that I and my anti-apartheid activities had been under surveillance. "That Mr Hopkins is very political," they said by way of explanation for the fact that permission from Pretoria for my visit would not be forthcoming.

If it was commonplace in those days for the complicated paths of sport and politics to be intertwined, it is no longer so. I am proud of what I wrote in 1980 but not half as proud as I am of the multicultural society of modern South Africa, the Rainbow Nation.

Last week I was welcomed to Sun City with a broad smile and an out-stretched hand. "Howzit, man?" Ernie Els asked in that typical South African greeting, extending a hand that seemed big enough to dwarf both of mine.

The talk turned to rugby and the forthcoming game between England and South Africa at Twickenham. "Two hundred rand that the 'Boks beat you," Els said. "Done," I replied. Els is proud of the new look of his country and that smile and long loping walk of his draw support from black and white, young and old. When he is at his house in Wentworth during England's summer, Els brings a touch of South Africa to Berkshire. He watches cricket, devours the amount of sport that is available in British newspapers and on television and fires up the barbecue as often as the weather permits.

One afternoon 20 years ago, a group of us had tea with Alan Paton, the novelist. He was a small, wiry man with a lick of silvery hair that flopped down over his face to collide with the smoke spiralling upwards from his cigarette.

The man who had spoken out against apartheid and written so movingly of his beautiful homeland now presented his visitors with an optimistic vision of his country. As we left he shook hands with us one by one and presented each of us with a mango. I kept mine until it became putrid.

To our visiting ears Paton's optimism had struck a jarring note. The sound of gunfire was common at night. The Lions were spirited out of their hotel in Johannesburg in pitch darkness and antagonism between whites and non-whites was everywhere. Cry indeed for Paton's beloved country.

South Africa is a juxtaposition of ancient and modern. The South Africa we saw that cool afternoon in 1980 is old South Africa, the country where coelacanths, the world's oldest fish, were discovered off the coast of Durban last week. Old South Africa is the Pilanesberg mountains that house one of only two volcanic craters in the world that have alkaline bedrock. Old South Africa is the broad-beamed weather-beaten Afrikaaner, face and hands tanned the colour and texture of a saddle. Old South Africa is Simon Masilo, the coloured caddie of Ernie Els. Old South Africa is biltong and *Die Stem*.

New South Africa is Sun City, which has been built in a fold in these same Pilanesberg mountains. It is the new anthem, incorporating *Nkosi Sikelel' iAfrika*, *Die Stem* and *Call of South Africa*. New South Africa is Ernie Els.

It has been a long and highly successful season for Els and it is winding down in this surreal place, a monument to gambling where thousands are bused in with their pockets jangling and bused out again with their pockets emptied of all their cash. It was here, in 1981, that Sean Connery came and, in most un-James Bond-like fashion, had to be shown how to play Punto Banco, and Telly Savalas is believed to have run up a gambling debt of over a million rand.

Last Thursday evening I sat in the bar of my hotel reading a newspaper stuck on a wooden stick and drinking a glass of white wine from the Cape. Beyond the French doors leading to a verandah, every bird in Africa was singing to me, or so it seemed. The bar was a large airy room where two fake elephant tusks met at the apex of the ceiling. Outside the bar was a statue of a huge elephant, one foot raised slightly.

A few weeks earlier I had listened to a radio adaptation of Evelyn Waugh's novel, *Scoop*, and now, in this environment, I found myself thinking of William Boot going to Africa to cover a revolution. Mental pictures came easily to mind of moustachioed men wearing pith helmets, shorts, knee-length socks and carrying messages in cleft sticks, who mopped their brow with a red spotted handkerchief.

Earlier that evening I had been given directions to a function in this enormous complex. The five key words of my instructions, words that made me smile then and still make me smile now, were: "Turn left at the elephant." Boot would have smiled at them. So, too, might Lord Copper.

Big this week

The Times, December 12, 2009

So, when are we going to see Tiger Woods on a golf course again? Best guesses are at the end of next month at a tournament at Torrey Pines, north of San Diego.

He likes that course. It is where he won the 2008 US Open. A more relevant question is: when are we going to see Tiger? Only a handful of people have since his car crash on November 27 and one of those – Elin, his wife – probably wishes she hadn't.

When are we going to see him again? Funny you should ask me that. I don't know. He is said to be having dental treatment to repair a tooth broken when Elin threw his mobile phone at him after catching him texting a woman just before his car crash.

How many more women are going to say they have had affairs with Tiger? Don't know that either, but two minutes ago it was up to 13.

So, beating 18 is still a possibility, is it? When you say beating 18, do you mean beating Jack Nicklaus's 18 professional major victories or the number of women who have slept with him?

Both, actually. Well, the number of women who claim relationships with him is rising faster than his total of major wins, which stands at 14 – and he didn't win one this year. In fact, his last was 18 months ago. So he is adding conquests off the course much quicker than on it.

Oh dear. What are the sponsors of this hitherto clean-cut athlete saying? So far, most are not cancelling their deals. But if his strike-rate continues to rise, they may reconsider their loyalty.

So Tiger might soon be out of the Woods then? Ha ha. No, er, yes, er, perhaps. Who knows?

Tiger Woods needs to cut out spit and polish act if he is to present the right image

The Times, December 7, 2009

The man clearly had his tongue in his cheek. He wanted the *Any Questions* panel to say when it thought Tiger would be out of the woods? None could.

Easier to answer is when Woods is likely to return to playing competitive golf again. Best guesses at this stage are at the Buick International at Torrey Pines on the cliffs north of San Diego, California, in February, a tournament where he has enjoyed great success.

As a result of what has gone on these past few days, Woods will not return next year as his former self. The public will not regard him as they once did and nor will the players. Indeed there is even a possibility that he may not play as well as he has done in the past because some of the previous certainties can no longer apply.

Since so many things will have changed by February, here are a few more alterations Woods could make to his personality, behaviour and entourage in an attempt to rebuild his image.

Stop swearing, spitting and throwing and banging golf clubs Tiger must realise how many people find spitting to be unattractive, even if he does not, likewise his obvious inability to control his temper. A reader calls him "the US's spitter-in-chief".

He is normally good at understanding the rhythms and rituals of the countries he is visiting. For example, when in Britain he understands why it is wrong to talk of the British Open and traps when he means the Open and bunkers. He knows it is good manners to remove his cap when he shakes hands with an opponent.

No one admires his swearing – neither the regularity of it nor his choice of words. It is a widely commented-on aspect of his game. There are those who say that Woods's use of the f-word on a golf course is the dark side of a man with his enormous gifts as a golfer. Have one and you have to have the other. One question: if Woods can, on occasions, almost will a putt into a hole, how is he unable to will himself to stop swearing?

Smile more Woods must interact more with the spectators and, dare one say it, the press. Be more humble. Sign autographs. This could make spectators change their minds about him and show genuine affection towards him as crowds in the US clearly do for Phil Mickelson, for example, and as they do here for Padraig Harrington and Rory McIlroy. Woods is respected; Mickelson is liked, loved even.

Until now Woods has seemed pretty indifferent to almost everything. He looks as though he is intent on playing golf with as few distractions as possible. He hides behind a mask of inscrutability, declining to engage with the people who have paid to watch him.

Stop behaving as though he is not bound by the normal rules A friend of mine calls this Woods's "I am God" attitude. "He believes he can control almost everything, hence the tantrums. If that inner conviction is broken, he won't win the major championships he needs to overtake Jack Nicklaus's record of 18." Beating this total is tantamount to being Woods's life work.

Sack Steve Williams Woods needs to find a sympathetic caddie who is not rude about his player's peers, as Williams was recently when he referred to Mickelson as a p***k. However good a job Williams does for Woods, and one assumes it is very good because otherwise he would not still be working for him, it is bad for Woods's image to have such an abrasive man as his caddie. Working for the world's best golfer has given Williams a manifest air of superiority to which he is not entitled.

Billy Foster, presently working for Lee Westwood, would fit the bill as Woods's new caddie. He has worked for Woods before, albeit briefly. Foster is very knowledgeable and does not seek the limelight. He has a deft touch, knowing when to goad his man on, as he did to Westwood on the eve of the Dubai World Championship that Westwood won so convincingly last month, and when to stand back. Foster would be the perfect employee for the completely professional player.

Mind you, so might Fanny Sunesson. If she was good enough to be selected by Nick Faldo when he was the best, she is certainly good enough to carry Woods's bag. Sunesson is discreet, loyal and hard-working. In view of what has happened, however, it may be a little too soon in the minds of many for Woods to have a Swedish female bag carrier.

Seek new professional advisers Woods has been shaped into a bland, aloof and clean-as-a-whistle athlete, good enough to attract huge sponsorship deals reported to be worth an annual $100 million. He entered into a pact with his advisers. If he undertook to try to play his best golf as often as he could, to work hard, to appear to be clean-cut, then in return they would control his image, marketing him skilfully and building him up into the world's best-known, highest-earning sportsman.

Although Woods has become very rich and famous, his image is in tatters. The man who was trained to become the best golfer from the age of two has been marketed and presented as something he might have once been but no longer is. So the policy has not worked. Woods needs help now and the people in Team Tiger who have advised him have not earned the right to continue to advise him in future.

A strait-laced sport? No, a little hanky-panky has always been par for the course

The Times, December 10, 2009

The scene: an hotel in Scotland on the evening of the third round of the Open Championship in July. The participants: an American multi-time major tournament winner and his wife. Alongside them, one of the most popular European players of recent times and someone other than his wife, who looked as though she could have been nanny to his children. Except that she wasn't exactly acting like Mary Poppins.

It happens in life, why not in golf, even though the perception of the game suggests that it shouldn't. One of the sport's two governing bodies is the Royal and Ancient Golf Club of St Andrews in Scotland and such a name contributes to its image of a high-bred old game that dates back centuries. This sepia-tinted view should not make golf and the men who play it any less likely to contain its share of broken marriages, illicit liaisons, new marriages.

"All my exes wear Rolexes," sang John Daly, the former US PGA winner and veteran of four marriages, years of treatment for alcoholism and several million dollars worth of punts with fellow gamblers. But even he could find it difficult to keep time on the comings and goings of modern professional golf.

The European Tour, and the PGA Tour in the US for that matter, is a nomadic circus of 150 men, most of whom are young, fit and rich, moving from one hotel and golf course to another on a weekly basis. Fly out on a Tuesday, play a pro-am Wednesday, compete in the tournament from Thursday to Sunday and, with a bit of luck, get home on Sunday night ready to leave again in two days. Often they are away for two or three weeks at a stretch, perhaps longer.

The golfers are the honey and the bees don't take long to arrive. On occasions though, the golfers are the bees and can't wait for the honey. At a recent tournament the organisers were offended by the requests of a leading player who wanted not only a free room but some prostitutes to be provided as well.

The story is also told of a golfer's wife taking friends to look at the new yacht her husband had just bought and moored at a jetty at the bottom of the garden, only to find him in bed with a neighbour.

For bachelors, golf can be the life of Riley. The young Australian golfer Adam Scott, 29, had a fling with Kate Hudson, Goldie Hawn's daughter, before beginning a very public relationship with Ana Ivanovic, the Serbian tennis player who was once voted one of the world's most beautiful women.

Nor is sex a contemporary phenomenon of the game. Harry Vardon, perhaps the greatest of all British golfers because he won the Open Championship six times and the US Open once at the end of the nineteenth century and in the early years of the twentieth, fathered an illegitimate son.

Nick Faldo has been prolific at more than just winning. In addition to six major championships, he has had three wives and four children, the births of three of whom were induced so as not to disrupt important golf events in which he was competing.

After separating from Melanie, his first wife, he and Gill, who would become his second wife, were being pursued around the US by journalists wanting interviews and photographs. Faldo successfully put off a reporter telephoning from London when he pretended to be a butler and answered the phone by saying: "Mr Faldo's residence."

When Faldo was between his second and third wives he had a relationship with a young American named Brenna Cepelak. She was so angry when he ended it that she took a nine-iron to the bonnet of his Porsche and is said to have done £15,000 worth of damage. Ring any bells?

Road Hole bunker kicks up sandstorm

The Times, December 5, 2002

So was it all a storm in a tee after all? Did the outcry in golf that followed suggestions that changes were to be made to the bunker to the left of the 17th green on the Old Course at St Andrews occur too soon? Have those who shouted "Fore!" at what they considered to be sacrilege to the Road Hole bunker, the most famous bunker on the most famous hole of the most famous golf course in the world, been guilty of playing out of turn? It would appear so.

Yesterday afternoon, a wintry sun shone on a group of officials from the St Andrews Links Trust, the body that oversees all the golf courses in the old town, as it made its way to the 17th green, the scene of the alleged crime. The members of the greens' sub-committee wanted to examine the work on the bunker and its surrounding area and to judge whether or not they liked what they saw.

They felt completely at ease in doing this because work on the Road Hole bunker was a site inspection of a project that is very much work in progress. The committee inspected what its greenkeeping staff had done. It noted how the size of the gathering area in which a ball will be swept up and sent rolling into the sand of the bunker had been increased, making it easier than ever to putt into the bunker.

It looked at the bunker's face, which had been reduced by two feet, back to the level it was in the sixties, after complaints by the players that it was difficult to get the ball out and after revelations that as the sand was deposited on the bunker's face from golfers flailing to extricate their balls, so the face had built up over the years.

It decided that this modification was too much and so it ordered the green-keeping staff to rebuild the bunker's face to within six inches of how it was when the Open was held at St Andrews in 2000 and how it was when Ernie Els took an eight in it as recently as October during the Dunhill Links Championship. In other words, suggestions that the face of this bunker was being reduced by two feet were 18 inches wide of the mark.

This activity followed a hectic few hours after news of the proposed changes to the bunker leaked out on a website. This, in turn, prompted golfers from around the world to raise their sand wedges in anger. This is not surprising as golf has been played at St Andrews since the fifteenth century and golfers come from all parts of the world to compete at the Home of Golf.

Dr David Malcolm, a past captain of the New Club in St Andrews, alleged that the bunker had been moved four feet farther away from the green and reduced in size. He also alleged that it would be harder to putt into the bunker now than it used to be. "The whole town is in uproar," Malcolm said. "Tampering with the bunker is going too far. A lot of players have cursed it through the years, but a lot more will mourn its passing like a dear and familiar friend."

Peter Dawson, the secretary of the Royal and Ancient Golf Club of St Andrews, said he was not sure that anybody would like the changes very much and the R & A would be discussing them with the Links Trust shortly. Among players, José María Olazábal said that if the bunker had been moved back from the putting surface and made shallower then officials were "… taking the personality from the hole – its character".

"I categorically deny we have moved the bunker," Peter Mason, the external affairs director of the Links Trust, said. "It is going to be easier to putt into it than it was before because the gathering area is bigger than it was. But we are considering reducing the face of the bunker because the course has 42,000 rounds played over it every year and everyone who tries to hit out of that bunker deposits sand on top of it. Over the years this has built up.

The Road Hole bunker on the 17th of the Old Course at St Andrews is
famous as one of the most difficult to escape from in the game.

"The critics remind me of the people who disagreed with us when we said we wanted to resurface the road at the back of the green. They said it would ruin the hole. We did it nonetheless and it has made no difference. It is still an exciting hole. Do you honestly think we would deliberately make a mess of the most famous bunker on the most famous hole of the most famous course in golf?

"Anyway this is work in progress. It is not finished. We have meetings with the R & A next week to talk about things to do with the 2005 Open and I am sure our proposals will come up for discussion then and all views will be taken into account. What we are doing is not painting a moustache on the face of the Mona Lisa, as some people allege. All we are doing is moving one hair on her head from one side of her parting to another."

Open wounds

1921 J.H. Taylor, five times a winner of the Open between 1894 and 1913, took 13 strokes in the bunker.

1978 Tommy Nakajima, of Japan, took five attempts to get his ball out during the 1978 Championship. Nakajima's travails led to the bunker being known as The Sands of Nakajima.

1990 José María Olazábal putted off the green into the bunker and only escaped from the sand on his second attempt.

1995 In the play-off for the Championship at the Old Course, Costantino Rocca took three strokes in the bunker and lost to John Daly.

2000 David Duval took four strokes to get his ball out of the bunker in the last round of the 2000 Open, the last time the Championship was held at St Andrews.

New courses in trouble as golf boom turns sour
The Sunday Times, December 16, 1990

Two of Britain's most ambitious golf developments are in financial trouble. A £52 million project for two championship courses and a luxury hotel on the banks of Loch Lomond is in the hands of administrators and up for sale. The equally lavish £32.5 million East Sussex National Golf Club near Gatwick airport, which also has two championship courses, has failed to attract sufficient members while building costs have mounted, and is undergoing a financial restructuring.

The two projects have much in common. Both were conceived during an unprecedented boom in golf as a leisure activity. Both were the heady dreams of ambitious men who insisted that no expense should be spared. Both made bids to stage the 1993 Ryder Cup. Both involved substantial borrowings, and both were hit by the rise in interest rates.

David Brench, chairman of Stirling Investments Ltd, the developers of the Loch Lomond project, hoped to build a complex to rival Gleneagles. A self-confessed golf nut, builder and property developer, Brench's plan involved two courses – the High Road and the Low Road – to be designed by Tom Weiskopf, the 1973 Open champion, a 200-bedroom five-star hotel, corporate golf cottages, a riding and shooting school, a 200-berth marina and a nature reserve. Rossdhu House, the 200-year-old former home of the Colquhoun family, was to become the clubhouse.

After years of negotiations, Stirling Investments secured planning permission from Dumbarton District Council, and a 128-year lease on a wooded peninsula guarded on three sides by Loch Lomond, a site which had been owned by the Clan Colquhoun since time immemorial. Sir Ivar Colquhoun of Luss, 32nd chief of the clan, a JP and former honorary sheriff of Dunbartonshire, joined the board of Stirling Investments.

Weiskopf described the site as "one of the greatest properties in the world". Its appeal lies in its stunning beauty and historical associations. In the Middle Ages the tenth chief Colquhoun was murdered on an island in Loch Lomond by a band of Hebridean marauders. Centuries later, Sir James Colquhoun, 28th chief, and four gillies drowned within earshot of Rossdhu while sailing home from a stalking expedition.

When Weiskopf last visited the site early in October, 15 of the holes on the High Road course had been finished. "We were hired to produce work that would make Loch Lomond one of the most beautiful in the world of golf," he said last week. By his account, they did. "They should be 18 wonderful holes," he said.

But work on other aspects had run into difficulties. Central to the project was the hotel. When it became clear that Stirling Investments was unable to attract a hotel developer, the Bank of Scotland, the main creditor, became worried.

On November 12, the bank announced it had requested an administrator to be appointed. "Stirling Investments based its plans on certain things happening," said Bruce Graham, of Cork Gully Chartered Accountants, who have been appointed administrators. "Some of these events did not take place, notably getting a hotel developer on site, and as a consequence the bank stepped in to protect the value of the property for the creditors."

Last week a suitably eerie mist hung over Loch Lomond. A makeshift road of thick mud, interrupted by seemingly bottomless potholes, led to Rossdhu House. There was not a workman in sight. A Land Rover, van and several cars stood outside the former stately home. There was no sign of activity behind its black empty windows and the only evidence of workmen was a portable building.

The project that would create 240 jobs has come almost to a halt. Only essential maintenance work is being done to the course and clubhouse. According to the administrators, only three sales staff and a caretaker remain on site.

The Colquhoun family remain sanguine. "One has time to get used to the idea that one's loved home is to be used as a golf course," Lady Colquhoun said. "One had thought it was going to be opened next summer, which is what one had been led to believe. So to hear suddenly that it wasn't was a disappointment."

Weiskopf, who has been fully paid for his work so far, hopes that he will be employed to design the second course. "The biggest disappointment in my career would not be finishing second four times in the Masters but not being able to conclude our work at Loch Lomond," he said.

At the East Sussex National club near Uckfield, the two championship courses are in play. But a financial cloud hangs over the project. Building work on the 200-bedroom hotel (estimated cost, £20 million) and clubhouse (cost, £2.5 million) has not begun and the professional's shop is doubling up as a locker room.

This is a far cry from the optimism and air of extravagance that was present when East Sussex was announced in February 1989. The brains and driving force was Brian Turner, a 54-year-old Canadian entrepreneur who had once been a scratch golfer.

Nothing was going to be too good for East Sussex National, which in name was fancifully modelled on the Augusta National course near Atlanta, Georgia. A type of bent grass common in America was sown, and 40 greenkeepers appointed to tend it. A 200-bedroom hotel was planned, together with a 35,000 square feet clubhouse, and a pro shop selling the best clothes and offering a hemming and tailoring service.

The club sought 1,000 members (debentures: £15,000; subscription: £1,000) but costs began to mount and membership was slow to rise. "Costs ran ahead of themselves," an insider said. "And it's no secret that membership sales were not as high as forecast." East Sussex had hoped to close membership well before May 1990 yet one source estimates that only 150 memberships have been taken up.

Most crucially of all, Turner failed to get the design for the clubhouse and hotel within budget. Building work was postponed while new plans were drawn up. "It was a big, big project, and it was simply too expensive, well over what we had allocated," Turner said. "There's nothing fishy about it, nothing went haywire. As far as I was concerned it wasn't financially viable to accept the architects' proposals."

Turner lost the support of his financial backers, Timeregal plc, a company owned by the Kuwaiti Investment Office. Timeregal assumed control of the project, restructured it financially and appointed Jimmy Hamilton, a chartered accountant, as general manager.

Turner has returned to Canada to raise further finance to regain control. His deadline is January 1. "I'm totally optimistic I can do it," Turner said last week.

Women's toughest opponents are in the clubhouse

Weekend FT, December 7, 1991

The name Joanne Morley probably does not strike a chord unless you follow women's amateur golf closely, in which case you will know that Morley was one of the outstanding players of the season that has just finished.

She won the English and British strokeplay titles; and her haul of three points out of four in the Great Britain and Ireland match against the Continent for the Vagliano Trophy was the best by a player from either side. In recognition of this success, Morley was named amateur woman golfer of the year last week.

Morley is a purposeful, assured 24-year-old who spends her winters working in Woolworths to earn enough money to pay for the competitive golf she plays all summer. She says she will turn professional at the end of next year but, for the moment, her sights are levelled at the Curtis Cup at Hoylake next June. And therein lies a story.

The Royal Liverpool Golf Club, at Hoylake on the tip of the Wirral peninsula, is among the oldest and most distinguished in the world. It was founded in Hoylake in 1864 and, 20 years later, started the amateur championship, the oldest event of its kind anywhere. It was at Hoylake in 1902 that Alex Herd won the Open with a rubber-core ball, thus killing off the gutty ball that had hitherto been used so successfully.

It was at Hoylake in 1921 that a match between the men amateurs of Britain and the US was played, an event for which the Walker Cup was presented the following year. And it was at Hoylake not long ago that women were told they could walk through the men's lounge to the dining room instead of, as previously, having to go outside the clubhouse. At the time of this historic pronouncement, it was made clear to the women that this concession was available only "so long as they look straight ahead".

If this chauvinism sounds remarkable in 1991, be assured it is not – or, rather, was not. Golf as a game, and the clubs its participants had to join in order to play, traditionally have remained the homes of racists and chauvinists.

Prejudice against Jews, for example, was such that they had great difficulty in joining golf clubs which operated a Jewish quota – and most of them did. This led to Jews founding their own clubs, of which Moor Allerton outside Leeds, Bonnyton in Glasgow and Hartsbourne, Potters Bar and Abridge near London are all good examples. Jews and Gentiles now mix harmoniously at most London clubs. The new outcasts in golf are the Japanese.

Their ambassador to Britain has playing facilities at Sunningdale, Berkshire, but many of his countrymen have to make-do with sessions at driving ranges and occasional outings at accommodating courses, of which there aren't many. This unwelcoming attitude has made the Japanese buy their own; recent acquisitions include Camberley Heath in Surrey, Old Thorns near Liphook, Hampshire, and the Turnberry hotel and course in south-west Scotland, the site of the 1986 Open.

Women, when faced with obvious discrimination, had no choice but to grin and bear it. When a man said: "Women don't play golf, they play *at* it", women had to like it or lump it. They had to do likewise until recently when they came across such indignities as a sign at the entrance to one golf club that read (and note the order of the nouns): "No dogs or women".

There are still clubs in Britain where the reaction of the men members is reminiscent of Robert Morley's in the film *Round the World in Eighty Days* when he saw a woman in the Reform Club. "A woman in the club!" exploded Morley. "It is the end."

That has had to change. It took the Equal Opportunities Commission to bring about that change. In 1988, and prompted by an average of one complaint a day for 13 years, the EOC proposed an amendment to the 1981 Sex Discrimination Act. The EOC wanted to bring into line those clubs that purported to offer membership to both sexes but, in reality, offered women limited rights.

"This absence of choice is particularly disadvantageous to women because of the restricted privileges attached to associate membership which may lead, for example, to prohibitions on the use of sporting facilities at weekends and on weekday evenings." This definition fits many of the 200 golf clubs in the UK where women have limited rights, little representation and pay a subscription not significantly lower than the men.

Although the government has so far declined to implement the recommendation of the EOC, the Ladies' Golf Union recently took it upon itself to become more militant. It announced in midsummer that it was boycotting the all-male clubs even if they had staged events for women in the past. This ruled out Royal St George's, Sandwich, site of the 1988 Curtis Cup match, and Muirfield, where the Curtis Cup was held in 1984. Both remain bastions of male chauvinism.

Mary Anderson, the chairman of the LGU and a woman of considerable charm and forcefulness, asked: "Why do men have the right to feel superior? I think women are far superior to men or, at any rate, we're all equal. I don't see why I can't have the same rights as a man."

To its credit, Hoylake is acceptable to the LGU. Next June when the Curtis Cup is held there, Morley, who will assuredly be playing for GB and Ireland, will be able to experience the historic links and the equally historic and imposing clubhouse. As she does so, I hope she does not have to look straight ahead.

Alliss support shows no sign of wavering

The Times, December 16, 2004

For an hour or so at lunchtime yesterday, Ottakar's bookshop in Bracknell, Berkshire, was where the Peter Alliss fan club went to worship and buy copies of their hero's autobiography. Men and women of all ages flocked through the doors. One man brought along a T-shirt he had bought at the first World Match Play Championship in 1961 for Alliss to sign. Some who had no interest in golf wanted the book for a friend, father or brother-in-law.

It was a valid demonstration of Alliss's popularity. More enthusiastic scenes had been enacted in Glasgow in October, where tickets for an evening with Alliss sold out in record time; in Bournemouth, where all available copies were bought in 15 minutes; in St Andrews, where he signed 300 copies in an hour. No doubt the queues will be longer in Farnham, Hampshire, near where he lives, today as sales move up towards 60,000 copies.

Karen Geary, of Hodder & Stoughton, watched yesterday and noted: "We knew he was popular, but this has exceeded our expectations. Everyone says to him, 'Don't give up commentating.' He's a national treasure."

Alliss, BBC TV's chief golf commentator, is described in an American magazine as "the best ... ever". But why exactly? The late Dan Maskell, a former colleague of Alliss, was admired for his tennis knowledge and all-round pleasant nature; Bill McLaren revered for his flinty rugby commentaries of unimpeachable authority; David Coleman hugely respected for his pugnacity and knowledge.

Alliss, 73, is different – adored by many, disliked by some. Some who watch sport on television think that he is bumbling, an out-of-touch geriatric, a reactionary to boot. Many more would leave home and crawl on their hands and knees to his side if he so much as lifted an eyebrow to encourage them.

In Bracknell, Alliss had them eating out of his hand the moment he walked towards the front of the shop to begin signing.

"I'm glad somebody has come," he joked as he passed a queue of 50 customers. "This is not gin by the way," he said of the glass of water he held in his right hand. "I wouldn't blame you if it was," a woman blurted out fiercely.

To these, the converted, Alliss can do no wrong. They could not care less that he said "bollocks" on television recently and was confused when Phil Mickelson won the Masters. "I'm more popular than ever because of saying bollocks," Alliss said. "I'm top of the pops in a punk golf magazine and I've had more people comment favourably to me about that. Doesn't bother me that I said it."

David Osborn is the rector of Bracknell and as an advocate for the pro-Alliss faction, a clergyman holds certain advantages. "He brings humanity to his broadcasts, he deflates egos," Osborn, who is a member at The Berkshire, said. "He is not afraid to say what he thinks and it is what everyone is thinking."

Many of those buying Alliss's book referred to the commentator's humour. "Peter is the only man I would willingly sit down and listen to for hours and hours," Mark Parker said. "He keeps me entertained – even on golf."

Daniel Mason was just passing the bookshop and decided on a whim to buy one for himself. "For me it is because I like Peter," he said. "If it is a choice between listening to Peter commentating on golf and watching something else on TV, I choose Peter."

Alliss had a word for everyone. "Have a good Christmas," he said again and again, adding, "don't overdo it, now." With one woman, a teacher, he lamented the changes in the education system. To another he said: "Hello, come closer." The woman said, quietly: "This is for my neighbour. He is 80."

"Shall I put, 'Well done on your 80th'?" Alliss asked.

"No," the woman replied. "It might have been his 81st."

And so it went on. An hour's work, 150 copies sold, more recruits added to Alliss's army of supporters to overcome those who feel that he should retire. It was another reassuring sign that Britain, famously a nation of shopkeepers, is also a nation of book buyers.

INDEX

Page numbers in *italic* refer to illustrations.